Yanmar

YANMAR MARINE DIESEL ENGINE 3JH2

Service Manual

Yanmar

YANMAR MARINE DIESEL ENGINE 3JH2

Service Manual

ISBN/EAN: 9783954272792
Erscheinungsjahr: 2013
Erscheinungsort: Bremen, Deutschland

© maritimepress in Europäischer Hochschulverlag GmbH & Co. KG, Fahrenheitstr. 1, 28359 Bremen. Alle Rechte beim Verlag und bei den jeweiligen Lizenzgebern.

www.maritimepress.de | office@maritimepress.de

Bei diesem Titel handelt es sich um den Nachdruck eines historischen, lange vergriffenen Buches. Da elektronische Druckvorlagen für diese Titel nicht existieren, musste auf alte Vorlagen zurückgegriffen werden. Hieraus zwangsläufig resultierende Qualitätsverluste bitten wir zu entschuldigen.

YANMAR
SERVICE MANUAL
MARINE DIESEL ENGINE

MODEL **3JH2** series

		Publication No.		A0A1015	
\multicolumn{3}{c}{**History of Revision**}		Page No	1
Manual Name			Service Manual for Marine Diesel Engine		
Engine Model :			**3JH2 series**		
Number of revision	Date of revision	Reason for correction	Outline of correction	Correction item No. (page)	Corrected by
1st	Apr. 2001	• Crank shaft V-pulley bolt tightening torque	• Added the standard V-pulley (material: casting iron) tightening torque and general use nuts & bolts tightening torque.	10-32	Quality Assurance Dept.
		• Clutch lever control cable connectlion.	• Added the tightening torque of nut for the remote control cable connection of clutch shifting lever.	8-3	
			• Injection timing changed.	1-3, 10-31	
2nd	Feb. 2003	• Add the model 3JH25A & 3JH30A	• Added the Exterior Views • Added the Specifieations • Added the Engine Outiine • Added the Pertomance Curves • Added the Piping Diagrams • Added the Fuel Injection Pump Sewice Data • Added the Intake and Exhaust System figure • Added the Lubrieation System figure • Added the Lube Oil Filter figure • Added theSea water line flgure • Added the Marine Gear Models KM3P1,KM3P3,KM35P1 • Added the Wiring diagrams	1-2-1, 1-2-2 1-3-1, 1-4-1 1-8-1 1-11-1, 1-11-2 1-14-1 3-1-1 4-1-1 5-2-1 5-6-1 6-3-1 7-29~7-56 9-4-1	Quality Assurance Dept.

Printed in Japan
A0A1015-0302

FOREWORD

This service manual has been compiled for engineers engaged in sales, service, inspection and maintenance. Accordingly, descriptions of the construction and functions of the engine are emphasized in this manual while items which should already be common knowledge are omitted.
One characteristic of a marine diesel engine is that its performance in a vessel is governed by its applicability to the vessel's hull construction and its steering system.
Engine installation, fitting out and propeller selection have a substantial effect on the performance of the engine and the vessel. Moreover, when the engine runs unevenly or when trouble occurs, it is essential to check a wide range of operating conditions—such as installation on the hull and suitability of the ship's piping and propeller − and not just the engine itself. To get maximum performance from this engine, you should completely understand its functions, construction and capabilities, as well as proper use and servicing.
Use this manual as a handy reference in daily inspection and maintenance, and as a text for engineering guidance.

CONTENTS

CHAPTER 1 GENERAL
1. Exterior Views 1-1
2. Specifications 1-3
3. Engine Outline 1-5
4. Performance Curves 1-10
5. Piping Diagrams 1-12

CHAPTER 2 BASIC ENGINE PARTS
1. CylinderBlock 2-1
2. Cylinder Head 2-4
3. Piston and Piston Pins 2-11
4. Connecting Rod 2-15
5. Crankshaft and Main Bearing 2-18
6. Camshaft and Tappets 2-21
7. Timing Gear 2-24
8. Flywheel and Housing 2-26

CHAPTER 3 FUEL INJECTION EQUIPMENT
1. Fuel Injection Pump Service Data 3-1
2. Governor 3-2
3. Disassembly Reassembly and Inspection of Fuel Injection Pump 3-11
4. Adjustment of Fuel Injection Pump and Governor .. 3-21
5. Fuel Feed Pump 3-27
6. FuelInjection Nozzle 3-29
7. Troubleshooting 3-33
8. Tools 3-35
9. Fuel Filter 3-37
10. Fuel Tank (Optional) 3-38

CHAPTER 4 INTAKE AND EXHAUST SYSTEM
1. Intake and Exhaust System 4-1
2. Turbocharger 4-3
3. Mixing Elbow 4-17

CHAPTER 5 LUBRICATION SYSTEM
1. Lubrication System 5-1
2. Lube Oil Pump 5-3
3. Lube Oil Filter 5-6
4. Oil Pressure Control Valve 5-8
5. Lube Oil Cooler 5-9
6. Piston Cooling Nozzle 5-10
7. Rotary Waste Oil Pump (Optional) 5-11

CHAPTER 6 COOLING WATER SYSTEM
1. Cooling Water System 6-1
2. Sea Water Pump 6-4
3. Fresh Water Pump 6-7
4. Heat Exchanger 6-10
5. Pressure Cap and Sub Tank 6-12
6. Thermostat 6-14
7. Kingston Cock (Optional) 6-16
8. Sea Water Filter (Optional) 6-17
9. Bilge Pump and Bilge Strainer (Optional) ... 6-18

CHAPTER 7 REDUCTION AND REVERSING GEAR
KM3A
1. Construction 7-1
2. Shifting Device 7-7
3. Inspection And Servicing 7-12
4. Disassembly 7-22
5. Reassembly 7-25

KM3P1, KM3P3, KM35P1
1. Construction 7-29
2. Shifting Device 7-35
3. Inspection And Servicing 7-40
4. Disassembly 7-48
5. Reassembly 7-53

CHAPTER 8 REMOTE CONTROL
1. Remote Control System 8-1
2. Remote Control Installation 8-2
3. Remote Control Inspection 8-5
4. Remote Control ADJUSTMENT 8-6
5. Disassembly 8-13

CHAPTER 9 ELECTRICAL SYSTEM
1. Electrical System 9-1
2. Battery 9-5
3. Starter Motor 9-8
4. Alternator 9-24
5. Instrument Panel 9-34
6. Warning Devices 9-36
7. Air Heater (Optional) 9-39
8. Electric Type Engine Stop Device (Optional) .. 9-40
9. Tachometer 9-42
10. Alternator 12V/80A(Optional) 9-45

CHAPTER 10 DISASSEMBLY AND REASSEMBLY
1. Disassembly and Reassembly Precautions ... 10-1
2. Disassembly and Reassembly Tools 10-2
3. Disassembly and Reassembly 10-9
4. Bolt/nut Tightening Torque 10-32
5. Test Running 10-33

CHAPTER 1
GENERAL

1. Exterior Views ······································ 1-1
2. Specifications ····································· 1-3
3. Engine Outline ···································· 1-5
4. Performance Curves ························· 1-10
5. Piping Diagrams ································ 1-12

1. Exterior Views
1-1. 3JH2E

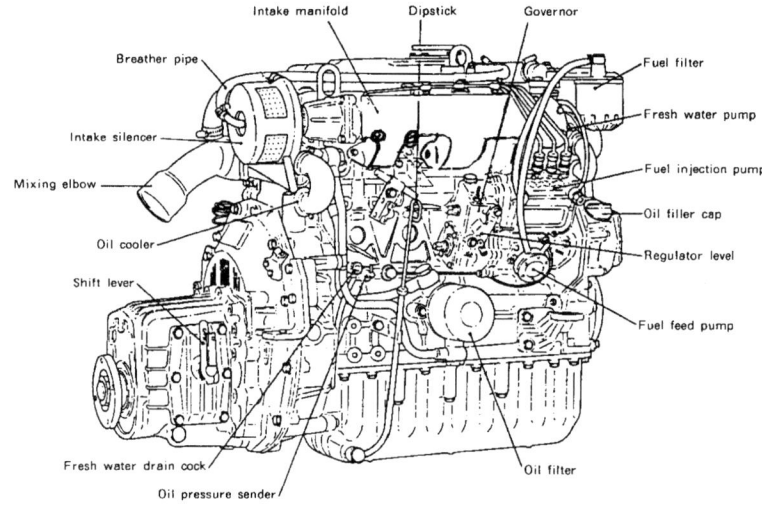

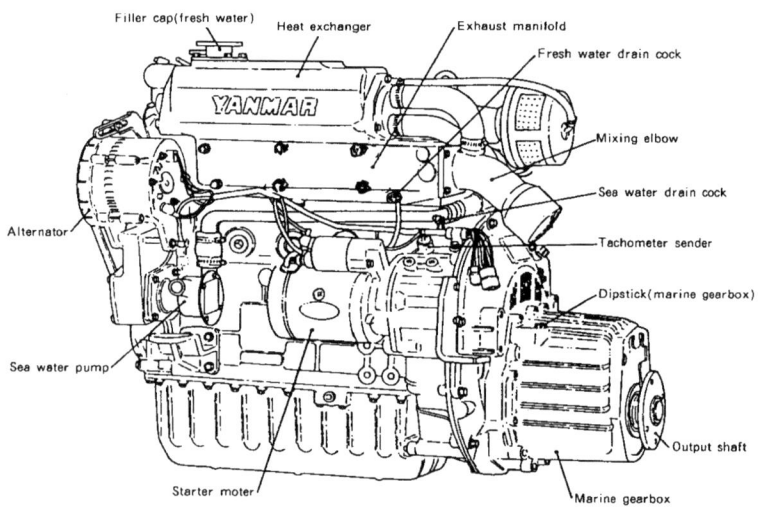

Chapter 1 General
1. Exterior Views
3JH2 Series

1-2. 3JH2-TE

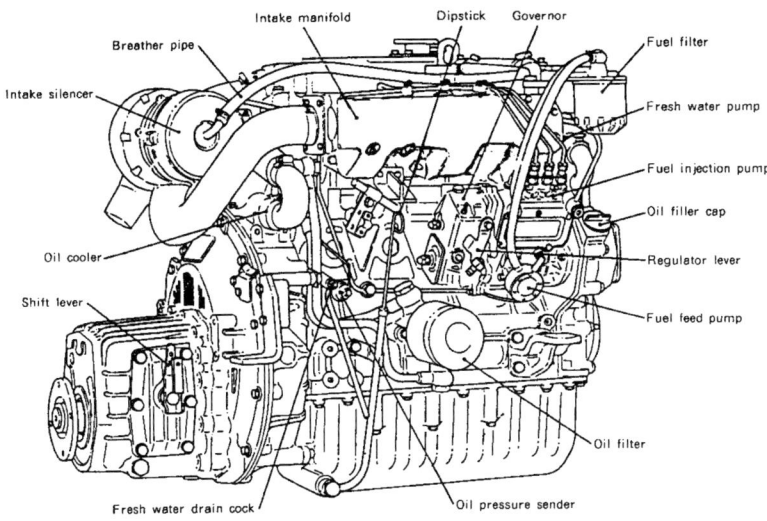

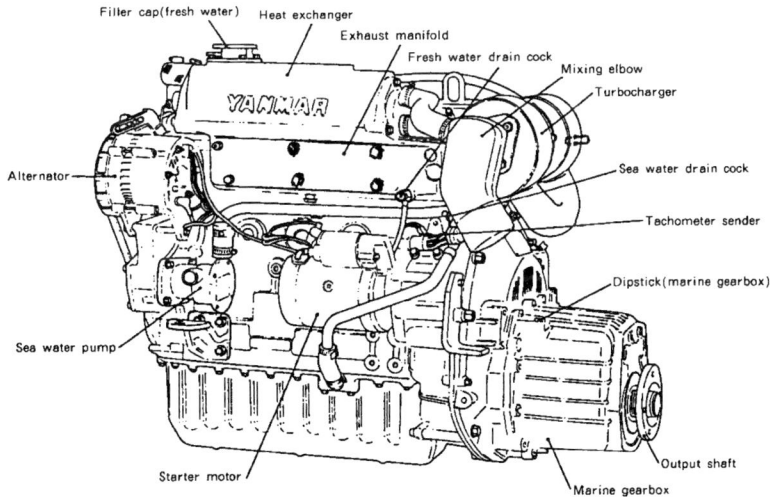

Chapter 1 General
I. Exterior Views

3JH2 Series

1-3 3JH25A/30A

<u>With KM3P3</u>

● Operating side

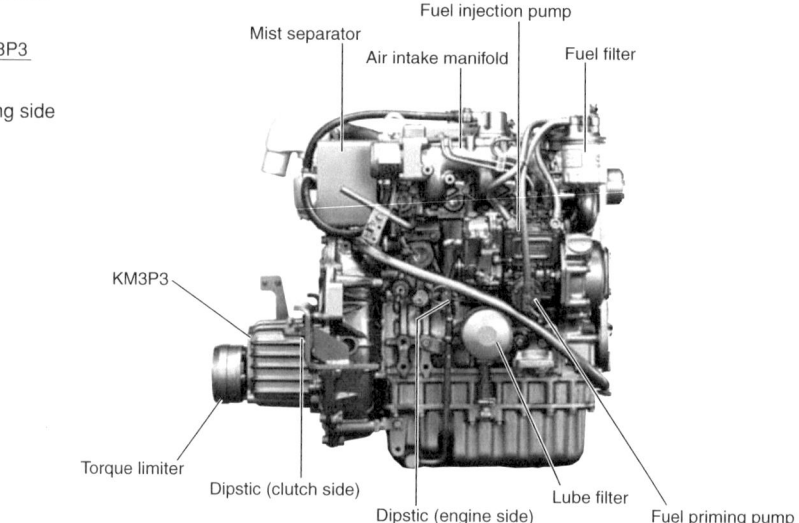

● Non-Operating side

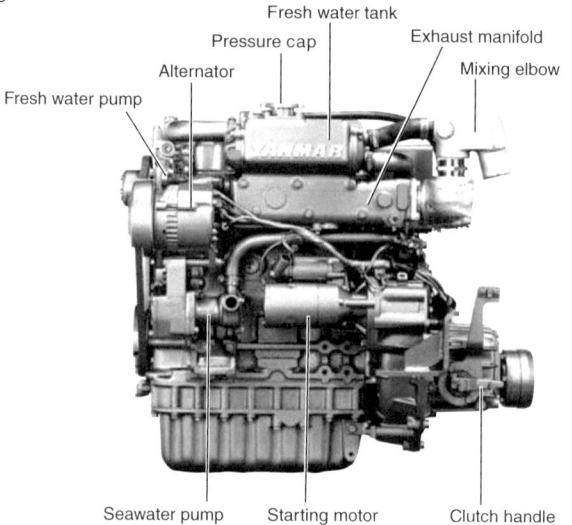

Chapter 1 General
1. Exterior Views
3JH2 Series

With KM3P1/ KM35P1

- Operating side

Mist separator
Fuel injection pump
Air intake manifold
Fuel filter
KM3P1
KM35P1
Dipstic (clutch side)
Dipstic (engine side)
Lube filter
Fuel priming pump

- Non-Operating side

Fresh water tank
Pressure cap
Exhaust manifold
Alternator
Mixing elbow
Fresh water pump
Seawater pump
Starting motor
Clutch handle

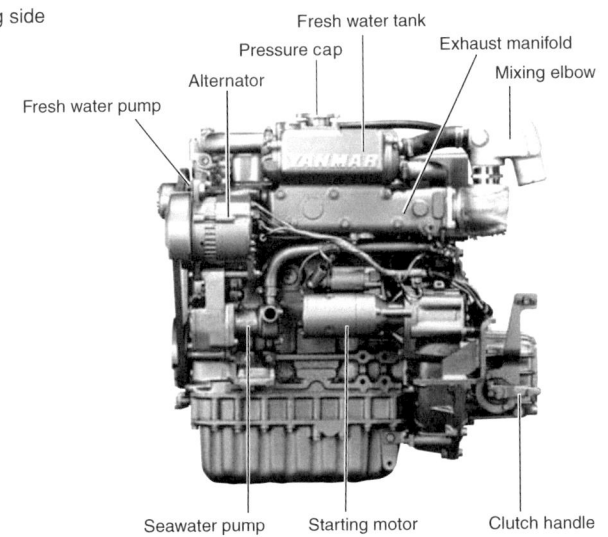

Chapter 1 General
2. Specifications

2. Specifications
2-1. Engine

Model			3JH2-(B)E	3JH2-T(B)E
Type			Vertical 4-cycle water cooled diesel engine	
Combustion system			Direct injection	
Aspiration			Normal aspiration	Exhaust gas turbocharger
Number of cylinders			3	
Bore × stroke		mm (in.)	82 × 86 (3.23 × 3.39)	
Displacement		ℓ (cu.in.)	1.363 (83.17)	
One hour rating output (DIN6270B) flywheel output	Output/crankshaft speed	kW/rpm (HP/rpm)	28.5/3600 (38.7/3600)	35.0/3600 (47.6/3600)
	Brake mean effective pressure	kgf/cm² (lb./in².)	6.97 (99.113)	8.62 (122.576)
	Piston speed	m/sec. (ft./sec.)	10.3	
Continuous rating output (DIN6270A) flywheel output	Output/crankshaft speed	kW/rpm (HP/rpm)	25.7/3400 (34.9/3400)	31.6/3400 (43.0/3400)
	Brake mean effective pressure	kgf/cm² (lb./in².)	6.80 (96.696)	8.35 (118.737)
	Piston speed	m/sec. (ft./sec.)	9.75	
Compression ratio			18.1	18.0
Fire order			1 $\xrightarrow{240°}$ 3 $\xrightarrow{240°}$ 2 $\xrightarrow{240°}$ 1	
Fuel injection pump			YPES-CL	
Fuel injection timing (b.T.D.C.)		degree	14°	17°
Fuel injection pressure		kgf/cm²(lb./in².)	200±5 (19.6±0.5)	
Fuel injection nozzle			Hole type	
Direction of rotaion	(Crankshaft)		Counter-clock wise viewed from stern	
Power take off			At Flywheel side	
Cooling system			Constant high temperature fresh water cooling Fresh water : Centrifugal pump Sea water : Rubber impeller pump	
Lubrication system			Forced lubrication with trochoid pump	
Starting system	Starting motor		DC 12V 1.4kW	
	AC generator		12V 55A (12V 80A : Option)	
Turbocharger	Type		—	RHB52 (I.H.I.)
	Model		—	
	Cooling system		—	Water cooling
Air cooler system	Type		—	—
	Radiation area	m² (in².)	—	—
Dimensions (with KMA)	Overall length	mm (in.)	760.2 (3JH2BE) / 782.3(3JH2E)	760.2 (29.93) / 782.3 (30.84)
	Overall width	mm (in.)	511.5	511.5 (20.65)
	Overall height	mm (in.)	587.5	587.5 (23.13)
Engine weight without marine gear (dry)		kg (lb.)	165	174
Lubricating oil capacity Effect/max.		ℓ (cu.in.)	2.1 / 4.9	
Cooling water capacity (Fresh water)	Fresh water tank	ℓ (cu.in.)	4.7	
	Sub tank	ℓ (cu.in.)	0.8 (48.82)	

Chapter 1 General
2. Specifications — 3JH2 Series

Model		Unit	3JH25A	3JH30A
Type		—	Vertical 4-cycle water cooled diesel engine	
Combustion system		—	Direct injection	
Aspiration		—	Normal aspiration	
Number of cylinders		—	3	
Bore × stroke		mm	82 × 86	
Displacement		ℓ	1.303	
One hour rating output (DIN6270B) flywheel output	Output/crankshaft speed	kW(PS)/rpm	20.2/3300 (27.5/3300)	24.3/3000 (33.0/3000)
	Brake mean effective pressure	MPa(kgf/cm^2)	0.539 (5.50)	0.713 (7.27)
	Piston speed	m/sec.	9.5	8.6
Continuous rating output (DIN6270A) flywheel output	Output/crankshaft speed	kW(PS)/rpm	18.4/3200 (25/3200)	22.1/2900 (30/2900)
	Brake mean effective pressure	MPa(kgf/cm^2)	0.506 (5.016)	0.670 (6.83)
	Piston speed	m/sec.	9.2	8.3
Compression ratio		—	18.1	
Fire order		—	1 — 3 — 2 — 1	
Fuel injection pump		—	YPES-CL	
Fuel injection timing (b.T.D.C.)		degree.	19±1	
Fuel injection pressure		MPa(kgf/cm^2)	19.6±0.5(200±5)	
Fuel injection nozzle		—	Hole type	
Direction of rotaion	(Crankshaft)	—	Counter-clock wise viewed from stern	
Power taka off		—	At Flywheel side	
Cooling system		—	Constant high temperature fresh water cooling Fresh water : Centrifugal pump See water : Rubber impeller pump	
Lubrication system		—	Forced lubrication with trochoid pump	
Starting system	Starting motor	V-kW	DC 12V-1.8kW	
	AC generator	V-A	12V-35A	
Dimensions (with KM35P1)	Overall length	mm	730	770
	Overall width	mm	545	
	Overall height	mm	680	
Engine weight without marine gear (dry)		kg	185	190
Lubricating oil capacity Effect/max.		ℓ	0.9 / 7.0	
Cooling water capacity (Fresh water)	Fresh water tank	ℓ	4.4	
	Sub tank	ℓ	0.8	

Printed in Japan
A0A1015-0302

Chapter 1 General
2. Specifications

3JH2 Series

2-2. Marine Gear

	Model		KBW-10E		KM3A		
Marine gear system	Type		Multiple friction disc cluth (Parallel drive)		Cone clutch (Angle drive)		
	Reduction ratio (Forward/Reverse)		2.14/2.50	2.45/2.50	2.33/3.04	2.64/3.04	3.21/3.04
	Direction of rotation (Forward) viewed from stern		Clock wise		Clock wise		
	Lubricating oil capacity Effect/max.	ℓ (cu.in.)	0.2/0.7 (12.204/42.714)		0.05/0.35 (3.051/21.357)		
	Lubricating oil						
	weight	kg (lb.)	17.5 (38.588)		13 (28.665)		

2-3. Applicability of Marine gear & Reduction ratio

●: Standard combination
○: Optional combination
×: Inapplicable

Marine gear		Engine model		3JH2F	3JH2-TE
Model	Reduction ratio	I.D Mark			
KBW10E	2.14	S		●	●
	2.45	G		●	●
	2.83	GG		●	×
KM3A	2.33	S		●	●
	2.64	G		●	●
	3.21	GG		●	×

1-4

Printed in Japan
A0A1015-9110SP

Chapter 1 General
2. Specifications
3JH2 Series

	Model		KM3P1	KM3P3	KM35P1
marine gear system	Clutch Type		Cone clutch		
	Reduction ratio (Forward/Reverse)		2.36 / 3.1 6		
	Direction of rotation(Forward) viewed from stern		Clock wise		
	Lubricating oil capacity min/max	ℓ	0.3 / 0.35		0.45 / 0.5
	Lubricating oil		SAE #30 API CC or CD		
	mas	kg	12	15	12
	Torque limiter		Not Eqipped	Eqipped	Eqipped

3. Engine Outline

3-1. 3JH2-E (KBW10-E)

Unit: mm

Chapter 1 General
3. Engine Outline

3-2. 3JH2-BE(KM3A)

Unit:mm

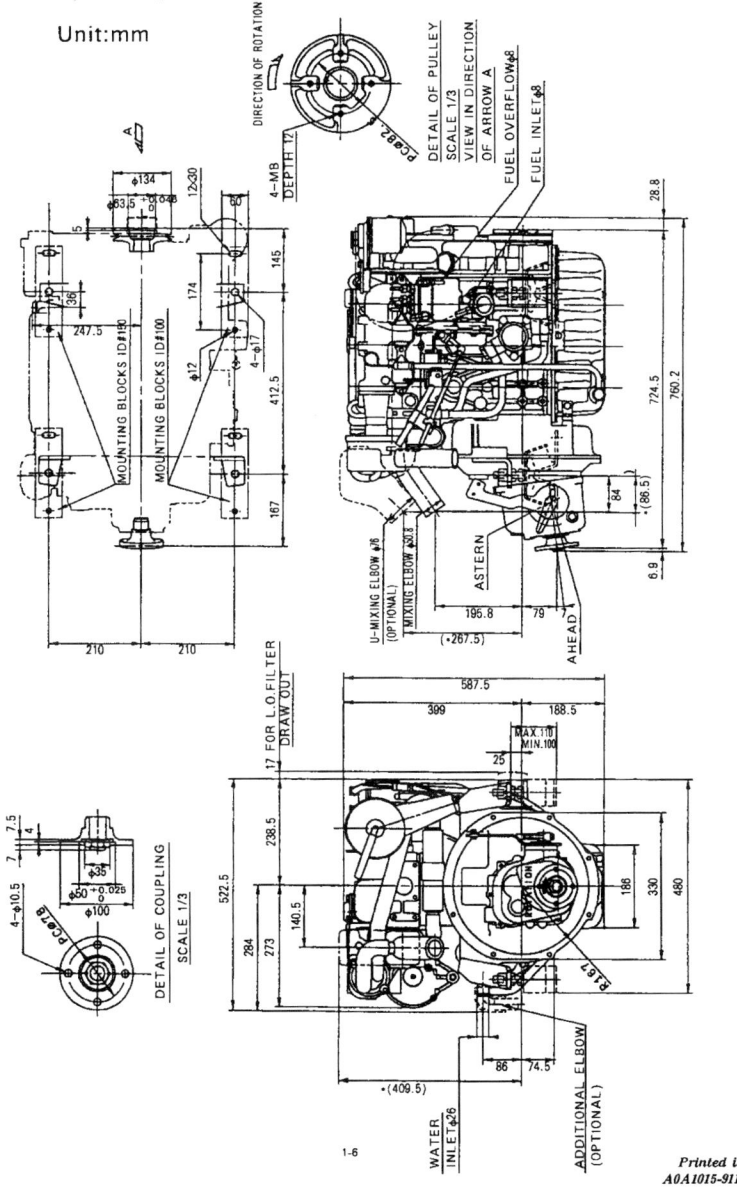

Chapter 1 General
3. Engine Outline

3JH2 Series

3-3. 3JH2TE(KBW10-E)

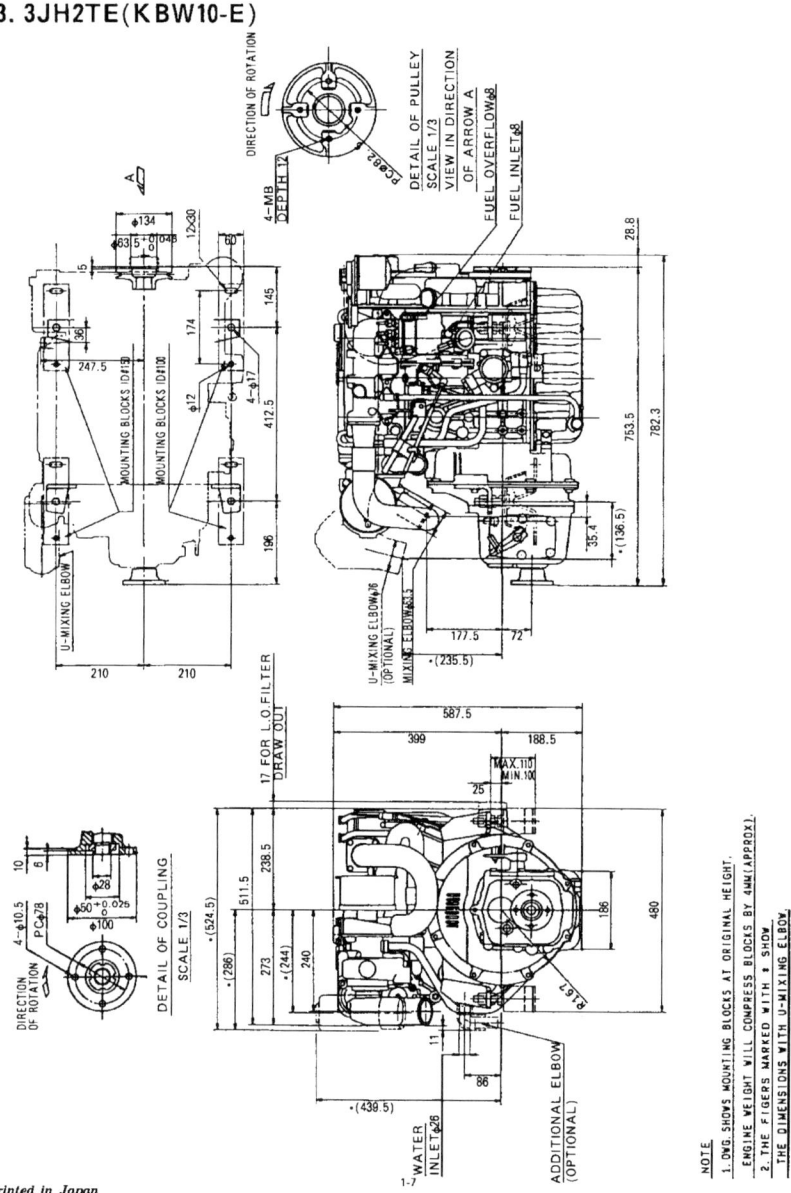

Chapter 1 General
3. Engine Outline 3JH2 Series

3-4. 3JH2-TBE(KM3A)

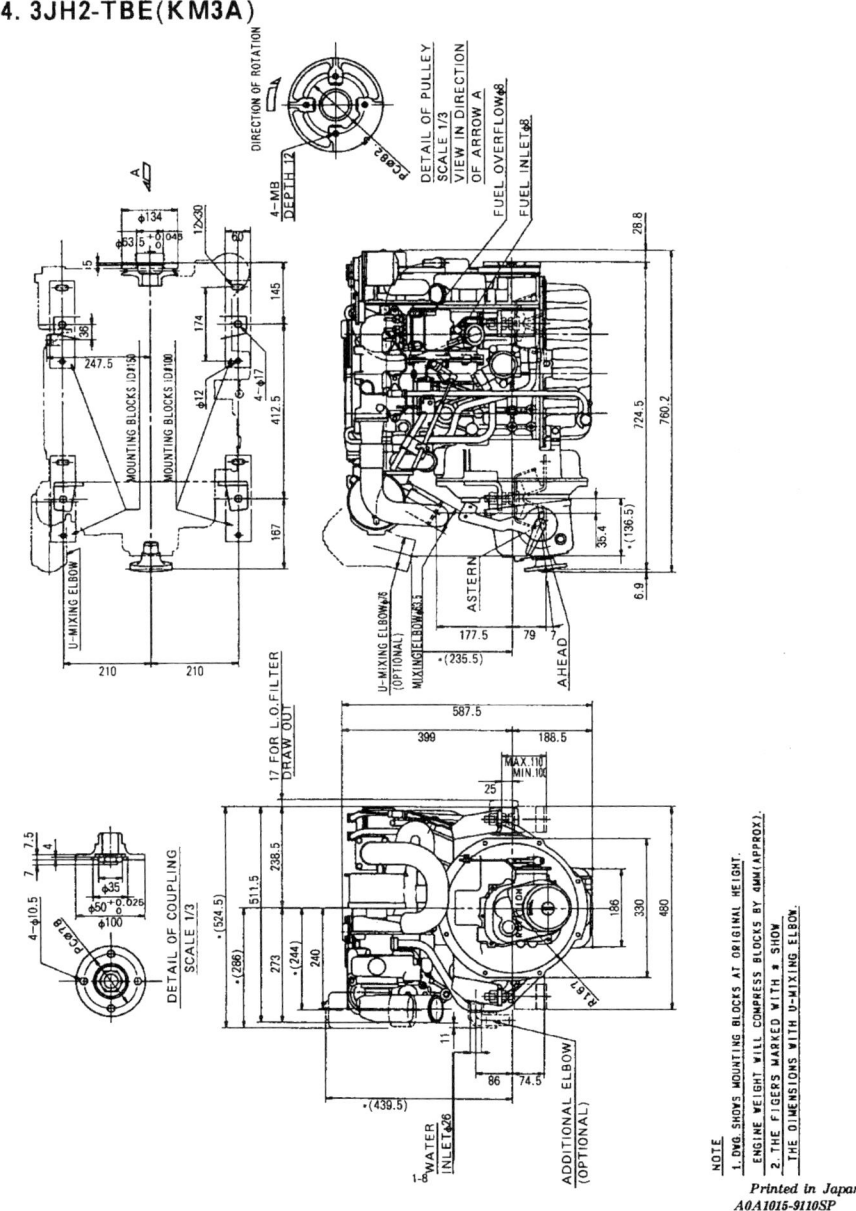

Chapter 1 General
3. Engine Outline
3JH2 Series

3JH25A/30A

Chapter 1 General
3. Engine Outline _____ 3JH2 Series

3-5. Dimensions of flywheel

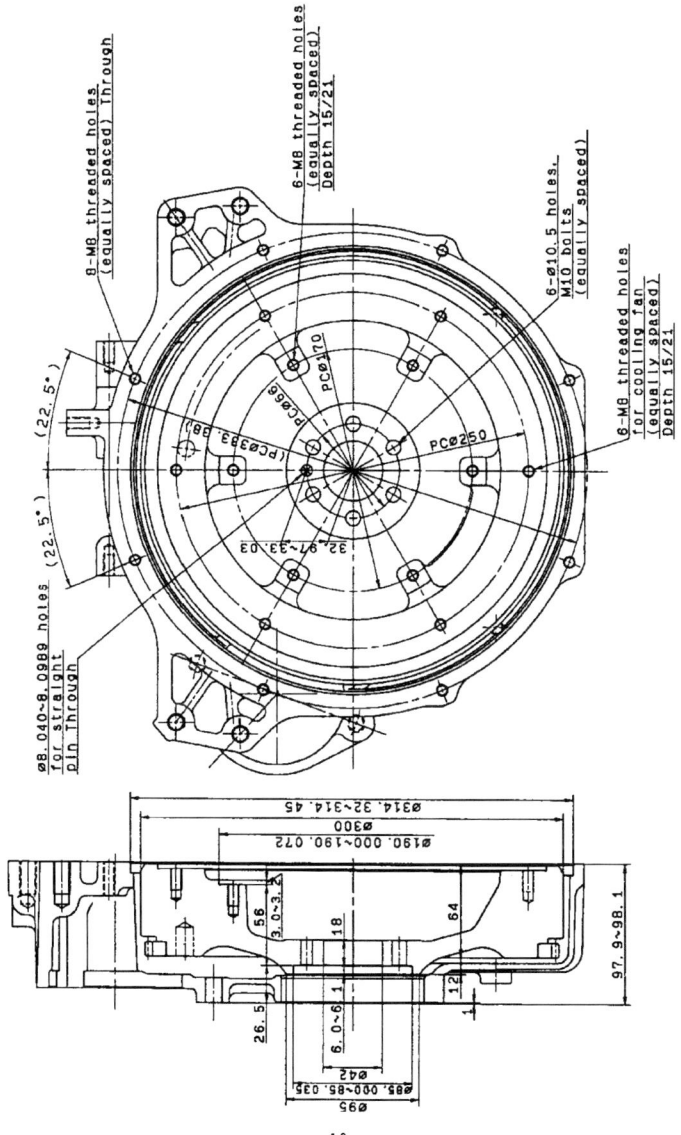

4. Performance Curves

4-1 3JH2-(B)E

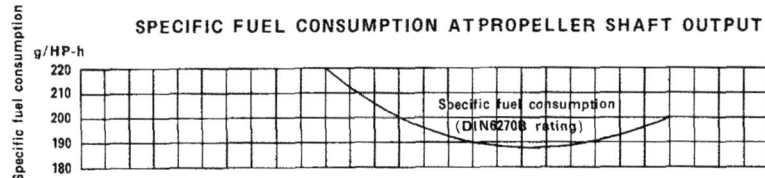

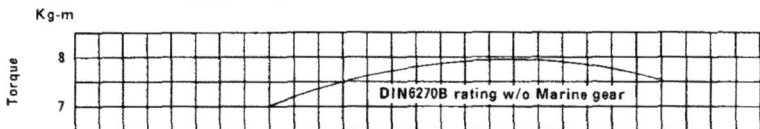

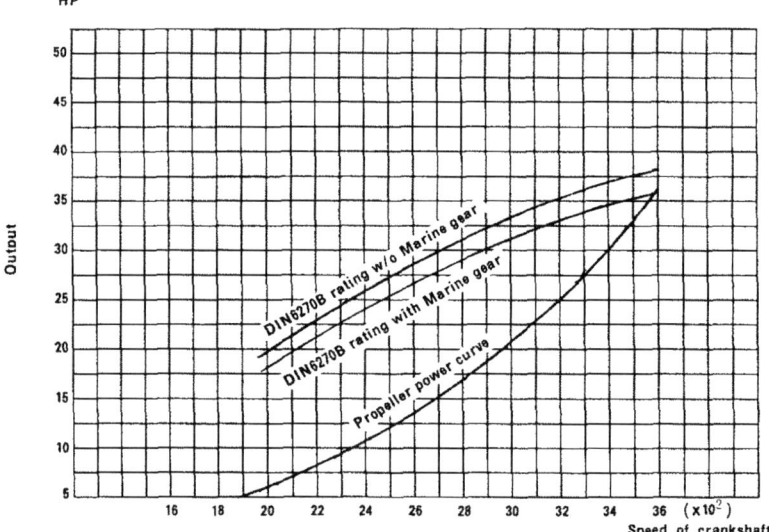

THE ENGINE FLYWHEEL OUTPUT IS APPROX 3% HIGHER

Chapter 1 General
4. Performance Curves   3JH2 Series

4-2. 3JH2-T(B)E

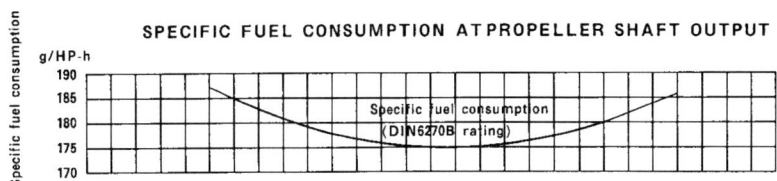

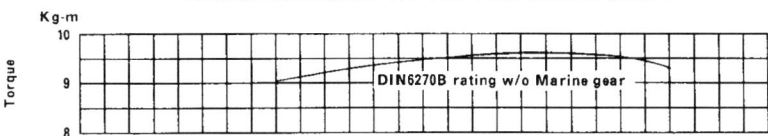

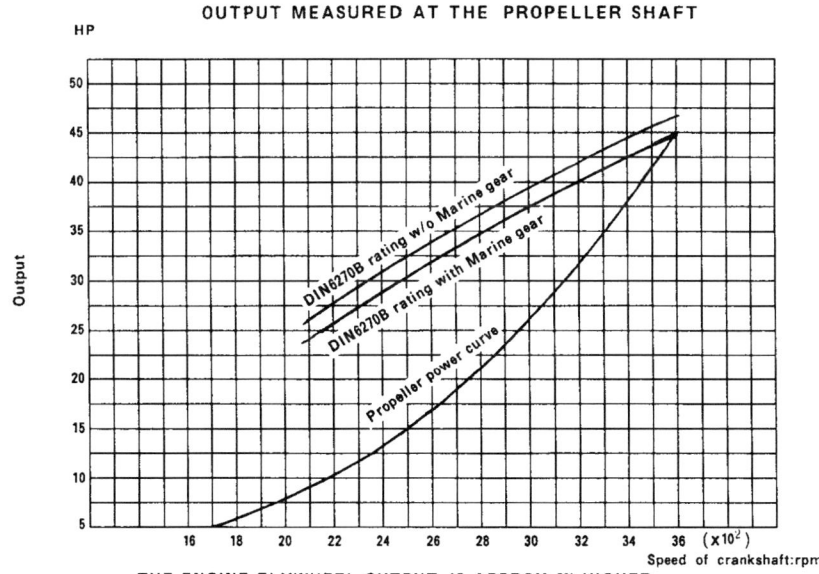

THE ENGINE FLYWHEEL OUTPUT IS APPROX 3% HIGHER

Chapter 1 General
4. Performance Curves

3JH2 series

3JH25A Performance Curve

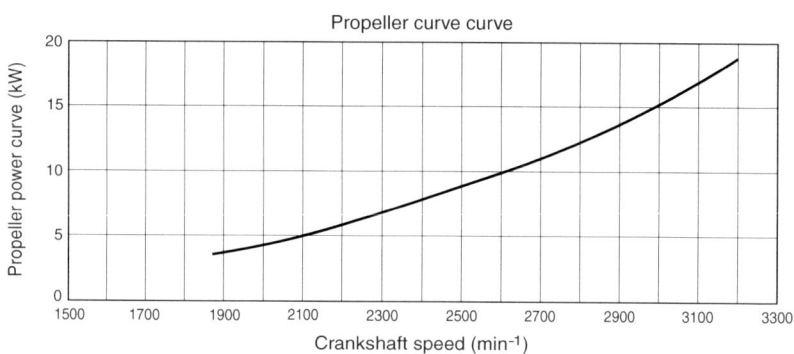

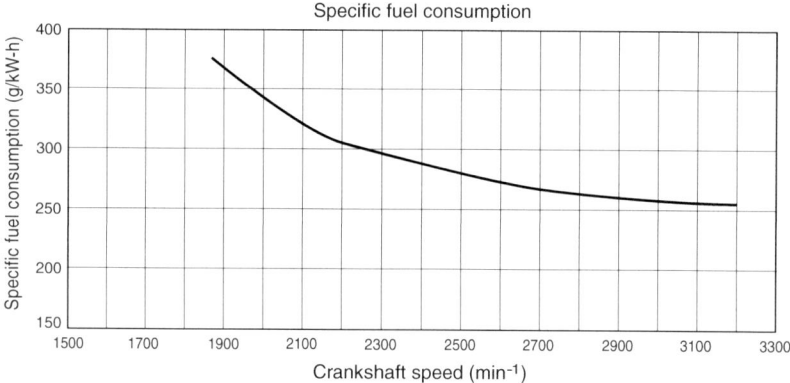

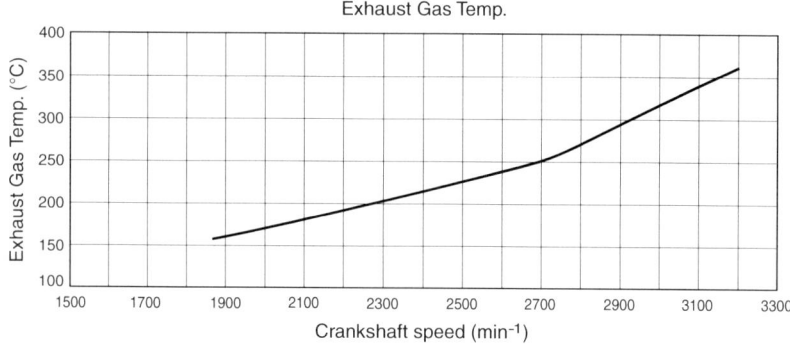

Chapter 1 General
4. Performance Curves

3JH30A Performance Curve

Propeller curve curve

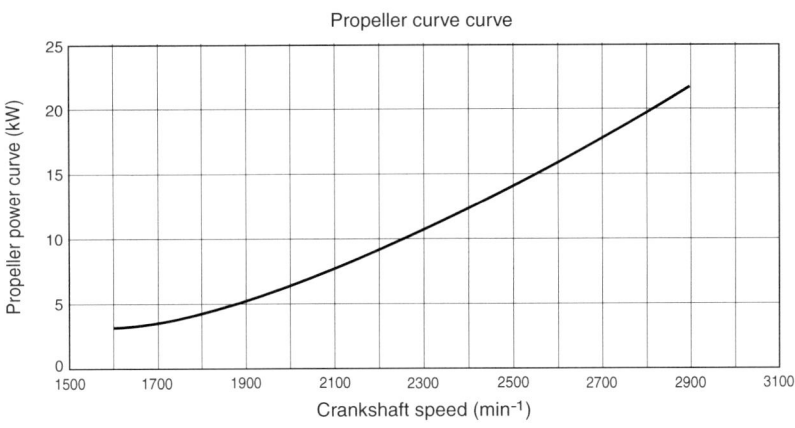

Specific fuel consumption

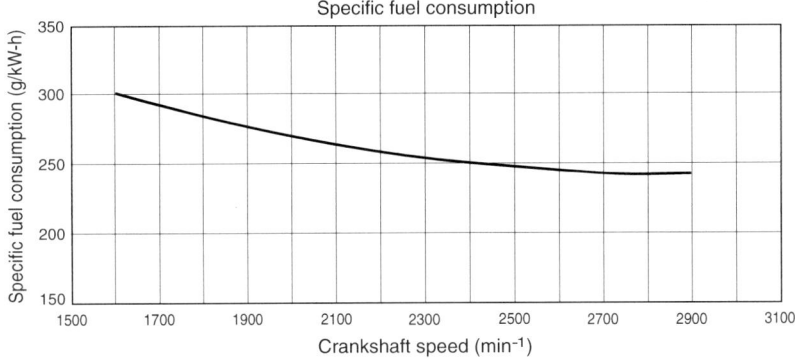

Exhaust Gas Temp.

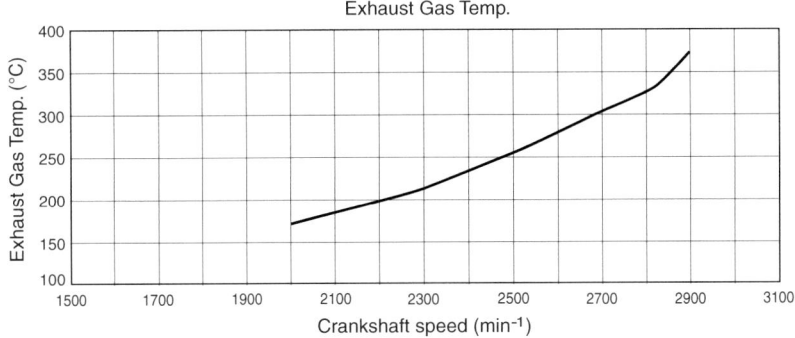

Chapter 1 General
5. Piping Diagrams

5. Piping Diagrams

5-1. 3JH2-(B)E × (KBW10E / KM3A)

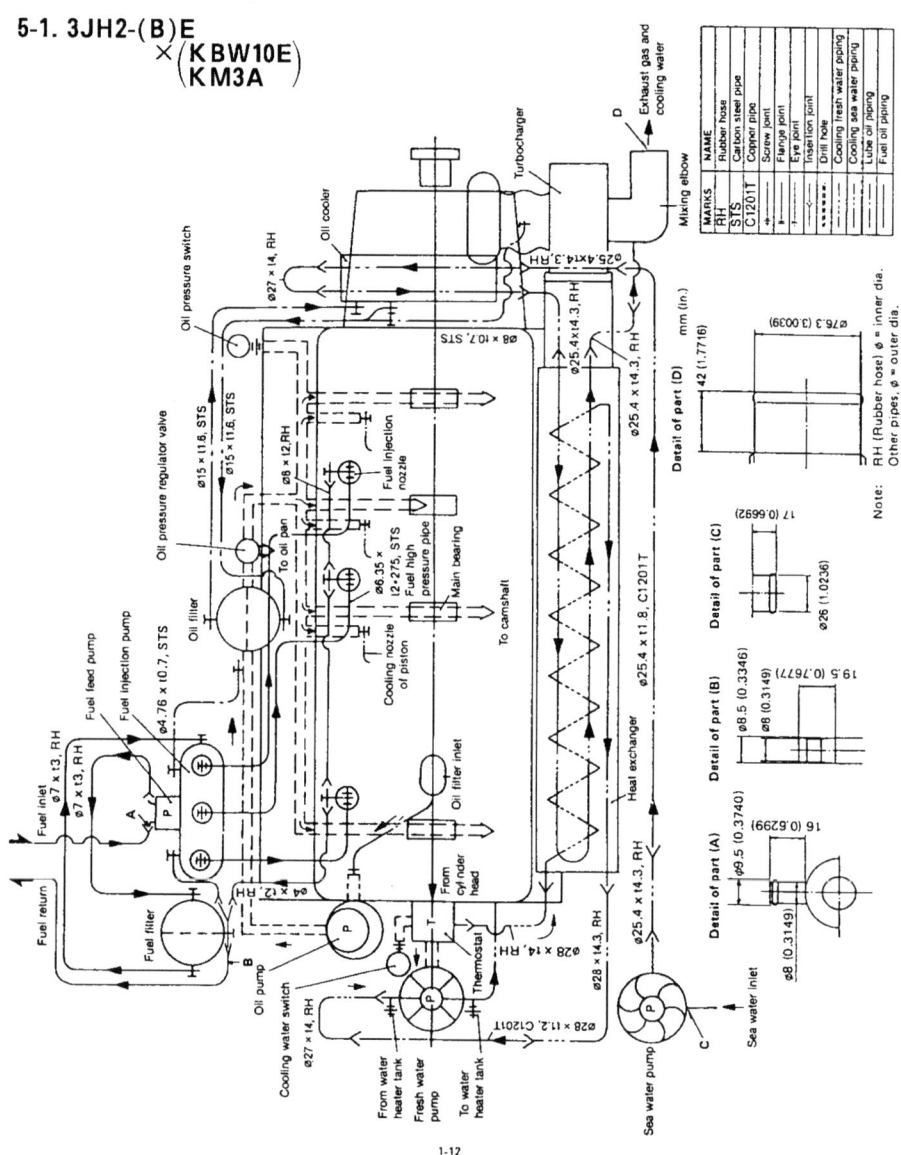

1-12

Chapter 1 General
5. Piping Diagrams

3JH2 Series

5-2. 3JH2-TE(KBW10-E)

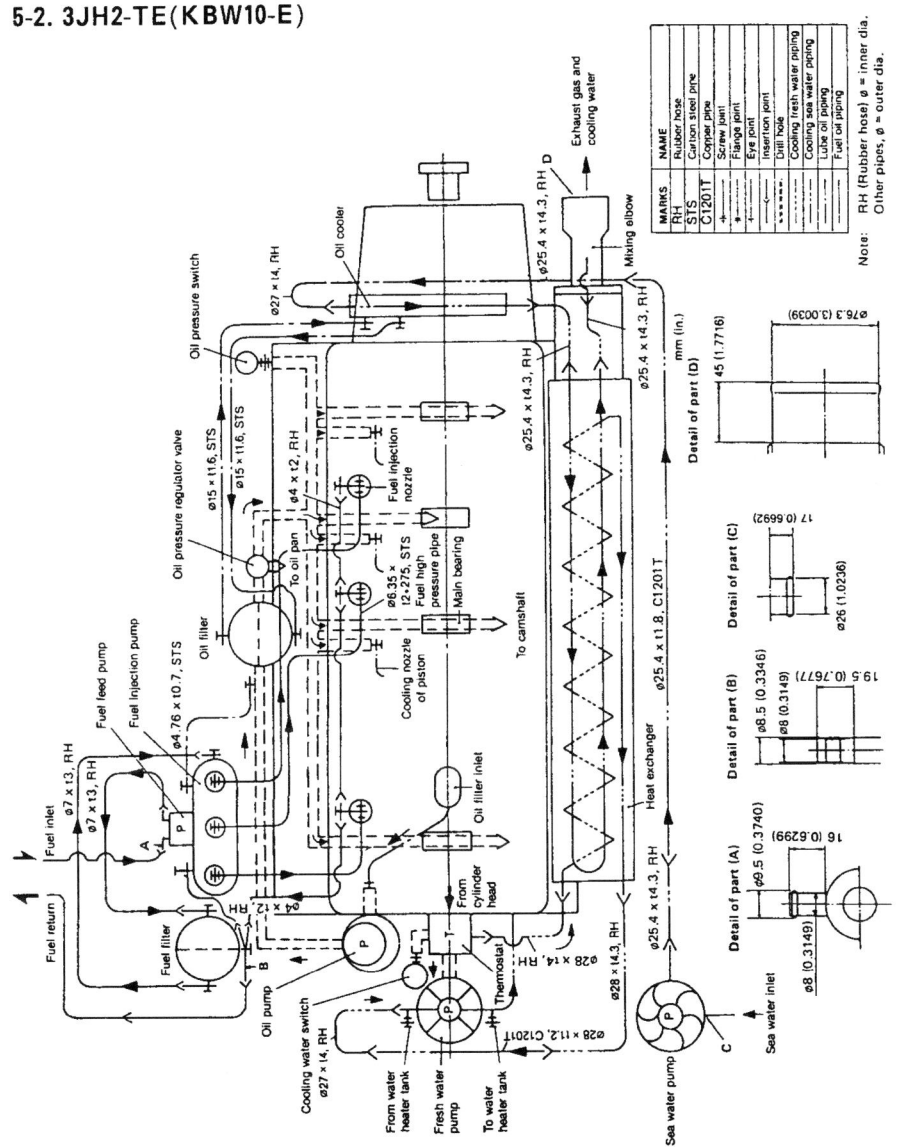

Chapter 1 General
5. Piping Diagrams

3JH2 Series

5-3. 3JH2-TBE(KM3A1)

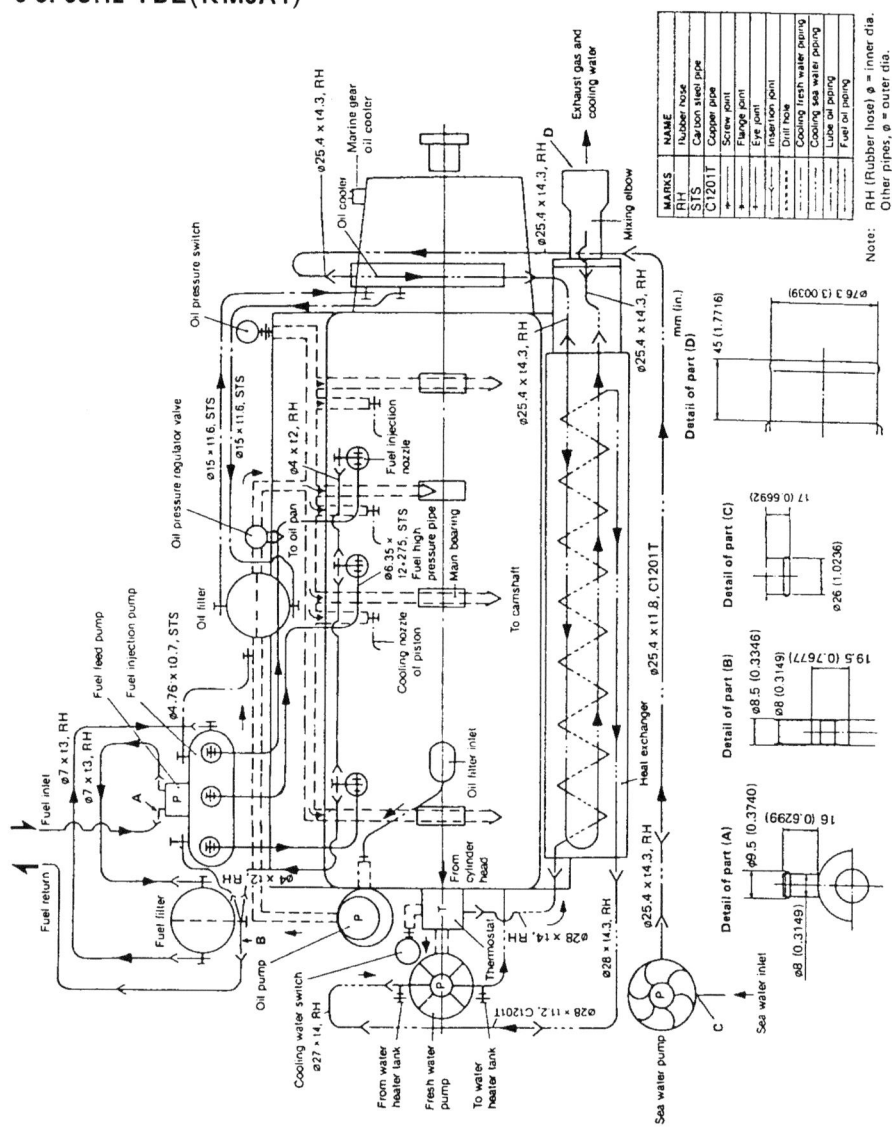

Chapter 1 General
5. Piping Diagrams

3JH2 series

3JH25A/30A

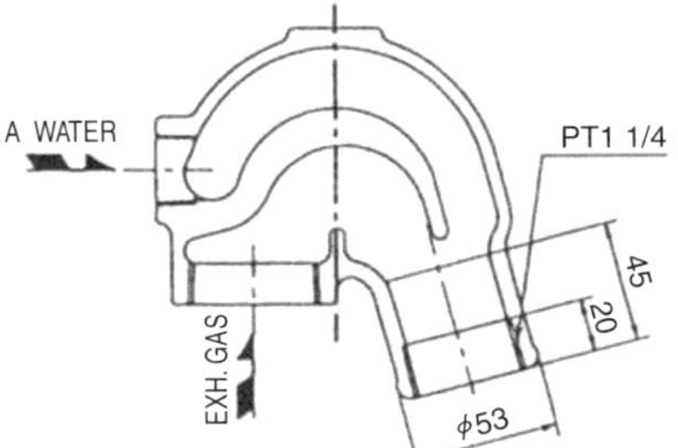

Marks of PIPING	NAME
R H	RUBBER HOSE
SGP	STEEL PIPE
STS	
C1201T	COPPER PIPE
	UNION SCREW JOINT
	FLANGE JOINT
	EYE JOINT
	INSERTION JOINT
	DRILL HOLE
	COOLING FRESH WATER PIPING
	COOLING SEA WATER PIPING
	LUB. OIL PIPING
	FUEL OIL PIPING
	MIST PIPE

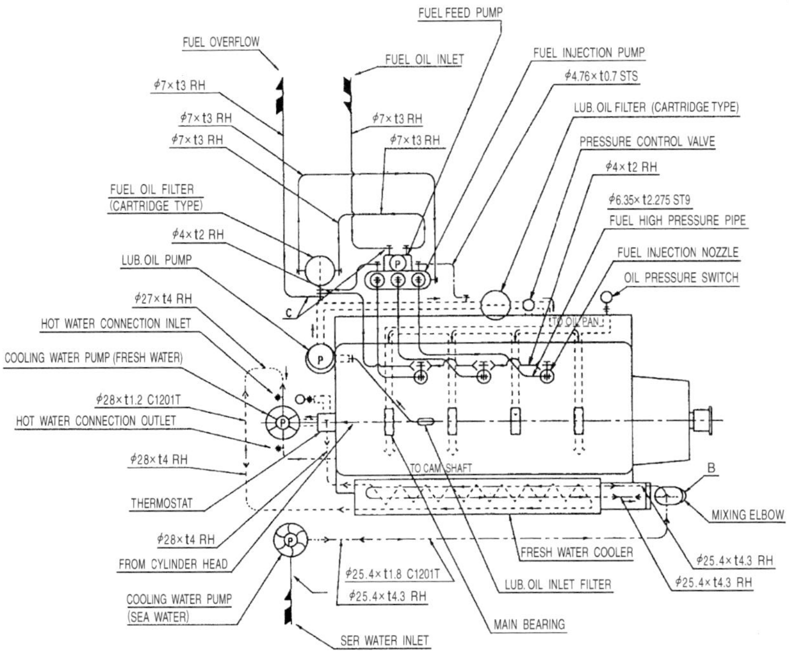

1-14-1

Printed in Japan
A0A1015-0302

CHAPTER 2
BASIC ENGINE PARTS

1. Cylinder Block ⋯⋯⋯⋯⋯⋯⋯⋯⋯⋯⋯⋯⋯⋯⋯ 2-1
2. Cylinder Head ⋯⋯⋯⋯⋯⋯⋯⋯⋯⋯⋯⋯⋯⋯⋯ 2-4
3. Piston and Piston Pins ⋯⋯⋯⋯⋯⋯⋯⋯⋯⋯ 2-11
4. Connecting Rod ⋯⋯⋯⋯⋯⋯⋯⋯⋯⋯⋯⋯⋯⋯ 2-15
5. Crankshaft and Main Bearing ⋯⋯⋯⋯⋯⋯⋯ 2-18
6. Camshaft and Tappets ⋯⋯⋯⋯⋯⋯⋯⋯⋯⋯⋯ 2-21
7. Timing Gear ⋯⋯⋯⋯⋯⋯⋯⋯⋯⋯⋯⋯⋯⋯⋯⋯ 2-24
8. Flywheel and Housing ⋯⋯⋯⋯⋯⋯⋯⋯⋯⋯⋯ 2-26

Chapter 2 Basic Engine
1. Cylinder block — 3JH2 Series

1. Cylinder Block

The cylinder block is a thin-skinned, (low-weight), short skirt type with rationally placed ribs. The side walls are wave shaped to maximize ridigity for strength and low noise.

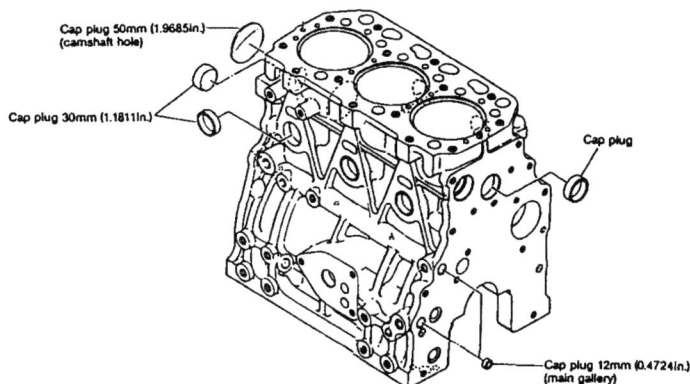

1-1 Inspection of parts

Make a visual inspection to check for cracks on engines that have frozen up, overturned or otherwise been subjected to undue stress. Perform a color check on any portions that appear to be cracked, and replace the cylinder block if the crack is not repairable.

1-2 Cleaning of oil holes

Clean all oil holes, making sure that none are clogged up and the blind plugs do not come off.

Color check kit
Part code No. 97550-004560

	Quantity
Penetrant	1
Developer	2
Cleaner	3

1-3 Color check procedure

(1) Clean the area to be inspected.
(2) Color check kit
    The color check test kit consists of an aerosol cleaner, penetrant and developer.
(3) Clean the area to be inspected with the cleaner.
    Either spray the cleaner on directly and wipe, or wipe the area with a cloth moistened with cleaner.
(4) Spray on red penetrant
    After cleaning, spray on the red penetrant and allow 5 ~ 10 minutes for penetration. Spray on more red penetrant if it dries before it has been able to penetrate.
(5) Spray on developer
    Remove any residual penetrant on the surface after the penetrant has penetrated, and spray on the developer. If there are any cracks in the surface, red dots or a red line will appear several minutes after the developer dries.
    Hold the developer 300 ~ 400mm (11.8110 ~ 15.7480in.) away from the area being inspected when spraying, making sure to coat the surface uniformly.
(6) Clean the surface with the cleaner.

NOTE: *Without fail, read the instructions for the color check kit before use.*

Chapter 2 Basic Engine
1. Cylinder block

3JH2 Series

I-4 Replacement of cup plugs

Step No.	Description	Procedure	Tool or material used
1.	Clean and remove grease from the hole into which the cup plug is to be driven. (Remove scale and sealing material previously applied.)	Remove foreign materials with a screw driver or saw blade.	• Screw driver or saw blade • Thinner
2.	Remove grease from the cup plug.	Visually check the nick around the plug.	• Thinner
3.	Apply Threebond No. 4 to the seat surface where the plug is to be driven in.	Apply over the whole outside of the plug.	• Threebond No. 4
4.	Insert the plug into the hole.	Insert the plug so that it sits correctly.	
5.	Place a driving tool on the cup plug and drive it in using a hammer.	Drive in the plug parallel to the seating surface.	• Driving tool • Hammer

2 ~ 3mm (0.0787 ~ 0.1181in.)

*Using the special tool, drive the cup plug so that the edge of the plug is 2mm (0.0787in.) below the cylinder surface.

3mm (0.1181in.)   100mm (3.9370in.)

mm (in.)

Plug dia.	d	D
ø12	ø11.9 ~ 12.0 (ø0.4685 ~ 0.4724)	ø20 (ø0.7874)
ø30	ø29.9 ~ 30.0 (ø1.1770 ~ 1.8110)	ø40 (ø1.5748)

Printed in Japan
A0A1015-9110SP

Chapter 2 Basic Engine
1. Cylinder block

3JH2 Series

1-5 Cylinder bore measurement

Measure the bore diameter with a cylinder gauge at the positions shown in the figure.
Replace the cylinder bore when the measured value exceeds the wear limit. Measurement must be done at least at 3 positions as shown in the figure, namely, top, middle and bottom positions in both directions along the crankshaft rotation and crankshaft center lines.

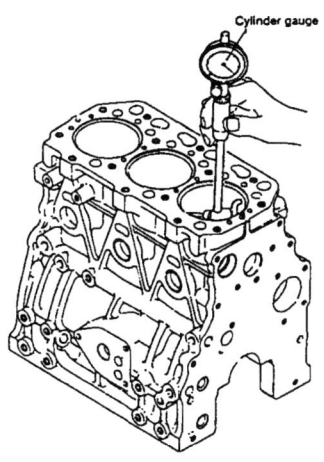

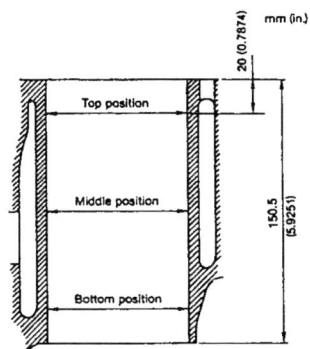

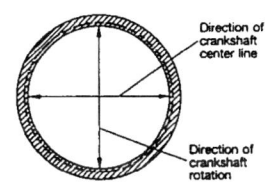

mm (in.)

	Standard	Wear limit
Cylinder bore dia.	ø82.00 ~ 82.03 (3.2283 ~ 3.2295)	ø82.06 (3.2307)
Cylinder roundness	0 ~ 0.01 (0 ~ 0.0004)	0.02 (0.0008)

Chapter 2 Basic Engine
2. Cylinder Head

2. Cylinder Head

The cylinder head is of 4-cylinder integral construction, mounted with 18 bolts. Special alloy stellite with superior resistance to heat and wear is fitted on the seats, and the area between the valves is cooled by a water jet.

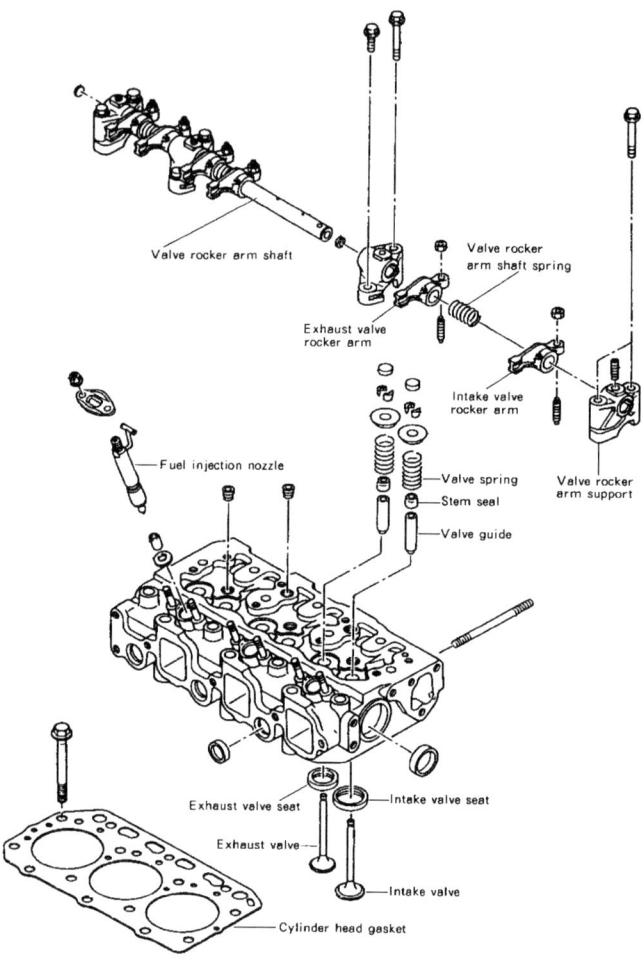

Chapter 2 Basic Engine
2. Cylinder Head

2-1 Inspecting the cylinder head

The cylinder head is subjected to very severe operating conditions with repeated high pressure, high temperature and cooling. Thoroughly remove all the carbon and dirt after disassembly and carefully inspect all parts.

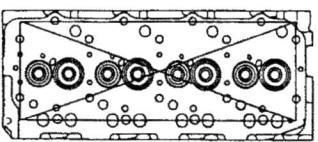

2-1.1 Distortion of the combustion surface

Carefully check for cylinder head distortion as this leads to gasket damage and compression leaks.
(1) Clean the cylinder head surface.
(2) Place a straight-edge along each of the four sides and each diagonal. Measure the clearance between the straight-edge and combustion surface with a feeler gauge.

Measurement procedure

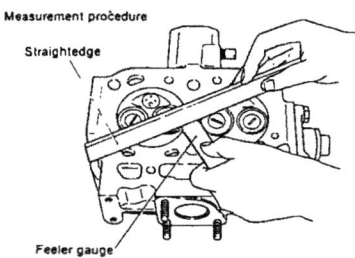

mm (in.)

	Standard	Wear limit
Cylinder head distortion	0.05 (0.0019) or less	0.15 (0.0059)

2-1.2 Checking for cracks in the combustion surface

Remove the fuel injection nozzle, intake and exhaust valve and clean the combustion surface. Check for discoloration or distortion and conduct a color check test to check for any cracks.

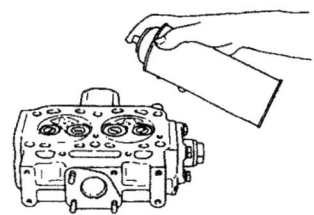

2-1.3 Checking the intake and exhaust valve seats

Check the surface and width of the valve seats.
If they are too wide, or if the surfaces are rough, correct to the following standards:

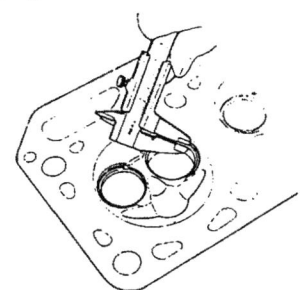

Seat angle	Intake	120°
	Exhaust	90°

mm (in.)

Seat width	Standard	Wear limit
Intake	1.28 (0.0504)	1.78 (0.0700)
Exhaust	1.77 (0.0697)	2.27 (0.0894)

Intake valve seat

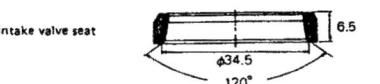

Exhaust valve seat

Standard dimension

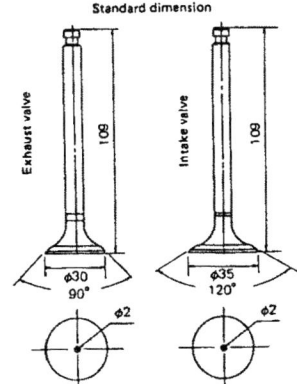

Chapter 2 Basic Engine
2. Cylinder Head

2-2 Valve seat correction procedure

The most common method for correcting unevenness of the seat surface with a seat grinder is as follows:
(1) Use a seat grinder to make the surface even.
   As the valve seat width will be enlarged, first use a 70° grinder, then grind the seat to the standard dimension with a 15° grinder.

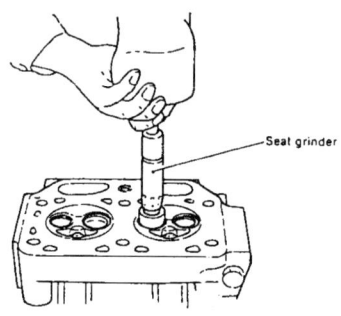

Seat grinder	Intake valve	30°
	Exhaust valve	45°

NOTE: When seat adjustment is necessary, be sure to check the valve and valve guide. If the clearance exceeds the tolerance, replace the valve or the valve guide, and then grind the seat.

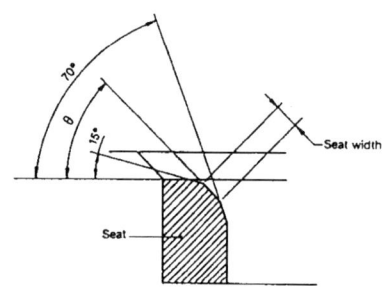

(2) Knead valve compound with oil and finish the valve seat with a lapping tool.
(3) Final finishing should be done with oil only.

Lapping tool
Use a rubber cap type lapping tool for cylinders without a lapping tool groove slit.

NOTE: Clean the valve and cylinder head with light oil or the equivalent after valve seat finishing is completed, and make sure that there are no grindings remaining.

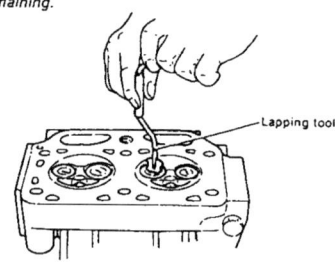

NOTE: 1. Insert adjusting shims between the valve spring and cylinder head when seats have been refinished with a seat grinder.
2. Measure valve distortion after valve seat refinishing has been completed, and replace the valve and valve seat if it exceeds the tolerance.

2-3 Intake/exhaust valves, valve guides
2-3.1 Wearing and corrosion of valve stem

Replace the valve if the valve stem is excessively worn or corroded.

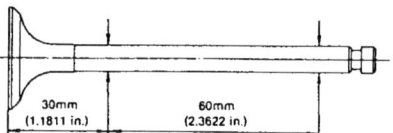

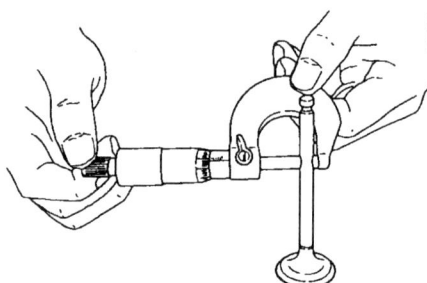

mm (in.)

Valve stem outside dia.	Standard	Wear limit
Intake	⌀7.960 ~ 7.975 (⌀0.3134 ~ 0.3140)	-0.13 (-0.0051)
Exhaust	⌀7.955 ~ 7.970 (⌀0.3132 ~ 0.3138)	-0.13 (-0.0051)

Chapter 2 Basic Engine
2. Cylinder Head

2-3.2 Inspection of valve seat wear and contact surface

Inspect for valve seat scratches and excessive wear. Check to make sure the contact surface is normal. The seat angle must be checked and adjusted if the valve seat contact surface is much smaller than the width of the valve seat.

NOTE: Keep in mind the fact that the intake and discharge valve have different diameters.

2-3.3 Valve sinking

Over long periods of use and repeated lappings, combustion efficiency may drop. Measure the sinking distance and replace the valve and valve seat if the valve sink exceeds the tolerance.

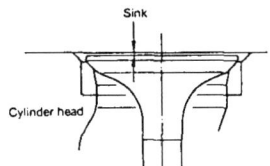

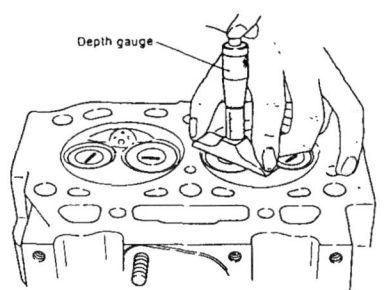

	Standard	Wear limit
Valve sink	0.4 ~ 0.6 (0.0157 ~ 0.0236)	1.5 (0.0590)

mm (in.)

2-3.4 Valve guide

(1) Measuring inner diameter of valve guide.
Measure the inner diameter of the valve guide and replace it if it exceeds the wear limit.

mm (in.)

		Standard	Wear limit
Valve guide inside dia.	Intake	ø8.010 ~ 8.025 (ø0.3154 ~ 0.3159)	+0.2 (0.0079)
	Exhaust	ø8.015 ~ 8.030 (ø0.3156 ~ 0.3161)	+0.2 (0.0079)

NOTE: The inner diameter standard dimensions assume a pressure fit.

(2) Replacing the valve guide
Use the insertion tool and tap in the guide with a mallet.

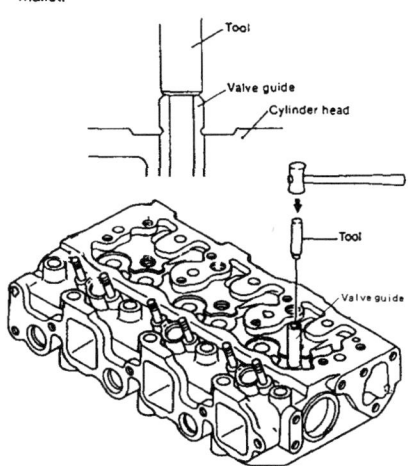

The intake valve guide and exhaust valve guide are of different shapes/dimensions. The one with a groove around it is the exhaust valve guide and the one without is the intake valve guide.

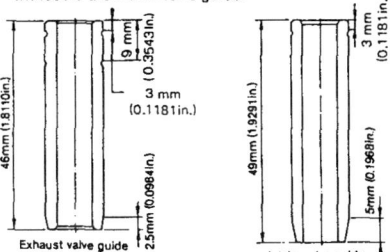

(3) Valve guide projection
The valve guide should project 15mm from the top of the cylinder head.

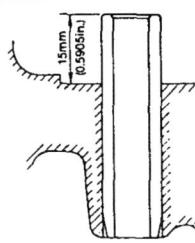

Chapter 2 Basic Engine
2. Cylinder Head

(4) Valve stem seals
The valve stem seals in the intake/exhaust valve guides cannot be re-used once they are removed—be sure to replace them.
When assembling the intake/exhaust valves, apply an adequate quantity of engine oil on the valve stem before inserting them.

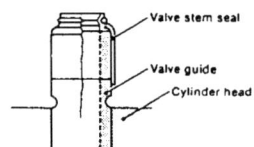

2-4 Valve springs
2-4.1 Checking valve springs
(1) Check the spring for scratches or corrosion.
(2) Measure the free length of the spring.

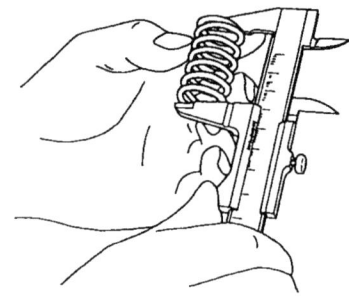

(3) Measure inclination.

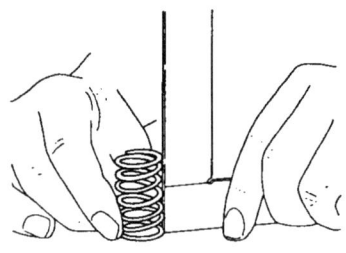

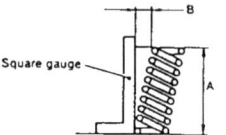

(4) Measure spring tension.

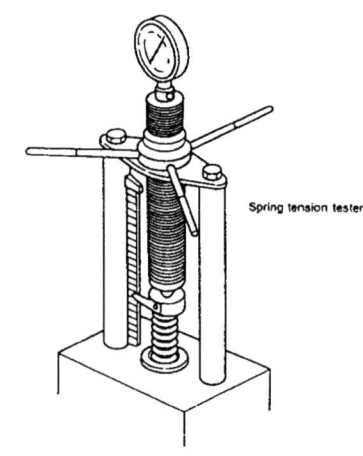

mm (in.)

Valve spring	Standard	Wear limit
Free length	44.4 (1.7480)	43 (1.6929)
Length when attached	40 (1.5748)	—
Load when attached	12kg (26.46 lb.)	10kg (22.05 lb.)

Assembling valve springs
The side with the smaller pitch (painted yellow) should face down (cylinder head).

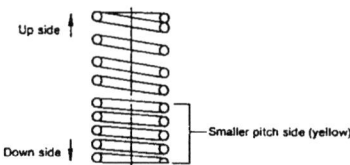

NOTE: *The pitch of the valve spring is not even. The side with the smaller pitch (yellow) should face down (cylinder head) when assembled.*

(5) Spring retainer and spring cotter
Inspect the inside face of the spring retainer, the outside surface of the spring cotter, the contact area of the spring cotter inside surface and the notch in the head of the valve stem. Replace the spring retainer and spring cotter when the contact area is less than 70%, or when the spring cotter has been recessed because of wear.

Chapter 2 Basic Engine
2. Cylinder Head

3JH2 Series

2-5 Assembling the cylinder head

Partially tighten the bolts in the specified order and then tighten to the specified torque, being careful that the head does not get distorted.
(1) Clean out the cylinder head bolt holes.
(2) Check for foreign matter on the cylinder head surface where it comes in contact with the block.
(3) Coat the head bolt threads and nut seats with lube oil.
(4) Use the positioning pins to line up the head gasket with the cylinder block.
(5) Match up the cylinder head with the head gasket and mount.

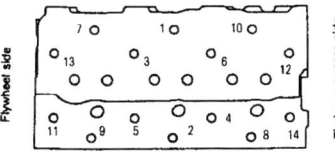

	First	Second
		kg-m (ft-lb)
Tightening torque	3.5 ~ 4.5 (25.32 ~ 32.55)	7.5 ~ 8.5 (54.25 ~ 61.48)

2-6 Measuring top clearance

(1) Place a high quality fuse (Ø1.5mm (0.0591in.), 10mm (0.3937in.) long) in three positions on the flat part of the piston head.
(2) Assemble the cylinder head gasket and the cylinder block and tighten the bolts in the specified order to the specified torque.
(3) Turn the crank, (in the direction of engine revolution), and press the fuse against the piston until it breaks.
(4) Remove the head and take out the broken fuse.
(5) Measure the three positions where each fuse is broken and calculate the average.
(0.71 ~ 0.75mm (0.0280 ~ 0.0295in.) is ideal)

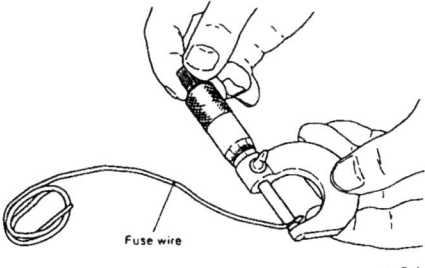

	mm (in.)
Top clearance	0.71 ~ 0.89 (0.0280 ~ 0.0350)

2-7 Intake and exhaust valve arms

Valve arm and valve arm bushing wear may change opening/closing timing of the valve, and may in turn affect engine performance according to the extent of the change.

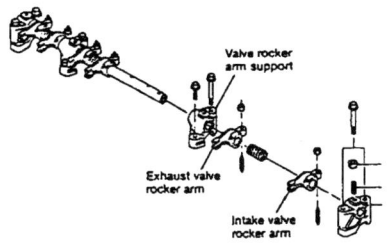

(1) Valve arm shaft and valve arm bushing
Measure the outer diameter of the shaft and the inner diameter of the bearing, and replace if wear exceeds the limit.

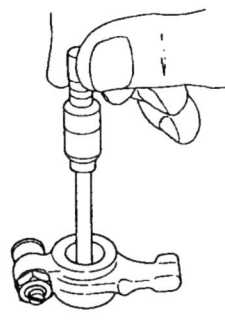

		Standard	Wear limit
			mm (in.)
Intake and exhaust valve rocker arm shaft outside dia.	A	15.966 ~ 15.988 (0.6285 ~ 0.6294)	15.955 (0.6281)
Intake and exhaust valve rocker arm inside dia.	B	16.000 ~ 16.027 (0.6299 ~ 0.6310)	16.090 (0.6334)
Valve rocker arm shaft and bushing clearance at assembly		0.012 ~ 0.061 (0.0005 ~ 0.0024)	0.135 (0.0053)

Replace the valve arm shaft bushing if it moves and replace the entire valve arm if there is no tightening clearance.

Chapter 2 Basic Engine
2. Cylinder Head

3JH2 Series

(2) Valve arm spring
   Check the valve arm spring and replace it if it is corroded or worn.
(3) Valve arm and valve top retainer wear
   Inspect the contact surface of the valve arm and replace it if there is abnormal wear or flaking.
(4) Inspect the contact surface of the valve clearance adjustment screw and push rod and replace if there is abnormal wear or flaking.

2-8 Adjustment of valve head clearance
(1) Make adjustments when the engine is cool.

	mm (in.)
Intake and exhaust head clearance	0.2 (0.0079)

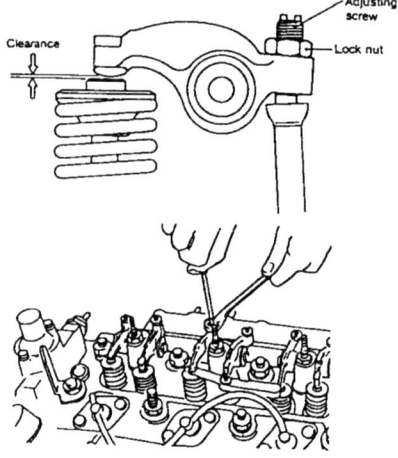

(2) Be sure that the opening and closing angles for both the intake and the exhaust valves are checked when the timing gear is disassembled (The gauge on the flywheel is read when the push rod turns the flywheel).

Model 3JH2-TE

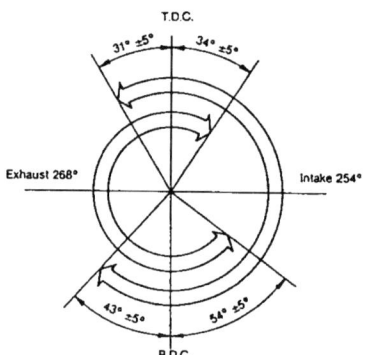

		3JH2E	3JH2-TE
Intake valve open	b. TDC	10° ~ 20°	26° ~ 36°
Intake valve closed	a. BDC	48° ~ 58°	38° ~ 48°
Exhaust valve open	b. BDC	51° ~ 61°	49° ~ 59°
Exhaust valve closed	a. TDC	13° ~ 23°	29° ~ 39°

3. Pistons and Piston Pins

Pistons are made of a special light alloy with superior thermal expansion characteristics, and the top of the piston forms a swirl type toroidal combustion chamber. The opposite face of the piston combustion surface is oil-jet cooled.

Pistons for engines with superchargers have a valve recess for the intake and exhaust valves.

The clearance between the piston and cylinder liner is kept at the proper value by the piston and cylinder liner property fit effected during assembly at the Yanmar factory.

IMPORTANT:
Piston shape differs among engine models. If an incorrect piston is installed, combustion performance will drop. Be sure to check the applicable engine model identification mark (I. D. Mark) on the piston to insure use of the correct part.

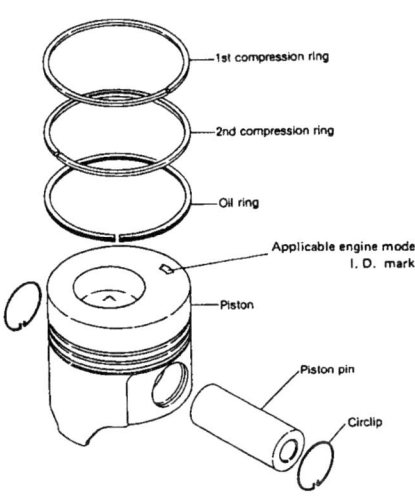
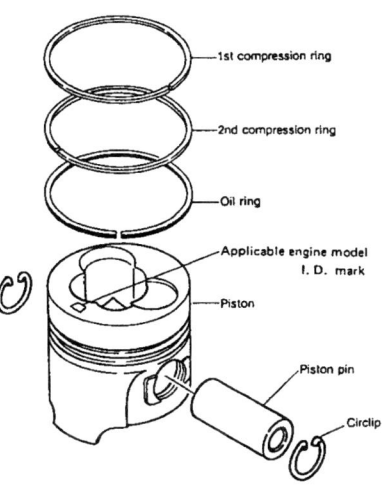

I.D.Mark for Piston

Engine Model	I.D.mark
3JH2E	–
3JH2–TE	3B

I.D.Mark for Piston pin

Engine Model	I.D.mark	Size	Part No.
3JH2E	–	φ26×66	129150-22300
3JH2–TE	3	φ26×69	129171-22300

Chapter 2 Basic Engine
3. Piston and Piston Pins

3-1 Piston
3-1.1 Piston head and combustion surface
Remove the carbon that has accumulated on the piston head and combustion surface, taking care not to scratch the piston. Check the combustion surface for any damage.

3-1.2 Measurement of piston outside diameter/inspection
(1) Replace the piston if the outsides of the piston or ring grooves are worn.
(2) Measure the piston 22mm (0.8661in.) from the bottom at right angles to the piston pin.

3-1.3 Replacing the piston
A floating type piston pin is used in this engine. The piston pin can be pressed into the piston pin hole at room temperature (coat with oil to make it slide in easily).

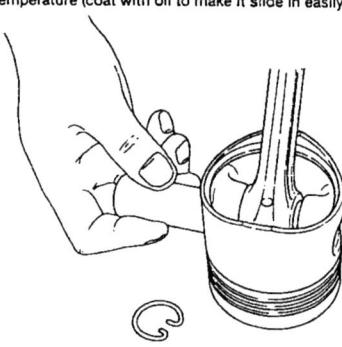

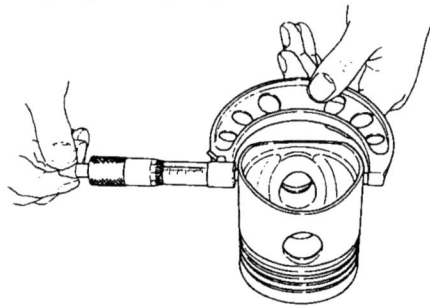

3-2 Piston pin
Measure the outer diameter and replace the pin if it is excessively worn.

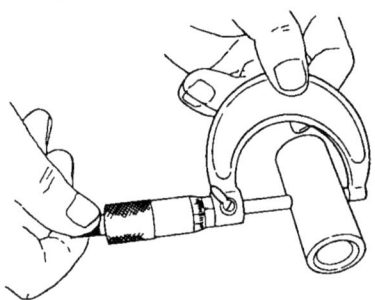

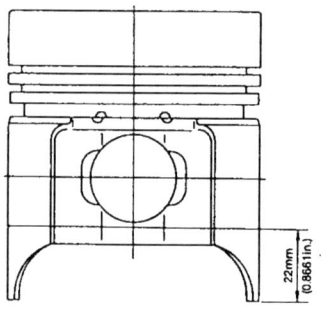

mm (in.)

Standard	Wear limit
81.919 ~ 81.949 (3.22515 ~ 3.22634)	77.81 (3.0633)

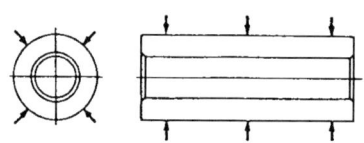

mm(in.)

	Standard	Wear limit
Piston pin insert hole dia.	φ26.000~26.009 (φ1.0236~1.0240)	+0.020 (0.0008)
Piston pin outside dia.	φ25.987~26.000 (φ1.0231~1.0236)	−0.025 (0.0009)
Standard clearance	0~0.022 (0~0.0009)	0.045 (0.0018)

3-3 Piston rings

There are 2 compression rings and 1 oil ring.
The absence of an oil ring on the piston skirt prevents oil from being kept on the thrust surface and in turn provides good lubrication.

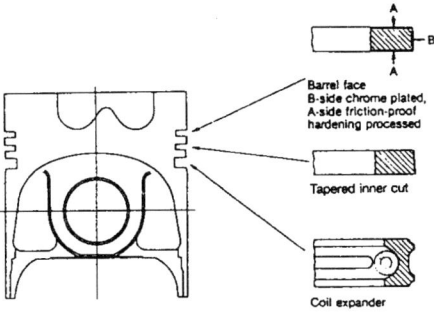

Barrel face
B-side chrome plated,
A-side friction-proof hardening processed

Tapered inner cut

Coil expander

3-3.1 Measuring the rings

Measure the thickness and width of the rings, and the ring-to-groove clearance after installation. Replace if wear exceeds the limit.

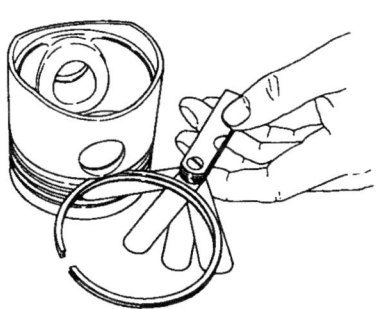

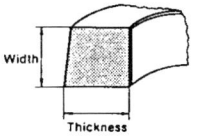

Width / Thickness

		Standard	mm (in.) Wear limit
First piston ring	Groove width	2.060 ~ 2.075 (0.0811 ~ 0.0816)	—
	Ring width	1.975 ~ 1.990 (0.0777 ~ 0.0783)	—
	Groove and ring clearance	0.070 ~ 0.100 (0.0027 ~ 0.0039)	0.2 (0.0078)
Second piston ring	Groove width	2.025 ~ 2.040 (0.0797 ~ 0.0803)	—
	Ring width	1.970 ~ 1.990 (0.0776 ~ 0.0783)	—
	Groove and ring clearance	0.035 ~ 0.070 (0.0013 ~ 0.0027)	0.2 (0.0078)
Oil ring	Groove width	4.020 ~ 4.035 (0.1582 ~ 0.1588)	—
	Ring width	3.975 ~ 3.990 (0.1564 ~ 0.1570)	—
	Groove and ring clearance	0.030 ~ 0.060 (0.0011 ~ 0.0023)	0.2 (0.0078)

3-3.2 Measuring piston ring gap

Press the piston ring onto a piston liner and measure the piston ring gap with a gauge. Press on the ring about 30mm (1.811in.) from the bottom of the liner.

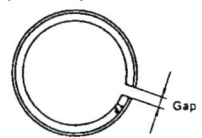

Gap

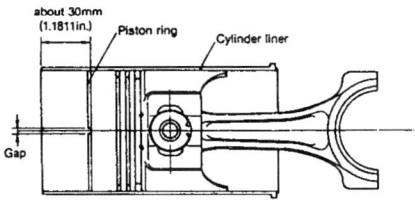

about 30mm (1.1811in.) Piston ring Cylinder liner

Gap

	Standard	mm (in.) Wear limit
First piston ring gap	0.25 ~ 0.40 (0.0098 ~ 0.0157)	1.5 (0.0590)
Second piston ring gap	0.20 ~ 0.40 (0.0078 ~ 0.0157)	1.5 (0.0590)
Oil ring gap	0.20 ~ 0.40 (0.0078 ~ 0.0157)	1.5 (0.0590)

3-3.3 Replacing the piston rings

(1) Thoroughly clean the ring grooves when replacing piston rings.
(2) The side with the manufacturer's mark (near piston ring gap) should face up.

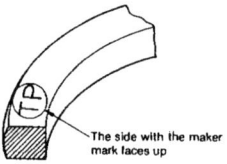

(3) After fitting the piston ring, make sure it moves easily and smoothly.
(4) Stagger the piston rings at 120° intervals, making sure none of them line up with the piston.

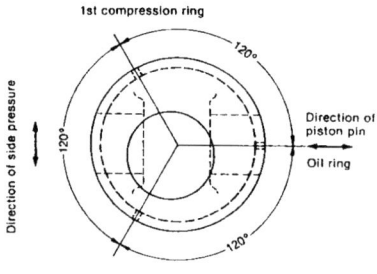

(5) The oil ring is provided with a coil expander. The coil expander joint should be opposite (staggered 180°) the oil ring gap.

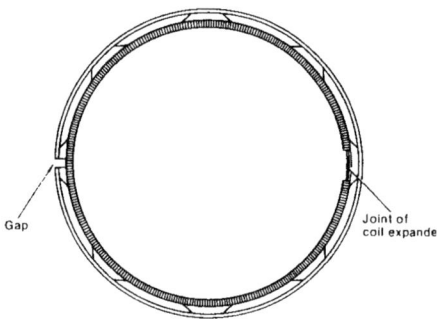

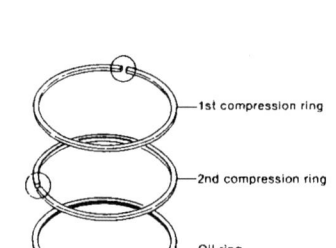

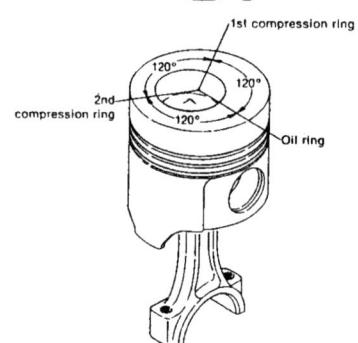

4. Connecting Rod

The connecting rod is made of high-strength forged carbon steel.
The large end with the aluminium metal can be separated into two and the small end has a 2-layer copper alloy coil bushing.

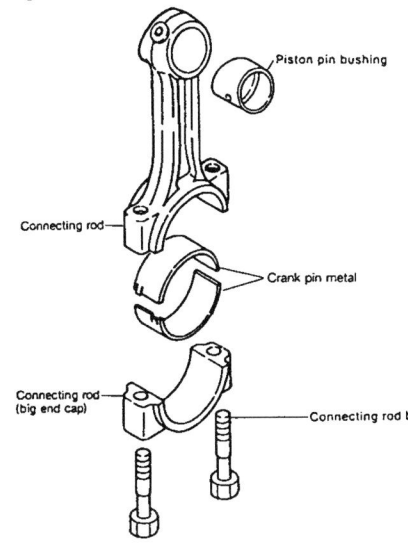

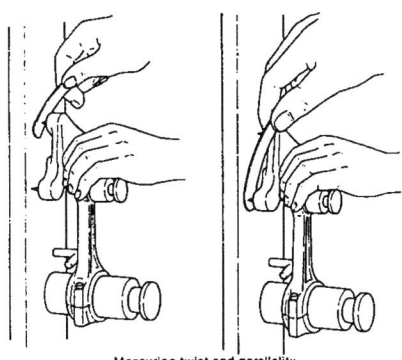

Measuring twist and parallelity

mm (in.)

	Standard	Wear limit
Connecting rod twist and parallelity	0.05 (0.0019)	0.07 (0.0027)

4-1.2 Checking thrust clearance

Fit the respective crank pins to the connecting rod and check to make sure that the clearance in the crankshaft direction is correct.

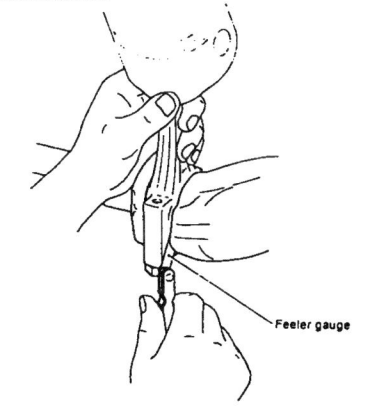

4-1 Inspecting the connection rod

4-1.1 Twist and parallelism of the large and small ends

Insert the measuring tool into the large and small ends of the connecting rod. Measure the extent of twist and parallelism and replace if they exceed the tolerance.

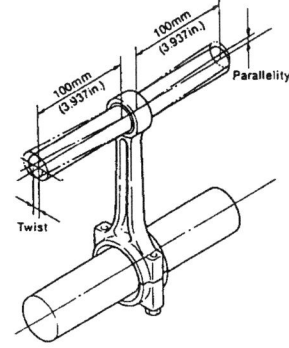

mm (in.)

	Standard	Wear limit
Connecting rod side clearance	0.20 ~ 0.40 (0.0078 ~ 0.0157)	0.55 (0.0216)

4-2 Crank pin bushing

4-2.1 Checking crank pin bushing

Check for flaking, melting or seizure on the contact surface.

4-2.2 Measuring crank pin oil clearance

Use a plastic gauge.

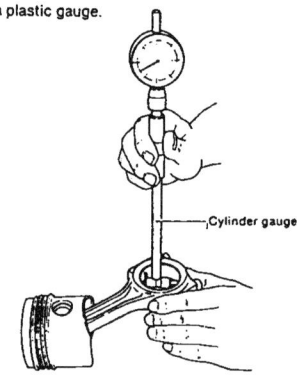

Procedure
(1) Use the press gauge (Plastigage) for measuring oil clearance in the crank pin.
(2) Mount the connecting rod on the crank pin (tighten to specified torque).

Connecting rod tightening torque	5.0 ~ 5.5 kg-m (36.15 ~ 39.77 ft-lb)

(3) Remove the connecting rod and measure the broken plastic gauge with measuring paper.

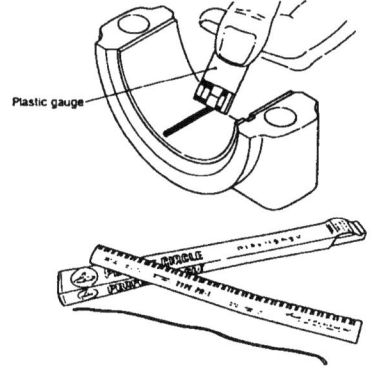

4-2.3 Precautions on replacement of crank pin bushing

(1) Wash the crank pin bushing.
(2) Wash the large end cap, mount the crank pin bushing and make sure that it fits tightly on the large end cap.
(3) When assembling the connecting rod, match up the large end and large end cap number. Coat the bolts with engine oil and gradually tighten them alternately to the specified torque.
If a torque wrench is not available, make match marks on the bolt heads and large end cap (to indicate the proper torque position) and retighten the bolts to those positions.

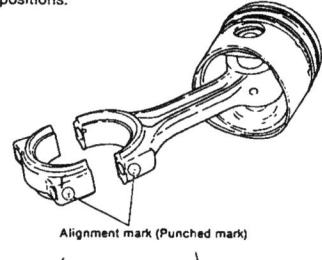
Alignment mark (Punched mark)

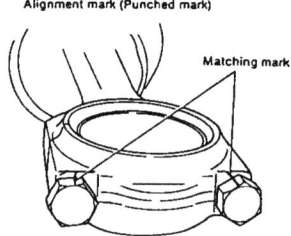
Matching mark

(4) Make sure there is no sand, metal cuttings or other foreign matter in the lube oil, and that the crankshaft is not scratched. Take special care in cleaning the oil holes.

4-3 Piston pin bushing

(1) Measuring piston pin clearance
Excessive piston pin bushing wear may result in damage to the piston pin or the piston itself.

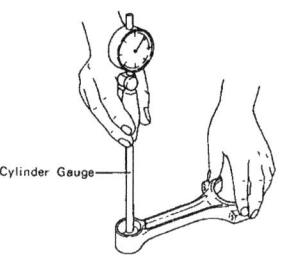
Cylinder Gauge

Chapter 2 Basic Engine
4. Connecting Rod

mm(in.)

	Standard	Wear limit
Piston pin bushing inside dia	26.025~26.038 (1.0246~1.0251)	26.1 (1.0275)
Piston pin and bushing oil clearance	0.026~0.051 (0.0009~0.002)	0.11 (0.0043)

Since the small end in 4JH2 Series is tapered, bush insertion is extremely difficult. Any minor mistake will cause abnormalities such as twist and bite. Do not insert the bush on-site.
(No piston pin bush spare part is available. It is included in the con-rod assembly supplied as a spare part.)

4-4 Assembling piston and connecting rod
The piston and connecting rod should be assembled so that the match mark on the connecting rod large end faces the fuel injection pump side and the combustion chamber above the piston is close to the fuel injection pump.

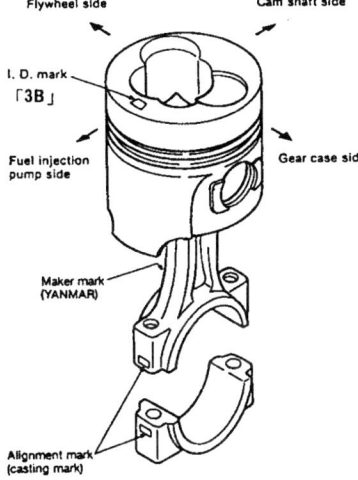

Chapter 2 Basic Engine
5. Crankshaft and Main Bearing

3JH2 Series

5. Crankshaft and Main Bearing

The crank pin and crank journal have been induction hardened for superior durability, and the crankshaft is provided with four balance weights for optional balance. The crankshaft main bearing is of the hanger type. The upper metal (cylinder block side) is provided with an oil groove. There is no oil groove on the lower metal (bearing cap side). The bearing cap (location cap) of the flywheel side has a thrust metal which supports the thrust load.

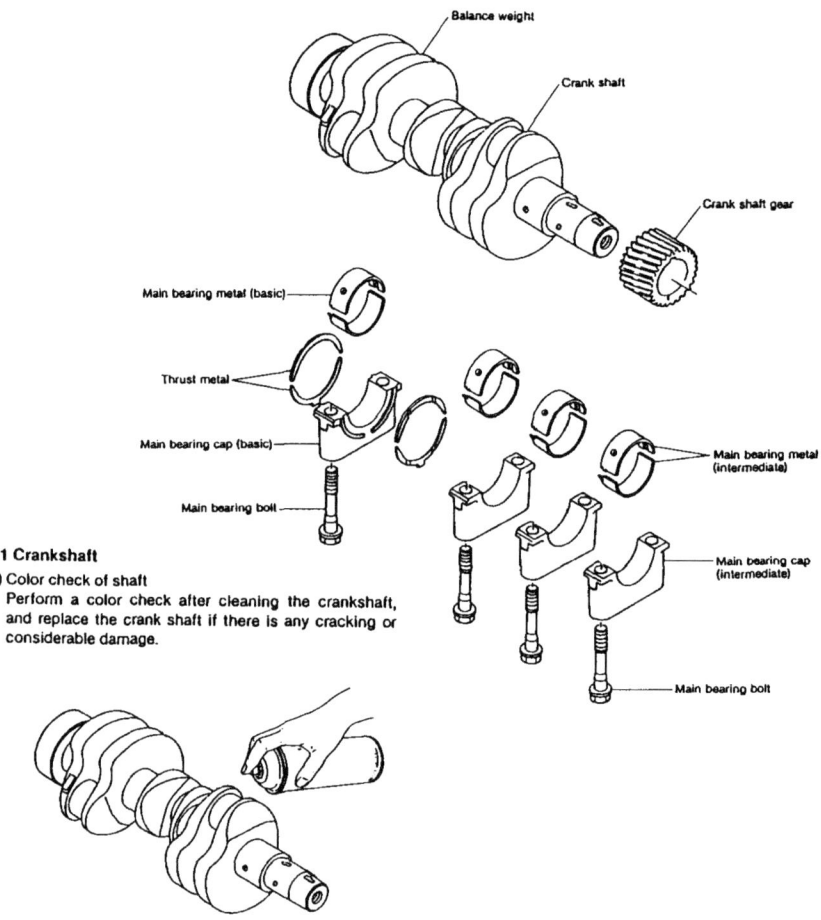

5-1 Crankshaft

(1) Color check of shaft

Perform a color check after cleaning the crankshaft, and replace the crank shaft if there is any cracking or considerable damage.

Printed in Japan
A0A1015-9110SP

Chapter 2 Basic Engine
5. Crankshaft and Main Bearing — 3JH2 Series

(2) Bending of the crankshaft
Support the crankshaft with V-blocks at both ends of the journals. Measure the deflection of the center journal with a dial gauge while rotating the crankshaft to check the extent of crankshaft bending.

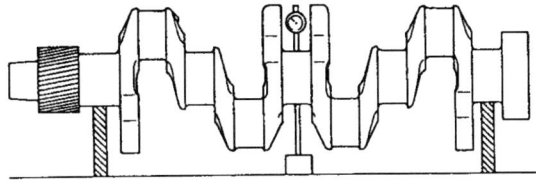
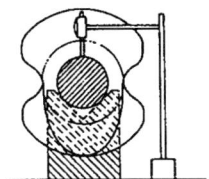

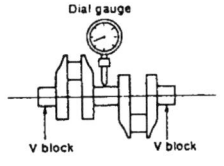
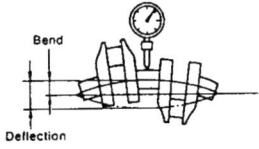

Crankshaft bend	Less than 0.03mm (0.0012 in.)

(3) Measuring the crank pin and journal
Measure the extent of journal wear (roundness, taper). Regrind it to the proper shape if it is within the outer diameter limit, and replace if not.

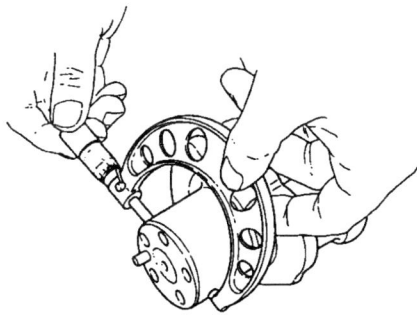
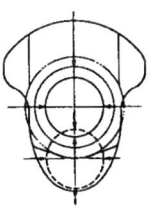
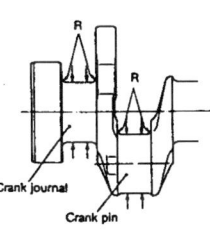

		Standard	Wear limit
			mm (in.)
Crank pin	Outside dia.	47.952 ~ 47.962 (1.8878 ~ 1.8882)	47.75 (1.8799)
	Bushing inside dia.	48.000 ~ 48.045 (1.8897 ~ 1.8915)	48.10 (1.8937)
	Crank pin and bushing oil clearance	0.038 ~ 0.093 (0.0014 ~ 0.0036)	0.25 (0.0098)
Crank journal	Outside dia.	49.952 ~ 49.962 (1.9666 ~ 1.9670)	49.75 (1.9586)
	Bushing inside dia.	50.000 ~ 50.045 (1.9685 ~ 1.9702)	50.10 (1.9724)
	Crank journal and bushing oil clearance	0.038 ~ 0.093 (0.0014 ~ 0.0036)	0.25 (0.0098)
Fillet rounding of crank pin and journal		3.500 ~ 3.800 (0.1377 ~ 0.1496)	

Chapter 2 Basic Engine
5. Crankshaft and Main Bearing

3JH2 Series

(4) Checking side clearance of the crankshaft
After assembling the crankshaft, tighten the main bearing cap to the specified torque, and move the crankshaft to one side, placing a dial gauge on one end of the shaft to measure thrust clearance.
This measurement can also be effected by inserting the gauge directly into the clearance between the thrust bearing and crankshaft thrust surface.
Replace the thrust bearing if it is worn beyond the limit.

mm (in.)

	Standard	Wear limit
Crankshaft side gap	0.090 ~ 0.271 (0.0035 ~ 0.0106)	0.30 (0.0118)

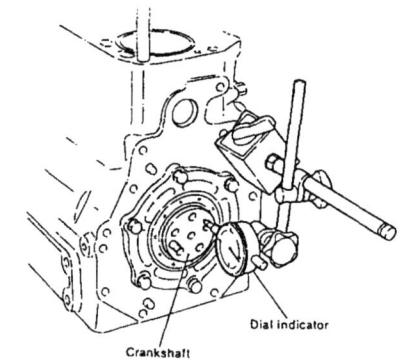

Dial indicator
Crankshaft

6-2 Main bearing

(1) Inspecting the main bearing
Check for flaking, seizure or burning of the contact surface and replace if necessary.
(2) Measuring the inner diameter of metal
Tighten the cap to the specified torque and measure the inner diameter of the metal.

Bearing cap bolt tightening torque	10.5 ~ 11.5 kg·m (75.92 ~ 83.15 ft-lb)

NOTE: When assembling the bearing cap, keep the following in mind.
1) The lower metal (cap side) has no oil groove.
2) The upper metal (cylinder block side) has an oil groove.
3) Check the cylinder block alignment No.
4) The "FW" on the cap lies on the flywheel side.

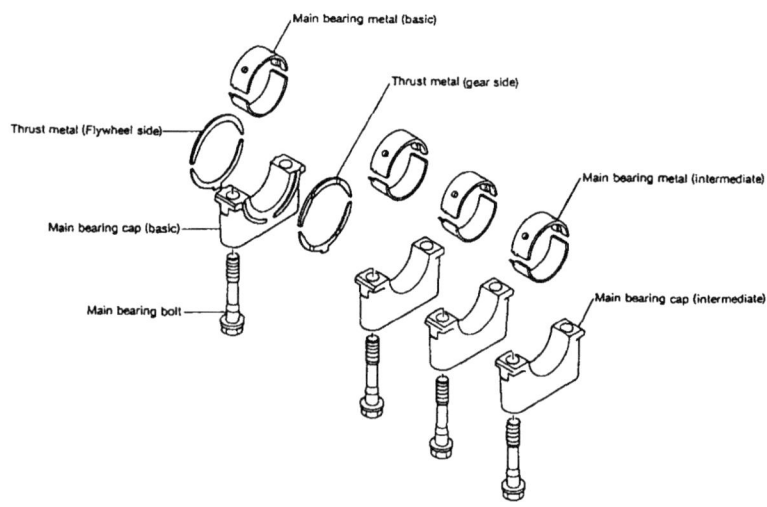

6. Camshaft and Tappets

6-1 Camshaft

The camshaft is normalized and the cam and bearing surfaces are surface hardened and ground. The cams have a curve that minimizes the repeated shocks on the valve seats and maximizes valve seat life.

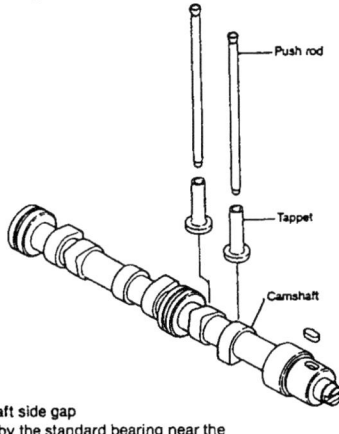

(1) Checking the camshaft side gap

The load is received by the standard bearing near the end of the camshaft by the cam gear, resulting in rapid wear of the end of the bearing and enlargement of the side gap. Therefore, measure the thrust gap before disassembly. As the cam gear is shrink-fitted to the cam, be careful when replacing the thrust bearing.

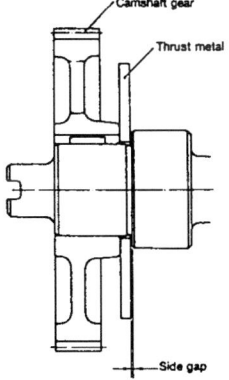

(2) Measure the camshaft height, and replace the cam if it is worn beyond the limit.

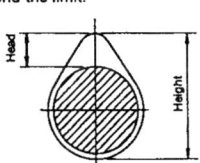

Camshaft height   mm (in.)

Engine model		Standard	Wear limit
3JH2E	Intake cam	38.66 ~ 38.74 (1.5220 ~ 1.5251)	38.4 (1.5118)
	Exhaust cam	38.66 ~ 38.74 (1.5220 ~ 1.5251)	38.4 (1.5118)
3JH2-TE	Intake cam	38.66 ~ 38.74 (1.5220 ~ 1.5251)	38.4 (1.5118)
	Exhaust cam	38.86 ~ 38.94 (1.5299 ~ 1.5330)	38.6 (1.5196)

mm (in.)

	Standard	Wear limit
Camshaft side gap	0.05 ~ 0.20 (0.0019 ~ 0.0079)	0.4 (0.0157)

Chapter 2 Basic Engine
6. Camshaft and Tappets
3JH2 Series

(3) Measure the camshaft outer diameter and the camshaft bearing inner diameter. Replace if they exceed the wear limit or are damaged.

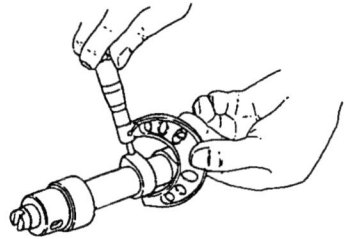

mm (in.)

	Standard			Wear limit
	Gear case side	Intermediate	Flywheel side	
Camshaft journal outside dia.	44.925 ~ 44.950 (1.7687 ~ 1.7696)	44.910 ~ 44.935 (1.7681 ~ 1.7690)	44.925 ~ 44.950 (1.7687 ~ 1.7696)	44.8 (1.7637)
Camshaft journal bushing inside dia.	44.990 ~ 45.050 (1.7712 ~ 1.7736)	—	—	—
Cylinder block bearing inside dia.	—	45.000 ~ 45.025 (1.7716 ~ 1.7726)	45.000 ~ 45.025 (1.7716 ~ 1.7726)	—
Oil clearance	0.040 ~ 0.125 (0.0015 ~ 0.0049)	0.065 ~ 0.115 (0.0025 ~ 0.0045)	0.050 ~ 0.100 (0.0019 ~ 0.0039)	0.2 (0.0078)

(4) Bending of the crankshaft
Support both ends of the crankshaft with V-blocks, place a dial gauge against the central bearing areas and measure bending. Replace if excessive.

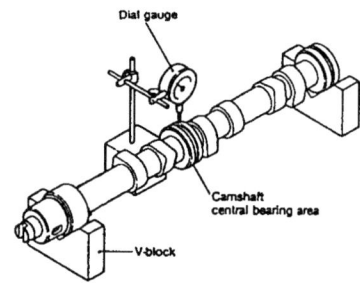

NOTE: The reading on the dial gauge is divided by two to obtain the extent of bending.

mm (in.)

	Wear limit
Camshaft deflection	0.02 (0.0007)

6-2 Tappets

(1) The tappets are offset to rotate during operation and thereby prevent uneven wearing. Check the contact of each tappet and replace if excessively or unevenly worn.

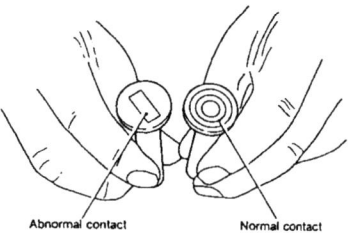

Abnormal contact   Normal contact

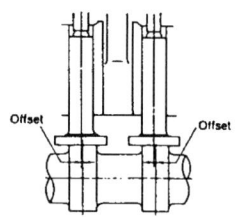

NOTE: When removing tappets, be sure to keep them separate for each cylinder and intake/exhaust valve.

Chapter 2 Basic Engine
6. Camshaft and Tappets

(2) Measure the outer diameter of the tappet, and replace if worn beyond the limit.

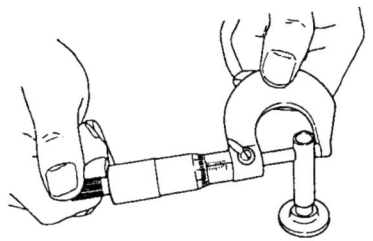

mm (in.)

	Standard	Wear limit
Tappet stem outside dia.	11.975 ~ 11.990 (0.4714 ~ 0.4720)	11.93 (0.4696)
Tappet guide hole inside dia. (cylinder block)	12.000 ~ 12.018 (0.4724 ~ 0.4731)	12.05 (0.4744)
Tappet stem and guide hole oil clearance	0.010 ~ 0.043 (0.0003 ~ 0.0016)	0.10 (0.0039)

(3) Measuring push rods.
Measure the length and bending of the push rods.

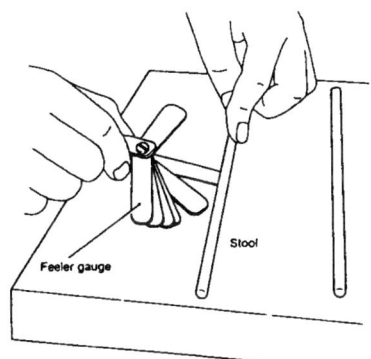

mm (in.)

	Standard	Wear limit
Push rod length	178.25 ~ 178.75 (7.0177 ~ 7.0374)	—
Push rod bend	Less than 0.03 (0.0011)	0.3 (0.0118)
Push rod dia.	8.5 (0.3346)	—

7. Timing Gear

The timing gear is helical type for minimum noise and specially treated for high durability.

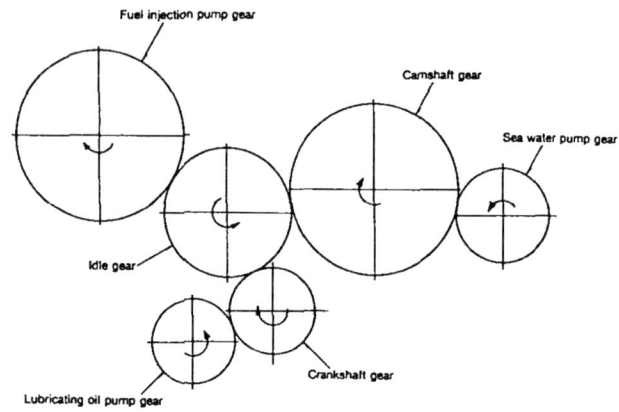

mm (in.)

	No. of teeth	Face width	Spiral angle	Center distance	Back lash	Back lash Wear limit
Sea water pump gear	31	12.0	right	92.544 ~ 92.592 (3.6434 ~ 3.6453)	0.04 ~ 0.12 (0.0015 ~ 0.0047)	0.2 (0.0078)
Camshaft gear	56	18.0	left	105.318 ~ 105.380 (4.1463 ~ 4.1488)	0.04 ~ 0.12 (0.0015 ~ 0.0047)	0.2 (0.0078)
Idle gear	43	18.0	right	75.525 ~ 75.573 (2.9734 ~ 2.9753)	0.04 ~ 0.12 (0.0015 ~ 0.0047)	0.2 (0.0078)
Crankshaft gear	28	40.0	left			
Lubricating oil pump gear	29	8.0	right	60.629 ~ 60.677 (2.3869 ~ 2.3888)	0.04 ~ 0.12 (0.0015 ~ 0.0047)	0.2 (0.0078)
Idle gear	43	18.0	right	105.254 ~ 105.316 (4.1438 ~ 4.1462)	0.04 ~ 0.12 (0.0015 ~ 0.0047)	0.2 (0.0078)
Fuel injection pump gear	56	10.0	left			

7-1 Inspecting the gears

(1) Inspect the gears and replace if the teeth are damaged or worn.
(2) Measure the backlash of all gears that mesh, and replace the meshing gears as a set if wear exceeds the limit.
  NOTE: If backlash is excessive, it will not only result in excessive noise and gear damage, but also lead to bad valve and fuel injection timing and a decrease in engine performance.

(3) Idling gear
  The bushing is pressure fitted into the idling gear. Measure the bushing inner diameter and the outer diameter of the shaft, and replace the bushing or idling gear shaft if the oil clearance exceeds the wear limit.
  A, B and C are inscribed on the end of the idling gear. When assembling, these marks should align with those on the cylinder block.

Chapter 2 Basic Engine
7. Timing Gear

3JH2 Series

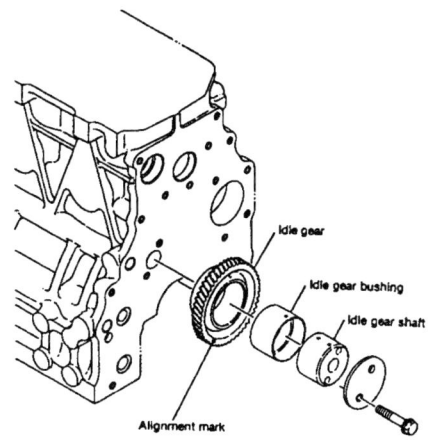

	Standard	Wear limit
Idle shaft dia.	45.950 ~ 45.975 (1.8090 ~ 1.8100)	45.88 (1.8062)
Idle shaft bushing inside dia.	46.000 ~ 46.025 (1.8110 ~ 1.8120)	—
Idle shaft and bushing oil clearance	0.025 ~ 0.075 (0.0009 ~ 0.0029)	0.15 (0.0059)

mm (in.)

7-2 Gear timing marks
Match up the timing marks on each gear when assembling (A, B and C).

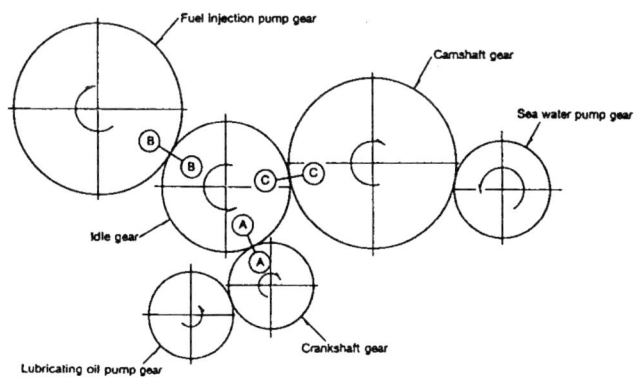

Chapter 2 Basic Engine
8. Flywheel and Housing

3JH2 Series

8. Flywheel and Housing

The function of the flywheel is, through inertia, to rotate the crankshaft in a uniform and smooth manner by absorbing the turning force created during the combustion stroke of the engine, and by compensating for the decrease in turning force during the other strokes.
The flywheel is mounted and secured by 6 bolts on the crankshaft end at the opposite end to the gear case; it is covered by the mounting flange (flywheel housing) which is bolted to the cylinder block.
The fitting surface for the damper disc is on the crankshaft side of the flywheel. The rotation of the crankshaft is transmitted through this disc to the input shaft of the reduction and reversing gear. The reduction and reversing gear is fitted to the mounting flange.
The flywheel's unbalanced force on the shaft center must be kept below the specified value for the crankshaft as the flywheel rotates with the crankshaft at high speed. To achieve this, the balance is adjusted by drilling holes in the side of the flywheel, and the unbalanced momentum is adjusted by drilling holes in the circumference.
The ring gear is shrink fitted onto the circumference of the flywheel, and this ring gear serves to start the engine by meshing with the starter motor pinion.
The stamped letter and line which show top dead center of each cylinder are positioned on the flywheel circumference, and by matching these marks with the arrow mark at the hole of the flywheel housing, the rotary position of the crankshaft can be ascertained in order to adjust tappet clearance or fuel injection timing.

8-1 Specifications of flywheel

Outside dia. of flywheel		mm	ϕ 300
Width of flywheel		mm	63
Weight of flywheel (including ring gear)		kg	20.0
GD^2 value		kg·m²	1.13
Circumferential speed		m/s	53.4 (3400rpm)
Speed fluctuation rate		δ	1 / 77 (3400rpm)
Allowable amount of unbalance		g-cm	35.5
Fixing part of damper disc	Pitch circle dia. of bolts	mm	170
	No. of bolts × bolt dia.		6-M8 thread equally spaced
Fixing part of crankshaft	Pitch circle dia. of bolts	mm	66
	No. of thread holes	mm	6-M10
	Fit joint dia.		ϕ 85.000 ~85.035
Model of reduction and reversing gear			KM3A, KBW10E
Mounting flange No.			SAE No.5 (in metric unit)
Ring gear	Center dia.	mm	289.56
	No of teeth		114

Chapter 2 Basic Engine
8. Flywheel and Housing _____ 3JH2 Series

8-2 Dimensions of flywheel and mounting flange

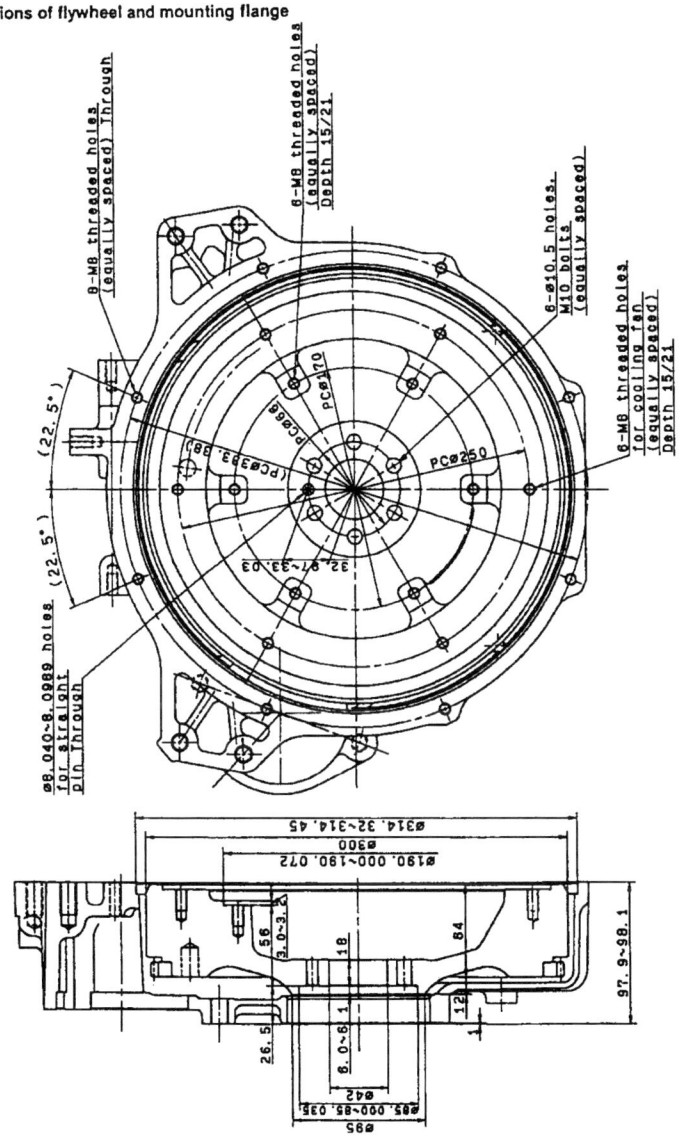

Chapter 2 Basic Engine
8. Flywheel and Housing

3JH2 Series

8-3 Ring gear

When replacing the ring gear due to excessive wear or damaged teeth, heat the ring gear evenly at its circumference, and after it has expanded drive it gradually off the flywheel by tapping it with a hammer, a copper bar or something similar around the whole circumference.

	mm (in.)
Interference of ring gear	0.21 ~ 0.45 (0.0083 ~ 0.0177)

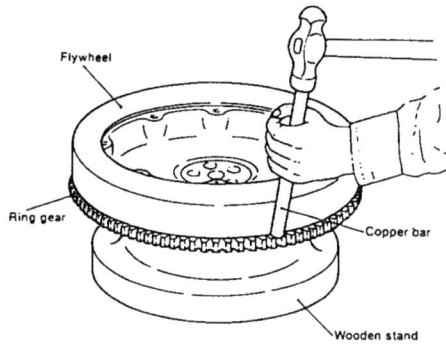

8-4 Position of top dead center and fuel injection timing

(1) Marking

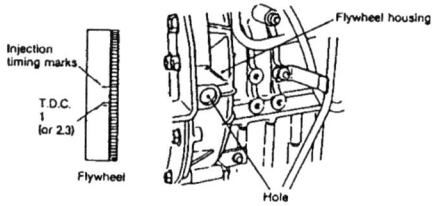

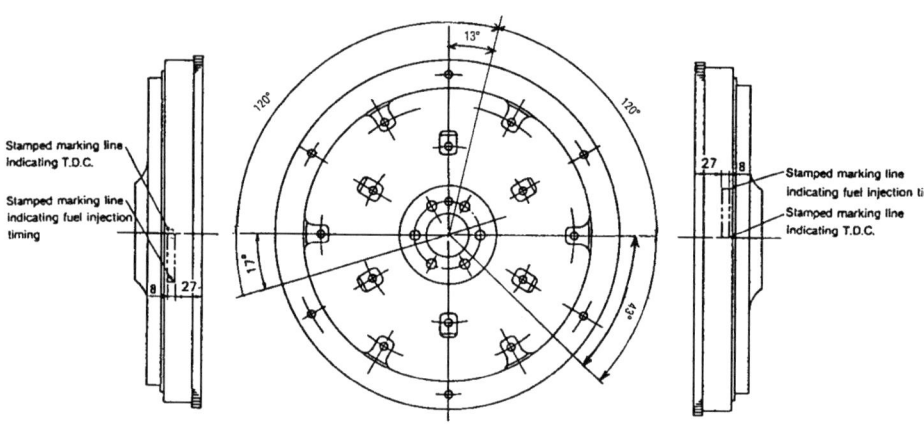

Chapter 2 Basic Engine
8. Flywheel and Housing
_____ 3JH2 Series

(2) Matching mark

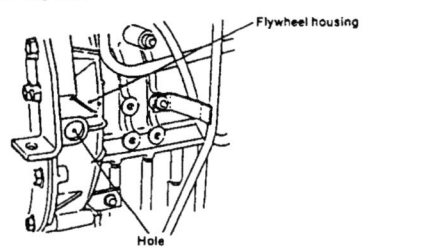

The matching mark is made at the hole of the flywheel housing.

8-5 Damper disc and cooling fan

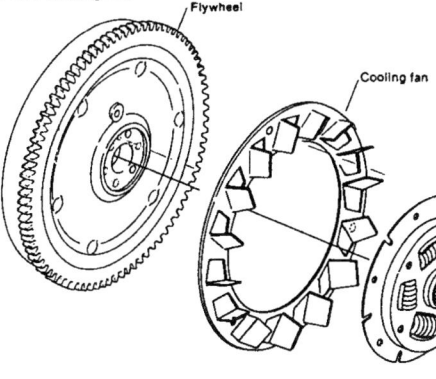

Applicability of Cooling Fan

	3JH2E	3JH2-TE
KM3A	○	–
KBW10E	○	○

* ○ Mark Combination Cooling Fan Equipipment

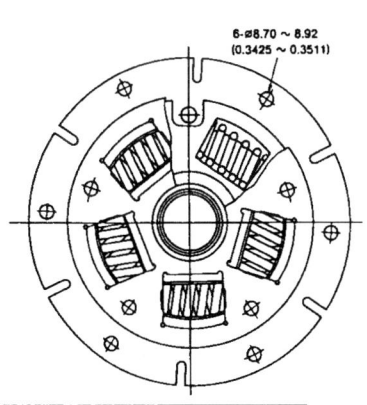

Torsional rigidity	421kg /rad (928.3 lb/rad)
Max. angle of torsion	7.3×10^{-3} rad
Stopper torque	37.7 kg·m (272.68 ft-lb)

CHAPTER 3
FUEL INJECTION EQUIPMENT

1. Fuel Injection Pump Service Data 3-1
2. Governor 3-2
3. Disassembly, Reassembly and Inspection
   of Fuel Injection Pump 3-11
4. Adjustment of Fuel Injection
   Pump and Governor 3-21
5. Fuel Feed Pump 3-27
6. Fuel Injection Nozzle 3-29
7. Troubleshooting 3-33
8. Tools 3-35
9. Fuel Filter 3-37
10. Fuel Tank (Optional) 3-38

Chapter 3 Fuel Injection Equipment
1. Fuel Injection Pump Service Data   3JH2 Series

1. Fuel Injection Pump Service Data (YANMAR TYPE : YPES-3CL)

Adjustment	Item		Engine model	3JH2E		3JH2-TE	
	Assemble cord		Part No.	729170-51300		729171-51300	
			I.D.mark	B634		B630	
	Adjustment specs			Engine specs	Calibration specs	Engine specs	Canbration specs
	Nozzle type I.D.mark			150P244HC0	DN-12SD12	140P255Z0	DN-12SD12
4-1-(1)	Injection starting pressure kg/cm² (lb/in2)			195~205 (2,773~2,915)	165~175 (2,346~2,489)	195~205 (2,773~2,915)	165~175 (2,346~2,489)
4-1-(2)	Fuelinjection pipe mm OD φ /ID φ ×L (in)			φ6/φ1.8×360 (0.2362/0.078 ×15.748)	φ6/φ2.8×600 (0.2362/0.078 7 ×23.622)	φ6/φ1.8×360 (0.2362/0.070 8 ×15.748)	φ6/φ2 ×600 (0.2362/0.078 7 ×23.622)
4-2	Top clearance mm /Prestroke (in)			0.45~0.55/3.0 (0.018~0.022/0.118)		0.45~0.55/3.0 (0.018~0.022/0.118)	
4-7-1	Rated load		Pump rpm:N1 rpm	1,800		1,800	
			Rack position:R1 mm(in)	7(0.276)		7(0.276)	
			Measuring stroke St	1,000		1,000	
			Injection volume cc	27.5	40	34.5	40
			Nonunifomity %	±3		±3	
4-7-2	No load		Pump rpm:N2 rpm	19,50		19,50	
			Rack position:R2 mm(in)	(4)		(3.5)	
4-7-3	Idling		Pump rpm:N3 rpm	400		400	
			Measuring stroke St	1,000		1,000	
			Injection volume cc	9~10	9~10	9~10	9~10
			Nonunifomity %	±10		±10	
4-7-4	Starting		Pump rpm:N4 rpm	200		200	
			Rack position mm(in)	11.5~12.5(0.453~0.492)		11.5~12.5(0.453~0.492)	
			Measurig stroke St	1,000		1,000	
			Injection volume cc	41.5~48.5	34~41	41.5~48.5	34~41
	Boost compensater		Standad	Non		Non	
			Pump rpm	–		–	
			Measuring stroke St	–		–	
			Injection volume cc	–	–	–	–
Ref.			F.ITiming (F.I.D)deg	17		17	

Chapter 3 Fuel Injection Equipment
1. Fuel Injection Pump Service Data

3JH2 series

Item				3JH25A		3JH30A	
		Engine					
Assemble code	Part No			729198-51300		729198-51320	
	I.D. mark			B450		B451	
Adjustment specs				Engine spec.	Cal. Spec.	Engine spec.	Cal. Spec.
Nozzle type I.D. mark				150P244HCO	DN-12SD12	150P244HCO	DN-12SD12
Injection starting pressure			(kg/cm²)	200~210	165~175	200~210	165~175
Fuel injection pipe			(OD φ × ID φ × L)	φ6 × φ1.8 × 360	φ6 × φ2.0 × 600	φ6 × φ1.8 × 360	φ6 × φ2.0 × 600
Top clearance/Pre stroke			(mm)	0.95~1.05/2.5		0.95~1.05/2.5	
Rated load	Pump rpm:N1		(rpm)	1650		1500	
	Rack position:R1		(mm)	6		6	
	Measuring stroke		(St)	1000		1000	
	Injection volume		(cm³)	21.5	28.2	27	—
	Non uniformity		(%)	±3		±3	
No load	Pump rpm:N2		(rpm)	—		—	
	Rack position:R2			—		—	
Idling	Pump rpm:N3		(rpm)	325		325	
	Measuring stroke		(St)	1000		1000	
	Injection volume		(cm³)	6~7	7~8	6~7	7~8
	Non uniformity		(%)	±20		±20	
Starting	Pump rpm:N4		(rpm)	200		200	
	Rack position		(mm)	11.5~1.25		11.5~1.25	
	Measuring stroke		(St)	1000		1000	
	Injection volume		(cm³)	60~70	56~66	60~70	56~66

Chapter 3 Fuel Injection Equipment
2. Governor

3JH2 Series

2. Governor

2-1. Disassembly, Reassembly and Inspection of Governor

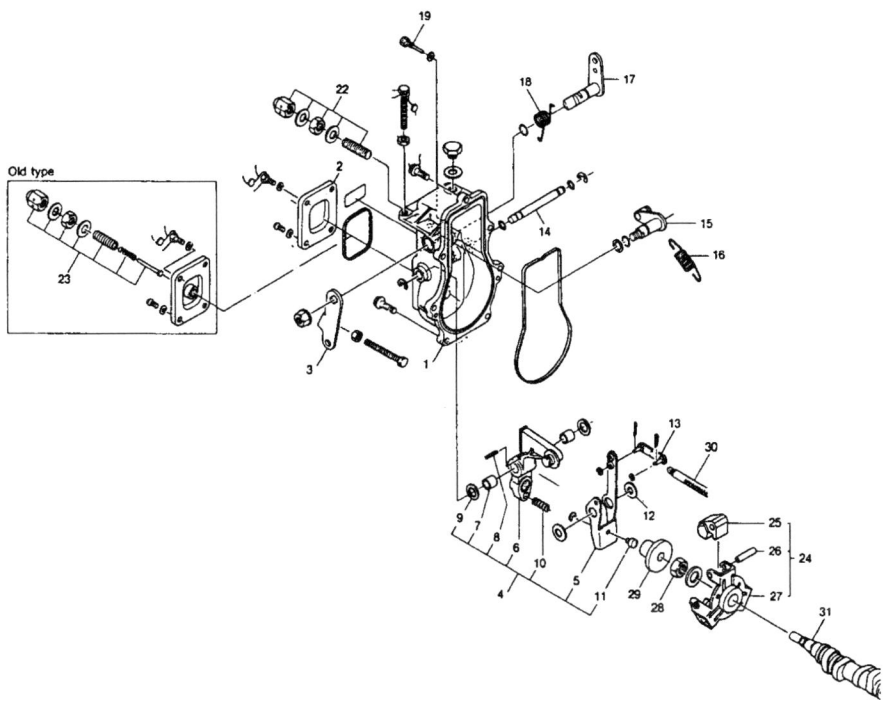

Old type

1. Governor case
2. Governor case cover
3. Control lever
4. Governor lever assembly 5. Governor lever
6. Tension lever
7. Bushing
8. Spring pin
9. Shim
10. Throttle spring
11. Shifter
12. Washer
13. Governor link
14. Governor shaft
15. Control lever shaft
16. Governor spring
17. Stop lever
18. Stop lever return spring
19. Stop lever stop pin
22. Fuel stopper (limit bolt) assembly
23. Adjusting spring assembly
24. Governor weight
25. Governor weight
26. Pin
27. Governor weight support
28. Governor weight nut
29. Governor sleeve
30. Control rack
31. Fuel pump cam shaft

2-1-1 Governor disassembly

(1) Remove the governor case.

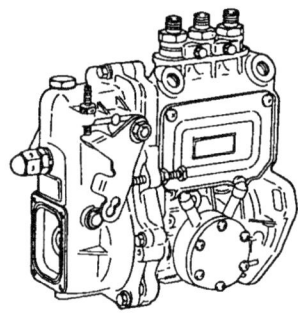

NOTE: Loosen the hex bolt on models with an angleich spring.

(2) Remove the control lever hex nut, and pull out the control lever from the control lever shaft.

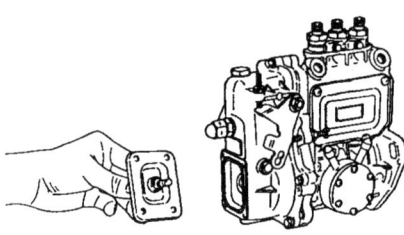

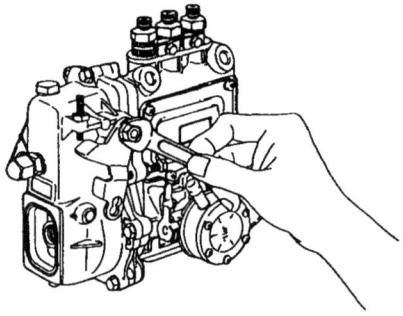

(3) Remove the governor case bolt. Remove the governor case (parallel pin) from the fuel pump until while lightly tapping the governor case with a wooden hammer. Create a gap between the governor case and fuel pump by moving parts of the governor lever.

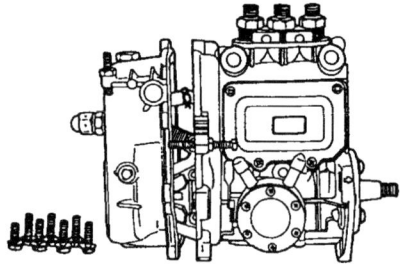

(4) Pull out the governor link snap pin by inserting needle nosed pliers between the fuel pump and governor case. case.

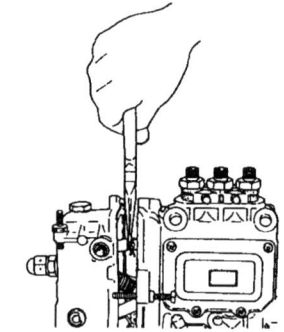

(5) The governor and fuel pump come apart by sliding the governor case and fuel pump apart and pulling out the link pin of the fuel control rack.

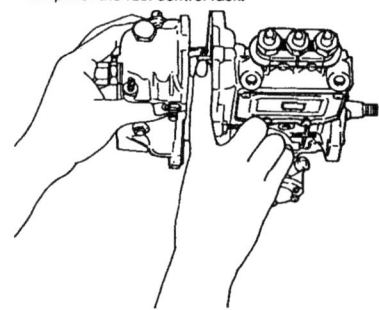

Chapter 3 Fuel Injection Equipment
2. Governor

3JH2 Series

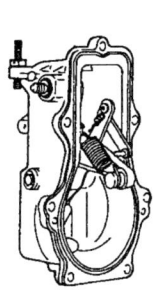 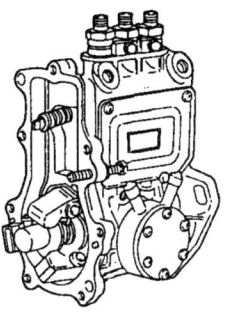

(6) Remove the stop lever return spring from the governor lever shaft.

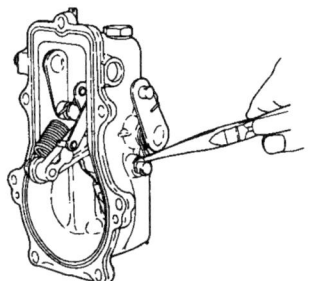

(7) Use needle nose pliers to unhook the governor spring from the tension lever and control lever shaft.

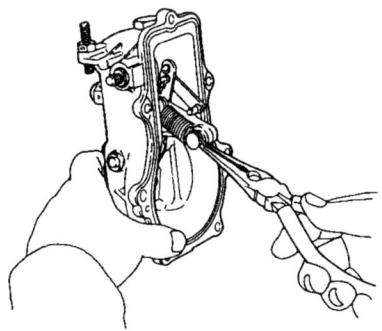

(8) Remove the snap-rings on both ends of the governor lever shaft.

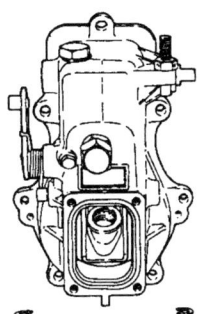

(9) Put a rod 8mm (0.3150in.) in dia. or less in one end of the governor lever shaft, and tap the governor shaft until the O-ring comes out the other side of the governor case.

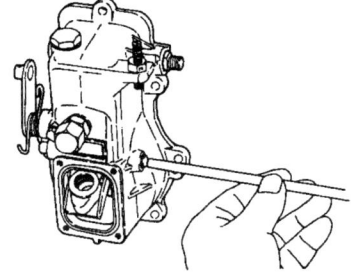

(10) After removing the O-ring, lightly tap the end of the shaft that you removed the O-ring from, and remove the governor lever shaft. Then remove the governor shaft assembly and washer.

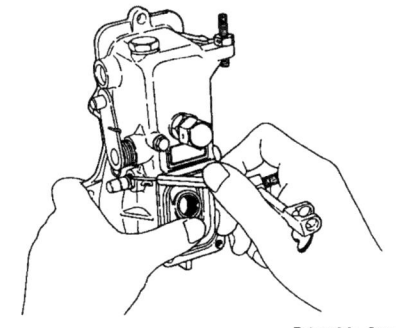

Printed in Japan
A0A1015-9110SP

Chapter 3 Fuel Injection Equipment
2. Governor

3JH2 Series

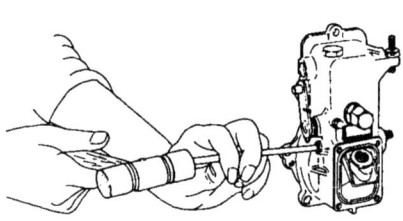

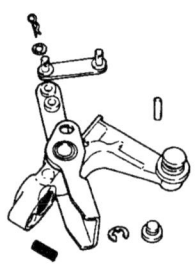

NOTE: The governor assembly consists of the governor lever, tension bar, bushing, throttle spring and shifter, and is normally not disassembled.
The spring pin is removed when you replace the shifter or throttle spring.

(12) When you need to pull out the stop lever, remove the stop lever shaft stop pin, and lightly tap the inside of the governor case.

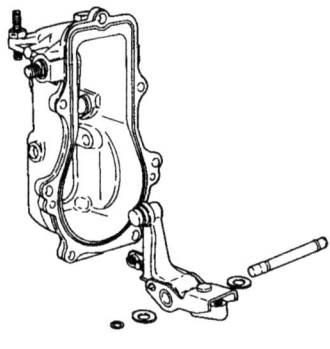

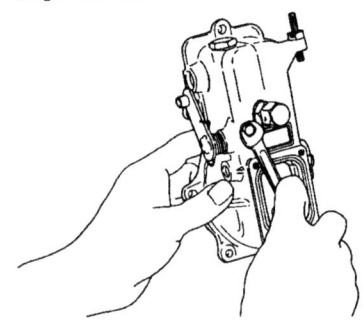

(11) Remove the governor link from the governor lever.

(13) When you need to pull out the control lever shaft, tap the end of the shaft with a wood hammer.

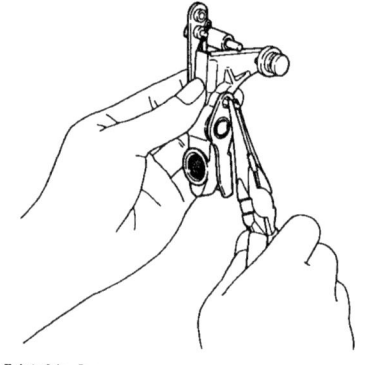

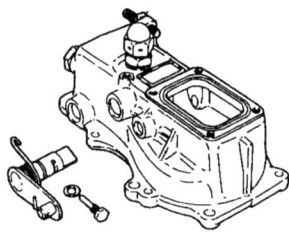

NOTE: 1. Do not remove the fuel limit nut from the governor case unless necessary.

Chapter 3 Fuel Injection Equipment
2. Governor _____ *3JH2 Series*

(14) Pull out the governor sleeve on the end of the fuel camshaft by hand.

(16) Remove the governor weight assembly from the fuel pump cam using the governor weight pulling tools.

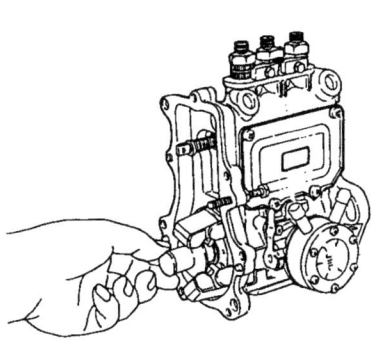

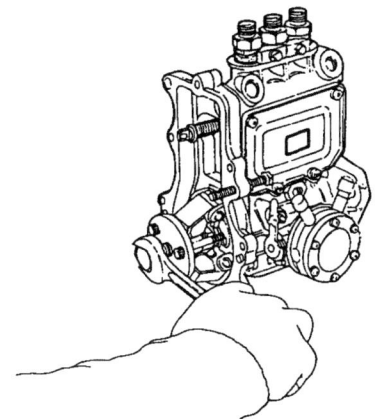

(15) Turn the governor weight with a box spanner two or three times to loosen it, stopping it with the hole in the fuel coupling ring or holding the coupling with a vise.

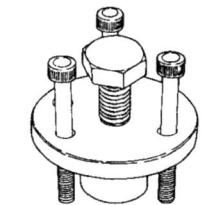

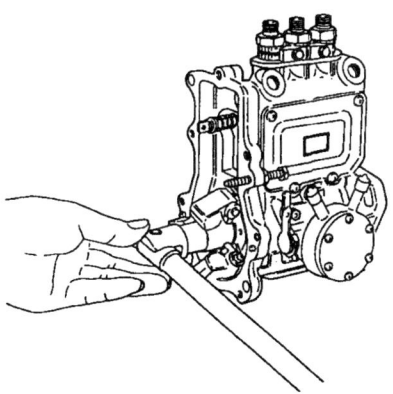

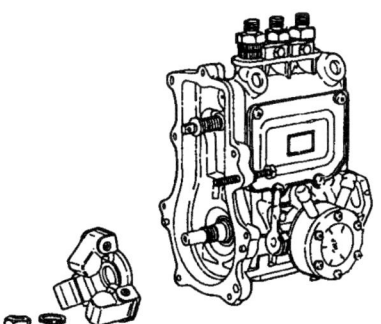

NOTE: When the taper fit comes apart after you have removed the nut, the governor weight may fly out —Be Careful.

NOTE: The governor weight assembly is made up of the governor weight, support and pin. Do not disassemble.

Printed in Japan
A0A1015-9110SP

Chapter 3 Fuel Injection Equipment
2. Governor

3JH2 Series

2-1-2 Inspection of governor
Inspection of governor weight assembly
(1) Replace the governor weight if it does not open and close smoothly.

(2) Replace the governor weight if the contact surface with governor sleeve is extremely worn.
(3) Replace if there is governor weight support/pin wear or the caulking is loose.
(4) Replace if the governor weight support stopper is excessively worn.

Inspection of governor sleeve

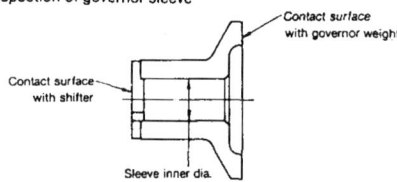

(1) Replace the governor sleeve if the contact surface with governor weight is worn or there is pitching.
(2) Replace the governor sleeve if the contact surface with shifter is considerably worn or there is pitching.
(3) If the governor sleeve does not move smoothly above the cam shaft due to governor sleeve inner dia. wear or other reasons, replace.

Inspection of governor shaft assembly
(1) Measure the clearance between the governor shaft and bushing, and replace if it exceeds the limit.

mm (in.)

	Standard Dimension	Standard Clearance	Limit
Governor shaft outer dia.	7.986 ~ 7.995 (0.3144 ~ 0.3147)	0.065 ~ 0.124 (0.0025 ~ 0.0048)	0.5 (0.0196)
Bushing inner dia.	8.060 ~ 8.110 (0.3173 ~ 0.3192)		

(2) Inspect the shifter contact surface, and replace the shifter (always by removing the pin to disassemble) if it is worn or scorched.
(3) Disassemble and replace throttle springs that are settled, broken or corroded by pulling the spring pin.
(4) Check link parts for bends or kinks that will cause malfunctioning, and replace any parts as necessary.

NOTE: 1. Side gap on top of governor lever shaft.

mm (in.)

Standard side gap	0.4 (0.0157)

2. Replace the governor lever, tension bar, bushing, shifter and throttle spring as an assembly.

(5) Inspection of springs
1) Check the governor spring and other springs and replace if they are broken, settled or corroded.
2) Measure the free length of the governor spring, and replace if it exceeds the limit.
See service data sheet for free length of governor spring.

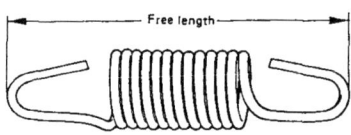

Governor spring spec. table

Engine model	3JH2E	3JH2-TE
Part No.	129470-61650	129100-61730
Spring constant kg/mm	0.32	4.22
Free length mm	12	42

2-2 Assembling governor
Inspect all parts after disassembly and replace any parts as necessary. Before starting reassembly, clean new parts and parts to be reused, and put them in order.
Make sure to readjust the unit after reassembly to obtain the specified performance.

(1) Insert the governor weight assembly in the taper portion at the end of the fuel pump camshaft, stopping it with the hole in the fuel coupling ring or holding the coupling with a vise, mount the rest, and tighten the governor weight nut.

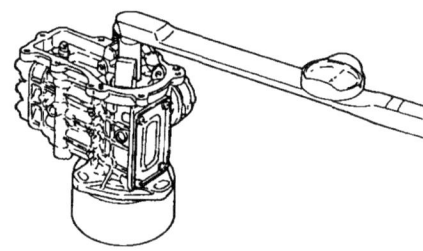

kg-m (ft-lb)

Governor weight nut tightening torque	4.5 ~ 5.0 (32.54 ~ 36.16)

Chapter 3 Fuel Injection Equipment
2. Governor
3JH2 Series

(2) Open the governor weight to the outside, and insert the sleeve in the end of the fuel pump camshaft.

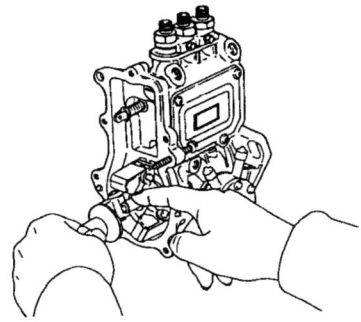

NOTE: Make sure that the sleeve moves smoothly after inserting it.

(3) When the stop lever has been disassembled, mount the stop lever return spring on the stop lever, tap the stop lever lightly with a wooden hammer to insert it, and tighten the stop lever stop pin.

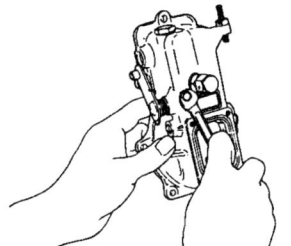

(4) When the control lever shaft has been removed, lightly tap the control lever shaft and washer from inside the governor case, using an appropriate plate.

(5) If the governor has been disassembled, tap in the spring pin.

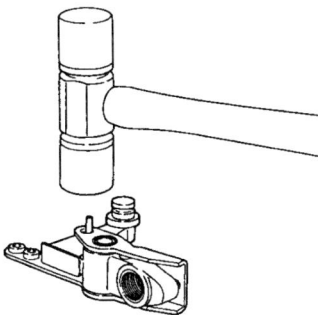

(6) Mount the governor lever assembly to the governor link.

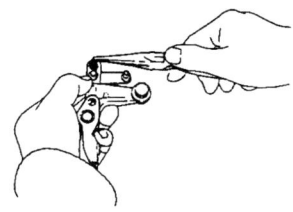

NOTE: 1. Make sure that the correct governor link mounting holes are used, and that it is mounted in the correct direction.
2. Make sure that the governor link moves smoothly.

(7) Put the governor lever shaft assembly in the governor case, insert the governor lever shaft, and tap it in until the O-ring groove comes out the opposite side of the governor case.

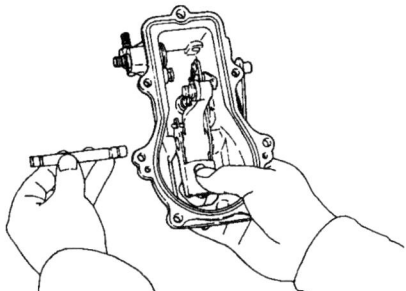

NOTE: 1. Fit the O-ring to the side you have tapped in.

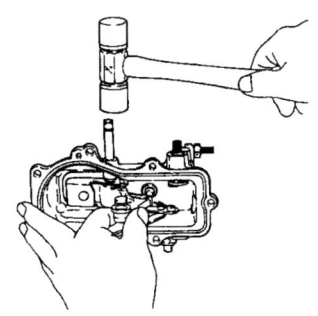

2. Be sure to insert the governor lever shaft in the correct direction.

Printed in Japan
A0A1015-9110SP

Chapter 3 Fuel Injection Equipment
2. Governor

3JH2 Series

3. Don't forget to mount the washers to both sides of the governor lever.

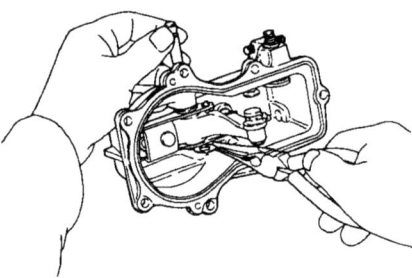

(8) After you have mounted the O-ring, tape the governor lever in the opposite direction, and mount the E-shaped stop rings on the grooves at both ends.

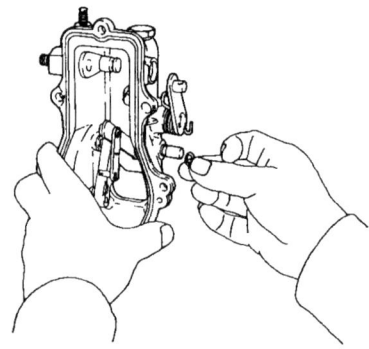

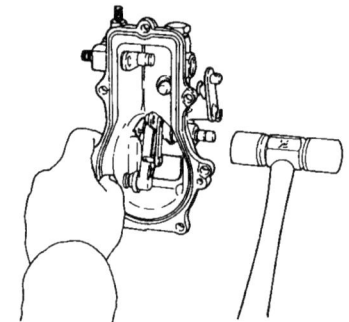

NOTE: After mounting the governor lever assembly, make sure the governor lever assembly moves smoothly.

(9) Fit the stop lever return spring to the end of the governor lever shaft.

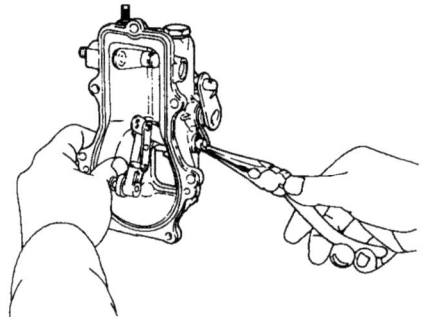

(10) Hook the governor spring on the control lever shaft and tension lever hook with radio pliers.

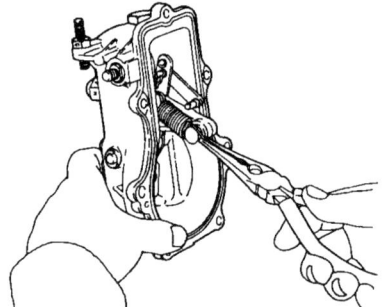

(11) Pull the governor link as far as possible towards the governor case mounting surface, insert the governor link pin in the fuel control rack pin hole and fit the snap pin on it.

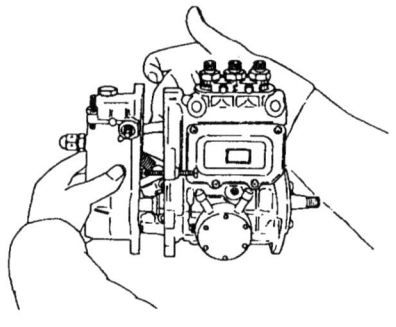

Printed in Japan
A0A1015-9110SP

Chapter 3 Fuel Injection Equipment
2. Governor

(12) Mount the governor case to the fuel pump unit while lightly tapping it with a wooden hammer, and tighten the bolts.
(13) Place the adjusting spring and adjusting rod on the governor case cover adjusting bolt, and mount the governor case cover.

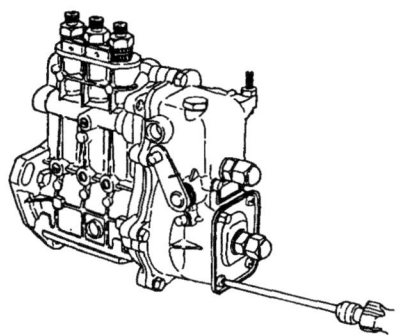

(14) Insert the control lever in the control lever shaft, and tighten the nut.

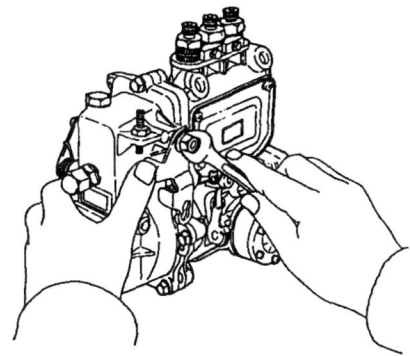

NOTE: Move the control lever back and forth to make sure that the entire link moves smoothly.

3. Disassembly, Reassembly and Inspection of Fuel Injection Pump

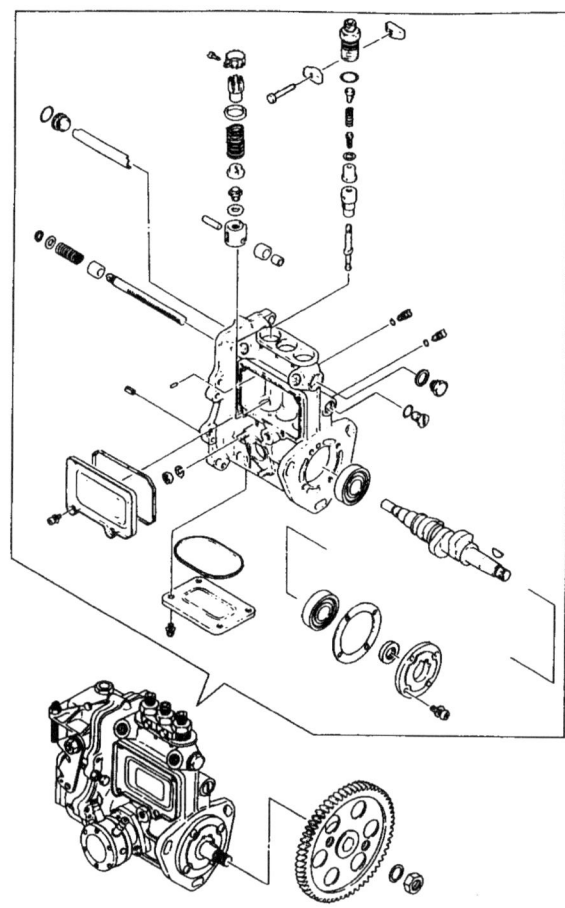

Chapter 3 Fuel Injection Equipment
3. Disassembly, Reassembly and Inspection of Fuel Injection Pump   *3JH2 Series*

3-1 Disassembly of fuel injection pump

When disassembling the fuel pump, separate the parts for each cylinder and be careful not to get them mixed up.
Be especially careful to keep the plunger/plunger barrel, delivery valve/delivery valve seat and other assemblies separate for each cylinder (the parts of each assembly must be kept with that assembly and put back in the same cylinder).

Preparation

1. Wash off the dirt and grease on the outside of the pump with cleaning oil (kerosene or diesel oil) before disassembly.
2. Perform work in a clean area.
3. Take off the fuel pump bottom cover and remove lubricant oil.
4. Turn the fuel pump upside down to drain fuel oil.

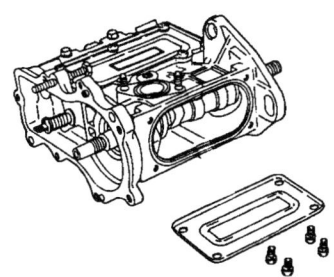

(1) Loosen the nut with a box spanner and take it off, holding it with the hole in the fuel coupling ring or holding the coupling with a vise and take out the governor weight assembly.

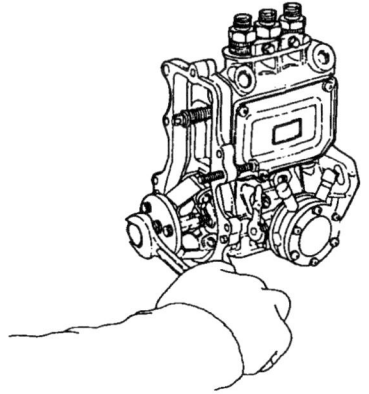

(2) Remove the fuel feed pump.
NOTE: Do not disassemble the fuel feed pump. See instructions for fuel feed pump for details.

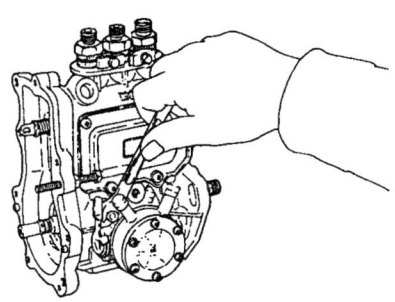

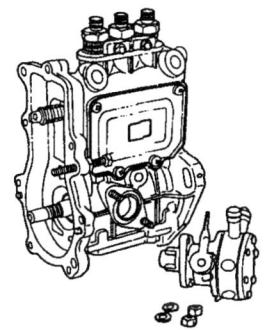

(3) Remove the fuel pump side cover.

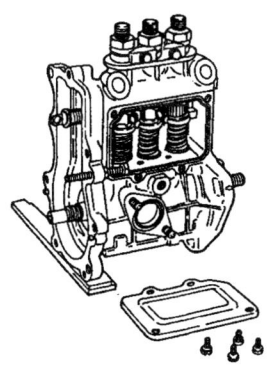

Printed in Japan
A0A1015-9110SP

Chapter 3 Fuel Injection Equipment
3. Disassembly, Reassembly and Inspection of Fuel Injection Pump

3JH2 Series

(4) Turn the camshaft until the roller guide is at the maximum head, and insert the plunger spring support plate in between the plunger spring washer B (lower side) and fuel pump unit.

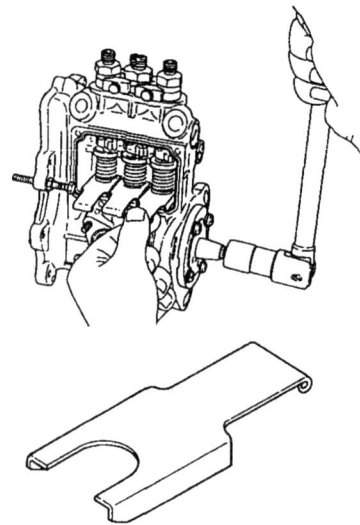

Plunger spring support plate

NOTE: If the camshaft does not turn, put double nuts on the end of the cam shaft or remove the coupling.

(5) Remove the camshaft wood ruff key.
(6) Put a screwdriver in the two grooves on the camshaft bearing holder mounting surface, and pull out the camshaft bearing holder.

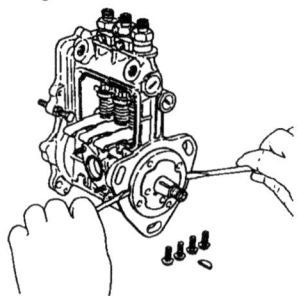

NOTE: 1. Be sure not to damage the oil seal with the threaded part of the camshaft.
2. Be careful not to loosen the shims in between the pump and bearing holder.

(7) Turn the fuel pump upside down, move all the roller guides to the plunger side, and then put the pump on its side. Turn the camshaft to a position so that none of the cylinder cams hit the tappets.
(8) Put a plate against the governor end side of the camshaft and lightly tap it, and pull out the camshaft and drive side bearing.

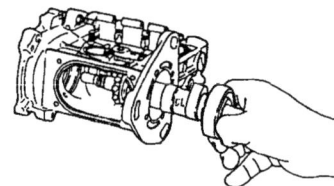

(9) Remove the roller guide stop.

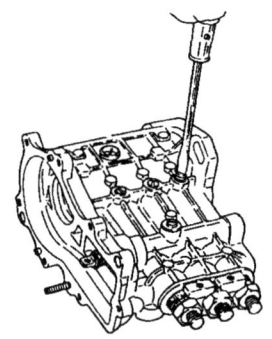

(10) Use a hammer handle or the like to push up the roller guide from the bottom of the pump, and remove the plunger spring support plate.

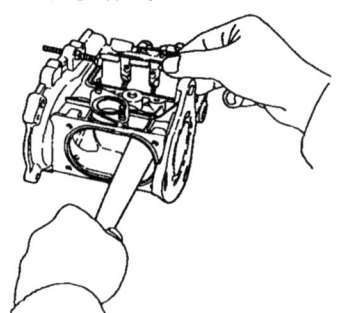

NOTE: The plunger spring may make the roller guide and plunger, etc. fly out when the plunger support plate is removed.

Printed in Japan
A0A1015-9110SP

3-13

Chapter 3 Fuel Injection Equipment
3. Disassembly, Reassembly and Inspection of Fuel Injection Pump — 3JH2 Series

(11) Remove the roller guide.

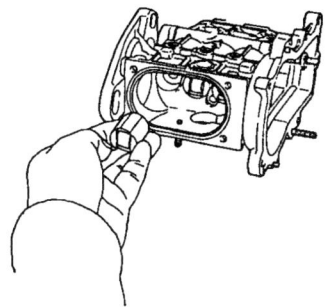

NOTE: When you stand the fuel pump up, all of the roller guides drop out at one time. Therefore, first remove the stop bolt for one cylinder at a time, and then the roller guide for each cylinder—continue this process.

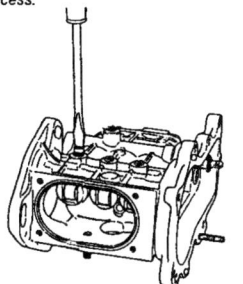

(12) Remove the plunger, plunger spring and lower washer from the lower part of the pump.

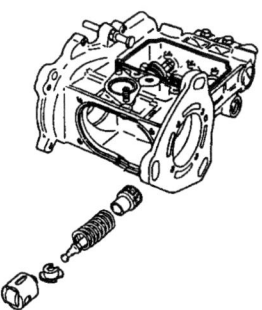

NOTE: Keep the parts separate for each cylinder.

(13) Loosen the small screw on control pinion.

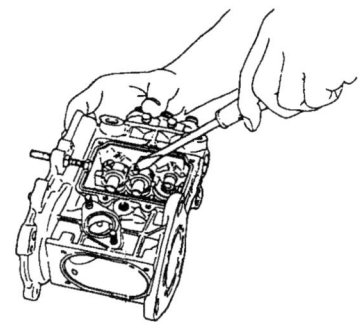

NOTE: 1. Check to make sure the match marks on the pinion/sleeve are correct before loosening the small screw on the control pinion, as the pinion and sleeve come apart when the screw is loosened. If the mark is hard to read or off center, lightly inscribe a new mark. This will serve as a guide when adjusting injection volume later.

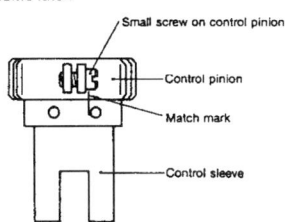

2. Keep parts separate for each cylinder.

(14) Remove the control pinion, sleeve and upper rest.

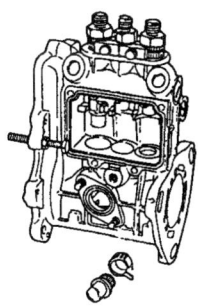

NOTE: Keep parts separate for each cylinder.

Chapter 3 Fuel Injection Equipment
3. Disassembly, Reassembly and Inspection of Fuel Injection Pump _____ 3JH2 Series

(15) Remove the control rack stop bolt and remove the rack.

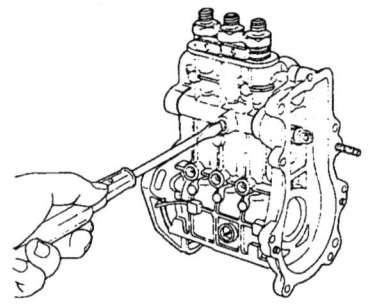

NOTE: Be careful not to lose the spring or rest on the control rack.

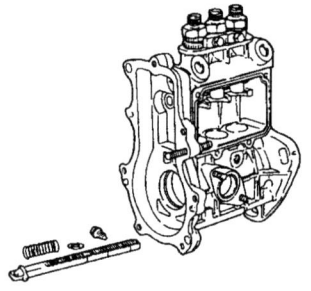

(16) Loosen the delivery valve retainer stop bolt, and remove the delivery valve holder stop.

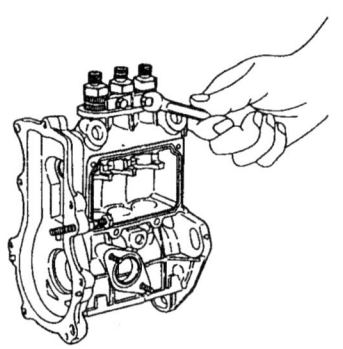

(17) Remove the delivery valve holder.

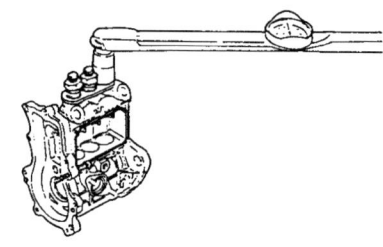

(18) Remove the delivery valve assembly.

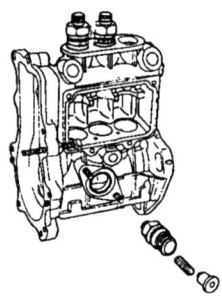

NOTE: 1. Be careful not to lose the delivery valve packing, delivery valve spring, delivery valve stopper or other small parts.
2. Keep the delivery valve assemblies for each cylinder clearly separated.

(19) Take the plunger barrel out from the top of pump.

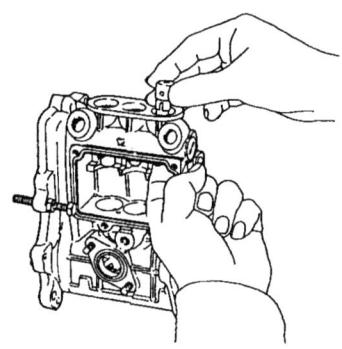

NOTE: Keep it as a set with the plunger that was removed earlier.

Chapter 3 Fuel Injection Equipment
3. Disassembly, Reassembly and Inspection of Fuel Injection Pump   *3JH2 Series*

3-2 Inspection of fuel injection pump

(1) Inspection of plunger
1) Thoroughly wash the plungers, and replace plungers that have scratches on the plunger lead or are discolored.
2) The plunger is in good condition if it slides down smoothly when it is tilted about 60°. Repeat this several times while turning the plunger. Repair or replace if it slides down too quickly or if it stops part way.

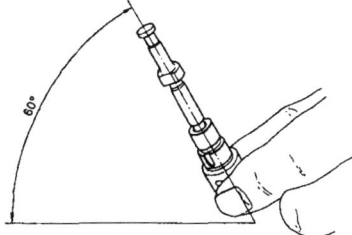

(2) Inspection of delivery valve

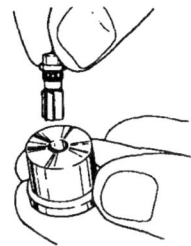

1) Replace as a set if the delivery valve suck-back collar or seat are scratched, scored, scuffed, worn, etc.
2) The valve is in good condition if it returns when released after being pushed it down with your finger (while the holes in the bottom of the delivery guide seat are covered). Replace if necessary.
3) Likewise, the valve should completely close by its own weight when you take your finger off the holes in the bottom of the delivery guide sheet.

NOTE: When fitting new parts, wash with diesel oil and perform the above inspection.

(3) Inspection of pump
1) Inspect for extreme wear of roller guide sliding surface. Scratches on the roller pin sliding surface are not a problem.
2) Inspect the plunger barrel seat.
If there are burrs or discoloration, repair or replace as this will lead to dilution of the lubricant.

(4) Inspection of fuel camshaft and bearings
1) Fuel camshaft
Inspect for scratches or wear of camshaft, deformation of key grooves and deformation of screws on both ends, and replace if necessary.
2) Bearings
Replace if the taper rollers or outer race surface is flaked or worn.

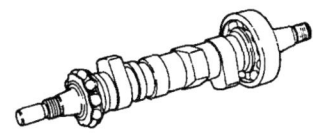

NOTE: Replace fuel camshafts and bearings together.

(5) Inspection of roller guide assembly
1) Roller

Replace if the surface is worn or flaked.
2) Roller Guide
Replace if the outer roller pin hole is extensively worn or there are many scratches.
3) Replace if the play of the roller guide assembly pin/roller is 0.2mm (0.0078in.) or more.
4) Injection timing adjustment bolt
Replace if the surface in contact with the plunger side is unevenly or excessively worn.

(6) Inspection of rack and pinion
1) Rack

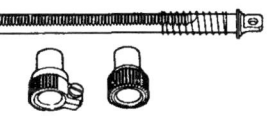

Inspect for bending of rack and wear or deformation of fit with pinion.
2) Pinion
Inspect for wear or deformation of fit with rack.

NOTE: If the tooth surface or sliding surface is not in good working order, rack resistance increases, affecting the condition of the engine (rough rpm, over running, etc.).

(7) Inspection of plunger spring and delivery spring
Inspect springs for scratches, cracks, breakage, uneven wear and rust.

Chapter 3 Fuel Injection Equipment
3. Disassembly, Reassembly and Inspection of Fuel Injection Pump _____ 3JH2 Series

(8) Inspection of oil seals
Inspect oil seals to see if they are burred or scratched.
(9) Inspection of roller guide stop
Inspect the side of the tip, replace if excessively worn.
(10) Inspection of O-rings
Inspect and replace if they are burred or cracked.

3-3 Reassembly of fuel injection pump

Preparation
After inspection, put all parts in order and clean.
See Inspection of Fuel Pump for inspection procedure.

(1) Put in the plunger barrel from the top of pump.

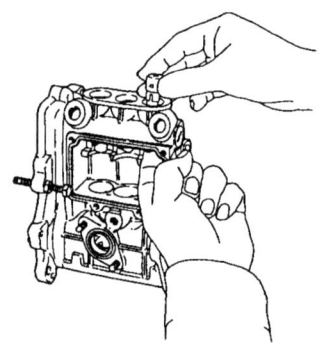

NOTE: Make sure the barrel key groove is fitted properly to the barrel stop pin.

(2) Place the delivery valve assembly, packing, spring and stopper from the top of the pump, in that order.

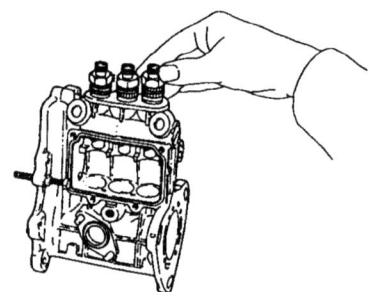

NOTE: Replace the delivery valve packing and O-ring.

(3) Place the control rack, and tighten the control rack stop bolt.

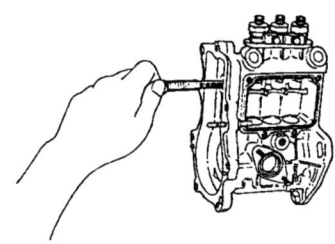

NOTE: 1. Do not forget the rack aux. spring.
2. Make sure the rack moves smoothly through a full cycle.

(4) Place the rack set screw (using the special tool) in the rack stop bolt screw hole to fix the rack.
(5) Looking from the bottom of pump, align the match marks on the rack and pinion.

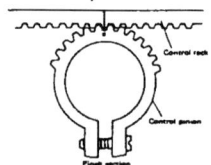

(6) While holding the pinion with one hand and keeping it aligned with the match mark, fit in the sleeve, and lightly tighten the small pinion screw.

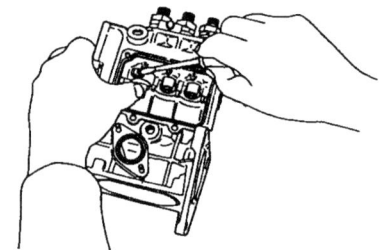

NOTE: Fitting of sleeve; Face towards small pinion screws and align with match mark.

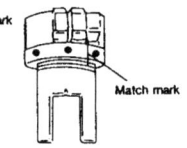

Printed in Japan
A0A1015-9110SP

Chapter 3 Fuel Injection Equipment
3. Disassembly, Reassembly and Inspection of Fuel Injection Pump

(7) Mount the plunger spring upper rest.

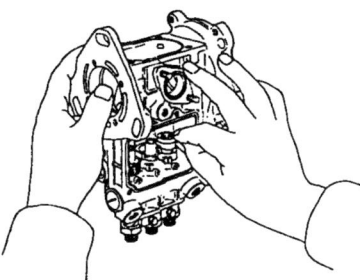

NOTE: 1. Be sure to mount the upper rest with the hollow side facing down.
2. Recheck to make sure that the rack moves easily.

(8) Mount the plunger spring.
(9) Mount the lower rest on the head of the plunger, and fit the plunger in the lower part of pump while aligning the match marks on the plunger flange and the sleeve.

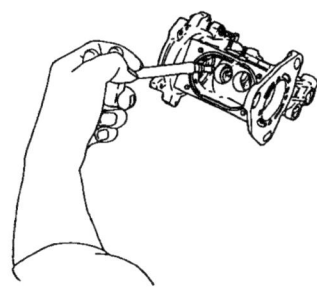

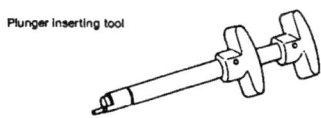

Plunger inserting tool

NOTE: If the plunger is mounted in the opposite direction, the injection volume will increase abnormally and cannot be adjusted.

(10) Insert the plunger spring support plate between the plunger spring seat B (lower) and fuel pump, by putting the handle of a hammer in the lower part of pump and pushing the roller guide up.

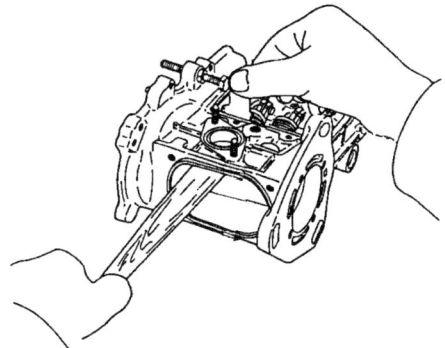

NOTE: 1. Face the roller guide stop groove upwards, and align it with the stop screw hole on the pump.

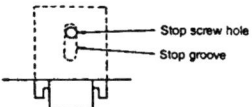

Stop screw hole
Stop groove

2. Check the movement of the rack. The plunger spring may be out of place if the movement is heavy — insert a screwdriver and bring it to the correct position.
3. When replacing the roller guide assembly, fit shims and lightly tighten:

Standard shim thickness	1.2 mm (0.0472 in.)
Part code number	129155-51600

(11) Make sure that the roller guide stop groove is in the correct position, and tighten the roller guide stop bolt.

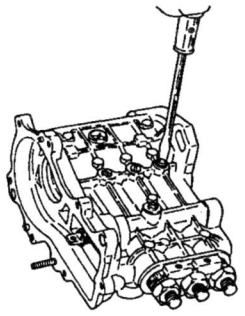

(12) Fit the bearings to both ends of the camshaft, and insert from the drive side by tapping lightly.

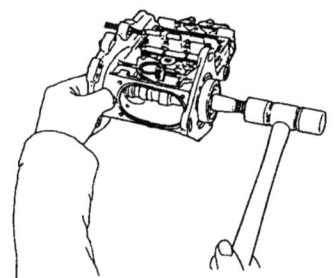

NOTE: Turn the pump upside down, and tap in the camshaft while moving the roller guide to the plunger spring side.

(13) Fit the oil seal on the inside of the bearing retainer and mount the bearing retainer.

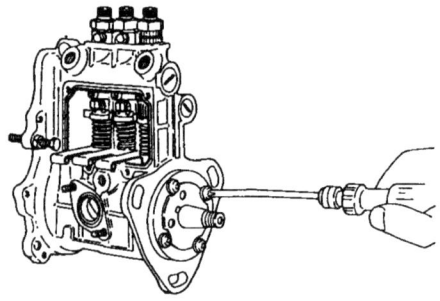

NOTE: Coat the camshaft and oil seal with oil to prevent the oil seal from being scratched.

(14) Fix the pump, lightly tap both ends of the cam shaft with a wooden hammer, and adjust the cam shaft side clearance with the adjustment shims while checking with a side clearance gauge.

	mm (in.)
Camshaft side clearance	0.02 ~ 0.05 (0.0007 ~ 0.0019)

Adjusting
Pull out the adjusting shims if the clearance is too small, and add adjusting shims if it is too large.

	mm (in.)
Adjusting shim thickness	0.50 (0.0196)
	0.40 (0.0157)
	0.30 (0.0118)
	0.15 (0.0059)

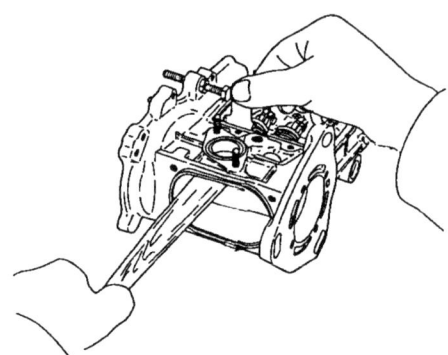

(15) Mount the fuel pump side cover.
(16) Tap in the camshaft wood ruff key.
(17) Turn the camshaft, and pull out the plunger spring support plate.

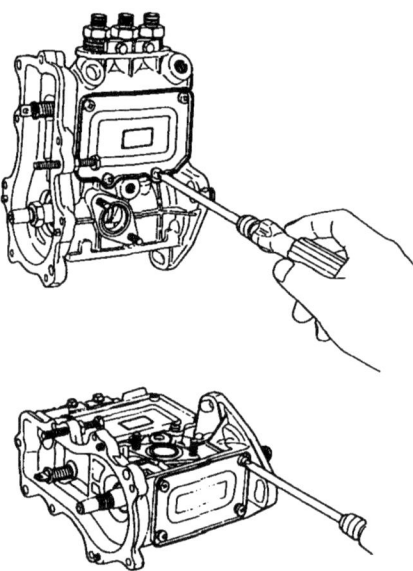

NOTE: Fit double nuts to turn the camshaft.

Chapter 3 Fuel Injection Equipment
3. Disassembly, Reassembly and Inspection of Fuel Injection Pump

(18) Tighten the delivery valve retainer.

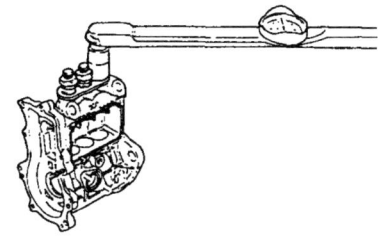

	kg-m (ft-lb)
Tightening torque	3.5 ~ 4.0 (25.31 ~ 28.93)

NOTE: 1. Tighten the retainer as far as possible by hand—if the bolt gets hard to turn part way, the packing or delivery valve are out of place. Remove, correct, and start tightening again.
2. Overtightening can result in malfunctioning of the rack.

(19) Fit the delivery retainer stop and tighten the stop bolt.

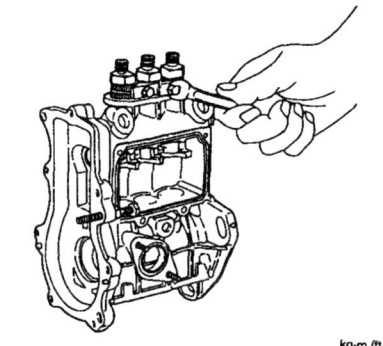

	kg-m (ft-lb)
Tightening torque	0.3 (2.16)

NOTE: Overtightening can upset the delivery retainer and cause oil leakage.

(20) Mount the fuel feed pump

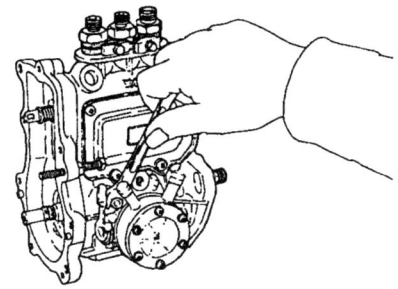

NOTE: Refer to the instructions for reassembly of the fuel feed pump.

4. Adjustment of Fuel Injection Pump and Governor

Adjust the fuel injection pump after you have completed reassembly. The pump itself must be readjusted with a special pump tester when you have replaced major parts such as the plunger assembly, roller guide assembly, fuel camshaft, etc. Procure a pump tester like the one illustrated below.

4-1 Preparations

Prepare for adjustment of the fuel injection pump as follows:

(1) Adjusting nozzle assembly and inspection of injection starting pressure.

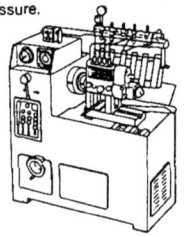

kg/cm² (lb/in.²)

Adjusting nozzle type	YDN-12SD12
Injection starting pressure	165 ~ 175 (2346.85 ~ 2489.08)

(2) Adjusting injection pipe.

mm (in.)

Inner dia./outer dia. × length	2.0/6.0 × 600 (0.0787/0.2362 × 23.6220)
Minimum bending radius	25 (0.9842)

(3) Mount the fuel injection pump on the pump tester platform.

mm (in.)

Tester used	l_1	l_2	Part code number
Yanmar	110 (4.3307)	150 (5.9055)	158090-51010
Robert Bosch	125 (4.9212)	165 (6.4960)	158090-51020

(4) Remove the control rack blind cover and fit the rack indicator.

Next, turn the pinion from the side of the pump until the control rack is at the maximum drive side position, and set it to the rack indicator scale standard position. Then make sure that the control rack and rack indicator slide smoothly.

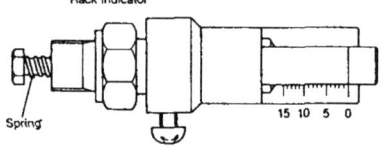

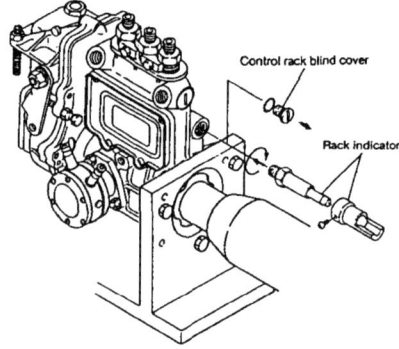

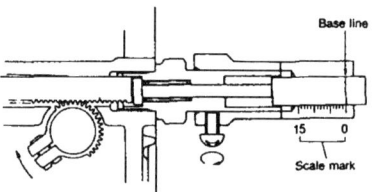

Part code number	158090-51500

Chapter 3 Fuel Injection Equipment
4. Adjustment of Fuel Injection Pump and Governor

(5) Check control rack stroke
Make sure the rack position is at 11.5 ~ 12.5mm (0.4527 ~ 0.4921in.) on the indicator scale when the governor control lever is set at the maximum operating position. If it is not at this value, change the link connecting the governor and control rack to adjust it.

NOTE: Links are availabe in 1mm (0.0394in.) increments.

(6) Remove the plug in the oil fill hole on the top of the governor case, and fill the pump with about 200cc of pump oil or engine oil.

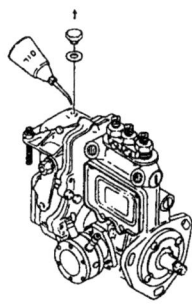

(7) Complete fuel oil piping and operate the pump tester to purge the line of air.
(8) Set the pressure of oil fed from the pump tester to the injection pump at 0.2 ~ 0.3kg/cm^2 (2.84 ~ 4.26 ln/in.^{2}).

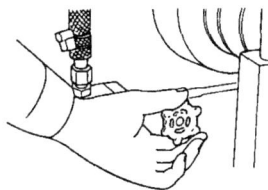

4-2 Adjustment of top clearance

Adjust the top clearance (the clearance between the top of plunger and the top of barrel with the cam at top dead center) of each cylinder plunger to bring it to the specified value by changing the thickness of the shims.

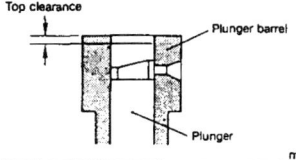

mm (in.)

Top clearance	0.95–1.05 (0.0374–0.0413)
Pre-stroke	2.5 (0.0984)
Standard shim thickness	1.2 (0.0472)

Relation between top clearance, standard shim thickness and pre-stroke.
mm (in.)

Adjusting shim thickness	1.0 (0.0394)
	1.2 (0.0472)
	1.3 (0.0512)
	1.4 (0.0551)
	1.5 (0.0591)
	1.6 (0.0630)
Part Code No.	129155–51600

(1) Place the top clearance gauge on a level surface and set the gauge to zero.

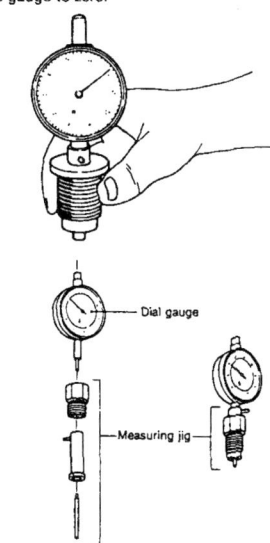

(2) Remove the injection pump delivery retainer, take out the delivery valve assembly, insert the top clearance gauge and tighten by hand.

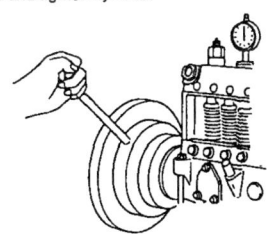

(3) Turn the camshaft, and bring the cam to the top dead center while watching the gauge needle.

Chapter 3 Fuel Injection Equipment
4. Adjustment of Fuel Injection Pump and Governor
3JH2 Series

(4) Read the gauge at this position, and adjust until the clearance is at the specified value by changing adjusting shims.
Tighten the adjusting screw after completing adjustment.

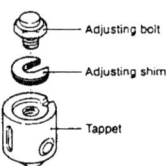

(Greater shim thickness decreases top clearance and smaller shim thickness increases top clearance).

NOTE: *Adjust while watching gauge, and then tighten.*

(5) After adjustment is completed, insert the delivery valve assembly and tighten the delivery retainer.

	kg·m (ft-lb)
Delivery retainer tightening torque	3.5 ~ 4.0 (25.31 ~ 28.93)

Repeat the above procedure to adjust the top clearance of each cylinder.

4-3 Adjusting of injection timing

After adjusting the top clearance for all cylinders, check/adjust the injection timing.

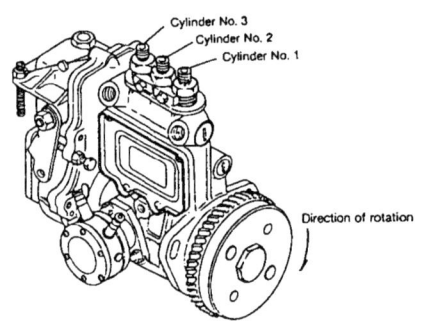

(1) Set the governor control lever to the operating position and fix (bring plunger to the effective injection range), turn the camshaft clockwise, and check the injection starting time (FID) of cylinder No.1 (start of discharge of fuel from the delivery retainer).

Cylinder no.	Count from the drive side
Direction of rotation	Right looking from drive side

(2) In the above state, set the tester needle to a position easy to read on the flywheel scale, and check the injection timing several times by reading the flywheel scale, according to the injection order.

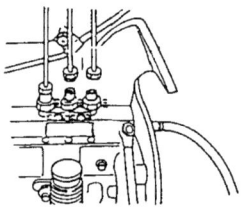

Injection order	1—3—4—2—1
Injection timing	90°
Allowable deviation	±30'

(3) Readjust the top clearance of cylinders that are not within the allowable deviation (increasing adjusting shim thickness makes injection timing faster, and decreasing makes it slower).
The change in injection timing effected by adjusting shims is as follows:

Change in shim thickness	Change in injection timing	
	Cam angle	Crank angle
0.1mm (0.0039in.)	0.5°	1.0°

(4) When you have readjusted top clearance, make sure it is within allowable values after completing adjustment.

mm (in.)

Allowable top clearance	0.3 (0.0118)

NOTE: 1. *All cylinders must be readjusted it any one shows less than the allowable value.*
2. *If the top clearance is less than the allowable value, the plunger will hit the delivery valve or the plunger flange will hit the plunger barrel.*

Chapter 3 Fuel Injection Equipment
4. Adjustment of Fuel Injection Pump and Governor

4-4 Plunger pressure test

(1) Mount the pressure gauge to the delivery retainer of the cylinder to be tested.

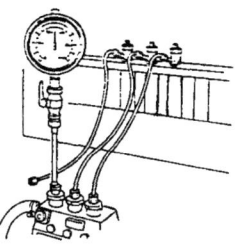

Max. pressure gauge reading	1000 kg/cm² (14223 lb/in.²)
Connecting screw dimensions	M12 × 1.5

(2) Set the governor control lever to the stop position, operate the injection pump at about 200 rpm, and make sure that the pressure gauge reading is 500 kg/cm² (7110 lb/in.²) or more while lightly moving the control pinion gear towards full throttle (drive side) from the pump.
Replace the plunger if the pressure does not reach this value.

(3) Immediately release the gear after the pressure rises to stop injection.
At the same time, check to see that oil is not leaking from the delivery retainer or fuel injection piping, and that there is no extreme drop in pressure.

4-5 Delivery valve pressure test

(1) Perform the plunger pressure test in the same way, bringing the pressure to about 120 kg/cm² (1706 lb/in.²), and then stopping injection.

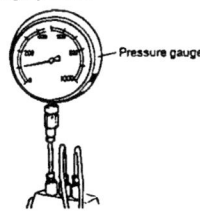
Pressure gauge

(2) After pressure rises to the above value, measure the time it takes to drop from 100 ~ 90 kg/cm² (1422 ~ 2702 lb/in.²).

100 → 90 kg/cm² (1422 ~ 1280 lb/in.²)	5 seconds (to drop 10 kg/cm² (142 lb/in.²))

If the pressure drops faster than this, wash the delivery valve, and retest. Replace the delivery valve if the pressure continues to drop rapidly.

4-6 Adjusting injection volume (uniformity of each cylinder)

The injection volume is determined by the fuel injection pump rpm and rack position. Check and adjust to bring to specified value.

4-6.1 Measuring injection volume

(1) Preparation
Set the pump rpm, rack position and measuring stroke to the specified value and measure:

Pump RPM	1800 rpm
Pump rotating direction	Right looking from drive side
Rack indicator scale reading	7mm (0.2756 in)

Remove the rack stop bolt behind the pump and screw in the rack fixing bolt to fix the rack.

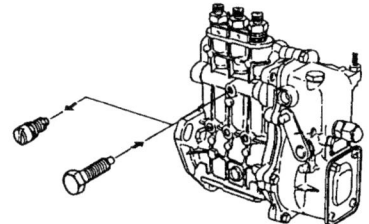

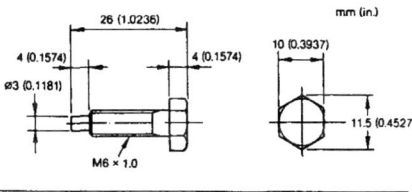

Part Code No.	158090-51510

(2) Measuring injection volume
Measure the injection volume at the standard stroke, and adjust as follows if it is not within the specified value.

Measuring stroke	1,000 st
Specified injection volume at standard rack position	See injection pump service data
Nonuniformity of cylinders	±3%

4-6.2 Adjustment of injection volume

Measure the injection volume in measuring cylinders for each cylinder, and adjust if necessary to obtain the specified values.
(1) Push the control rack all the way to the drive side, stop with the rack fixing bolt, and loosen the pinion/sleeve fixing bolt 1/3 of a revolution.

Chapter 3 Fuel Injection Equipment
4. Adjustment of Fuel Injection Pump and Governor

(2) When the control sleeve is turned to the right or left, the plunger is turned through the same angle to increase or decrease injection volume.
The injection volume is increased when the control sleeve is turned in the − direction and decreased when turned in the − direction in the following figure.

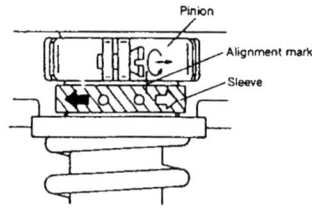

(3) Measure the injection volume of each cylinder again. Repeat this process until the injection volume for every cylinder is the same (within the specified limit).
(4) Next, measure the injection volumes under different conditions, and make sure the injection volume for every cylinder is within the specifications.
Replace the plunger if the injection volume is not within specifications.

NOTE: See adjustment data for the specified injection volume value at other measuring points.

(5) After completing measurement, firmly tighten the piston/sleeve fixing screw.
(6) If not aligned with the match mark, make a new match mark.

4-7 Adjustment of governor
4-7.1 Adjusting fuel limit bolt
(1) Adjust the tightness of the fuel limit bolt to bring the rack position to the specified value (R_1) with the governor control lever all the way down towards the fuel increase position, while keeping the pump at rated rpm N_1.

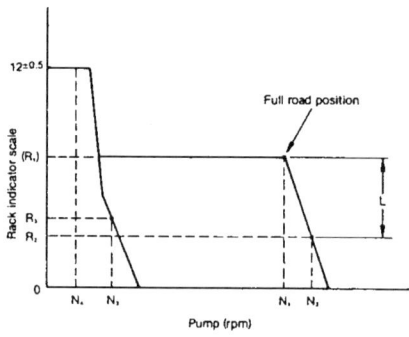

(2) Measure fuel injection volume at rack position (R_1). Tightening of fuel limit bolt.
(3) If the injection volume is at the specified value, tighten the fuel limit bolt lock nut at that position.

4-7.2 Adjusting RPM limit bolt
(1) Gradually loosen the governor control lever while keeping the pump drive condition in the same condition as when the fuel limit bolt was adjusted, and adjust the tightness of the RPM limit bolt to the point where the rack position just exceeds the specified value (R_1).

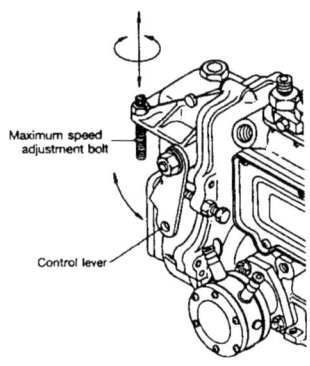

(2) Check maximum RPM at no load
Further increase rpm, and make sure that rack position ($R_2 = R_1 − L$) corresponding to maximum rpm at no load is within specified value (N_2).

No load max. RPM (Pump RPM)	1950 rpm

4-7.3 Adjusting idling
(1) Maintain the pump rpm at specified rpm (N_3).

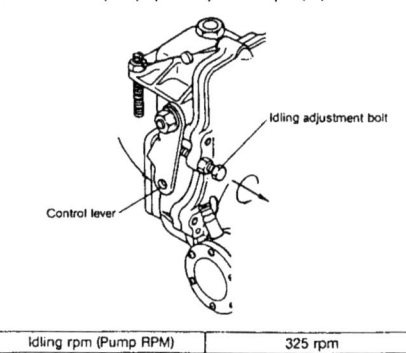

Idling rpm (Pump RPM)	325 rpm

Chapter 3 Fuel Injection Equipment
4. Adjustment of Fuel Injection Pump and Governor

(2) Measure the injection volume while lowering the governor control lever to the idling position, and adjust the position of the control lever with the idling adjustment bolt to bring it to the specified value.

Measuring stroke	1000 st
Idling injection volume	See injection pump service data

4-7.4 Check injection volume when starting

(1) Make sure the control rack moves smoothly while gradually reducing idling rpm.
(2) Next, fix the governor control lever at the full load position with the pump at the specified rpm (N_4). Make sure that control rack is at the maximum rack position (11.05 ~ 12.05).
Measure the injection volume and check to make sure it is within the specified value.

Pump rpm (N^4)	200 rpm
Rack indicator scale	11.5~12.5mm(0.4527~0.4921 in.)
Measuring stroke	1000 st
Injection volume	See injection pump service data

Checking injection stop
Drive the pump at rated rpm (N_1) and standard rack position (R_1) with the governor control lever at the full load position, operate the stop lever on the back of the governor case, and make sure that injection to all cylinders is stopped.

NOTE: Be sure to remove the rack fixing bolt when doing this.

5. Fuel Feed Pump

The fuel feed pump pumps fuel from the fuel tank, passes it through the fuel filter element, and supplies it to the fuel injection pump.

The fuel feed pump is mounted on the side of this engine and is driven by the (eccentric) cam of the fuel pump camshaft. It is provided with a manual priming lever so that fuel can be supplied when the engine is stopped.

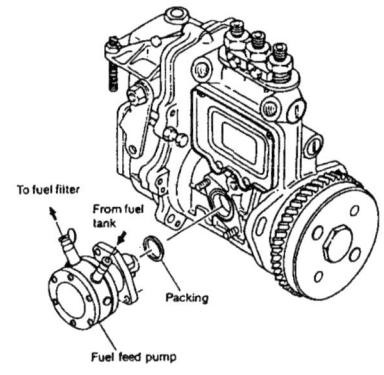

5-1 Construction of fuel feed pump

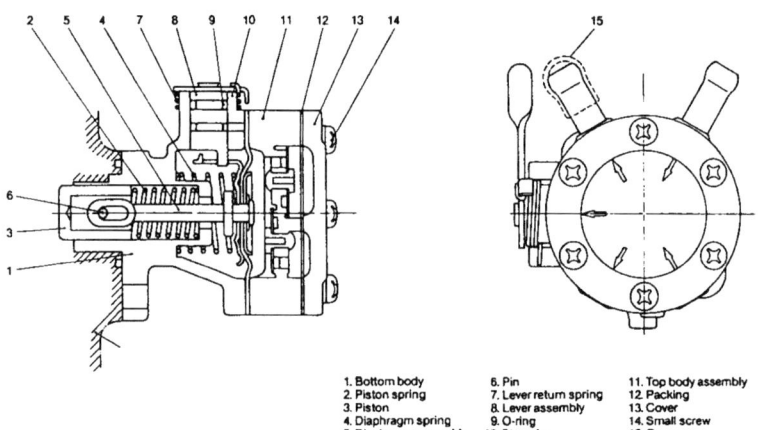

1. Bottom body
2. Piston spring
3. Piston
4. Diaphragm spring
5. Diaphragm assembly
6. Pin
7. Lever return spring
8. Lever assembly
9. O-ring
10. Stop pin
11. Top body assembly
12. Packing
13. Cover
14. Small screw
15. Cap

5-2 Fuel feed pump specifications

Head	1m (3.28 ft)
Discharge volume	230 cc/min (14.03 in.³/min) at 1500 cam rpm, discharge pressure of 0.2 kg/cm² (2.84 lb/in.²)
Closed off pressure	0.3 kg/cm² (4.26 lb/in.²) or more (at 400 cam rpm)

Chapter 3 Fuel Injection Equipment
5. Fuel Feed Pump

5-3 Disassembly and reassembly of fuel feed pump

5-3.1 Disassembly
(1) Remove the fuel feed pump mounting nut, and take the fuel feed pump off the fuel injection pump.
(2) Clean the fuel feed pump assembly with fuel oil.
(3) After checking the orientation of the arrow on the cover, make match marks on the upper body and cover, remove the small screw, and disassemble the cover, upper body and lower body.

5-3.2 Reassembly
(1) Clean all parts with fuel oil, inspect, and replace any defective parts.
(2) Replace any packings on parts that have been disassembled.
(3) Make sure that the intake valve and discharge valve on upper body are mounted in the proper direction, and that you don't forget the valve packing.
(4) Assemble the diaphragm into the body, making sure the diaphragm mounting holes are lined up (do not force).
(5) Align the match marks on the upper body of the pump and cover, and tighten the small screws evenly.

	kg-cm (ft-lb)
Tightening torque	15 ~ 25 (1.08 ~ 1.80)

5-4 Fuel feed pump inspection
(1) Place the fuel feed pump in kerosene, cover the discharge port with your finger, move the priming lever and check for air bubbles (Repair or replace any part which emits air bubbles).

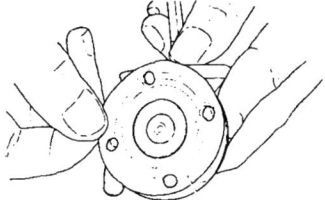

(2) Attach a vinyl hose to the fuel feed pump intake, keep the pump at the specified depth from the fuel oil surface, move the priming lever by hand and check for sudden spurts of fuel oil from the discharge port. If oil is not spurted out, inspect the diaphragm and diaphragm spring and repair/replace as necessary.
(3) Diaphragm inspection
Parts of the diaphragm that are repeatedly burned will become thinner or deteriorate over a long period of time. Check the diaphragm and replace if necessary.

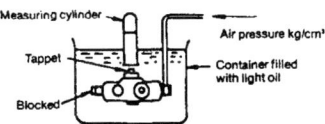

(4) Valve contact/mounting
Clean the valve seat and valve with air to remove any foreign matter.

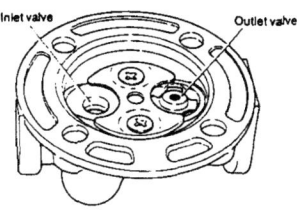

(5) Inspect the diaphragm spring and piston spring for settling and the piston for wear, and replace as necessary.

NOTE: Replace parts as an assembly.

6. Fuel Injection Nozzle

When fuel oil pumped by the fuel injection pump reaches the injection nozzle, it pushes up the nozzle valve (held down by spring), and is injected into the combustion chamber at high pressure.
The fuel is atomized by the nozzle to mix uniformly with the air in the combustion chamber. How well the fuel is mixed with high temperature air directly affects combustion efficiency, engine performance and fuel economy.
Accordingly, the fuel injection nozzles must be kept in top. condition to maintain performance and operating efficiency.

6-1 Functioning of fuel injection nozzle

Fuel from the fuel injection pump passes through the oil port in the nozzle holder, and enters the nozzle body reservoir.
When oil reaches the specified pressure, it pushes up the nozzle valve (held by the nozzle spring), and is injected through the small hole on the tip of the nozzle body.
The nozzle valve is automatically pushed down by the nozzle spring and closed after fuel is injected.
Oil that leaks from between the nozzle valve and nozzle body goes from the hole on top of the nozzle spring through the oil leakage fitting and back into the fuel tank.
Adjustment of injection starting pressure is effected with the adjusting shims.

(1) Hole type fuel injection nozzle

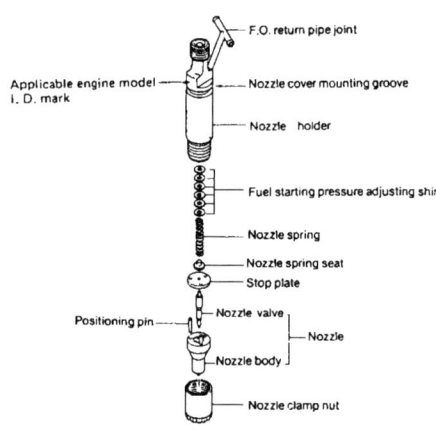

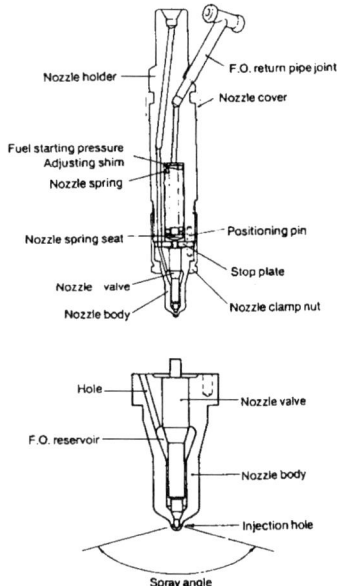

Engine model	3JH2E	3JH2-TE
Nozzle I.D. Mark	150P244HC0	140P255Z0
Spray angle	150°	140°
No. of injection hole × dia	4 × 0.24mm	5 × 0.25mm
Nozzle opening pressure	195 ~ 205kg/cm²(2.773 ~ 2.915lb/in.²)	

Chapter 3 Fuel Injection Equipment
6. Fuel Injection Nozzle

3JH2 Series

Nozzle body identification number
The type of nozzle can be determined from the number inscribed on the outside of the nozzle body.
1) Hole type fuel injection nozzles

Sample

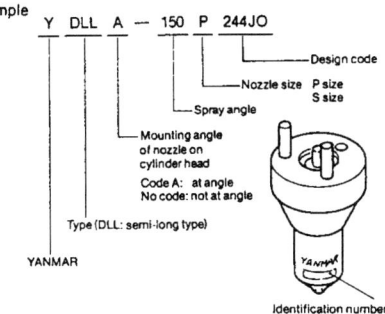

Y DLL A — 150 P 244JO
- Design code
- Nozzle size P size / S size
- Spray angle
- Mounting angle of nozzle on cylinder head
  Code A: at angle
  No code: not at angle
- Type (DLL: semi-long type)

YANMAR

Identification number

6-2 Fuel injection nozzle disassembly

NOTE: 1. Disassemble fuel injection nozzle in a clean area as for the fuel injection pump.
2. When disassembling more than one fuel injection nozzle, keep the parts for each injection nozzle separate for each cylinder (i.e. the nozzle for cylinder 1 must be remounted in cylinder 1).

(1) When removing the injection nozzle from the cylinder head, remove the high pressure fuel pipe, fuel leakage pipe, etc., the injection nozzle retainer nut, and then the fuel injection nozzle.

(2) Put the nozzle in a vise
NOTE: Use the special nozzle holder for the hole type injection nozzle so that the high pressure mounting threads are not damaged.
(3) Remove the nozzle nut

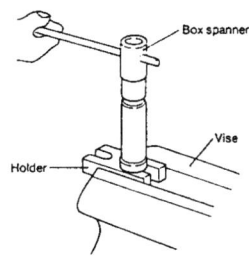

NOTE: Use a special box spanner for the hole type (the thickness of the two nozzle nuts is 15mm (0.5906in.)).

(4) Remove the inner parts
NOTE: Be careful not to loosen the spring seat, adjusting shims or other small parts.

6-3 Fuel injection nozzle inspection
6-3. 1 Washing

(1) Be sure to use new diesel oil to wash the fuel injection nozzle parts.
(2) Wash the nozzle in clean diesel oil with the nozzle cleaning kit.

Nozzle cleaning kit

1) Diesel Kiki nozzle cleaning kit:
   Type NP-8486B No. 5789-001
2) Anzen Jidosha Co., Ltd. nozzle cleaning kit:
   Type NCK-001

(3) Clean off the carbon on the outside of the nozzle body with a brass brush.

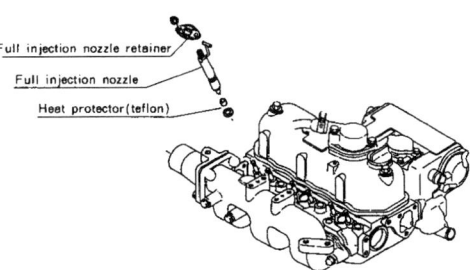

Full injection nozzle retainer
Full injection nozzle
Heat protector (teflon)

(4) Clean the nozzle seat with cleaning spray.

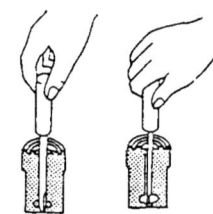

(5) Clean off the carbon on the tip of nozzle with a piece of wood.
(6) Clean hole type nozzles with a nozzle cleaning needle.

Nozzle cleaning needle (piano wire)
0.2mm dia. wire, 22mm long × 5 wires

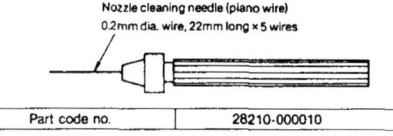

Part code no.	28210-000010

6-4. 2 Nozzle inspection

(1) Inspect for scratches/wear
Inspect oil seals for abnormal scratches or wear and replace the nozzle if the nozzle sliding surface or seat are scratched or abnormally worn.
(2) Check nozzle sliding
Wash the nozzle and nozzle body in clean diesel oil, and make sure that when the nozzle is pulled out about half way from the body, it slides down by itself when released.
Rotate the nozzle a little; replace the nozzle/nozzle body as a set if there are some places where it does not slide smoothly.

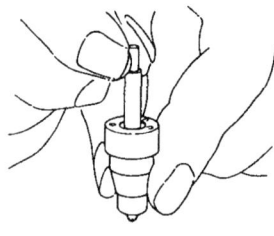

(3) Inspecting stop plate (inter-piece)
Check for scratches/wear in seals on both ends, check for abnormal wear on the surface where it comes in contact with the nozzle; replace if the stop plate is excessively worn.

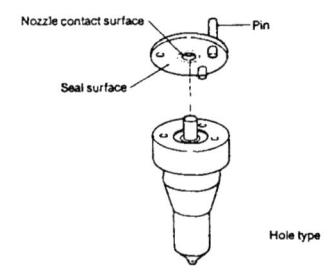

Hole type

	mm (in.)
Nozzle contact surface wear limit	0.1 (0.0039)

(4) Inspecting nozzle spring
Replace the nozzle spring if it is extremely bent, or the surface is scratched or rusted.

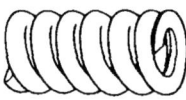

(5) Nozzle holder
Check the oil seal surface for scratches/wear; replace if the wear is excessive.

6-5 Fuel injection nozzle reassembly

The fuel injection nozzle is reassembled in the opposite order to disassembly.
(1) Insert the adjusting shims, nozzle spring and nozzle spring seat in the nozzle holder, mount the stop plate with the pin, insert the nozzle body/nozzle set and tighten the nut.
(2) Use the special holder when tightening the nut for the hole type nozzle as in disassembly.

Nozzle nut tightening torque	kg-m (ft-lb)
Hole type nozzle	4 ~ 4.5 (28.9 ~ 32.5)

6-6 Adjusting fuel injection nozzle

6-6. 1 Adjusting opening pressure

Mount the fuel injection nozzle on the nozzle tester and use the handle to measure injection starting pressure. If it is not at the specified pressure, use the adjusting shims to increase/decrease pressure (both hole and pintle types).

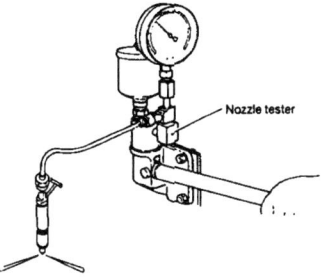

Nozzle tester

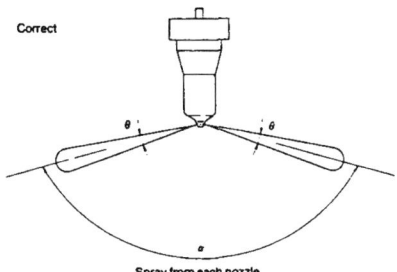

Correct

Spray from each nozzle hole is uniform

Poor

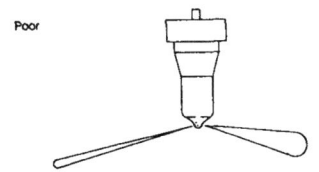

- Excessive difference in spray angle (θ)
- Excessive difference in injection angle (α)
- Incomplete atomization
- Sluggish starting/stopping of injection

Injection starting pressure

	kg/cm² (lb/in.²)
Injection starting pressure	195 ~ 205 (2773 ~ 2915)

7-6. 2 Injection test

After adjusting the nozzle to the specified starting pressure, check the fuel spray condition and seat oil tightness.

(1) Check seat oil tightness

After two or three injections, gradually increase the pressure up to 20 kg/cm² (284 lb/in.²) before reading the starting pressure, maintain the pressure for 5 seconds, and make sure that no oil is dripping from the tip of the nozzle.

Test the injection with a nozzle tester; retighten and test again if there is excessive oil leakage from the overflow coupling.

Replace the nozzle as a set if oil leakage is still excessive.

(2) Injection spray condition

Operate the nozzle tester lever once to twice a second and check for abnormal injection.

1) Hole type nozzles

Replace hole type nozzles that do not satisfy the following conditions:
- Proper spray angle (θ)
- Correct injection angle (α)
- Complete atomization of fuel
- Prompt starting/stopping of injection

7. Troubleshooting

7-1 Troubleshooting of fuel injection pump

Complete repair means not only replacing defective parts, but finding and eliminating the cause of the trouble as well. The cause of the trouble may not necessarily be in the pump itself, but may be in the engine or the fuel system. If the pump is removed prematurely, the true cause of the trouble may never be known. Before removing the pump from the engine, at least go through the basic check points given here.

Basic check points
- Check for breaks or oil leaks throughout the fuel system, from the fuel tank to the nozzle.
- Check the injection timings for all cylinders. Are they correctly adjusted? Are they too fast or too slow?
- Check the nozzle spray.
- Check the fuel delivery. Is it in good condition? Loosen the fuel pipe connection at the injection pump inlet, and test operate the fuel feed pump.

7-2 Major faults and troubleshooting

Fault		Cause	Remedy
1. Engine won't start.	Fuel not delivered to injection pump.	(1) No fuel in the fuel tank.	Resupply
		(2) Fuel tank cock is closed.	Open
		(3) Fuel pipe system is clogged.	Clean
		(4) Fuel filter element is clogged.	Disassemble and clean, or replace element
		(5) Air is sucked into the fuel due to defective connections in the piping from the fuel tank to the fuel pump.	Repair
		(6) Defective valve contact of feed pump	Repair or replace.
		(7) Piston spring of feed pump is broken.	Replace
		(8) Inter-spindle or tappets of feed pump are stuck.	Repair or replace
	Fuel delivered to injection pump.	(1) Defective connection of control lever and accel. rod of injection pump.	Repair or adjust
		(2) Plunger is worn out or stuck.	Repair or replace
		(3) Delivery valve is stuck.	Repair or replace
		(4) Control rack doesn't move.	Repair or replace
		(5) Injection pump coupling is damaged, or the key is broken.	Replace
	Nozzle doesn't work.	(1) Nozzle valve doesn't open or close normally.	Repair or replace
		(2) Nozzle seat is defective.	Repair or replace
		(3) Case nut is loose.	Inspect and tighten
		(4) Injection nozzle starting pressure is too low.	Adjust
		(5) Nozzle spring is broken.	Replace
		(6) Fuel oil filter is clogged.	Repair or replace
		(7) Excessive oil leaks from the nozzle sliding area.	Replace the nozzle assembly
	Injection timing is defective.	(1) Injection timing is retarded due to failure of the coupling.	Adjust
		(2) Camshaft is excessively worn.	Replace camshaft
		(3) Roller guide incorrectly adjusted or excessively worn.	Adjust or replace
		(4) Plunger is excessively worn.	Replace plunger assembly
2. Engine starts, but immediately stops.		(1) Fuel pipe is clogged.	Clean
		(2) Fuel filter is clogged.	Disassemble and clean, or replace the element.
		(3) Improper air-tightness of the fuel pipe connection, or pipe is broken and air is being sucked in.	Replace packing; repair pipe
		(4) Insufficient fuel delivery from the feed pump.	Repair or replace

Chapter 3 Fuel Injection Equipment
7. Troubleshooting
3JH2 Series

Fault		Cause	Remedy
3. Engine's output is insufficient.	Defective injection timing, and other failures.	(1) Knocking sounds caused by improper (too fast) injection timing. (2) Engine overheats or emits large amount of smoke due to improper (too slow) injection timing. (3) Insufficient fuel delivery from feed pump.	Inspect and adjust Inspect and adjust Repair or replace
	Nozzle movements is defective	(1) Case nut loose. (2) Defective injection nozzle performance. (3) Nozzle spring is broken. (4) Excessive oil leaks from nozzle.	Inspect and retighten Repair or replace nozzle Replace Replace nozzle assembly
	Injection pump is defective.	(1) Max. delivery limit bolt is screwed in too far. (2) Plunger is worn. (3) Injection amount is not uniform. (4) Injection timings are not even. (5) The 1st and 2nd levers of the governor and the control rack of the injection pump are improperly lined up. (6) Delivery stopper is loose. (7) Delivery packing is defective. (8) Delivery valve seat is defective. (9) Delivery spring is broken.	Adjust Replace Adjust Adjust Repair Inspect and retighten Replace packing Repair or replace Replace

4. Idling is rough.		(1) Movement of control rack is defective.
		  1) Stiff plunger movement or sticking.
		  2) Rack and pinion fitting is defective.
		  3) Movement of governor is improper.
		  4) Delivery stopper is too tight.
		(2) Uneven injection volume.
		(3) Injection timing is defective.
		(4) Plunger is worn and fuel injection adjustment is difficult.
		(5) Governor spring is too weak.
		(6) Feed pump can't feed oil at low speeds.
		(7) Fuel supply is insufficient at low speeds due to clogging of fuel filter.
			
			Repair or replace
			Repair
			Repair
			Inspect and adjust
			Adjust
			Adjust
			Replace
			Replace
			Repair or replace
			Disassemble and clean, or replace element

5. Engine runs at high speeds, but cuts out at low speeds.		(1) The wire or rod of the accel. is caught. (2) Control rack is caught and can't be moved.	Inspect and repair Inspect and repair
6. Engine doesn't reach max. rpm.		(1) Governor spring is broken or excessively worn. (2) Injection performance of nozzle is poor.	Replace Repair or replace
7. Loud knocking.		(1) Injection timing is too fast or too slow. (2) Injection from nozzle is improper. Fuel drips after each injection. (3) Injection nozzle starting pressure is too high. (4) Uneven injection. (5) Engine overheats, or insufficient compression.	Adjust Adjust Adjust Adjust Repair
3. Engine exhausts too much smoke.	When exhaust smoke is black:	(1) Injection timing is too fast. (2) Air volume intake is insufficient. (3) The amount of injection is uneven. (4) Injection from nozzle is improper.	Adjust Inspect and repair Adjust Repair or replace
	When exhaust smoke is white:	(1) Injection timing is too slow. (2) Water is mixed in fuel. (3) Shortage of lube oil in the engine. (4) Engine is over-cooled.	Adjust Inspect fuel system, and clean Repair Inspect

Chapter 3 Fuel Injection Equipment
8. Tools

8. Tools

Name of tool	Shape and size	Application
Pump mounting scale for Yanmar tester 158090-51010 for Bosch (tester) 158090-51020		
Measuring device (cam backlash) 158090-51050		
Plunger insert 158090-51100		
Tappet holder 158090-51200		
Weight extractor 158090-51400		

Chapter 3 Fuel Injection Equipment
8. Tools
_____ 3JH2 Series

Name of tool	Shape and size	Application
Rack indicator 158090-51500		
Rack lock screw 158090-51010		
Dummy nut 158090-51520		
Nozzle plate 158090-51700		
Plunger gauge 121820-92540		
Top clearance gauge 158090-51300		
Timer extraction tool		

9. Fuel Filter

The fuel filter is installed between the fuel feed pump and fuel injection pump, and removes dirt/foreign matter from the fuel pumped from the fuel tank.
The fuel filter element must be changed periodically. The fuel pumped by the fuel feed pump goes around the element, is fed through the pores in the filter and discharged from the center of the cover. Dirt and foreign matter in the fuel are deposited in the element.

9-1 Fuel filter specifications

Filtering method	filter paper
Filtering area	840cm² (130.20in.²)
Maximum flow	0.25 ℓ/min (15.25 in.³/min)
Pressure loss	100mm (3.9370in.) Hg or less
Max. dia. of unfiltered particle	5μ

9-2 Fuel filter inspection

The fuel strainer must be cleaned occasionally. If there is water or foreign matter in the strainer bowl, disassemble the strainer and wash with clean fuel oil to completely remove foreign matter. Replace the element every 300 hours of operation.
Replace the filter prior to this if the filter is very dirty, deformed or damaged.

Element changes	every 300 hours
Element part code number	129470-55700

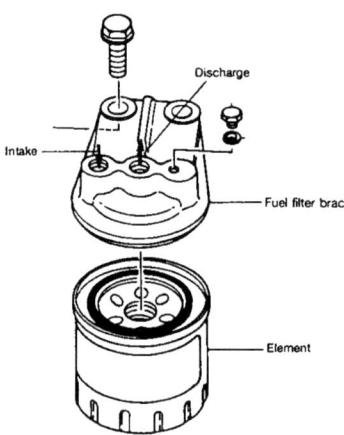

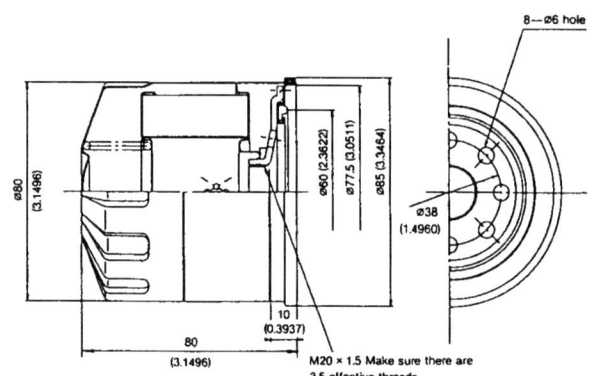

10. Fuel Tank

A triangular 30 liter fuel tank with a 2000mm (78.7402in.) rubber fuel hose to fit all models is available as an option. A fuel return connection is provided on top of the tank to which a rubber hose can be connected to return fuel from the fuel nozzles.

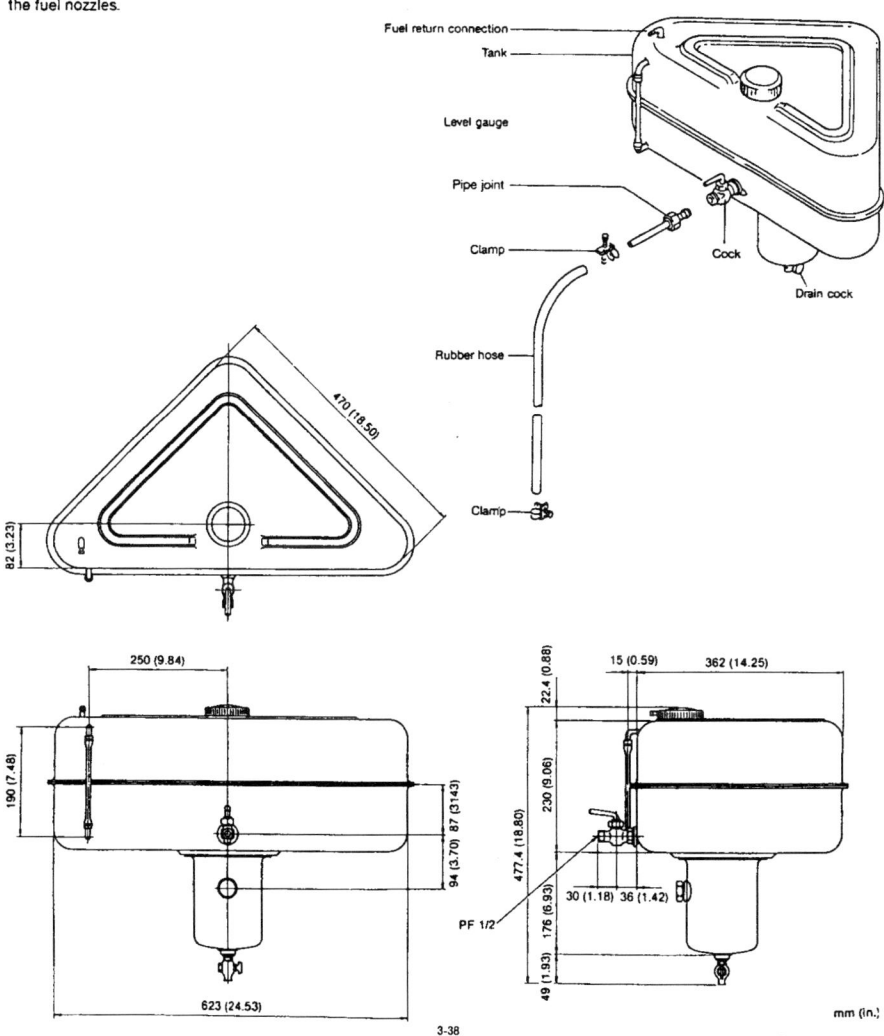

CHAPTER 4
INTAKE AND EXHAUST SYSTEM

1. Intake and Exhaust System 4-1
2. Turbocharger 4-3
3. Mixing Elbow 4-17

1. Intake and Exhaust System

1-1 3JHE engine

Air enters in the intake silencer mounted at the end of the intake manifold, is fed to the intake manifold and then on to each cylinder.

Exhaust gas goes into the exhaust manifold (in the fresh water tank) mounted on the cylinder head discharge. After cooling it enters the mixing elbow which is directly connected with the exhaust manifold, and is discharged from the ship along with waste cooling water.

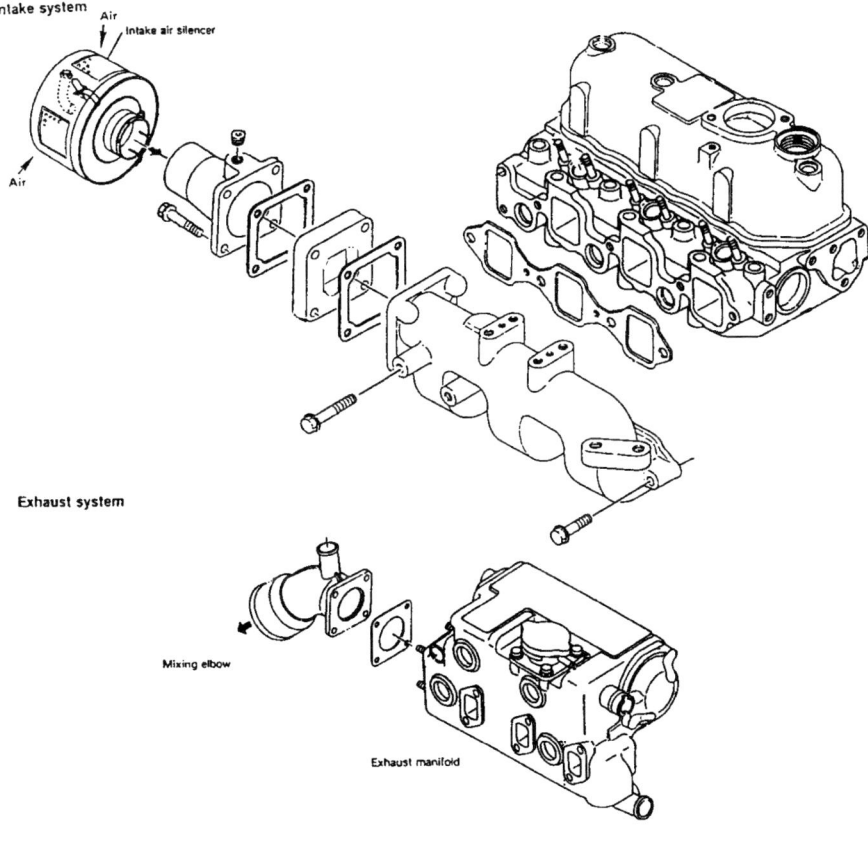

Chapter 4 Intake and Exhaust System
1. Intake and Exhaust System

3JH2 series

3JH25A/30A

Intake system

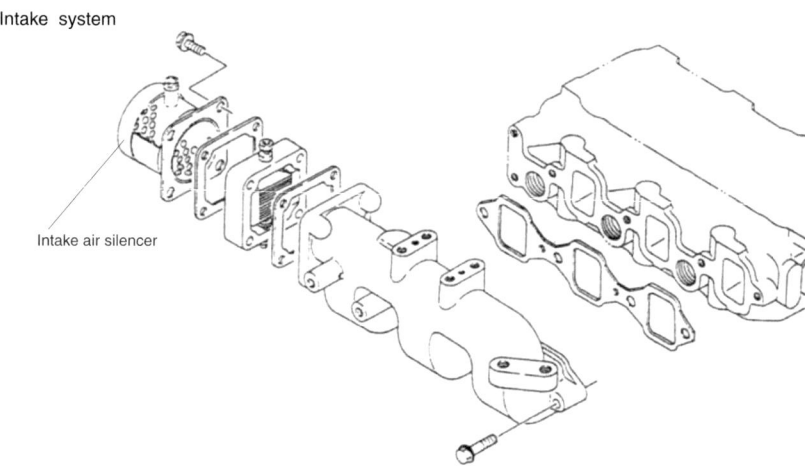

Intake air silencer

Exhaust system

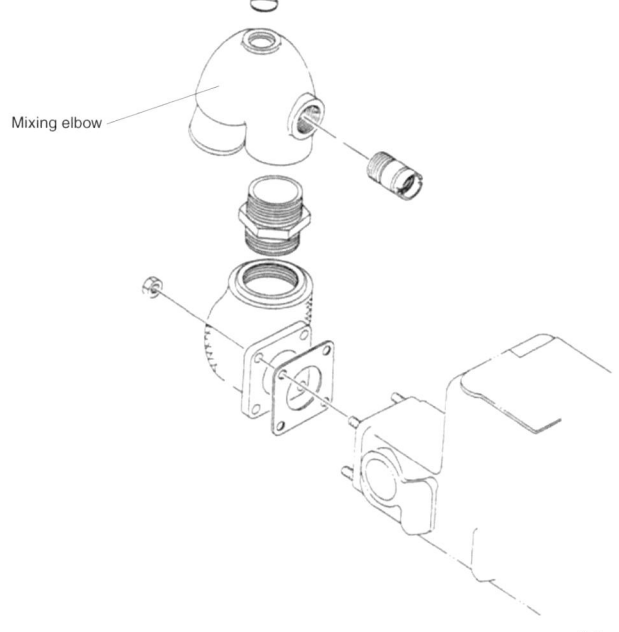

Mixing elbow

Chapter 4 Intake and Exhaust System
1. Intake and Exhaust System

1-2 3JH-TE engine
Intake system

Air goes from the intake manifold mounted to the turbocharger, through the turbocharger and a rubber hose to the intake manifold and is fed to each cylinder.

Exhaust gas goes from the exhaust manifold to the turbocharger connected to the exhaust manifold, to the mixing elbow mounted to the turbocharger, and is discharged from ship along with waste cooling water.

2. Turbocharger

2-1 Specifications

Turbocharger maker	ISHIKAWAJIMA-HARIMA HEAVY INDUSTRIAL CO.LTD.(IHI)	
Turbine type	Radial flow	
Blower type	Centrifugal	
Bearing type	Full foating	
Lubrication method	Outer lubrication	
Cooling method	Air cooled	
Continuous rated rpm	155,000	
Max.gas inlet temp. (continuous allowable)	700°C	
Dry weight, approx.	4.2kg(9.26 lb.)	
Turbocharger model	—	MY67
Applicable engine model	3JH2-TE	

2-2 Construction

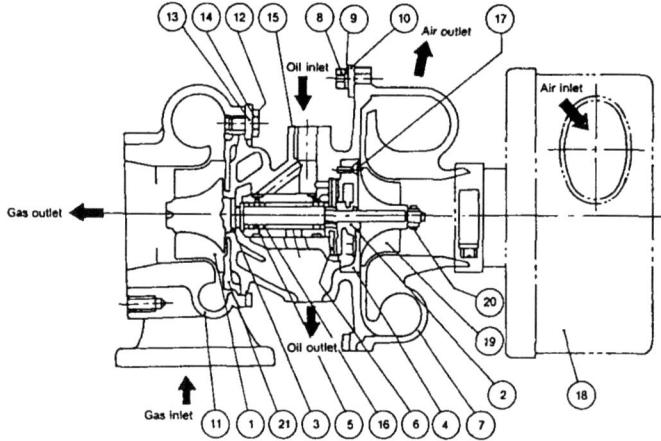

1. Turbine shaft
2. Oil thrower
3. Turbine side seal ring
4. Seal plate
5. Floating bearing
6. Thrust bearing
7. Blower wheel chamber
8. M5 hexagonal bolt
9. M5 lock washer
10. Blower side top plate
11. Turbine wheel chamber
12. M6 hexagonal bolt
13. Turbine side locking plate
14. Lock washer
15. Bearing chamber
16. Stop ring
17. Screw M3
18. Intake silencer
19. Blower wheel fixing nut
20. Blower wheel
21. Heat insulating board

Chapter 4 Intake and Exhaust System
2. Turbocharger

3JH2 Series

2-3 Interchangeability of turbochargers

The IHI-make turbocharger used for the 3JH2-TE differ according to the engine model. Care should therefore be taken to asemble only components for the turbocharger used in your engine when replacing parts. The use of incorrect turbocharger components will detract from the performance of the engine. Turbocharger models can be distinguished by their name plates.

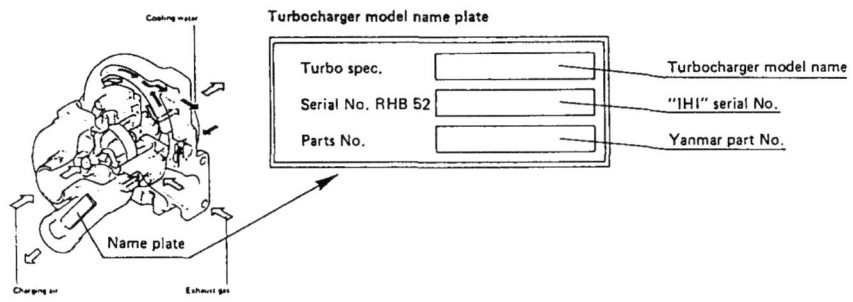

Engine model	Turbocharger model(spec.)	Yanmar parts No.	Turbine & Blower Spec.	
			Turbine	Blower
3JH2-TE	MY75	129171 - 180000	3400IHP12NW	BRLL338C

Printed in Japan
A0A1015-9110SP

2-4 Interchangeability of turbocharger components

The inspection procedures and adjustment standard are identical for all turbocharger models. Please note, however, that the asterisked (*) components differ according to the turbocharger model and are not interchangeable.

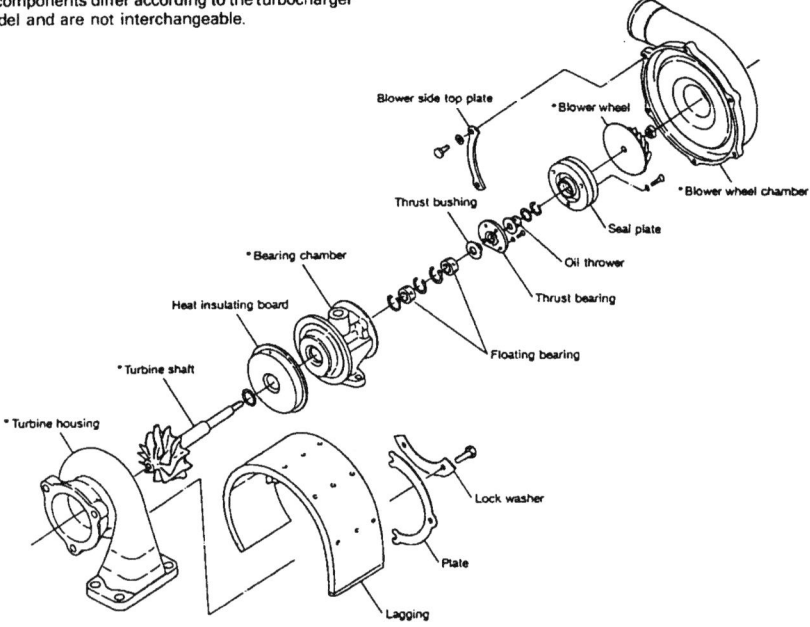

Components Parts No.

Parts name	RHB52HW
Turbine housing	NN138475
Bearing chamber	NN133359
Turbine shaft	NN131102
Blower wheel	NN136511
Blower wheel chamber	NN133792
Applicable engine model	3JH2-TE
Code number	129171-18000

Chapter 4 Intake and Exhaust System
2. Turbocharger
3JH2 Series

2-5 Disassembly, assembly
2-5.1 Preparations for disassembly
The following special tools are required for disassembly of the turbocharger, in addition to the standard tools.

Name of tool	Use	Illustration
Bar	To remove thrust metal and thrust bushings	mm (in.) 75 (2.9527), ⌀7.5 (0.2952) Material: Copper or brass
Pliers	To remove floating bushing stop ring	
Pliers	To remove seal ring	
Torque driver (Phillips) 5 ~ 50kg/cm² (71.11 ~ 711.16 lb/in.²)	To mount thrust metal and seal plate (+)	Standard Model
Box wrench	To tighten turbine shaft 10mm (0.3937in.) × 12 square	Box only may be used
Torque wrench	For following bolts M6: 10mm (0.3937in.) 110kg/cm² (1564.56 lb/in.²) M5: 8mm (0.3149in.) 45 kg/cm² (64.005 lb/in.²) M5: 8mm (0.3149in.) 20 kg/cm² (284.46 lb/in²)	
Gauge wire	To measure play in shaft and axial direction (horizontal and vertical)	mm (in.) R10 (0.3937), R5 (0.1968), ⌀5 (0.1968), 7 (0.2755) M26 P0.45, 1 (0.0393), 8 (0.3149), 40 (1.5748), 10 (0.3937), 15 (0.5905) Mount to dial gauge

Chapter 4 Intake and Exhaust System
2. Turbocharger — 3JH2 Series

2-5.2 Inspection prior to disassembly
(1) Make sure that the turbine and blower blades are not in contact and that the rotor rotates smoothly.
(2) Measuring rotor play.

mm (in.)

	Standard	Wear limit
Rotor play in direction of shaft	0.03 ~ 0.06 (0.0011 ~ 0.0023)	0.09 (0.0035)
Rotor play in axial direction	0.08 ~ 0.13 (0.0031 ~ 0.0051)	0.17 (0.0066)

2-5.3 Disassembly
Make match marks before disassembling the turbocharger to show how the super charger is mounted on the engine. This determines the angle at which the turbine chamber, bearing chamber and blower chamber are mounted.
(1) Removing blower chamber
  1) Remove the M5 mounting bolts, spring washers and blower side retaining plate.
  2) Remove the blower chamber.

NOTE: 1. *The blower chamber and bearing chamber mounting surfaces are coated with a liquid gasket.*
  2. *Be careful not to scratch the blower blade when disassembling the blower chamber.*

(2) Removing blower blade
  1) Fit a box wrench (10mm (0.3937in.)) to the end of the turbine side of the turbine shaft and remove the shaft end nut.

NOTE: *The box end nut has left handed threads.*

  2) Remove the blower blade.

(3) Removing turbine chamber, lagging.
  1) Remove the turbine chamber mounting bolts and the turbine side retaining plate for lagging.
  2) Remove the lagging and turbine chamber.

(4) Pulling the turbine shaft
  1) Lightly hold the heat shield by hand and pull out the turbine shaft.

NOTE: *If the turbine shaft is hard to pull out, lightly tap the blower side end of the shaft with a wooden mallet.*

  2) Remove the heat shield.

NOTE: *If the heat shield is hard to remove, tap it lightly with a caulking chisel.*

(5) Removing the seal plate
  1) Loosen the M3 flat seal plate mounting screws with a plus screwdriver and remove them along with the double grip (tooth) washers.
  2) Remove the seal plate.

NOTE: *The seal plate and bearing chamber mounting surfaces are coated with a liquid gasket.*

  3) Remove the oil ring seal from the seal plate.
(6) Removing the thrust metal and thrust bushing.
  1) Loosen the M3 flat seal plate mounting screws with a plus screwdriver and remove them along with the double grip washers.
  2) Use a copper rod to remove the thrust metal and thrust bushing.

(7) Removing the floating metal (bushing)
  1) Remove the round R stop ring from the bearing chamber with stop ring pliers.
  2) Remove the floating metal from the bearing chamber.
(8) Removing seal ring
  1) Remove the turbine side seal ring from the turbine shaft.
  2) Remove the large and small blower side seal rings from the oil seal.

2-5.4 Preparations for reassembly
(1) When the turbocharger is reassembled, special tools, liquid gasket (Three Bond No.1207S or Three Bond No.1215) and burning preventative agent are needed in addition to the standard tools.
(2) Always replace the following with new parts when reassembling the turbocharger:

  Turbine side seal rings
  Blower side seal rings (large)
  Blower side seal rings (small)
  M3 flat screws
  Bent washers
  Double grip washers

Near the turbine

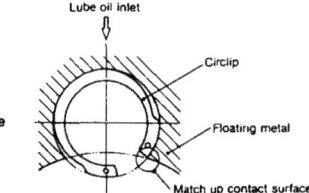

All other cases

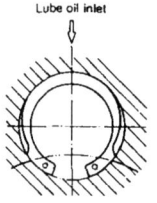

Looking from turbine side

Chapter 4 Intake and Exhaust System
2. Turbocharger

3JH2 Series

2-5.5 Reassembly

(1) Reassembly of floating metal
1) Mount the inside round R stop ring in the bearing chamber with stop ring pliers.
2) Fit the floating metal in the bearing chamber.
3) Mount the outside round R stop ring in the bearing chamber.

NOTE: 1. The round R stop ring opening should be mounted as shown in the illustration. The round part of the stop ring should be mounted on the metal.
2. When mounting, coat the floating metal with engine oil.

(2) Reassembly of the turbine shaft
1) Insert the seal ring in the turbine shaft.
2) Mount the heat shield on the turbine side bearing chamber.
3) Coat the journal of the turbine shaft with engine oil and insert from the turbine side of the bearing chamber.

NOTE: Take adequate care not to scratch the floating metal with the turbine shaft.
The seal ring opening should face the oil intake and be inserted aligned with the turbine shaft center.

(3) Reassembly of the thrust metal
1) Insert the thrust bushing in the turbine shaft.
2) Coat the thrust metal with engine oil and mount it in the bearing chamber.
3) Put the double grip washers on the thrust metal mounting M3 flat screws and tighten with the torque driver.

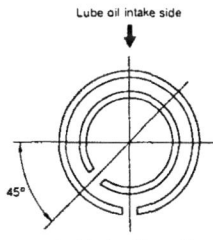

Lube oil intake side

45°

Looking from blower side

	kg-cm (ft-lb)
Tightening torque	12 ~ 14 (0.86 ~ 1.01)

(4) Mounting seal plate
1) Insert the seal ring in the oil drain.
2) Insert the seal plate in the oil drain.

NOTE: The seal ring opening should face the direction indicated in the upper right illustration.

3) Coat the blower side seal plate mounting surface of the bearing chamber (20) with the liquid gasket (Three Bond No.1207S or Three Bond No.1215).

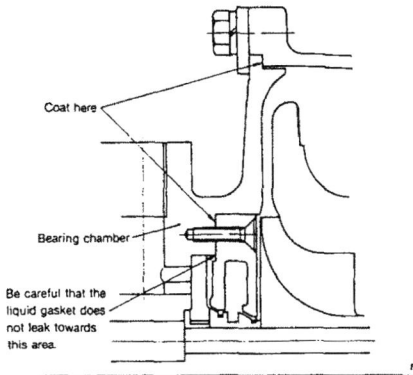

Coat here

Bearing chamber

Be careful that the liquid gasket does not leak towards this area.

	mm (in.)
Coating thickness	0.1 ~ 0.2 (0.0039 ~ 0.0078)

NOTE: See the illustration for where to coat it.

4) Mount the sealing plate on the bearing chamber.
5) Put the double grip washers on the sealing plate mounting M3 flat screws and tighten with the torque driver.

	kg-cm (ft-lb)
Tightening torque	12 ~ 14 (0.86 ~ 1.01)

(5) Mounting blower blade
1) Put the blower blade on the turbine shaft.
2) Tighten the turbine side shaft end nut of the turbine shaft with a box wrench (10mm (0.3937in.)).

NOTE: The shaft end nut has a left handed thread.

	kg-cm (ft-lb)
Tightening torque	18 ~ 22 (1.30 ~ 1.59)

(6) Mounting turbine chamber
1) Mount the turbine chamber, aligned with the match marks made before disassembly.

NOTE: When replacing parts, mount after checking the oil intake/discharge and exhaust gas intake positions.

2) Lugging
Put on the turbine side retainer plate for lugging and the bent washer, and tighten with the M6 hex bolt.
Make sure to bend the washer after tightening the M6 hex bolt.

	kg-cm (ft-lb)
Tightening torque	105 ~ 115 (7.59 ~ 8.31)

(7) Mounting blower chamber
1) Coat the blower side flange surface of the seal plate with the liquid gasket (Three Bond No.1207S or Three Bond No.1215).

NOTE: Refer to page (21) for where to coat.

	mm (in.)
Coating thickness	0.1 ~ 0.2 (0.0039 ~ 0.0078)

2) Align the match marks made before disassembly and mount the seal plate in the blower chamber.

Chapter 4 Intake and Exhaust System
2. Turbocharger

NOTE: When replacing parts, mount only after checking oil intake/discharge and air discharge positions.

3) Replace on the blower side retaining plate and spring washer and tighten with the M5 hex bolt.

	kg-cm (ft-lb)
Tightening torque	40 ~ 50 (2.89 ~ 3.61)

(8) Measuring rotor play
See item 3-2 on inspection procedure—the measuring procedure is the same.
Rotor play above the standard is usually due to improper assembly or use of the wrong part—reassemble.

mm (in.)

	Standard
Rotor play in direction of shaft	0.03 ~ 0.06 (0.0011 ~ 0.0023)
Rotor play in axial direction	0.08 ~ 0.13 (0.0031 ~ 0.0051)

2-5.6 Disassembly/reassembly precautions
Observe the following during and after mounting the turbocharger on the engine.
Be especially careful to prevent the entrance of foreign matter into the turbocharger.
(1) Precautions on mounting the turbocharger.

Lube oil system
1) Run new engine oil through the oil intake holes before mounting on the engine, turn the turbine shaft by hand and lubricate the journal metal (bushings) and thrust metal.
2) Wash the engine oil intake pipe and oil discharge pipe, check for damage and make sure it is not clogged up with dirt or other foreign matter.
3) Make sure that there is no oil leakage from the oil pipes and joints after assembly.

Intake system
1) Make sure that there is no dirt or other foreign matter in the air intake system.
2) Make sure that there is no air leakage from the air supply duct/air cleaner connections.

Exhaust system
1) Make sure that there is no dirt or other foreign matter in the exhaust gas system.
2) Make sure not to mix up the special heat resistant bolts and nuts with the regular bolts when mounting the parts. Coat the bolts, nuts, etc. with burning preventive agent.
(Heat resistant hex bolts are used for the turbine chamber.)
3) Make sure that there is no gas leakage from exhaust piping/connections.

2-6 Inpsection and maintenance
2-6.1 Washing

(1) Inspection prior to washing
Make a visual inspection of disassembled parts before washing to check for burning, wear, foreign, matter and carbon build-up. Make an especially thorough inspection in case of breakdowns as a step towards determining the cause of the breakdown.

Major items

Inspection	Location
Carbon build-up	1) Turbine shaft turbine side seal ring and back of blade.
	2) Around the heat shield mounting of the bearing chamber and the inside wall of the bearing chamber.
Lubrication (wear, burning, discoloration)	1) Turbine shaft journal, thrust bushing, oil drain.
	2) Floating metal and thrust metal.
	3) Around the inner bearing race of the bearing chamber.
Oil leakage	1) Inside wall of the turbine chamber.
	2) Outer circumference of the bearing chamber and around the heat shield mounting.
	3) Turbine side seal ring of the turbine shaft and the back of the blade.
	4) Inside wall of the blower chamber.
	5) Back of the blower blade.
	6) Back of the seal plate and place where the seal ring is inserted.

Chapter 4 Intake and Exhaust System
2. Turbocharger
3JH2 Series

(2) Washing procedure
Keep the following in mind when washing the parts.

Item	Tools/Cleaning Agent	Procedure

(1) Turbine shaft	1. Tools
	(1) Bucket
	(500 × 500)
	(2) Heat source
	    steam or gas burner
	(3) Brush
	2. Cleaning agent
	    Standard carbon removing agent
		(1) Boil the turbine shaft in the washing bucket. Do not hit the blade to remove the carbon.
		(2) Soak in the cleaning agent until the carbon and other materials adhering to the surface become soft.
		(3) Use a plastic scrubber or hard hair brush to remove the softened foreign matter.
		(4) Be very careful not to scratch the turbine shaft bearing surface or the seal ring grooves.
		(5) Any foreign matter will unbalance the turbine shaft, so be sure to clean it well. Do not use a wire brush.

(2) Turbine chamber	1. Tools
	    same as for turbine shaft
	2. Cleaning agent
	    same as for turbine shaft
		(1) Boil the turbine chamber in the washing bucket.
		(2) Soak in the cleaning agent until all the material adhering to the surface becomes soft.
		(3) Use a plastic scrubber or hard hair brush to remove the foreign matter.

(3) Blower blade, blower chamber	1. Tools (1) Bucket (500 × 500) (2) Brush 2. Cleaning agent	(1) Soak in the cleaning agent until the foreign matter adhering to the surface becomes soft. (2) Use a plastic scrubber or hard hair brush to remove the softened foreign matter. Do not use a wire brush.
(4) Other parts	(1) Wash all other parts with diesel oil. (2) Clean all lube oil lines with compressed air. (3) Be careful not to scratch parts or allow them to rust.	

Chapter 4 Intake and Exhaust System
2. Turbocharger

2-6.2 Inspection procedure

(1) Blower chamber
Inspect for scratches caused by contact with the blower blade, scratches in the mounting surface, any galling or cracks.
Replace if necessary.

(2) Turbine chamber
Inspect for scratches caused by contact with the turbine blade, flaking due to oxidation of the skin, and deformation due to heat or cracks.
Replace if necessary.

(3) Blower blade
Inspect for scratches caused by contact, and for breakage, corrosion or deformation.
Replace if necessary.

(4) Turbine shaft
1) Inspect the portion around the turbine blade for scratches, breakage, discoloration or deformation, and inspect the shaft for bending, discoloration of journal, abnormal wear, seal ring groove scratches or wear.
Replace if necessary.
2) Measure the outer diameter of turbine shaft journal (A) and seal ring groove width (E), and replace if beyond the wear limit.

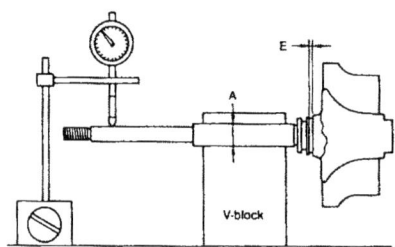

mm (in.)
		Wear limit
Journal outer dia.	A	7.98 (0.3141)
Seal ring groove width	B	1.29 (0.0507)

3) Measure turbine shaft undulation and replace if it exceeds 0.011mm (0.0004in.).

(5) Head shield
Inspect for scratches due to contact, deformation due to heat, and corrosion.
Replace if necessary.

(6) Thrust bushing, oil seal and thrust metal. Inspect for wear, scratches, discoloration, etc., and replace if necessary, even if they remain within the wear limit.

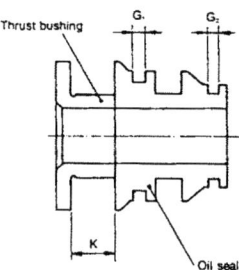

1) Thrust bush
Measure the thrust bush groove clearance (K), and replace if it exceeds the wear limit.

mm (in.)
		Wear limit
Thrust bush groove clearance	K	4.07 (0.1602)

2) Oil ring
Measure the seal ring groove width (G_1), (G_2) and replace if it exceeds the wear limit.

mm (in.)
		Wear limit
Seal ring groove width	G_1	1.31 (0.0515)
	G_2	1.11 (0.0437)

3) Thrust metal
Measure the thrust metal width (J), and replace if it exceeds the wear limit.

mm (in.)
		Wear limit
Thrust metal width	J	3.98 (0.1566)

(7) Floating metal
1) Inspect for abnormal wear, discoloration, scratches, etc., and replace if necessary.
2) Measure the inner diameter (C) and outer diameter (D) of the metal, and replace if either exceeds the wear limit.

mm (in.)
		Wear limit
Floating metal outer dia.	C	12.31 (0.4846)
Floating metal inner dia.	D	8.04 (0.3165)

(8) Bearing chamber
1) Inspect for flaking due to oxidation of the skin, galling and scratches, and replace if necessary.
2) Inspect the round R stop ring for breakage or cracks and replace if necessary.
3) Measure the (B) and (F) dimensions of the bearing chamber as shown in the illustration on the right, and replace if either exceeds the wear limit.

Chapter 4 Intake and Exhaust System
2. Turbocharger

2-6.3 Periodic inspection

(1) Periodically inspect the overall condition of supercharger and the amount of dirt build-up. Inspect at the intervals specified in the following chart.

Item	Interval		
	3 months or 1500 hours	6 months or 3000 hours	12 months or 6000 hours
Rotation of rotor	O		
Rotor play		O	
Disassembly, cleaning and inspection of entire unit			O
Cleaning and inspection of air filter	Every 300 hours		

(2) Inspection Procedure
 1) Rotation of rotor
  The rotation of the rotor is checked by listening for any abnormal noise when it is rotating. Use a listening bar, placing the tip of the bar firmly against the turbocharger and gradually increasing engine rpm. If a loud noise is emitted every 2 or 3 seconds, rotation is abnormal. The turbocharger should be replaced or repaired as something may be wrong with the metal or rotor.
 2) Rotor play
  Remove the turbocharger from the engine and check the play in the shaft axial and radial directions as shown below.
 3) Rotor play in the shaft axial direction.

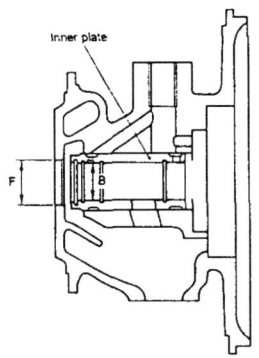

mm (in.)

		Wear limit
Bearing chamber inner dia.	B	12.42 (0.4889)
Turbine side seal ring area inner dia.	F	15.05 (0.5925)

(9) Seal plate
 1) Inspect for scratches due to contact, scratches in mounting surface, galling and cracks and replace if necessary.
 2) Measure the blower side seal ring area (H_1, H_2) and replace if either exceeds the wear limit.

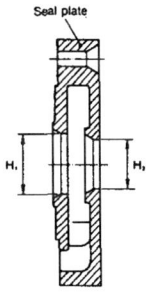

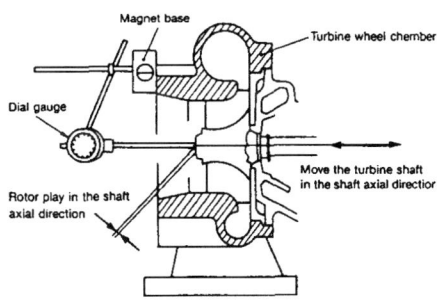

mm (in.)

	Standard	Wear limit
Rotor play in shaft axial direction	0.03 ~ 0.06 (0.0018 ~ 0.0023)	0.09 (0.0035)

mm (in.)

		Wear limit
Blower side seal ring area inner dia.	H_1	12.45 (0.4901)
	H_2	10.05 (0.3956)

(10) Seal ring
  Inspect for wear or deformation and replace if necessary.
(11) Inspect retaining plates, bolts and spring washers for deformation and replace if necessary. Always replace the M3 flat screw bend washer and grip washer.

Chapter 4 Intake and Exhaust System
2. Turbocharger

4) Rotor play in shaft radial direction.

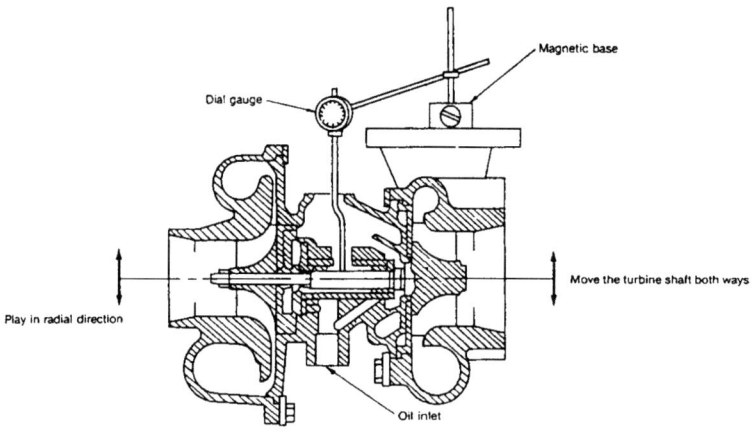

	Standard	Wear limit
		mm (in.)
Rotor play in the shaft radial direction	0.08 ~ 0.13 (0.0031 ~ 0.0051)	0.17 (0.0066)

Chapter 4 Intake and Exhaust System
2. Turbocharger _____ 3JH2 Series

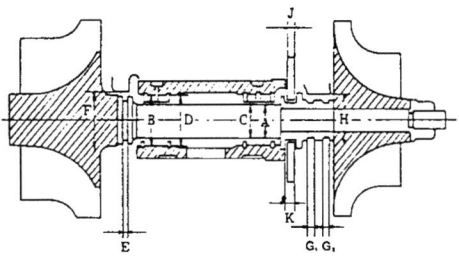

mm (in.)

	Items to check	Standard	Wear limit
Turbine shaft	Turbine shaft journal outer dia. (A)	7.99 ~ 8.00 (0.3145 ~ 0.3149)	7.980 (0.3141)
	Turbine side seal ring groove width (E)	1.25 ~ 1.28 (0.0492 ~ 0.0503)	1.210 (0.0476)
	Blower side seal ring groove width (G_1)	1.22 ~ 1.23 (0.0480 ~ 0.0484)	1.310 (0.0515)
	Blower side seal ring groove width (G_2)	1.02 ~ 1.03 (0.0401 ~ 0.0405)	1.110 (0.0437)
	Turbine shaft play	0.01 (0.0003)	0.011 (0.0004)
Bearing	Floating bearing inner dia. (C)	8.01 ~ 8.03 (0.3153 ~ 0.3161)	8.040 (0.3165)
	Floating bearing inner dia. (D)	12.32 ~ 12.33 (0.4850 ~ 0.4854)	12.310 (0.4846)
	Bearing set ring inner dia. (B)	12.40 ~ 12.41 (0.4881 ~ 0.4885)	12.420 (0.4889)
Thrust bearing	Thrust bearing width (J)	3.99 ~ 4.01 (0.1570 ~ 0.1578)	3.980 (0.1566)
	Thrust bushing groove dimension (K)	4.04 ~ 4.05 (0.1590 ~ 0.1594)	4.070 (0.1602)
Seal ring fixing area	Turbine side (bearing wheel chamber) (F)	15.00 ~ 15.02 (0.5905 ~ 0.5913)	15.050 (0.5925)
	Blower side (seal plate) (H_1)	12.40 ~ 12.42 (0.4881 ~ 0.4889)	12.450 (0.4901)
	Blower side (seal plate) (H_2)	10.00 ~ 10.02 (0.3937 ~ 0.3944)	10.050 (0.3956)
Play of rotor in shaft axial direction		0.03 ~ 0.06 (0.0011 ~ 0.0023)	0.090 (0.0035)
Play of rotor in radial direction		0.08 ~ 0.13 (0.0031 ~ 0.0051)	0.170 (0.0066)

Tightening torque

	Screw dia. mm	Tightening torque kg-cm (ft-lb)
Turbine chamber set bolt	M6	105 ~ 115 (7.59 ~ 8.31)
Blower chamber set bolt	M5	40 ~ 45 (2.89 ~ 3.25)
Thrust metal set screw	M3	12 ~ 14 (0.86 ~ 1.01)
Seal plate set screw	M3	12 ~ 14 (0.86 ~ 1.01)
Blower blade nut	left hand screw M5	18 ~ 22 (1.30 ~ 1.59)

Chapter 4 Intake and Exhaust System
2. Turbocharger

3JH2 Series

2-7 Troubleshooting

The engine will not produce the required output if the turbocharger breaks down. If the engine output drops, first check the engine to see if anything is wrong, and then check the turbocharger according to the following procedure if there is nothing wrong with the engine.

2-7.1 Excessive smoke

(1) Insufficient air intake

Cause	Remedy
1) Air cleaner is clogged up.	• Replace or wash the element.
2) Air intake is closed.	• Open to proper position.
3) Leakage from air intake system connections.	• Inspect and repair

(2) Turbocharger does not rotate

Cause	Remedy
1) Build-up of foreign matter in oil on seals inhibiting turbine shaft rotation.	• Disassemble and clean turbocharger and change engine oil.
2) Burned metal • Insufficient oil or clogging up of supply pipe. • Oil temperature too high. Rotating parts are out of balance. • Insufficient warming up or sharp stopping.	• Disassemble turbocharger and repair. • Inspect engine oil supply system, repair any parts as necessary and change the engine oil. • Wash or replace rotating parts. • Read operation manual and operate engine accordingly.
3) Turbine or blower blade knocking something or broken. • Excessive rpm • Excessive exhaust gas temperature rise. • Entrance of foreign matter. • Worn metal (bushings) • Improper reassembly	• Inspect engine parts and adjust. • Disassemble and thoroughly remove any foreign matter, inspect the air cleaner, and engine parts, and repair as necessary. • Disassemble turbocharger and repair. • Reassemble

(3) Excessive exhaust gas drag (resistance)

Cause	Remedy
1) Insufficient turbocharger rpm due to leakage of exhaust gas before entry into turbocharger.	• Inspect fittings and repair.
2) Insufficient turbocharger rpm due to deformation of exhaust system piping.	• Repair

2-7.2 White exhaust smoke

Cause	Remedy
1) Oil leaking on blower side or turbine side due to clogging or deformation of return piping.	• Repair or replace pipe.
2) Seal ring excessively worn or broken due to excessive metal wear.	• Disassemble turbocharger and repair.

2-7.3 Excessive oil consumption

Cause	Remedy
1) Seal ring excessively worn or broken due to excessive metal wear.	• Disassemble turbocharger and repair.

2-7.4 Decrease in (engine) output

Cause	Remedy
1) Gas leakage from exhaust gas system. 2) Air leakage from blower side discharge.	• Inspect parts and repair.
3) Air cleaner element clogged up.	• Clean or replace element.
4) Turbocharger dirty or damaged.	• Disassemble turbocharger and repair, or replace.

Chapter 4 Intake and Exhaust System
2. Turbocharger

2-7.5 Poor (slow) turbocharger responsiveness (starting)

Cause	Remedy
1) Carbon build-up on turbine side (blade seal) inhibiting turbine shaft rotation.	• Disassemble and wash turbocharger and replace engine oil.
2) Incomplete combustion.	• Inspect engine fuel system and improve combustion efficiency.

2-7.6 Abnormal noise or vibration

(1) Abnormal noise

Cause	Remedy
1) Blower discharge air flows back (surges) when the gas line area is considerably reduced due to closing of the turbine chamber nozzle or during acceleration.	• Disassemble and clean turbocharger.
2) Rotating parts knocking something.	• Disassemble turbocharger and repair or replace.

(2) Vibration

Cause	Remedy
1) Fittings connecting turbocharger and exhaust gas piping/oil pipe have become loose.	• Inspect fittings and retighten/repair as necessary.
2) Rotating parts making contact with surrounding parts because of metal failure, or turbine blade or blower blade damaged due to entrance of foreign matter.	• Disassemble turbocharger and repair or replace. Thoroughly remove any foreign matter.
3) Rotating parts out of balance.	• Repair or replace rotating parts.

2-8 Turbocharger blower washing procedure

2-8.1 General
(1) Use "Blower Wash" and clean water to wash the blower.
(2) Make it a general practice to wash the turbocharger blower when the air supply pressure has decreased by about 10 percent. The frequency of this will differ greatly depending on working conditions, but about once a week is generally sufficient.
(3) This prodecure cannot be used for cleaning the entire turbocharger. It must be periodically disassembled and cleaned.
(4) Only remove the inlet cap when washing the blower—it must not be removed under any other circumstances.

2-8.2 Procedure
(1) Run the engine at normal load (3/4 ~ 4/4 load) and apply Blower Wash for 4 ~ 5 seconds with a 20cc standard oiler.
(2) 3 ~ 5 minutes after application of the Blower Wash the dirt will be loosened up. Slowly put in 20cc of water (over about 4 ~ 10 seconds).
(3) Use a vinyl container to feed in the cleaning agent or water. If too much cleaning agent or water enters suddenly there might be a breakdown or breakage of the blower blade. Be sure to feed in the cleaning agent or water at the correct speed.
(4) If there is no change in the air supply pressure or exhaust gas temperature after washing, repeat the washing after about 10 minutes.
No change after washing the blower 3 ~ 4 times indicates that either the blower is extremely dirty or something else is out of order. Disassemble and clean the washer, and take any other action as necessary.
(5) Run the engine under load to dry for at least 15 minutes after feeding in the agent or water.

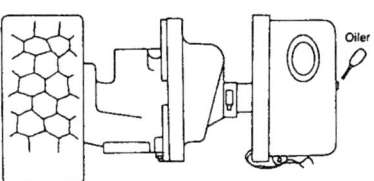

Clean the blower: Every 150 hours

3. Mixing Elbow

3-1 Construction
Threre are two types of mixing elbows for the 3JH3E engine: the L and U types. Both types are bolted to the exhaust mainfold.
There are also L and U types for the 3JH-TE, engine.
Both are mounted on the turbocharger discharge.

3-2 Mixing elbow inspection
(1) Clean dirt and scale out of the air and cooling water lines.
(2) Repair cracks or damage to welds, or replace.
(3) Inspect the gasket packing and replace as necessary.

For model 3JH2E (Option)

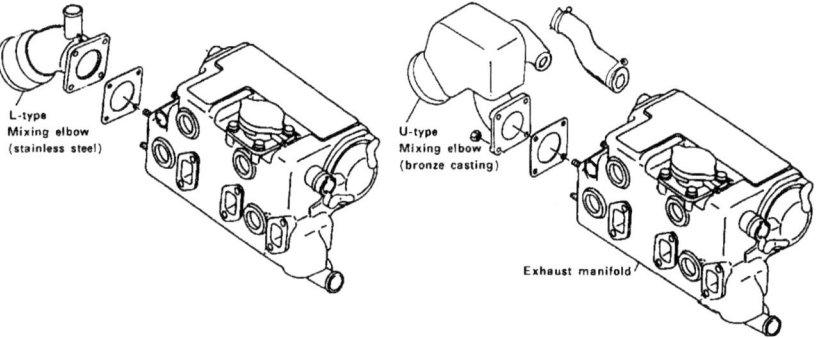

For models 3JH2-TE (Option)

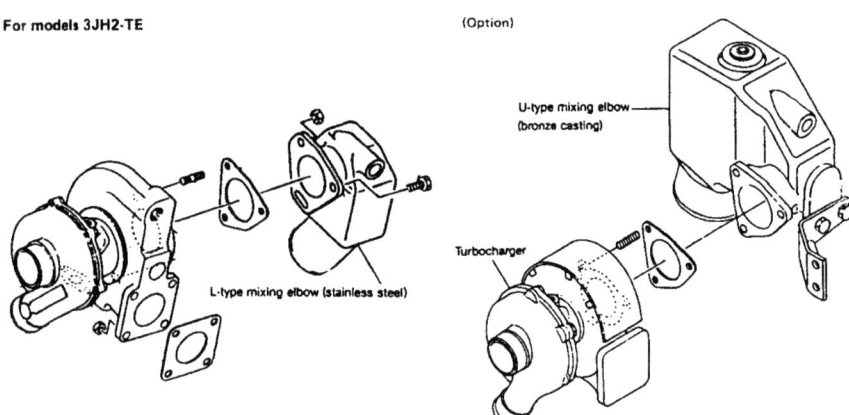

CHAPTER 5
LUBRICATION SYSTEM

1. Lubrication System ······················· 5-1
2. Lube Oil Pump ···························· 5-3
3. Lube Oil Filter ···························· 5-6
4. Oil Pressure Control Valve ··············· 5-8
5. Lube Oil Cooler ··························· 5-9
6. Piston Cooling Nozzle ···················· 5-10
7. Rotary Waste Oil Pump (Optional) ········ 5-11

Chapter 5 Lubrication System
1. Lubrication System   3JH2 Series

1. Lubrication System

The lube oil in the oil pan is pumped up through the intake filter and intake piping by the lube oil pump, through the holes in the cylinder body and on to the discharge filter.

The lube oil which flows from the holes in the cylinder body through the bracket to the oil element is filtered and sent to the oil cooler. It returns from the oil cooler to the bracket, the pressure is regulated, and it is fed back to main gallery in the cylinder body.

The lube oil which flows in the main gallery goes to the crankshaft journal, lubricates the crank pin from the crankshaft journal, and a portion of the oil is fed to the camshaft bearings.

Oil is sent from the gear case camshaft bearings through the holes in the cylinder body and cylinder head to the valve arm shaft to lubricate the valve arm and valves.

Oil is also sent from the main gallery to the piston cooling nozzle to cool the piston surface, and is sent through the intermediate gear bearing (oil) holes to lubricate the intermediate gear bearings and respective gears.

Lube oil for the fuel injection pump is sent by pipe from the main gallery to the fuel injection pump.

Part of the lube oil is sent from the oil cooler discharge to the supercharger in engines fitted with one, and is then piped back from the supercharger to the oil pan.

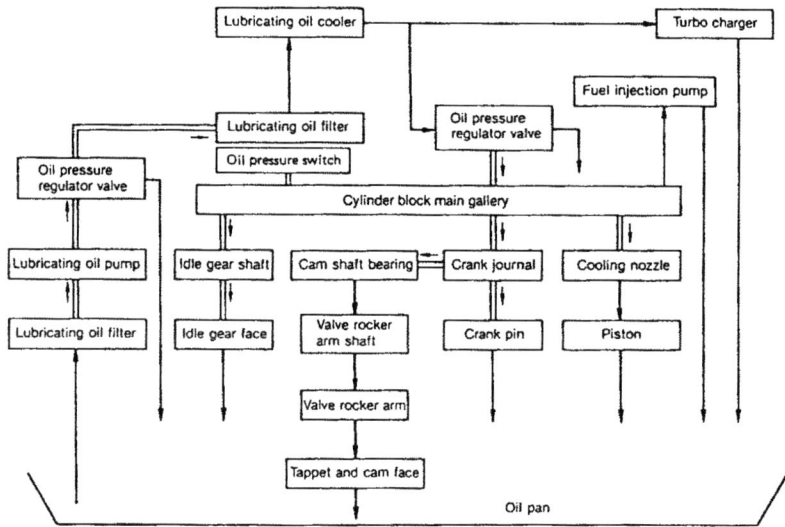

5-1

Chapter 5 Lubrication System
1. Lubrication System

3JH2 Series

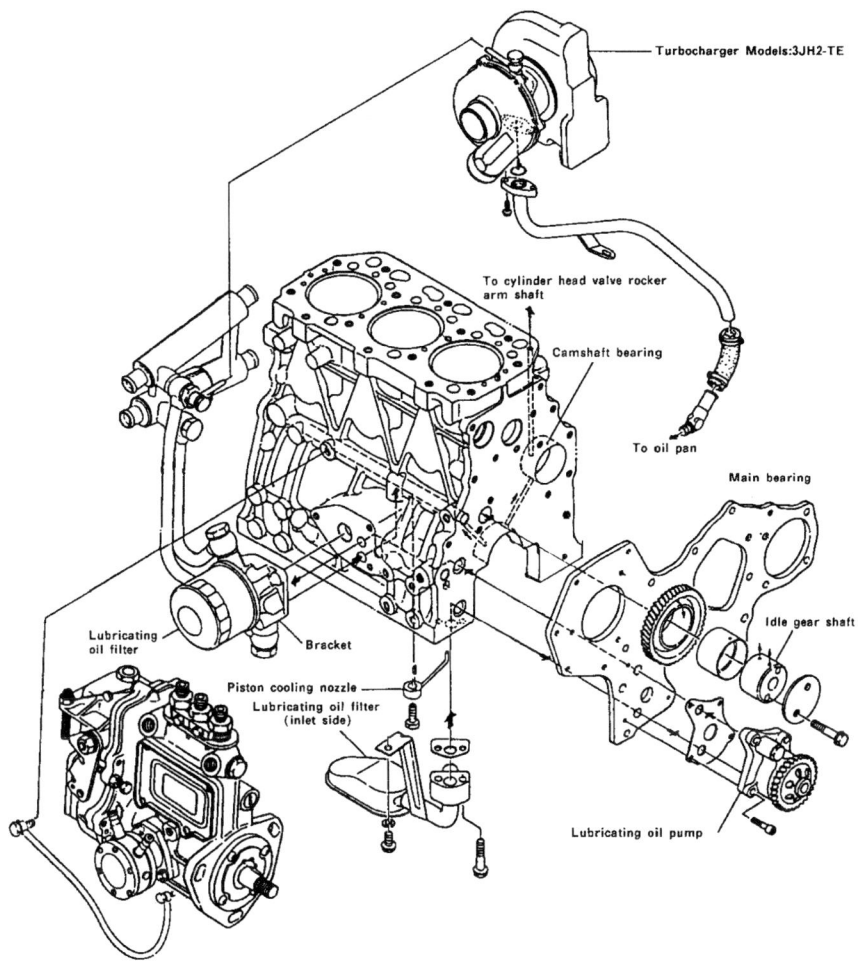

Chapter 5 Lubrication System
1. Lubrication System

3JH2 series

3JH25A/30A

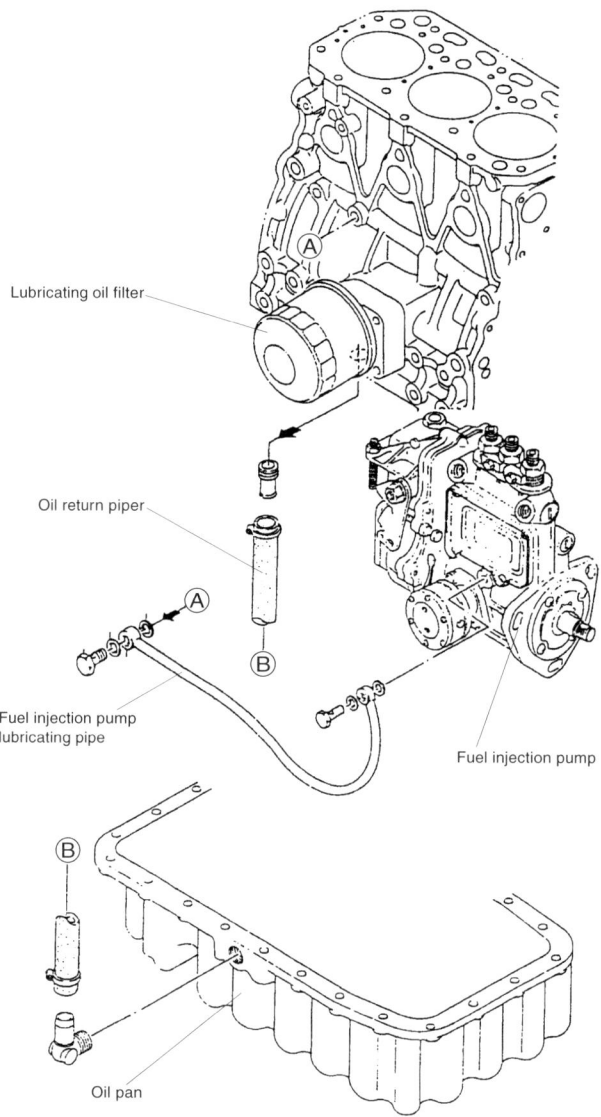

Chapter 5 Lubrication System
2. Lube Oil Pump _____ 3JH2 Series

2. Lube Oil Pump

2-1 Lube oil pump construction

The trochoid type lube oil pump is mounted on the gear case side engine plate, and the rotor shaft gear is driven by the crankshaft gear.

The lube oil flows from the intake filter mounted on the bottom of the cylinder body through the holes in the cylinder body and engine plate, and out from the holes in the engine plate and cylinder body to the discharge filter.

The lube oil pump is fitted with a pressure regulating valve which maintains the discharge pressure at 3kg/cm².

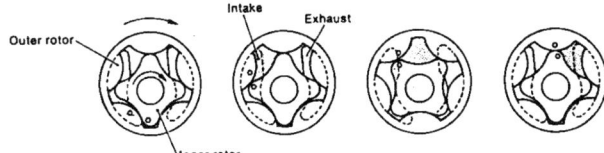

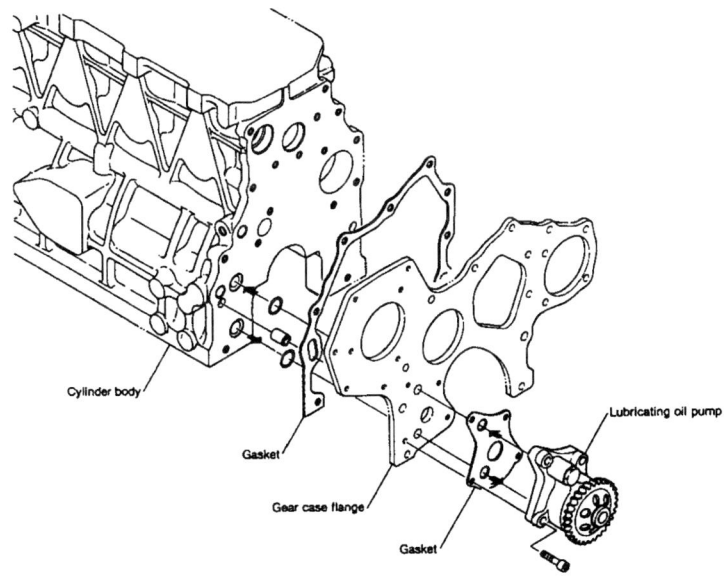

Chapter 5 Lubrication System
2. Lube Oil Pump

3JH2 Series

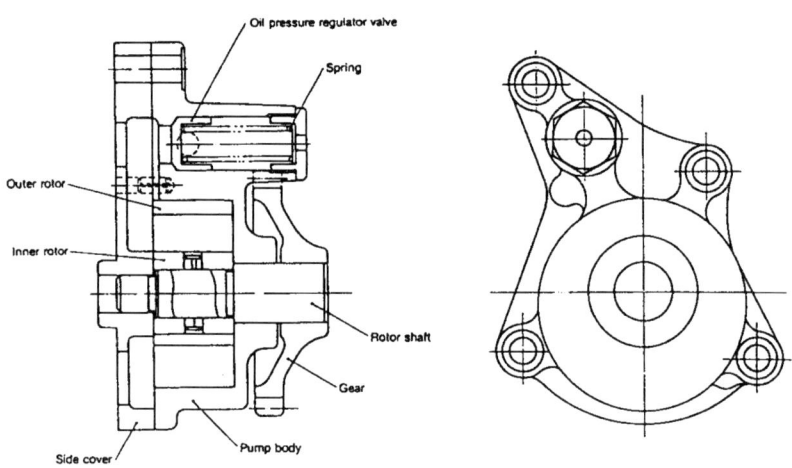

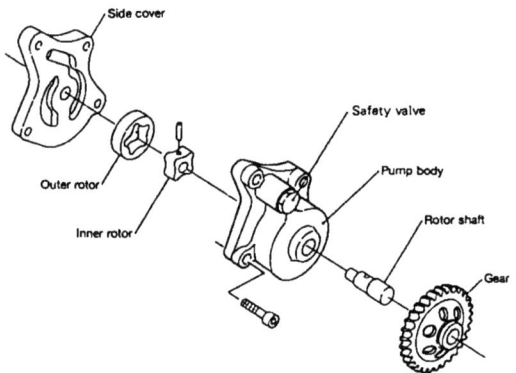

2-2 Specifications of lube oil pump

Engine speed	3600 rpm
Gear ratio (crank gear/pump gear)	28/29
Pump speed	3477 rpm

Chapter 5 Lubrication System
2. Lube Oil Pump

3JH2 Series

2-3 Lube oil pump disassembly

(1) Remove the lube oil pump assembly from the engine plate.
(2) The lube oil pump cover may be disassembled, but do not disassemble the rotor, rotor shaft or drive gear. The oil pressure regulating valve plug is coated with adhesive and screwed in, so it cannot be disassembled. These parts cannot be reused after disassembly. Replace if necessary as an assembly.

2-4 Lube oil pump inspection

(1) Clearance between outer rotor and pump body
Insert a feeler gauge between the outer rotor and pump body to measure the clearance, and replace if it exceeds the limit.

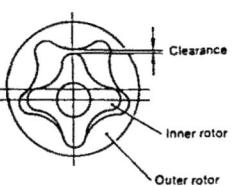

	Standard	Wear limit
Outer rotor and inner rotor clearance	0.050 ~ 0.105 (0.0019 ~ 0.0041)	0.15 (0.0059)

mm (in.)

(3) Clearance between pump body and inner rotor side of outer rotor
Place a straight-edge against the end of the pump body and insert a feeler gauge between the straight-edge and the rotor to measure side clearance. Replace the assembly if the clearance exceeds the limit.

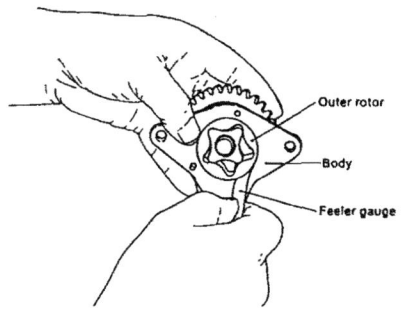

	Standard	Wear limit
Outer rotor and pump body clearance	0.100 ~ 0.170 (0.0039 ~ 0.0066)	0.25 (0.0098)

mm (in.)

(2) Clearance between outer rotor and inner rotor
To measure clearance, insert a feeler gauge between the top of the inner rotor tooth and the top of the outer rotor tooth, and replace if it exceeds the limit.

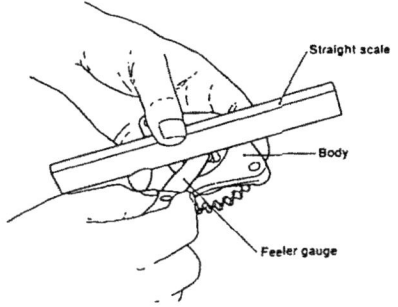

	Standard	Wear limit
Pump body and inner rotor, outer rotor clearance	0.03 ~ 0.09 (0.0011 ~ 0.0035)	0.13 (0.0051)

mm (in.)

(4) Clearance between rotor shaft and side cover
Measure the rotor shaft outer diameter and the side cover hole diameter, and replace the entire assembly if the clearance exceeds the limit.

mm (in.)

	Standard	Wear limit
Rotor shaft and body clearance	0.013 ~ 0.043 (0.0005 ~ 0.0016)	0.2 (0.0078)

(5) Check for looseness of driver gear/rotor shaft fitting, and replace the entire assembly if loose or wobbly.
(6) Push the oil pressure regulating valve piston from the oil hole side, and replace the assembly if the piston does not return due to spring breakage, etc.
(7) Make sure that the rotor shaft rotates smoothly and easily when the drive gear is rotated.

Turning torque	less than 1.5 kg-cm (0.108 ft-lb)

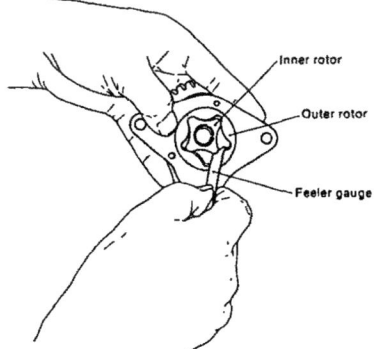

3. Lube Oil Filter

3-1 Lube oil filter construction
The lube oil filter is a full-flow paper element type, mounted to the side of the cylinder body with the filter bracket. The cartridge type filter is easy to remove.
To prevent seizure in the event of the filter clogging up, a bypass circuit is provided in the oil filter. The bypass valve in the filter element opens when the difference in the pressure in front and behind the paper element reaches $0.8 \sim 1.2 \text{kg/cm}^2$ ($11.38 \sim 17.06 \text{ lb/in.}^2$).

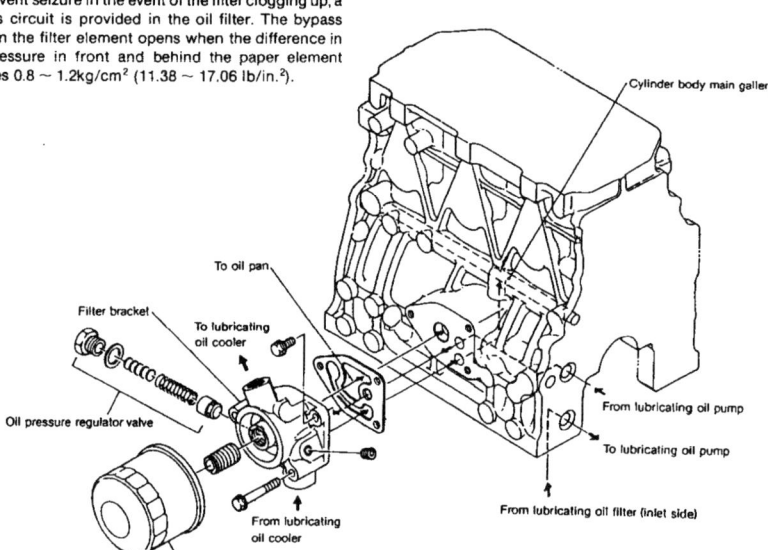

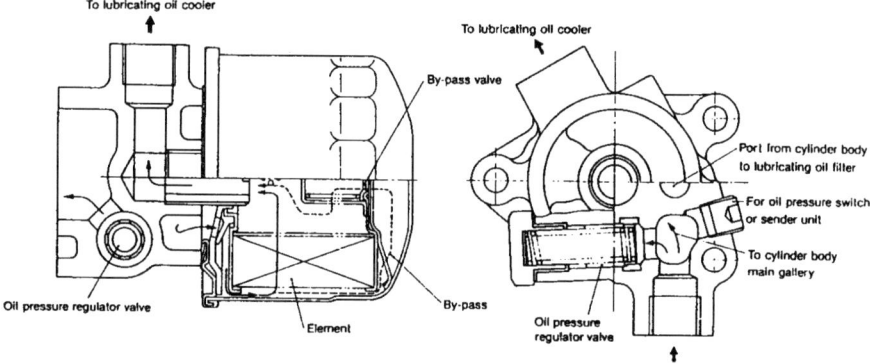

Chapter 5 Lubrication System
3. Lube Oil Filter

3JH2 series

3JH25A/30A

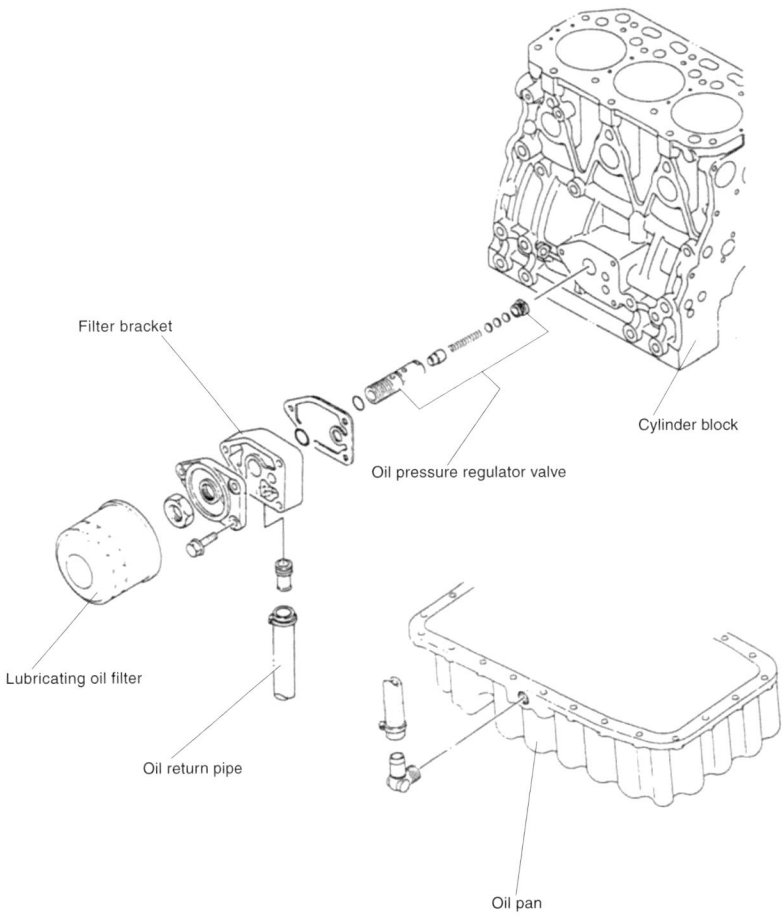

Chapter 5 Lubrication System
3. Lube Oil Filter

Type	Full flow, paper element
Filtration area	800cm² (124in.²)
Discharge volume	20 ℓ/min (1220 in³//min)
Pressure loss	0.1 ~ 0.3kg/cm² (1.422 ~ 4.266lb/in.²)
By-pass valve regulating pressure	0.8 ~ 1.2kg/cm² (11.37 ~ 17.06lb/in.²)

3-2 Lube oil filter replacement

(1) Period

The paper element will get clogged up with dirt after long hours of usage, and eventually unfiltered oil will be fed to the engine through the bypass circuit. Replace the filter according to the following standard, as the dirt in unfiltered oil will of course have a detrimental affect on the engine.

Oil filter replacement period	Every 300 hours of engine operation

(2) Replacement
1) Remove the lube oil filter with the special tool.
2) Clean the filter mounting surface on the filter bracket and mounting screws.
3) Coat the filter rubber packing with lube oil.
4) Screw in the filter until the rubber packing comes in contact with the bracket mounting surface, and then 2 ~ 3 turns more.
5) Run the engine after mounting the filter, and make sure that there is no oil leakage.

4. Oil Pressure Control Valve

4-1 Oil pressure control valve construction

The oil pressure control valve built into the oil filter bracket controls the oil pressure from the time the lube oil leaves the filter and is cooled in the lube oil cooler until just before it enters the cylinder body main gallery.

When the pressure of lube oil entering the cylinder body main gallery exceeds the setting, the control valve piston opens the bypass hole and lube oil flows back into the oil pan.

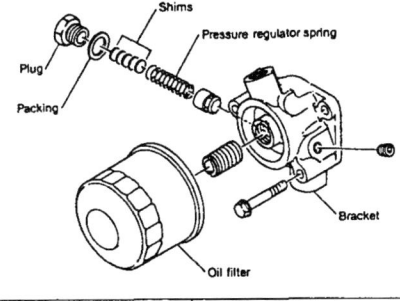

Regulating pressure	3.5 ~ 4.5 kg/cm² (49.78 ~ 64.00 lb/in.²)

4-2 Oil pressure control valve replacement

The control valve has been adjusted and assembled at the factory, so it should not be disassembled without good reason.

If the oil pressure control valve is disassembled due to spring trouble, etc., mount a pressure gauge on the oil pressure sender unit mounting washer, and adjust the pressure with adjustment shims until it is at the specified value.

Shim thickness	Shim part No.
0.2mm (0.0078 in.)	121850-35210
0.5mm (0.0196 in.)	121850-35220
1.0mm (0.0393 in.)	121850-35230

4-3 Vibration preventing damper

The filter bracket hydraulic (oil pressure) sender unit mount is constructed so that a vibration preventing damper can be mounted on it.
The hydraulic sender unit is mounted on the damper.

5. Lube Oil Cooler [Applicable Engine Model 3JH2(T)E]

5-1 Lube oil cooler construction

The spiral thread of the inner pipe is in contact with the inner surface of the outer pipe. This forms a spiral passageway.
The lube oil flows through this passageway and is cooled by the cooling water (sea water) flowing through the inner pipe.

There are two such pipes, connected side by side, designed so that the lube oil and sea water flow in the opposite directions.

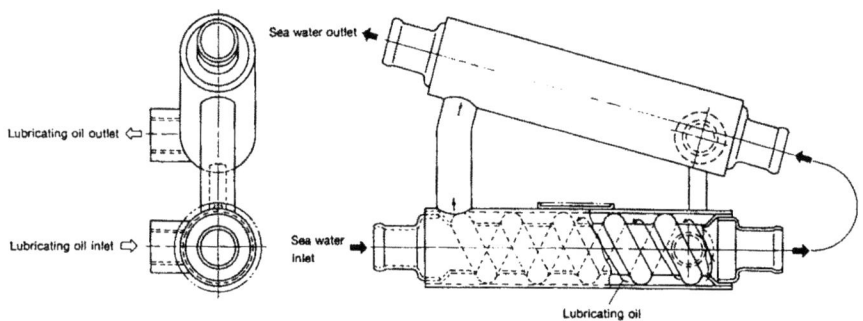

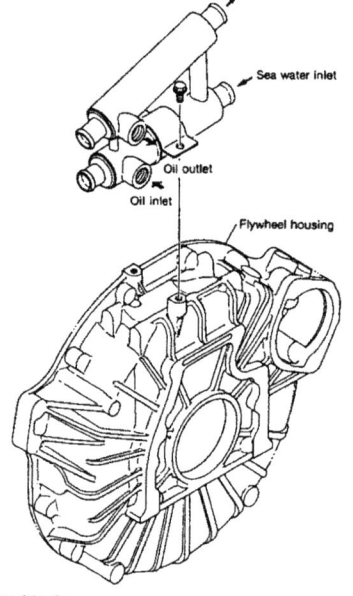

Engine Model	3JH2E	3JH2-TE
Cooling area	0.0096 m² (29.76 in.²)	0.0192 m² (29.76 in.²)
Cooling water discharge volume	3773 ℓ/hr (230228 in.³/h)	
Lubricating oil discharge volume	2160 ℓ/hr (131803 in.³/h)	
Lubricating oil temperature at 40°C room air	Model 3JH2E: 110°C or below Model 3JH2-TE: 115°C or below	

5-2 Inspecting the lube oil cooler

(1) Clean the inside of the sea water pipes with a wire brush to prevent the build-up of scale.
(2) If the rubber hose connection or welds are corroded, repair or replace the cooler.
(3) Apply the following water pressures to the sea water and lube oil lines to check for any leakage. Repair or replace the cooler if there are any leaks.

	Test pressure
Lubricating oil circuit	8 kg/cm² (113.78 lb/in.²)
Sea water circuit	4 kg/cm² (56.89 lb/in.²)

Chapter 5 Lubrication System
6. Piston Cooling Nozzle

6. Piston Cooling Nozzle (only 3JH2TE)

6-1 Piston cooling nozzle construction
A nozzle made from steel piping is mounted on the lower part of cylinder body main gallery. Lube oil from the main gallery is sprayed out in a jet from the steel tip (Ø1.77mm (0.0697in.)) of this pipe.
This jet spray cools the piston surface when the piston goes down.

6-2 Inspection of piston cooling nozzle
(1) Check the nozzle tip hole to see if it is clogged up with dirt or other foreign matter, and clean.
(2) Inspect the pipe mounting to see if it is or may become loose or come off due to vibration, etc., and replace if necessary.

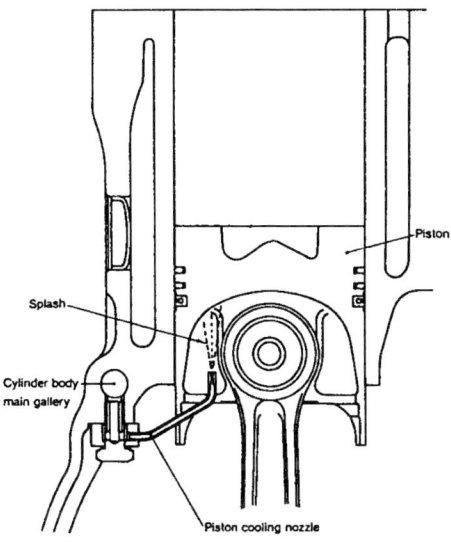
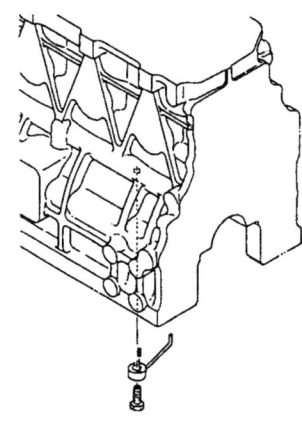

Oil injection volume	1.3 ℓ/min. (79.32 in.³/min)
Oil injection pressure	3.5 kg/cm² (49.78 lb/in.²)

7. Rotary Waste Oil Pump (Optional)

A rotary waste oil pump to pump out waste oil during oil changing is available as an option.
This is a vane type pump. Turning the handle rotates the vanes and pumps out lube oil.

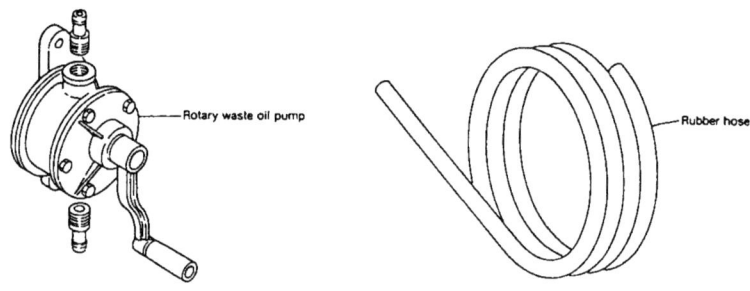

7-1 Construction

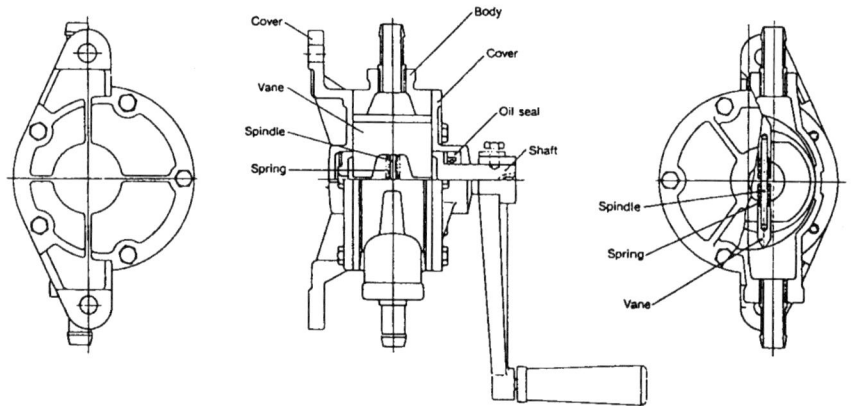

Rotary waste oil pump

Delivery capacity of one stroke	0.13ℓ (7.93 in.³)
Delivery pressure	1.5 kg/cm² (21.33 lb/in.²) or below
Suction head	less than 1m (39.37 in.)
Part No.	43600-002311

Rubber hose

Inner dia. × length	ø12 × 1000mm (0.4724 × 39.37 in.)
Part No. of rubber hose	43720-001220

7-2 Inspecting the waste oil pump

(1) Disassemble the waste oil pump and check for spring breakage or vane damage when there is an extreme drop in discharge volume, and replace if necessary.
(2) Replace the oil seal if there is excessive oil leakage from the handle shaft.
(3) Replace the impeller if there is an excessive gap between the impeller and the covers on both sides of casing. This will cause a drop in discharge volume.
(4) The hose coupling is coated with adhesive and screwed in. It therefore cannot be disassembled.

CHAPTER 6
COOLING WATER SYSTEM

1. Cooling Water System ··· 6-1
2. Sea Water Pump ··· 6-4
3. Fresh Water Pump ··· 6-7
4. Heat Exchanger ··· 6-10
5. Pressure Cap and Sub Tank ··· 6-12
6. Thermostat ··· 6-14
7. Kingston Cock (Optional) ··· 6-16
8. Sea Water Filter (Optional) ··· 6-17
9. Bilge Pump and Bilge Strainer (Optional) ··· 6-18

Chapter 6 Cooling Water System
1. Cooling Water System

3JH2 Series

1. Cooling Water System

The cooling water system is of the indirect sea water cooled, fresh water circulation type. The cylinders, cylinder heads, turbocharger and exhaust manifold are cooled with fresh water, and the lube oil cooler air cooler and fresh water cooler (heat exchanger) use sea water.

Sea water pumped in from the sea by the sea water pump cools the intercooler the lube oil in the lube oil cooler and then goes to the heat exchanger, where it cools the fresh water. Then it is sent to the mixing elbow and is discharged from the ship with the exhaust gas.

Fresh water is pumped by the fresh water pump from the fresh water tank to the cylinder jacket to cool the cylinders, the cylinder head and then turbocharger. The fresh water pump body also serves as a discharge passageway (line) at the cylinder head outlet, and is fitted with a thermostat.

The thermostat is closed when the fresh water temperature is low, immediately after the engine is started and during low load operation, etc. Then the fresh water flows to the fresh water pump inlet, and is circulated inside the engine without passing through the heat exchanger.

When the temperature of the fresh water rises, the thermostat opens, fresh water flows to the heat exchanger, and it is then cooled by the sea water in the tubes as it flows through the cooling pine. Then temperature of the fresh water is thus kept within a constant range by the thermostat.

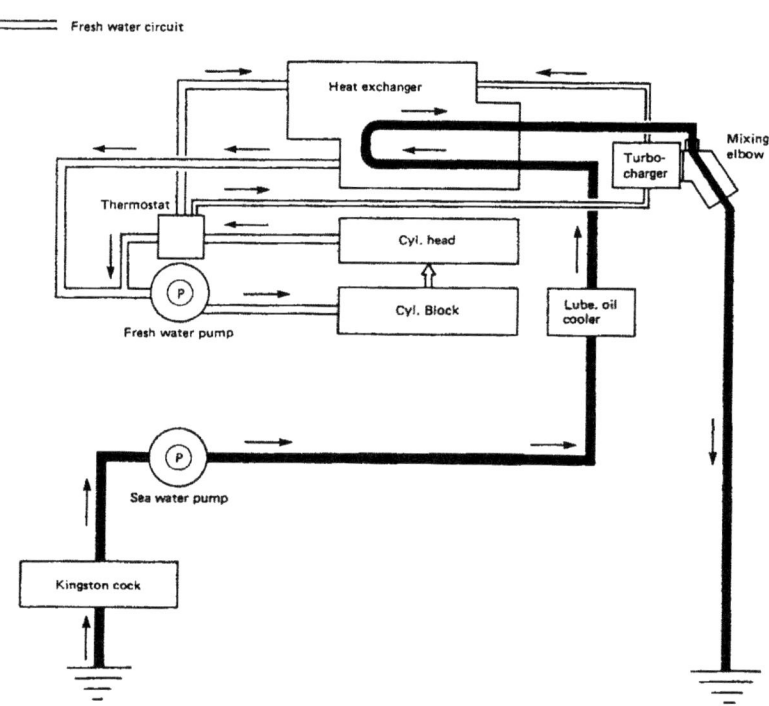

Chapter 6 Cooling Water System
1. Cooling Water System   3JH2 Series

Fresh water line [ENGINE MODEL: 4JH2E&4JH2-TE]

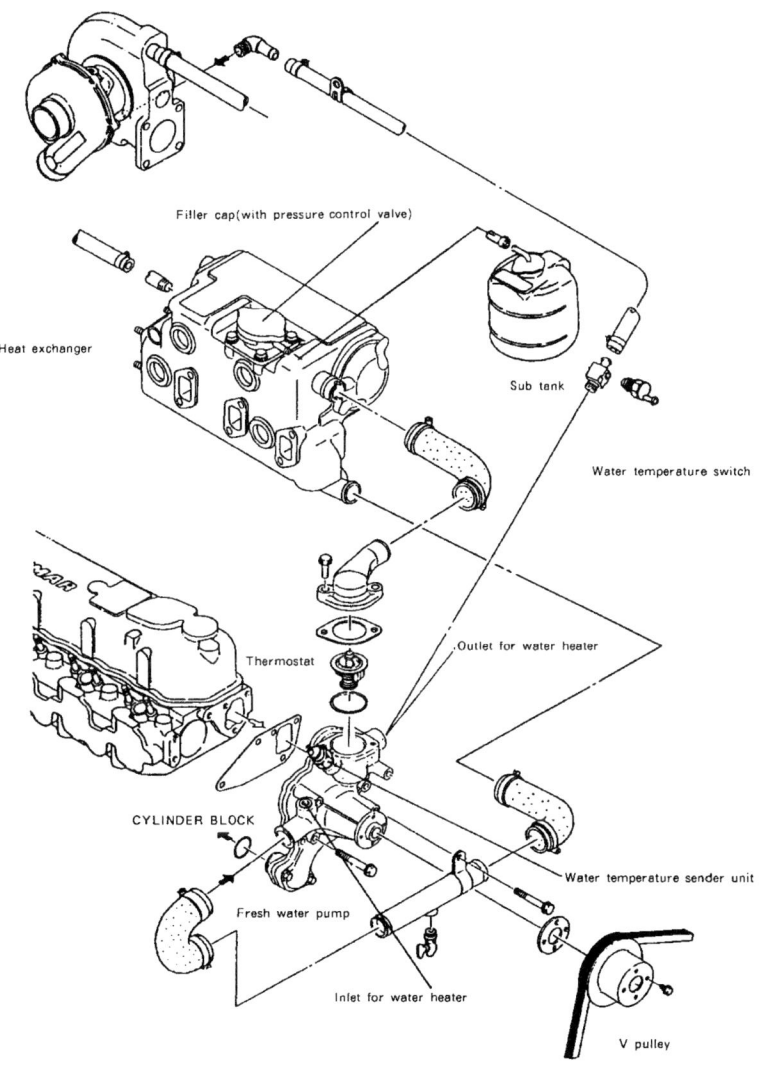

Chapter 6 Cooling Water System
1. Cooling Water System

Sea water line [ENGINE MODEL: 3JH2E & 3JH2-TE]

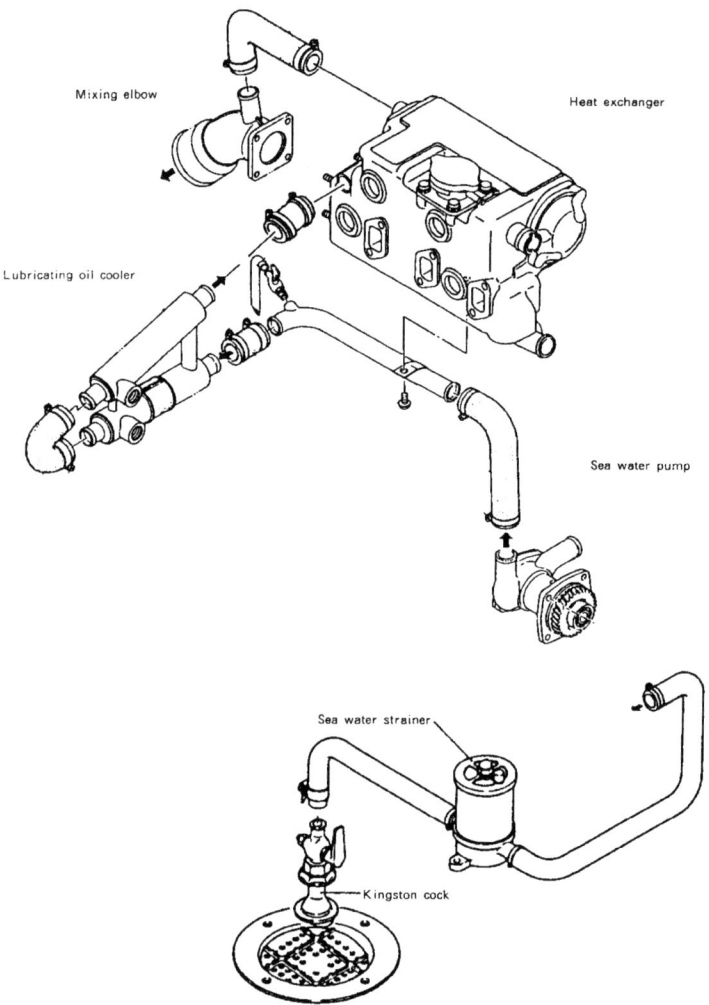

Chapter 6 Cooling Water System
1. Cooling Water System

3JH2 series

3JH25A/30A

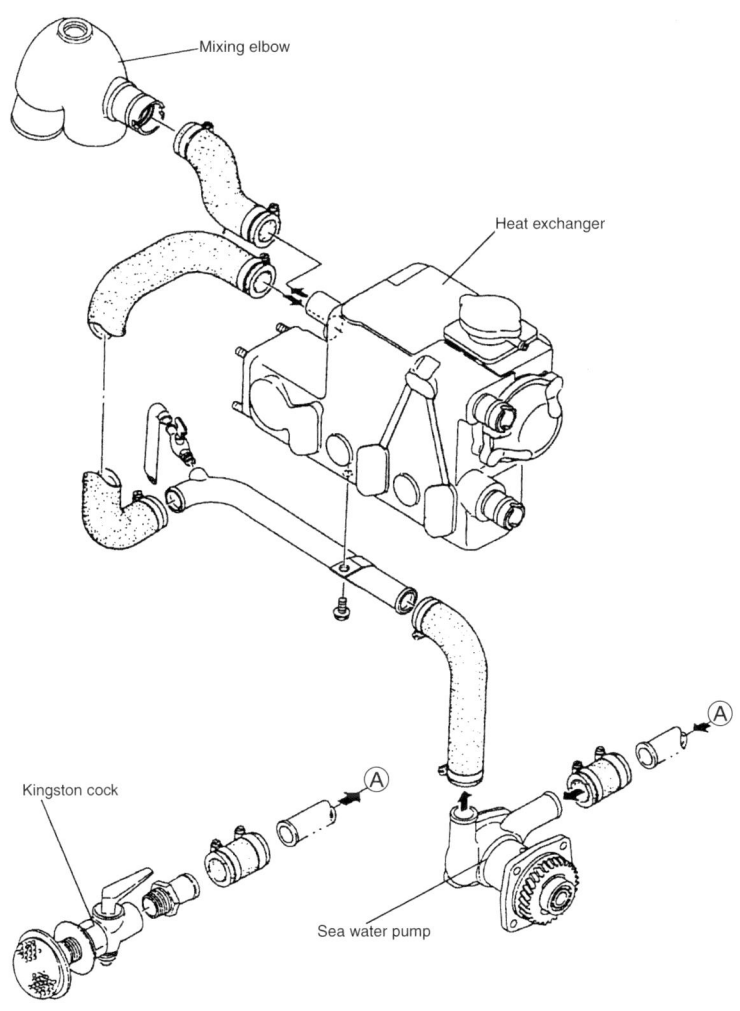

Chapter 6 Cooling Water System
2. Sea Water Pump

3JH2 Series

2. Sea Water Pump

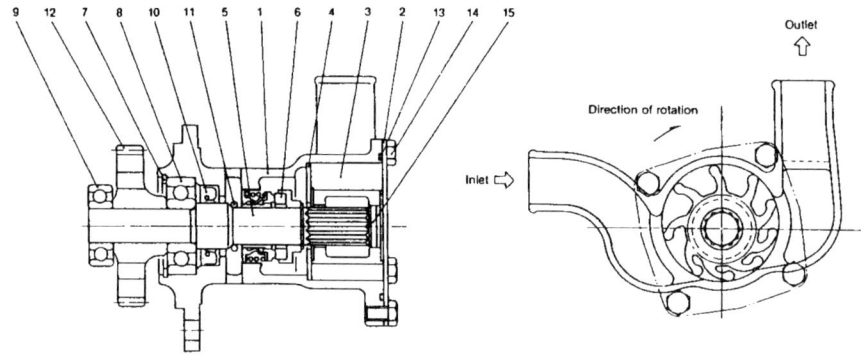

1. Sea water pump body
2. Side cover
3. Impeller (C-type)
4. Wear plate
5. Pump shaft
6. Mechanical seal
7. Circlip
8. Bearing
9. Bearing
10. Oil seal
11. Water seal ring
12. Gear
13. O ring
14. Hexagonal bolt
15. Impeller blind cover

2-2 Specifications of sea water pump

Engine speed (max.)	3600 rpm
Gear ratio (crank gear/pump gear)	28/31
Pump speed	3252 rpm
Suction head	0.5m (1.66 ft)
Total head	9.5m (31.16 ft)
Delivery capacity	3250 ℓ/h (198315 in.³/h)

2-3 Sea water pump disassembly

(1) Remove the rubber hose from the sea water pump outlet and then the sea water pump assembly from the gear case.
(2) Remove the sea water pump cover and take out the O-ring, impeller and wear plate.
(3) Remove the mechanical seal side stop ring.
(4) Insert pliers from the drive gear long hole and remove the stop ring that holds the bearings.
(5) Lightly tap the pump shaft from the impeller side and remove the pump shaft, bearings, and drive gear as a set.
(6) Remove the oil seal and mechanical seal if necessary.

2-4 Sea water pump inspection

(1) Inspect the rubber impeller, checking for splitting around the outside, damage or cracks, and replace if necessary.

mm (in.)

	Standard	Clearance at assembly	Maximum allowable clearance	*Wear limit
Impeller width	31.6 ~ 31.8 (1.2440 ~ 1.2519)	0 ~ 0.3 (0 ~ 0.0118)	0.8 (0.0314)	31.3 (1.2322)
Wear plate thickness	2 (0.0787)			1.8 (0.0708)
Housing width	33.8 ~ 33.9 (1.3307 ~ 1.3346)			—
Side plate thickness	2 (0.0787)			1.8 (0.0708)

Printed in Japan
A0A1015-9110SP

Chapter 6 Cooling Water System
2. Sea Water Pump

3JH2 Series

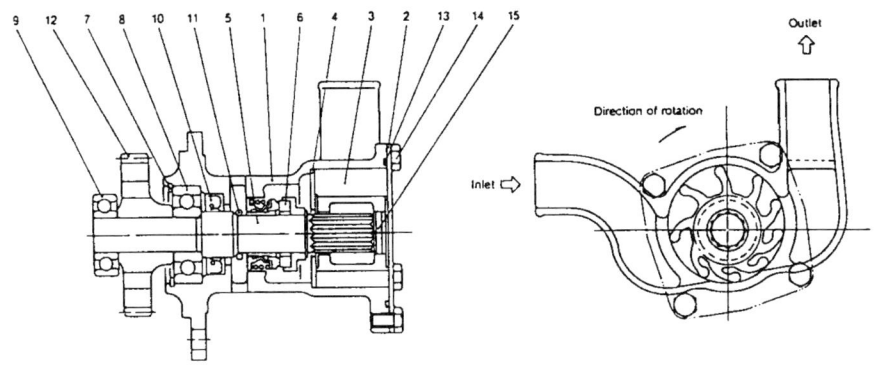

1. Sea water pump body
2. Side cover
3. Impeller (C-type)
4. Wear plate
5. Pump shaft
6. Mechanical seal
7. Circlip
8. Bearing
9. Bearing
10. Oil seal
11. Water seal ring
12. Gear
13. O ring
14. Hexagonal bolt
15. Impeller blind cover

2-2 Specifications of sea water pump

Engine speed (max.)	3600 rpm
Gear ratio (crank gear/pump gear)	28/31
Pump speed	3252 rpm
Suction head	0.5m (1.66 ft)
Total head	9.5m (31.16 ft)
Delivery capacity	3750 l/h (228825in.³/h)

2-3 Sea water pump disassembly

(1) Remove the rubber hose from the sea water pump outlet and then the sea water pump assembly from the gear case.
(2) Remove the sea water pump cover and take out the O-ring, impeller and wear plate.
(3) Remove the mechanical seal side stop ring.
(4) Insert pliers from the drive gear long hole and remove the stop ring that holds the bearings.
(5) Lightly tap the pump shaft from the impeller side and remove the pump shaft, bearings, and drive gear as a set.
(6) Remove the oil seal and mechanical seal if necessary.

2-4 Sea water pump inspection

(1) Inspect the rubber impeller, checking for splitting around the outside, damage or cracks, and replace if necessary.

mm (in.)

	Standard	Clearance at assembly	Maximum allowable clearance	Wear limit
Impeller width	31.6 ~ 31.8 (1.2440 ~ 1.2519)	0 ~ 0.3 (0 ~ 0.0118)	0.8 (0.0314)	31.3 (1.2322)
Wear plate thickness	2 (0.0787)			1.8 (0.0708)
Housing width	33.8 ~ 33.9 (1.3307 ~ 1.3346)			—
Side plate thickness	2 (0.0787)			1.8 (0.0708)

Chapter 6 Cooling Water System
2. Sea Water Pump

_____ 3JH2 Series

(3) Inspect the mechanical seal and replace if the spring is damaged, or the seal is corroded. Also replace the mechanical seal if there is considerable water leakage during operation.

Cooling water leakage	less than 3 cc/h (0.18 in.³/h)
Parts No. of oil seal	129795-42670

(4) Make sure the ball bearings rotate smoothly. Replace if there is excessive play.

2-5 Sea water pump reassembly

(1) When replacing the mechanical seal, coat the No.1101 oil seal and pressure fit. Coat the sliding surface with a good quality silicon oil, taking sufficient care not to cause any scratches.
(2) When replacing the oil seal, coat with grease and insert.
(3) Mount the pump shaft, ball bearing and gear assembly to the pump unit and fit the bearing stop ring. Be sure not to forget the water O-ring when doing this.

NOTE: Coat the shaft with grease.

(4) After inserting the mechanical seal stop ring, mount the wear plate and impeller.

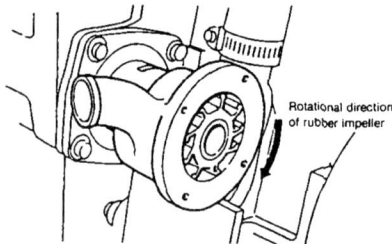

Rotational direction of rubber impeller

NOTE: 1. When inserting the impeller in the pump, make sure that the impeller lies in the proper direction.
 2. Coat the inside of pump body impeller housing with grease.

(5) Mount the O-ring side cover.

NOTE: Replace the O-ring.

3. Fresh Water Pump

3-1 Fresh water pump construction

The fresh water pump is of the centrifugal (volute) type, and circulates water from the fresh water tank to the cylinders and cylinder head.
The fresh water pump consists of the pump body, impeller, pump shaft, bearing unit and mechanical seal. The V pulley on the end of the pump shaft is driven by a V belt from the crankshaft.
The bearing unit assembled in the pump shaft uses grease lubricated ball bearings and cannot be disassembled.
The totally enclosed mechanical seal spring presses the impeller seal mounted on the impeller side away from the pump body side. This prevents water from leaking along the pump shaft.
As the impeller and pulley flanges are press fit assembled, they cannot be disassembled.

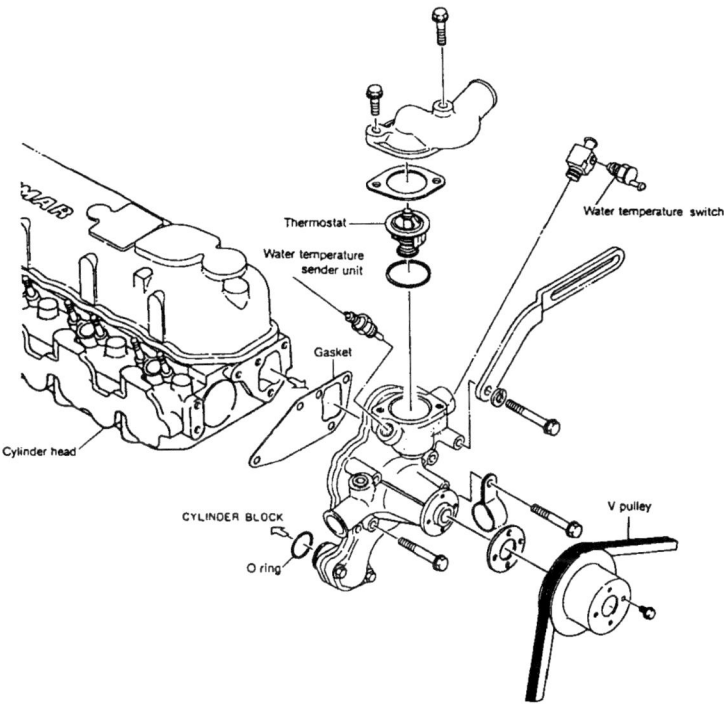

Chapter 6 Cooling Water System
3. Fresh Water Pump

3JH2 Series

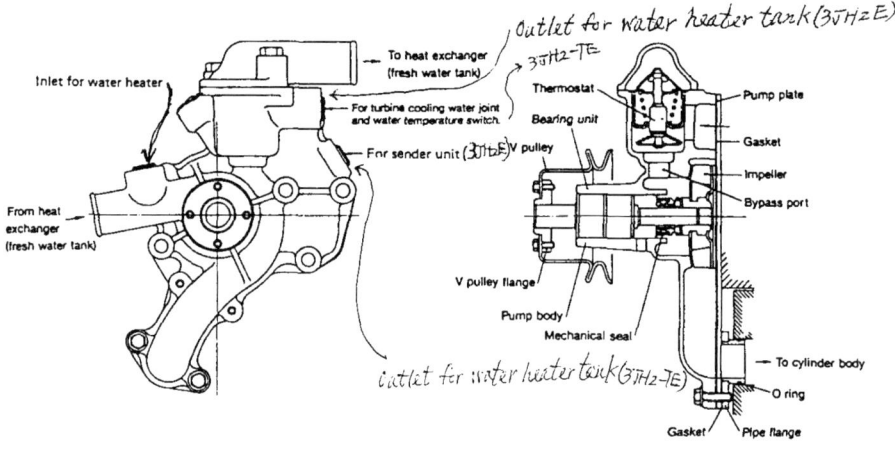

3-2 Specifications of fresh water pump

Crank shaft speed (max.)	3600 rpm
Pulley ratio (crank shaft/pump shaft)	Ø134/Ø120
Pump shaft speed	4020 rpm
Delivery capacity	86.6 ℓ/min (5284 in.³/min)
Total head	4m (13.12 ft)

3-3 Fresh water pump disassembly

(1) Do not disassemble the fresh water pump. It is difficult to disassemble and, once disassembled, even more difficult to reassemble. Replace the pump as an assembly in the event of trouble.
(2) When removing the fresh water pipe as an assembly from the cylinder and cylinder head, replace the cylinder intake pipe O-ring.
(3) When the fresh water pump body and cylinder intake flange and/or fresh water pump and pump plate are disassembled, retighten to the specified torque.

Tightening torque for pump setting bolts	70 ~ 110 kg-cm (5.06 ~ 7.94 ft-lb)

3-4 Fresh water pump inspection

(1) Bearing unit inspection
Rotate the impeller smoothly. If the rotation is not smooth or abnormal noise is heard due to excessive bearing play or contact with other parts, replace the pump as an assembly.
(2) Impeller inspection
Check the impeller blade, and replace if damaged or corroded, or if the impeller blade is worn due to contact with pump body.

(3) Check the holes in the cooling water and bypass lines, clean out any dirt or other foreign matter and repair as necessary.
(4) Replace the pump as an assembly if there is excessive water leakage due to mechanical seal or impeller seal wear or damage.
(5) Inspect the fresh water pump body and flange, clean off scale and rust, and replace if corroded.
(6) Measure the clearance between the impeller and the pump body, and the impeller and the plate.
Measure the clearance between the impeller and the pump body by pushing the impeller all the way towards the body, and inserting a thickness gauge diagonally between the impeller and the body.
Measure the clearance between the impeller and the plate (pump body bracket) by placing a straight-edge against the end of the pump body and inserting a thickness gauge between the impeller and the straight-edge.

Printed in Japan
A0A1015-9110SP

Measuring clearance between impeller and pump body.

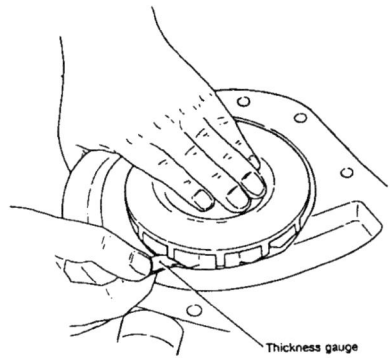

Measuring clearance between impeller and pump body bracket.

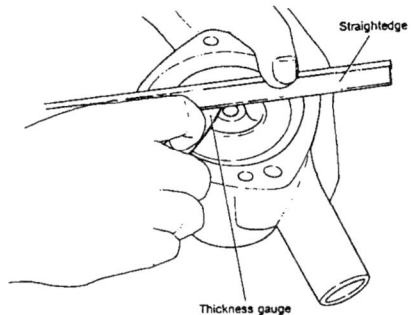

	Standard	Wear limit
Clearance between impeller and body	0.3 ~ 1.1 (0.0118 ~ 0.0433)	1.5 (0.0590)
Clearance between impeller and plate	1.5 (0.0590)	—

mm (in.)

4. Heat Exchanger

4-1. Heat exchanger construction

The heat exchanger cools the hot fresh water that has cooled the inside of the engine with sea water.
The inside of the heat exchanger cooling pipe consists of 36 small dia. tubes and baffle plates.
The sea water flows through the small dia. tubes and the fresh water flows through the maze formed by the baffle plates.
There is a reservoir at the bottom of the cooling pipe which serves as the fresh water tank. There is an exhaust water passageway (line) in the reservoir which forms water cooled exhaust gas manifold.
The filler cap on top of the heat exchanger has a pressure valve, which lets off steam through the overflow pipe when pressure in the fresh water system exceeds the specified value. It also takes in air from the overflow pipe when pressure in the fresh water system drops below the normal value.

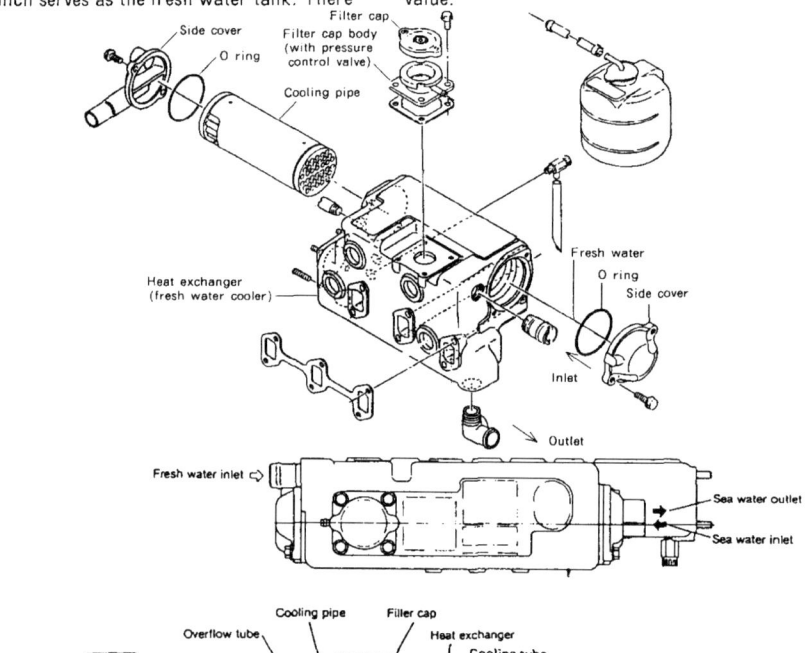

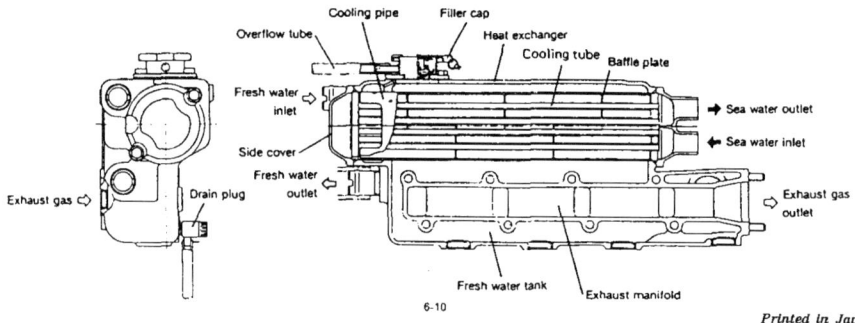

6-10

Chapter 6 Cooling Water System
4. Heat Exchanger

3JH2 Series

4-2 Specifications of heat exchanger

Model of engine		3JH2E	3JH2-TE
Output(DIN6270 B rating)	HP/rpm	50/3600	62/3600
Pipe dia. x pieces	mm(in.)	$\phi 6.4/\phi 8 \times 36$ (0.2519/0.3149)	
Radiation area	m^2(in.^{2})	0.298	0.298
Radiation area/HP	m^2/HP(in.^{2}/HP)	0.00596(9.24)	0.00481(7.457)
Fresh water discharged volume	ℓ/hr(in.^{3}/hr)	5562(339393)	
Sea water discharged volume	ℓ/hr(in.^{3}/hr)	3500(213570)	
Fresh water flow speed in cooling pipe	m/s(ft/s)	1.53(5.02)	
Sea water flow speed in cooling tube	m/s(ft/s)	1.34(4.39)	
Fresh water capacity	ℓ/(in.^{3})	6.7(408.8)	

4-3 Disassembly and reassembly of the heat exchanger

(1) Remove the covers on both sides and take out the cooling pipe and O-ring(s).

NOTE: Replace the O-ring(s) when you have removed the cooling pipe.

(2) Remove the filler assembly.

4-4 Heat exchanger inspection

(1) Cooling pipe inspection
 1) Inspect the inside of the tubes for rust or scale build-up from sea water, and clean with a wire brush if necessary.

NOTE: Disassemble and wash when the cooling water temperature reaches 85°C.

 2) Check the joints at both ends of the tubes for looseness or damage, and repair if loose. Replace if damaged or corroded.
 3) Check tubes and replace if leaking.
 4) Clean any scale or rust off the outside of the tubes.

(2) Heat exchanger body inspection
 1) Check heat exchanger body and side cover for dirt and corrosion. Replace if excessively corroded, or cracked.
 2) Inspect sea water and fresh water inlets and outlets, retighten any joints as necessary and clean the insides of the pipes.
 3) Check the exhaust gas intake flange and line, and replace if corroded or cracked.

(3) Heat exchanger body water leakage test
 1) Compressed air/water tank test
  Fit rubber covers on the fresh water and sea water inlets and outlets. Place the heat exchanger in a water tank, feed in compressed air from the overflow pipe and check for any (water) leakage, (air bubbles).

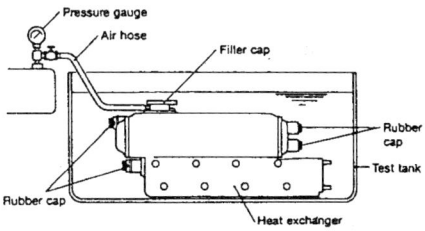

Test pressure	2 kg/cm^2 (28.44 lb/in.^{2})

 2) Use of the tester
  Fit the fresh and sea water inlets and outlets with rubber covers and fill the fresh water tank with fresh water. Fit a pressure cap tester in place of the pressure cap, operate the pump for one minute and set the pressure at 1.5kg/cm^2 (21.33lb/in.^{2}). If there are any leaks the pressure will not rise. If there are no leaks the pressure will not fall.

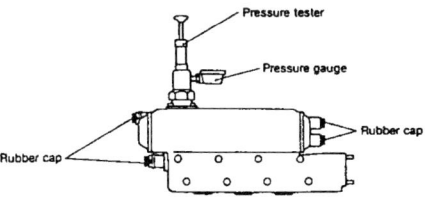

5. Pressure Cap and Sub Tank

5-1 Pressure cap construction

The pressure cap mounted on the fresh water filler neck incorporates a pressure control valve. The cap is mounted on the filler neck cam by placing it on the rocking tab and rotating. The top seal of the cap seals the top of the filler neck, and the pressure valve seals the lock seat.

5-2 Pressure cap pressure control

The pressure valve and vacuum seal both seal the valve seat when the pressure in the fresh water system is within the specified value of $0.9 kg/cm^2$ ($12.80 lb/in.^2$). This seals the fresh water system.
When the pressure within the fresh water system exceeds the specified value, the pressure valve opens, and steam is discharged through the overflow pipe. When the fresh water is cooled and the pressure within the fresh water system drops below the normal value, atmospheric pressure opens the vacuum valve, and air is drawn in through the overflow pipe.

5-3 Pressure cap inspection

Precautions

Do not open the pressure cap while the engine is running or right after stopping because high temperature steam will be blown out. Remove the cap only after the water has had a chance to cool down.

(1) Remove scale and rust, check the seat and seat valve, etc. for scratches or wear, and the spring for corrosion or settling. Replace if necessary.

NOTE: Clean the pressure cap with fresh water as it will not close completely if it is dirty.

(2) Fit the adapter on the tester to the pressure cap. Pump until the pressure gauge is within the specified pressure range ($0.75 \sim 1.05 kg/cm^2$ ($10.67 \sim 14.91 lb/in.^2$)) and note the gauge reading. The cap is normal if the pressure holds for six seconds. If the pressure does not rise, or drops immediately, inspect the cap and repair or replace as necessary.

Pressure valve operation

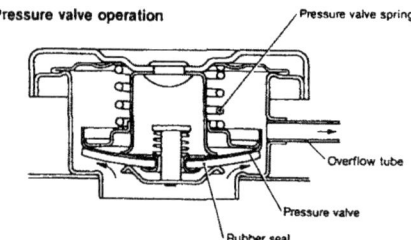

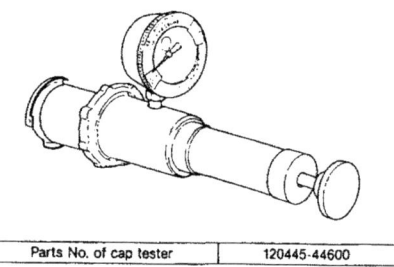

Parts No. of cap tester	120445-44600

Vacuum valve operation

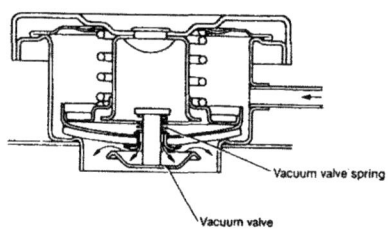

The sub tank, (which will be described later), keeps the water level from dropping due to discharge of steam when the pressure valve opens.

5-4 Function of the sub tank

The pressure valve opens to discharge steam when the steam pressure in the fresh water tank exceeds $0.9 kg/cm^2$ ($12.80 lb/in.^2$).
This consumes water. The sub tank maintains the water level by preventing this discharge of water.
The steam discharged into the sub tank condenses into water, and the water level in the sub tank rises.
When the pressure in the fresh water system drops below the normal value, the water in the sub tank is sucked back into the fresh water tank to raise the water back to its original level.
The sub tank facilitates long hours of operation without water replacement and eliminates the possibility of burns when the steam is ejected from the filler neck becase the pressure cap does not need to be removed.

Action of pressure control valve

Pressure valve	Open at $0.9 kg/cm^2 G$ ($12.80 lb/in.^2$)
Vacuum valve	Open at $0.05 kg/cm^2 G$ ($0.71 lb/in.^2$) or below

Chapter 6 Cooling Water System
5. Pressure Cap And Sub Tank

5-7 Precautions on usage of the sub tank
(1) Check the sub tank when the engine is cool and refill with fresh water as necessary to bring the water level between the low and full marks.
(2) Check the overflow pipe and replace if bent or cracked. Clean out the pipe if it is clogged up.

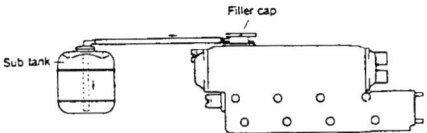

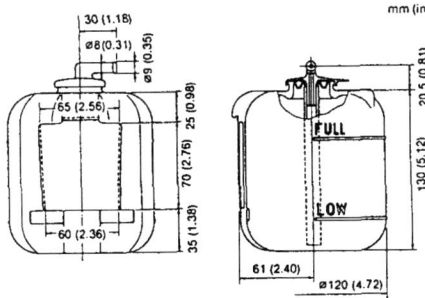

5-5 Specifications of sub tank

	Overall capacity	1.25ℓ (76.27 in.³)
Subtank capacity	Full-scale position	0.8ℓ (48.81 in.³)
	Low-scale position	0.2ℓ (12.20 in.³)
Part No. of subtank		120445-44530

5-6 Mounting the sub tank
(1) The sub tank is mounted at approximately the same height as the heat exchanger (fresh water tank).
(allowable difference in height: 300mm (11.8110in.) or less)
(2) The overflow pipe should be less than 1000mm (39.3701in.) long, and mounted so that it does not sag or bend.

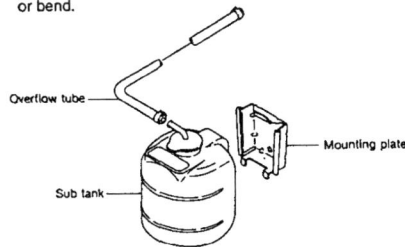

NOTE: Make sure that the overflow pipe of the sub tank is not submerged in bilge. If the overflow pipe is submerged in bilge, water in the bilge will be siphoned into the fresh water tank when the water is being cooled.

6. Thermostat

6-1 Functioning of thermostat

The thermostat opens and closes a valve according to changes in the temperature of the fresh water inside the engine, controlling the volume of water flowing to the heat exchanger from the cylinder head, and in turn maintaining the temperature of the fresh water in the engine at a constant level.

The thermostat is bottom bypass type. It is located in a position connected with the cylinder head outlet line at the top of the top of fresh water pump unit.

When the fresh water temperature is low (75.0 ~ 78.0°C or less), the thermostat is closed, and fresh water goes from the bypass line to the fresh water pump intake and circulates in the engine.

When the fresh water temperature exceeds the above temperature, the thermostat opens, and a portion of the water is sent to the heat exchanger and cooled by sea water, the other portion going from the bypass line to the fresh water pump intake.

The bypass line is closed off as the thermostat valve opens, and is completely closed when the fresh water temperature reaches 81.5°C (valve lifts 4mm (0.1575in.)), sending all of the water to the heat exchanger.

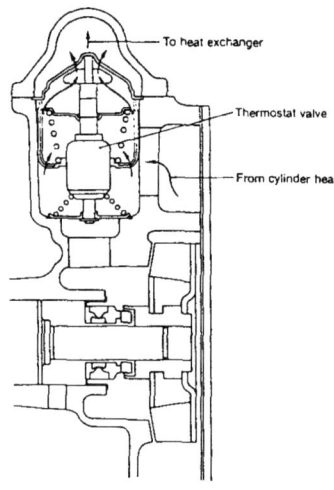

When valve is opened (by-pass passage is closed)

6-2 Thermostat construction

The thermostat used in this engine is of the wax pellet type, with a solid wax pellet located in a small chamber. When the temperature of the cooling water rises, the wax melts and increases in volume. This expansion and construction is used to open and close the valve.

6-3 Characteristics of thermostat

Opening temperature	75 ~ 78°C (167 ~ 174°F)
Full open temperature	90° (194°F)
Valve lift at full open	8mm (0.3149 in.)
By-pass valve lift	3.7mm (0.1456 in.)
By-pass valve close temperature	81.5°C (178°F)

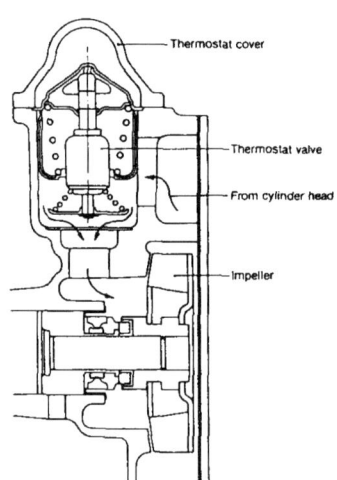

When valve is closed (by-pass passage is opened)

6-4 Thermostat inspection

Remove the thermostat cover on top of the fresh water pump and take out the thermostat. Clean off scale and rust and inspect, and replace if the characteristics (performance) have changed, or if the spring is broken, deformed or corroded.

6-5 Testing the thermostat

(1) Put the thermostat in a beaker with fresh water, and heat it on an electric stove. The thermostat is functioning normally if it starts to open between 75 ~ 78°C, and opens 8mm (0.3150in.) or more at 90°C. Replace the thermostat if it is not functioning normally.
(2) Normally, the thermostat should be inspected every 500 hours of operation, but, it should be inspected before this if the cooling temperature rises abnormally or white smoke is emitted for a long time after engine starting.
(3) Replace the thermostat every year or 2000 hours of operation (whichever comes first).

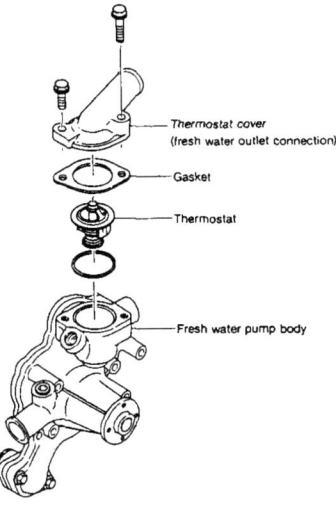

Thermostat cover (fresh water outlet connection)
Gasket
Thermostat
Fresh water pump body

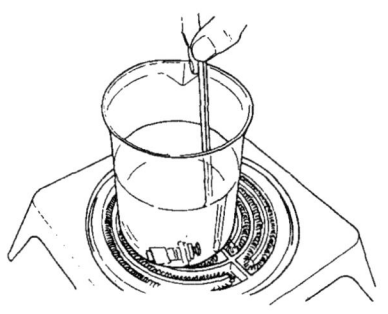

Part No. of thermostat	129470-49800

Chapter 6 Cooling Water System
7. Kingston Cock (Optional) — *3JH2 Series*

7. Kingston Cock (Optional)

7-1 Construction

The Kingston cock, installed on the bottom of the hull, controls the intake of cooling water into the boat. The Kingston cock serves to filter the water so that mud, sand, and other foreign matter in the water does not enter the water pump.

Numerous holes are drilled in the water side of the Kingston cock, and a scoop strainer is installed to prevent the sucking in of vinyl, etc.

7-3 Inspection

When the cooling water volume has dropped and the pump is normal, remove the vessel from the water and check for clogging of the Kingston cock.

If water leaks from the cock, disassemble the cock and inspect if for wear, and repair or replace it.

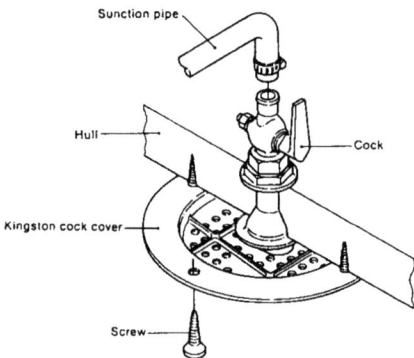

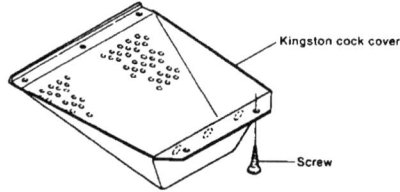

7-2 Handling precautions

Caution the user to always close the Kingston cock after each day of use and to confirm that it is open before beginning operation.

If the Kingston cock is left open, water will flow in reverse and the vessel will sink if trouble occurs with the water pump.

On the other hand, if the engine is operated with the Kingston cock closed, cooling water will not be able to get in, resulting in engine and pump trouble.

8. Sea Water Filter (Optional)

When operating the engine in areas where the sea water contains a large amount of mud, sand or other foreign matter, a sea water filter should be provided between the kingston cock and the sea water pump.
Occasionally inspect the sea water filter and clean the dirt and scale off the element. Remove the dirt and sand from the bottom of the filter.

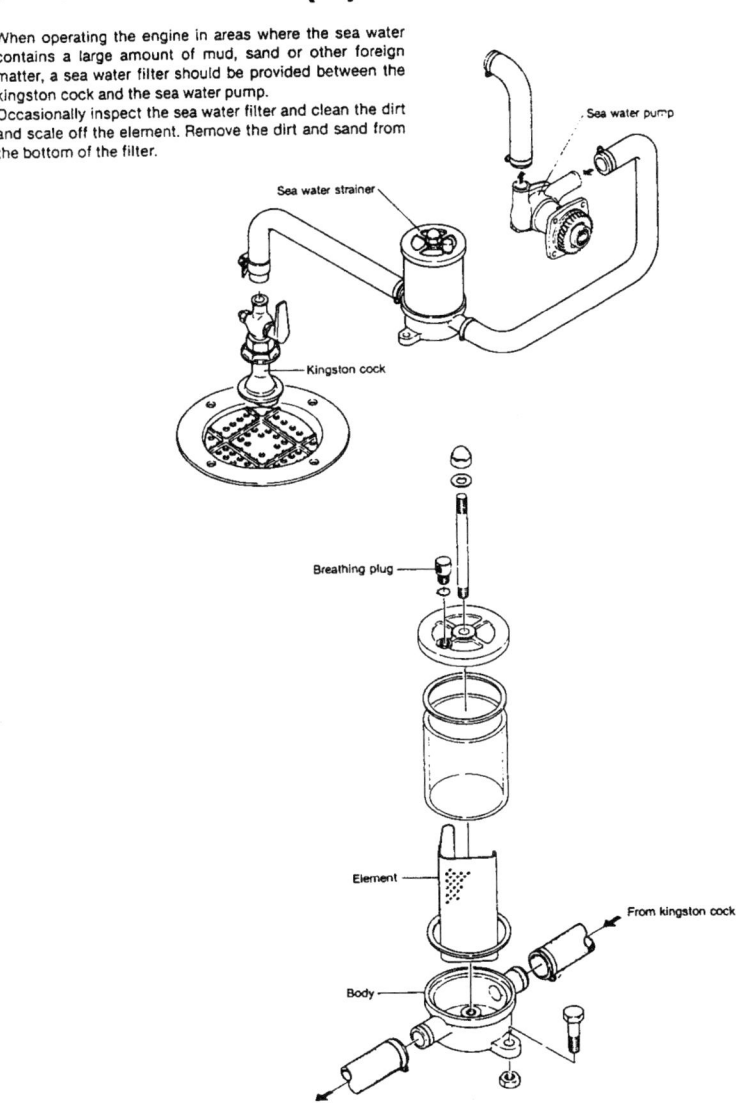

9. Bilge Pump and Bilge Strainer (Optional)

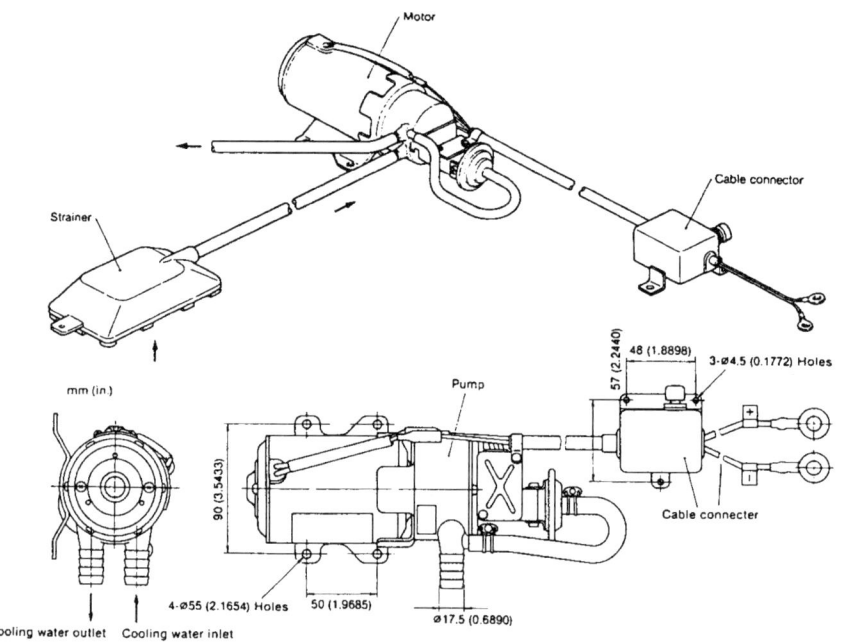

9-1 Bilge pump
9-1.1 Specifications

Code No.	120345-46010 (with strainer)
Model No.	BP190-10
Rating	60 min.
Voltage	12V
Output	90W
Weight	3.0kg (6.6 lb)

9-1.2 Performance of pump (in pure water)

	Voltage	11.5V
Suction performance	Max. suction lift	1.2m (3.94 ft)
	Suction time	4 sec.
	Voltage	11.5V
Pumping lift performance	Current	8A
	Total lift	1m (3.28 ft)
	Lifting volume of water	17 ℓ/min

9-2 Bilge strainer

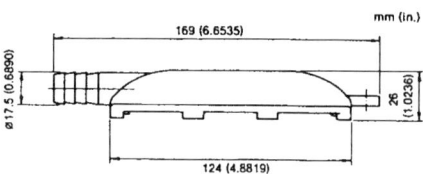

CHAPTER 7
REDUCTION AND REVERSING GEAR

1. Construction ·· 7-1
2. Shifting Device ··· 7-7
3. Inspection And Servicing ······························ 7-12
4. Disassembly ·· 7-20
5. Reassembly ·· 7-25

Chapter 7 Reduction and Reversing Gear
1. Construction

Marine Gear Models
KM3A
for Engine Models 3JH2BE
3JHE-TBE

1. Construction

1-1. Construction

This clutch is a cone-type, mechanically operated clutch.
When the drive cone (which is connected to the output shaft by the lead spline) is moved forward or backward, its taper contacts with the large gear and transfers power to the output shaft.

The construction is simple when compared with other types of clutch and if serves to reduce the number of components, making for a lighter, more compact unit which can be operated smoothly. Although it is small, the power transmission efficiency is high even under a heavy load. Its durability is high and it is also reliable because high grade materials are used for the shaft and gear, and a taper roller bearing is incorporated. Power transmission is smooth because connection with the engine is made through the damper disc.

- The drive cone is made from special aluminum bronze which has both higher wear-resistance and durability. The drive cone is connected with the output shaft through the thread spline. The taper angle, diameter of the drive cone, twist angle, and diameter of the thread spline, are designed to give the greatest efficiency, thus ensuring that the drive cone can be readily engaged or disengaged.
- Helical gears are used for greater strength. The intermediate shaft is supported at 2 points to reduce deflection and gear noise.
- The clutch case and mounting flange are made from an aluminum alloy of special composition to reduce weight.

It is also anticorrosive against seawater.
- As the damper disc is fitted to the input shaft, power can be transmitted smoothly.
- There is small clearance between the dipstick and the inside of the dipstick tube. A small hole in the dipstick works as a breather.
- When the load on the propeller is removed, the engagement of the drive cone and the large gear is maintained by the shifter and V-groove of the drive cone. Even when the drive cone's tapered area and V-groove are worn, this engagement is maintained by the shift lever device and accordingly no adjustment of the remote control cable is required.
- The cup spring on the rear of the larger gear absorbs rotational fluctuations and stabilizes the engagement of the drive cone and the larger gear. Thus, the durability of the cone against wear is enhanced.

Chapter 7 Reduction and Reversing Gear
1. Construction

3JH2 Series

1-2 specifications

Model			KM3A				
For engine models			3JH2BE			3JH2-TBE	
Clutch			Constant mesh gear with servo cone clutch (wet type)				
Reduction ratio	Forward		2.33	2.64	3.21	2.33	2.64
	Reverse		3.04	3.04	3.04	3.04	3.04
Propeller shaft rpm(Forward)			1457	1290	1059	1457	1290
Direction of rotation	Input shaft		Counter-clockwise, viewed from stern				
	Output shaft	Forward	Clockwise, viewed from stern				
		Reverse	Counter-clockwise, viewed from stern				
Remote control	Control head		Single lever control				
	Cable		Morse, 33-C (cable travel 76.2mm or				
	Clamp		YANMAR made, standard accessory				
	Cable connector		YANMAR made, standard accessory				
Output shaft coupling	Outer diameter		ϕ100mm (3.93")				
	Pitch circle diameter		ϕ78mm (3.07")				
	Connecting bolt holes		4-ϕ10.5mm (4-ϕ0.41")				
Position of shift lever			Right side, viewed from stern				
Lubricating oil			SAE 20/30				
Lubricating oil capacity			0.45 ℓ				
Dry weight			12kg (26.5lbs)				

Note
In the case of clutch model KM3A, when are larger propeller or moment of inertia of the propeller than those listed in the table bellow is used, install the limiter (Option).

Reduction ratio	No. of blade	Diameter of the propeller	Moment of inertia (GD^{2}kg-m^2)	Material
2.33	3	450 (17.5)	$\leq$ 0.15	
	4	425 (16.5)		
2.64	3	470 (18.5)	$\leq$ 0.19	Bronze
	4	440 (17.5)		
3.21	3	490 (19)	$\leq$ 0.23	
	4	460 (18)		

Chapter 7 Reduction and Reversing Gear
1. Construction _____ *3JH2 Series*

1-3 Power transmission system
1-3-1 Arrangement of shafts and gears

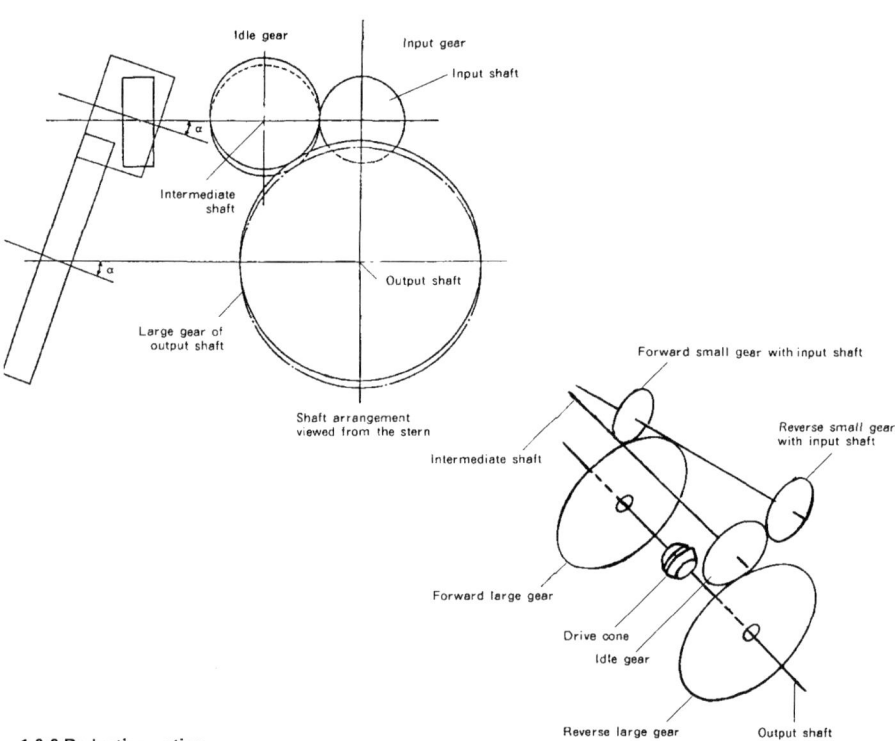

1-3-2 Reduction ration

Forward

Model	No. of teeth of forward small gear Zif	No. of teeth of forward large gear Zof	Reduction ratio Zof/Zif
KM3A	24	56	56/24 = 2.33
	22	58	58/22 = 2.64
	19	61	61/19 = 3.21

Reverse

Model	No. of teeth of reverse small gear Zif	No. of teeth of intemediate shaft gear Zi	No. of teeth of reverse large gear Zdr	Reduction ratio Zi/Zir·Zdr/Zl
KM3A	23	36	70	70/23 = 3.04

Chapter 7 Reduction and Reversing Gear
1. Construction _____ *3JH2 Series*

1-3-3 Power transmission routine-Forward

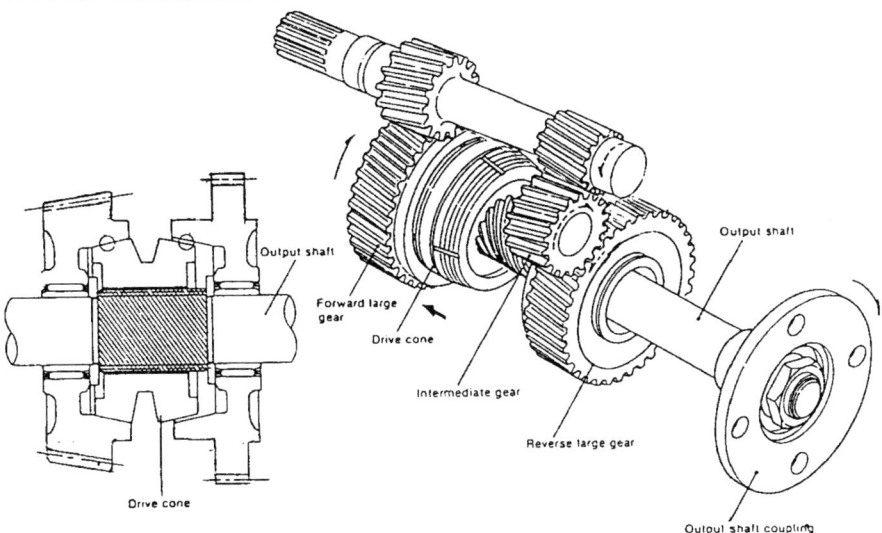

1-3-4 Power transmission routine-reverse

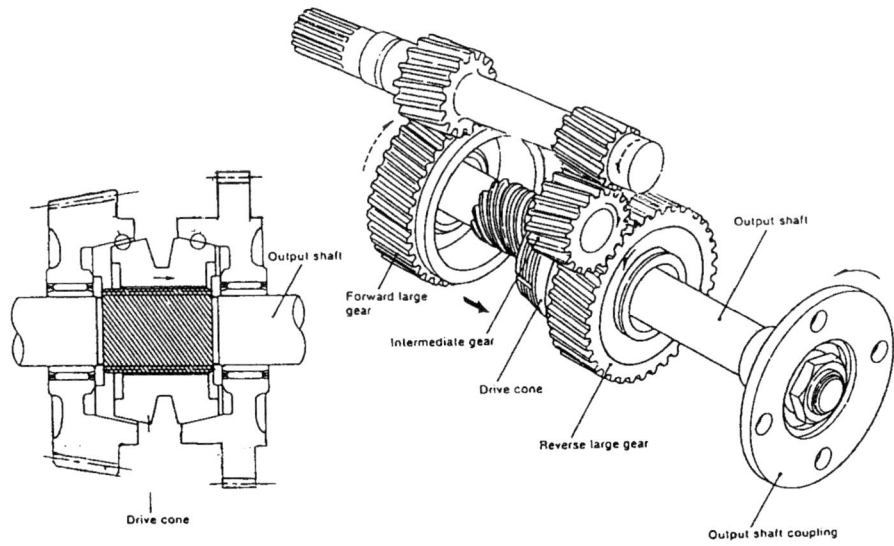

Chapter 7 Reduction and Reversing Gear
1. Construction _____ *3JH2 Series*

1-4 Drawing

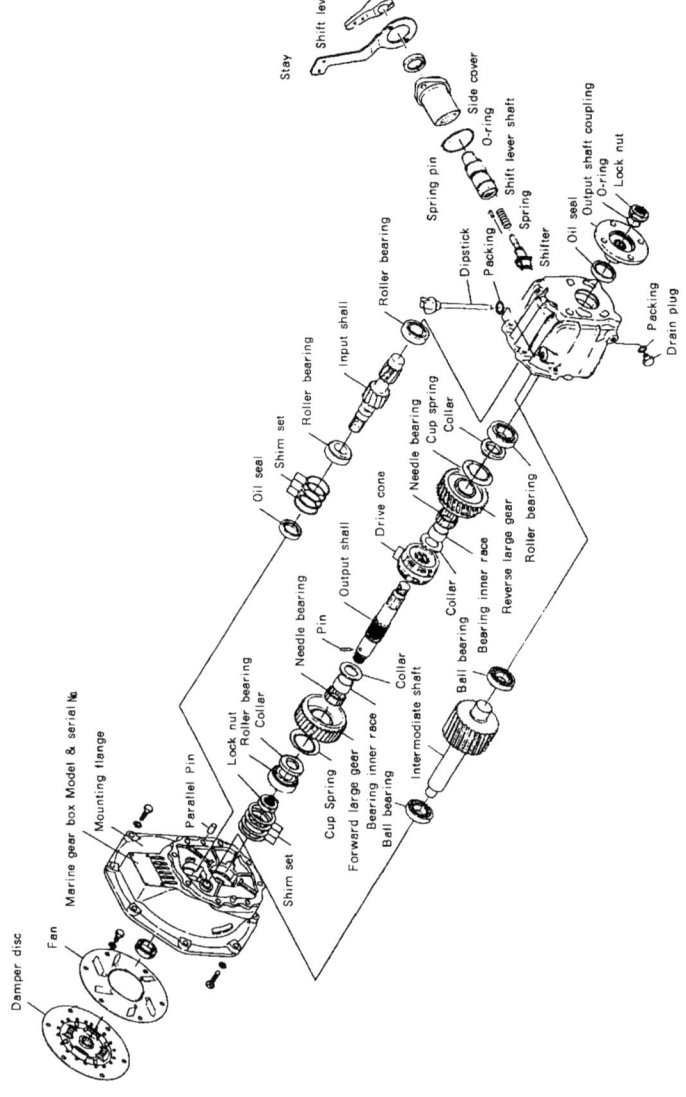

Chapter 7 Reduction and Reversing Gear
1. Construction _____ *3JH2 Series*

1-5 Sectional view

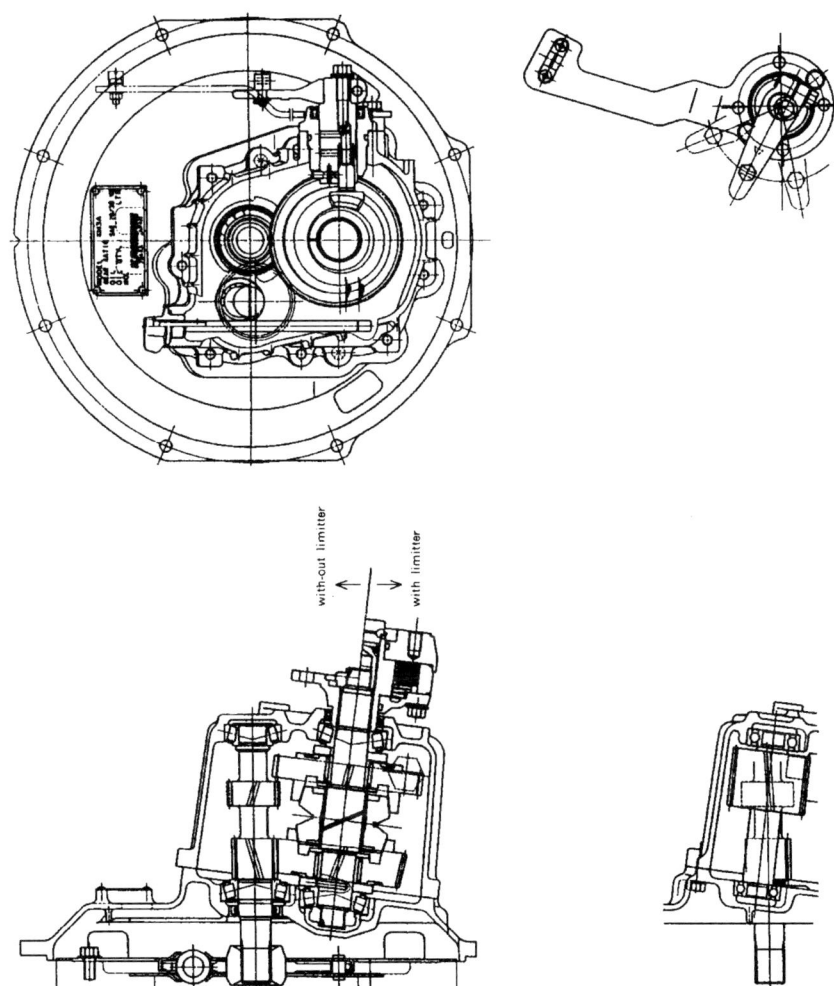

2. Shifting Device

2-1 Construction of shifting mechanism

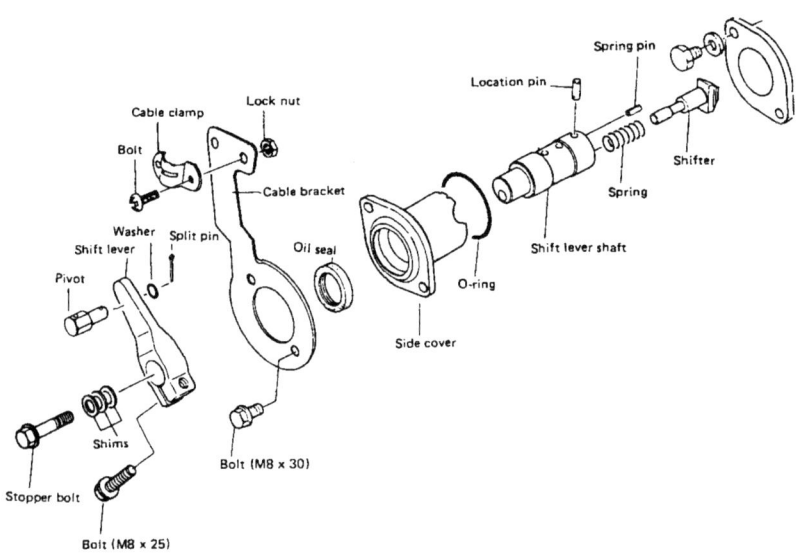

The shift lever shaft is installed on the side cover with neutral, forward and reverse positions provided on this cover. The neutral, forward and reverse location pins of the shift lever shaft are constantly inserted into their respective grooves on the shift lever by the tension of the shifter spring. The shifter is set on the eccentric hole of the shift lever shaft and moves the drive cone in the neutral position either to the forward or reverse positions, and then back to the neutral positions. (The shift lever shaft moves slightly to the shift lever or drive cone side when the shift lever is placed in the forward on reverse positions.)

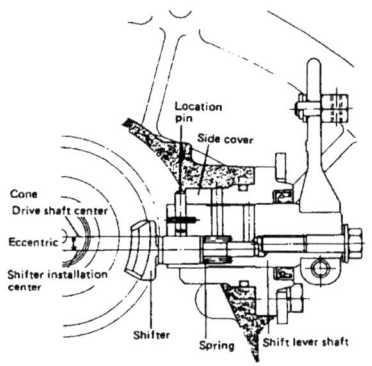

Chapter 7 Reduction and Reversing Gear
2. Shifting Device _____ *3JH2 Series*

2-2 Forward and reverse clutch operation
(Neutral ⇨ Forward; Neutral ⇨ Reverse)
When the shift lever is moved to forward position from the neutral position, the shift lever shaft starts to revolve, and the location pin disengages from the neutral V-groove position of the side cover.(Shift lever moves approx. 0.5mm to the drive cone side.) At this time the shifter, moves the drive cone's V-groove to the forward large gear.

When the location pin of the shift lever shaft falls in the forward position groove of the side cover, the shift lever shaft moves approx. 3mm to the shift lever side, and the shifter stars to press the drive cone V-groove to the forward large gear side through the spring force.

2-3 Engagement and disengagement of clutch
(Forward ⇨ Neutral; Reverse ⇨ Neutral)

When the shift lever is moved to the forward position from the neutral position, the shift lever shaft starts to revolve, and the location pin disengages from the forward position groove of the side cover. (The shift lever shaft moves approx. 3mm to the drive cone side.) At this time, the shifter which is set on the eccentric hole of the shift lever shaft is moved to the neutral side (reverse large gear side). The drive cone, however, is engaged with the forward large gear through the torque force produced by the revolving centrifugal force.

Further, when the shift lever shaft starts to revolve, and the positioning pin falls in to the neutral V-groove position of the side cover (the shift lever shaft travels approx. 5mm to the shift lever side), the shifter moves to the shift lever side(to the spring side) while moving the V-groove of the drive cone to the reverse large gear side. The movement of the shifter to the shift lever side, however, is stopped when the shifter end contacts the stopper bolt. The shifter only works to press the V-groove of the drive cone to the reverse large gear side. Thus, the drive cone is disengaged from the forward large gear. After this disengagement, the transmission torque of the drive cone is decreased to zero and the shift lever is returned to the neutral position by the spring force.

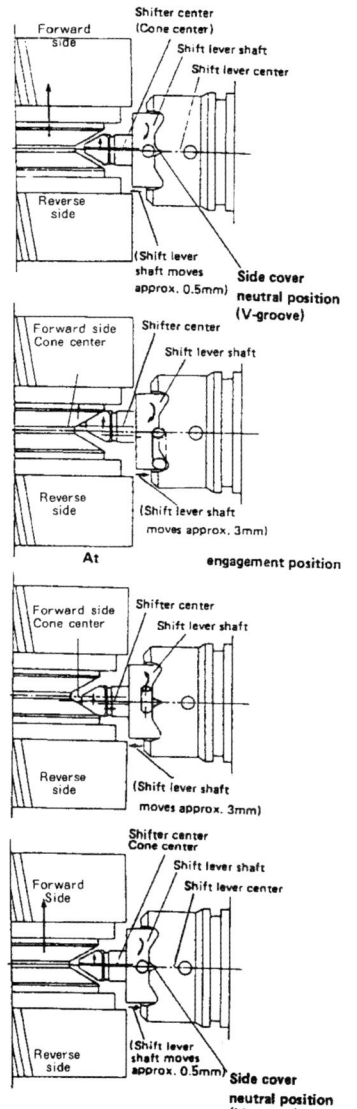

Printed in Japan
A0A1015-9110SP

Chapter 7 Reduction and Reversing Gear
2. Shifting Device

2-4 Clutch shifting force

Shifting position / shifting direction	Shifting lever position at 56mm	Remote control handle postition at 170mm (Cable length, 4m)
Engaging force at 1000rpm	3 ~ 4kg (6.6 ~ 8.8lbs)	4 ~ 5kg (8.8 ~ 11.0lbs)
Disengaging force at 1000rpm	3.5 ~ 5kg (7.7 ~ 11.0lbs)	4 ~ 6kg (8.8 ~ 13.2lbs)

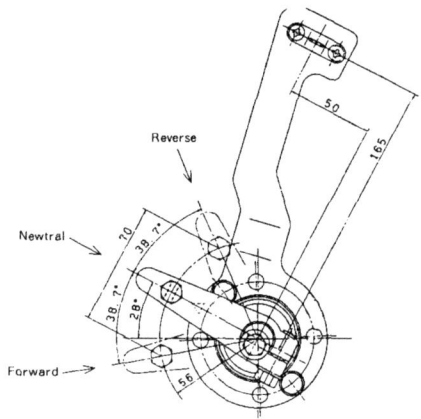

2-5 Adjustment of shifting device

Whenever the side cover, shift lever shaft, shifter, stopper bolt or drive cone is replaced, be sure to adjust the clearance between the shifter end and the stopper bolt by using shims. When the adjustment of this clearance is not proper the drive cone may be improperly fitted when the shift lever is moved to the neutral position from either the forward or the reverseposition.

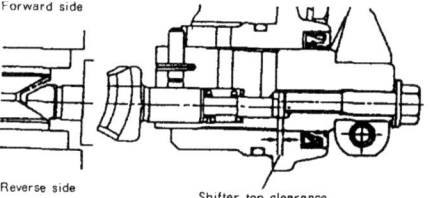

Chapter 7 Reduction and Reversing Gear
2. Shifting Device _____ 3JH2 Series

2-5-1 Measurement and adjustment of clearance

(1) Assemble the shifting mechanism (without installing the stopper bolt of the shifter) to the marine gear case.

NOTE: Ensure the correct alignment of the shifter before assembly.

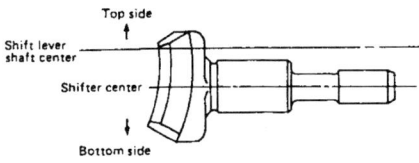

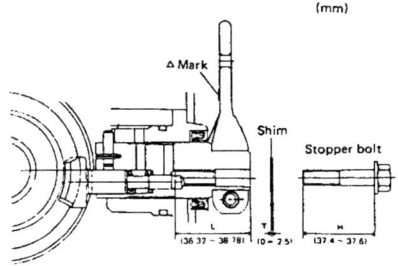

(2) Turn the shift lever 10~15 degree either to the forward or reverse position from the neutral position.
(3) Measure the L-distance between the shift lever shaft end surface and the shifter end and measure the minimum L (Lmin).
(4) Measure the H-distance (the distance from the neck of the stopper bolt to its end).
(5) Obtain the shim thickness "T" by the following formula.

$$T = (H - Lmin + 1.25) \pm 0.1mm(0.0039in.)$$

NOTE: Shim set includes one each of 1_{mm}, 0.4_{mm}, 0.3_{mm}, 0.25_{mm} shims.
(YANMAR Part No. 177088-06380)

(6) Insert shim (s) of proper thickness to the stopper bolt side and tighten to the shift lever shaft.

NOTE: When tightening the stopper bolt, apply either a non-drying type liquid packing (THREE BOND No.1215), or a seal tape around the bolt threads.

2-5-2 Inspect for the following points
(to be inspected every 2-3 months)

(1) Looseness at the connection of the cable connector and the remote control cable.

(2) Looseness of the attaching nut of the cable connector and the shift lever.

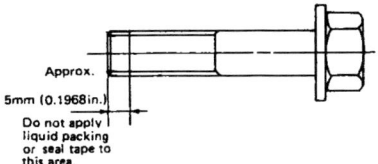

Chapter 7 Reduction and Reversing Gear
2. Shifting Device

2-6 Adjustment of the remote control head Marine gear box control side

(1) Equal distribution of the control lever stroke.

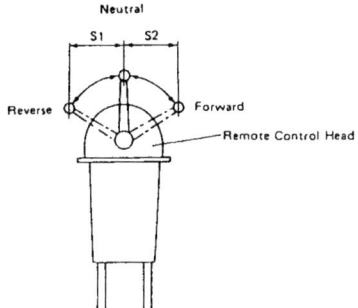

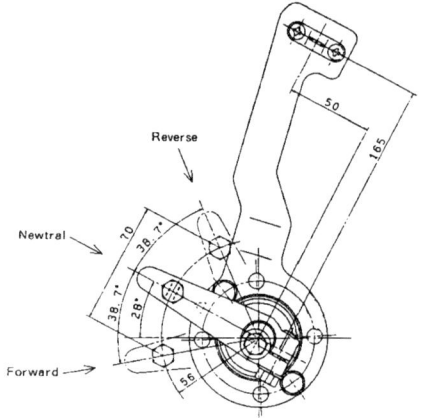

The stroke between the neutral position → forward position (S2), and the neutral position → reverse position (S1) must be equalized.
When either stroke is too short, clutch engagement becomes faulty.

(2) Equalizing the travel distance of the control cable.
After ensuring the equal distribution of the stroke described in (1), connect the cable to the control head.
Adjust so that the cable shift travel of the S_1 and S_2 control lever strokes becomes identical.

2-7 Cautions

(1) Always stop the engine when attaching, adjusting, and inspecting.
(2) When conducting inspection immediately after stopping the engine, do not touch the clutch. The oil temperature is often raised to around 90°C (194°F).
(3) Half-clutch operation is not possible with this design and construction. Do not use with the shift lever halfway to the engaged position.
(4) Set the idling engine speed at between 650 and 800rpm.

NOTE: The dual(Two) lever remote control device cannot be usded.

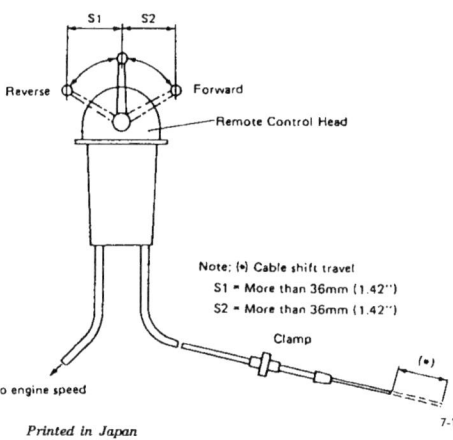

Note: (•) Cable shift travel
S1 = More than 36mm (1.42")
S2 = More than 36mm (1.42")

Chapter 7 Reduction and Reversing Gear
3. Inspection and Servicing
_____ 3JH2 Series

3. Inspection and Servicing

3-1 Clutch case
(1) Check the clutch case with a test hammer for cracking.
Perform a color check when required.
If the case is cracked, replace it.
(2) Check for staining on the inside surface of the bearing section.
Also, measure the inside diameter of the case. Replace the case if it is worn beyond the wear limit.

3-2 Bearing
(1) Rusting and damage.
If the bearing is rusted or the taper roller retainer is damages, replace the bearing.
(2) Make sure that the bearings rotates smoothly.
If rotation is not smooth, if there is any binding, or if any abnormal sound is evident, replace the baring.

3-3 Gear
Check the surface, tooth face conditions and backlash of each gear. Replace any defective part.
(1) Tooth surface wear.
Check the tooth surface for pitting, abnormal wear, dents, and cracks. Repair the lightly damaged gears and replace heavily damaged gears.
(2) Tooth surface contact.
Check the tooth surface contact. The amount of tooth surface contact between the tooth crest and tooth flank must be at least 70% of the tooth width.
(3) Backlash.
Measure the backlash of each gear, and replace the gear when it is worn beyond the wear limit.

mm(in.)

	Maintenance standard	Wear limit
Input shaft forward gear and output shaft forward gear	0.05 ~ 0.14 (0.0020 ~ 0.0055)	0.2 (0.0079)
Input shaft reverse gear and intermediate gear	0.06 ~ 0.12 (0.0024 ~ 0.0047)	0.2 (0.0079)
Intermediate gear and output shaft reverse gear	0.06 ~ 0.12 (0.0024 ~ 0.0047)	0.2 (0.0079)

3-4 Forward and reverse large gears
(1) Contact surface with drive cone.
Visually inspect the tapered surface of the forward and reverse large gears where they make contact with the drive cone to check if any abnormal condition or sign of overheating exists. If any defect is found, replace the gear.

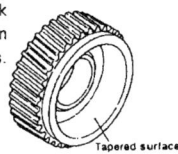
Tapered surface

(2) Forward/reverse gear needle bearing.
When an abnormal sound is produced at the needle bearing, visually inspect the rollers; replace the bearing if the rollers are faulty.

Rollers

3-5 Drive cone
(1) Visually inspect that part of the surface that comes into contact with the circumferential triangular slot to check for signs of scoring, overheating or wear. If deep scoring or signs of overheating are found, replace the cone.

contact surface

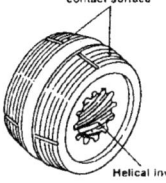
Helical involute spline

(2) Check the helical involute spline for any abnormal condition on the tooth surface, and repair or replace the part should any defect be found.
(3) Measure the amount of wear on the tapered contact surface of the drive cone, and replace the cone when the wear exceeds the specified limit.

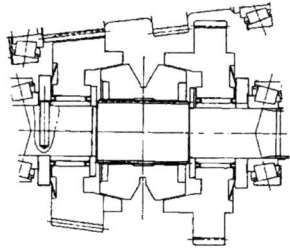

7-12

Printed in Japan
A0A1015-9110SP

Chapter 7 Reduction and Reversing Gear
3. Inspection and Servicing

mm(in.)

		Standard dimensions	Limited dimensions
Dimensions ℓ	KM3A	29.2-29.8(1.1496-1.1732)	28.1(1.1063)

NOTE: When dismantled, the forward or reverse direction of the drive cone must be clearly identified.

(4) If the wear of the V-groove of the drive cone is excessive, replace the part.

NOTE: When replacing the dive cone, the drive cone and forward large gear and reverse large gear must be lapped prior to assembly.
The lapping procedure is described below.

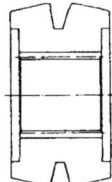

3-5-1 Lapping Procedure for Drive Cone

(1) Coat the lapping powder onto the cave of the clutch gear (Lapping powder: 67 micron silicon carbide #280)

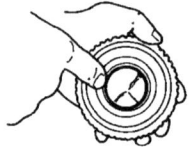

(2) Set the large gear on the clutch shaft with a needle bearing and then set the drive cone on the clutch shaft.

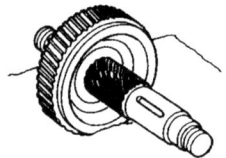

(3) Lap the large gear's cave and drive cone, pushing them together by hand.

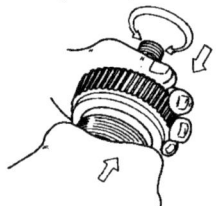

(4) Push and turn the clutch gear about 5 times both clockwise and counter-clockwise.

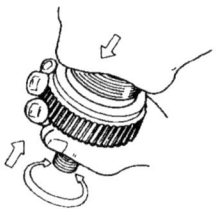

(5) After lapping them, wash them with washing oil. The lapped parts should be cleaned completely.

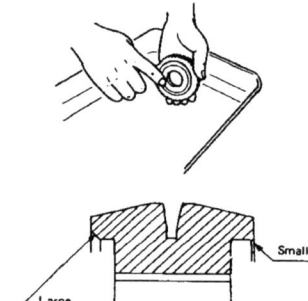

NOTE: Do not mix the combination of the lapped parts. The washing oil should be changed frequently in order to prevent residual powder being left on the parts. When assembling the drive cone, be sure to check its alignment. The larger chamferring face should be on the forward large gear side.

Chapter 7 Reduction and Reversing Gear
3. Inspection and Servicing _____ *3JH2 Series*

3-6 Thrust collar

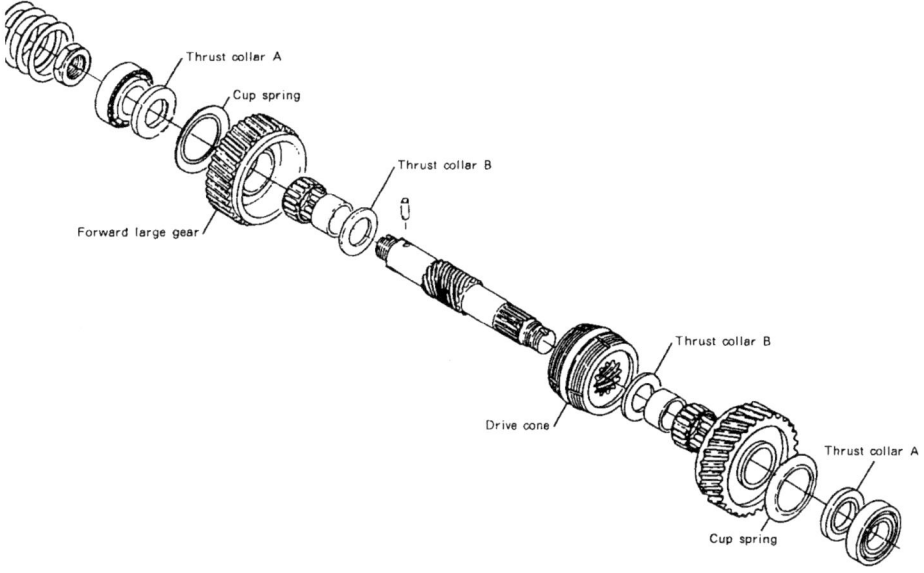

Chapter 7 Reduction and Reversing Gear
3. Inspection and Servicing
3JH2 Series

(1) Visually inspect the sliding surface of thrust collar A or B to check for signs of overheating, scoring, or cracks.
Replace the collar if any abnormal condition is found.

(2) Measure the thickness of thrust collar A or B, and replace it when the dimension exceeds the specified limit.

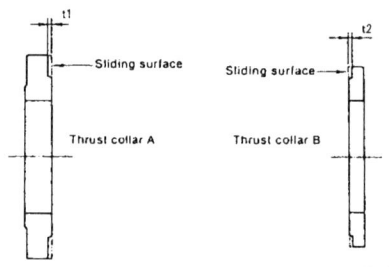

Stepped wear	Limit for use
Thrust collar A, t1	0.05(0.0020)
Thrust collar B, t2	0.20(0.0079)

mm(in.)

3-7 Cup spring

(1) Check for cracks and damage to the cup spring. Replace the part if defective.
(2) Measure the free length of the cup spring. If the length or the thickness deviates from the standard size, replace the part.

Cup spring

	Standard	Limit
Cup spring, T	2.8~3.1 (0.1102~0.1220)	2.6 (0.1024)

mm(in.)

3-8 Oil seal of output shaft

Visually inspect the oil seal of the output shaft to check if there is any damage or oil leakage; replace the seal when any abnormal condition is found.

3-9 Input shaft

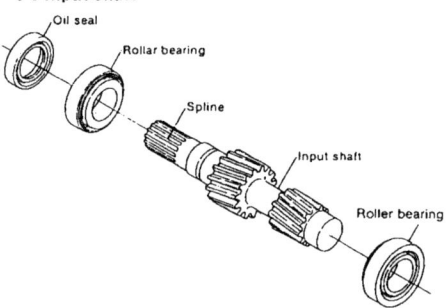

(1) Spline part
Whenever uneven wear and/or scratches are found, replace with a new part.
(2) Surface of oil seal.
If the sealing surface of the oil seal is worn or scratched, replace.

3-10 Output shaft

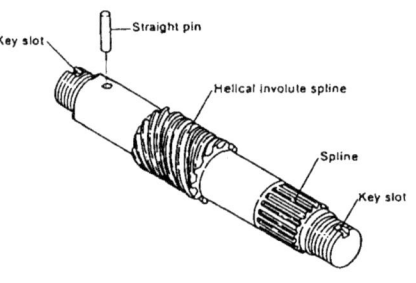

(1) Visually inspect the spline and the helical involute spline, and repair or replace a part when any abnormal condition is found on its surface.

Printed in Japan
A0A1015-9110SP

Chapter 7 Reduction and Reversing Gear
3. Inspection and Servicing _____ 3JH2 Series

3-11 Intermediate shaft

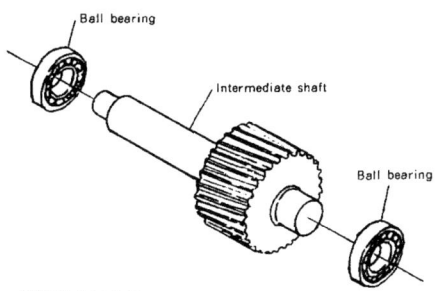

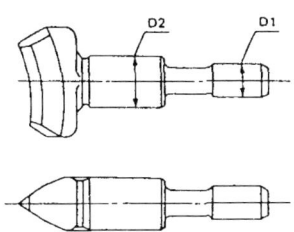

(1) Ball bearing
Check the turning condition with gently rotate, and when bearing is sticked or damaged. Replace if necessary.

	Standard	Limit
D 1	6.69~6.70 (0.2634~0.2638)	6.60 (0.2559)
D 2	11.966~11.984 (0.4711~0.4718)	11.95 (0.4706)
Shift lever shaft, Shifter insert hole	12.0~12.018 (0.4724~0.4731)	12.05 (0.4744)

mm(in.)

3-12 Shifting device

3-12-1 Shifter

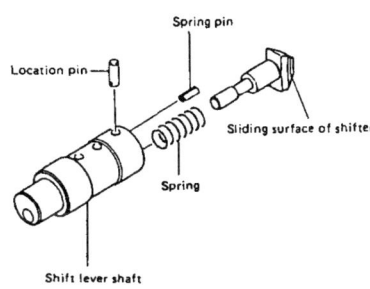

3-12-2 Shift lever shaft and location pin
(1) Check the shift lever shaft and location pin for damage or distortion, and replace defective parts. If the location pin must be replaced, replace it together with the shift lever shaft.
(2) Measure the diameter of the shift lever shaft and the shifter insertion hole. Replace the part if the size deviates from the standard value.

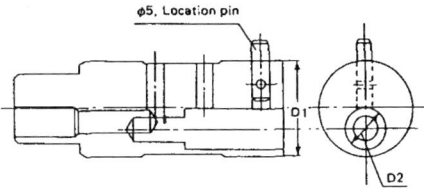

(1) Visually inspect the surface in contact with the drive cone, and replace the shifter when signs of overheating, damage or wear are found.
(2) Measure the shaft diameter of the shifter. Replace the shaft if the size deviates from the standard.

mm(in.)

	Standard	Limit
D 1	27.959~27.98 (1.1001~1.1016)	27.90 (1.0984)
D 2	12.0~12.018 (0.4724~0.4731)	12.05 (0.4744)
Side cover, Shift insert hole	28.0~28.021 (1.1024~1.1032)	28.08 (1.1055)

Printed in Japan
A0A1015-9110SP

Chapter 7 Reduction and Reversing Gear
3. Inspection and Servicing

3-12-3 Shifter spring
(1)Check the spring for scratches or corrosion.
(2)Measure the free length of the spring.

Shifter spring	Standard	Limt
Free length	22.6mm (0.890in.)	19.8mm(0.780in.)
Spring constant	0.854kg/mm(1.88lbs/0.04in.)	–
Length when attached	14.35mm (0.5650 in.)	–
Load when attached	7.046kg (15.54 lbs)	6.08kg (13.41lbs)

3-12-4 Stopper bolt
Check the stopper bolt. If it is worn or stepped, replace.

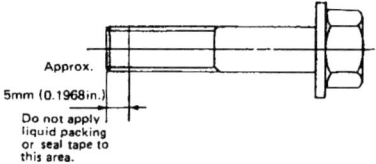

3-12-5 Side cover and oil seal
(1)Check the neutral, forward and reverse position grooves.
Replace if the grooves are worn.
(2)Measure the insertion hole of the shift lever s haft.
Replace if the size deviates from the standard value.
(3)Check the oil seal and the O-ring for damage.
Replace if the part is defective.

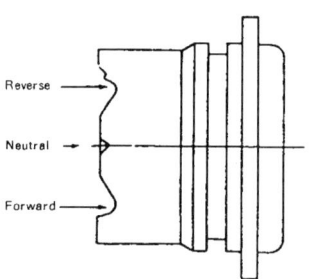

3-13 Damper disc

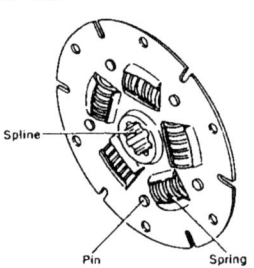

(1)Spline part.
Whenever uneven wear and/or scratches are found, replace with a new part.
(2)Spring.
Whenever uneven wear and/or scratches are found, replace with a new part.
(3)Pin wear
Whenever uneven wear and/or scratches are found, replace with a new part.
(4)Whenever a crack or damage to the spring slot is found replace the defective part with a new one.

3-14 Shim adjustment for output and input shafts
Check the thickness of shims for both input and output shafts. When the component parts are not replaced after dismantling, the same shims can be reused. When the clutch case and flange or any one of the following parts is replaced the thickness of the shim must be determined in the following manner.

For input shaft part: input shaft, bearing.
For output shaft parts: output shaft, thrust collar A, thrust collar B, gear, bearing.

Chapter 7 Reduction and Reversing Gear
3. Inspection and Servicing
3JH2 Series

(1) Shim thickness (T2, T3) measurement of output shaft
  (a) Measure the bearing insertion hole depth (A) of the mounting flange, and the bearing insertion hole depth (A') of the clutch case.
  (b) Measure the length (B) between the bearing outer race.

NOTE: Tighten the mounting flange nut of the output shaft assembly with the specified torque. Press-fit the inner race of the clutch case roller bearing to the large gear side.

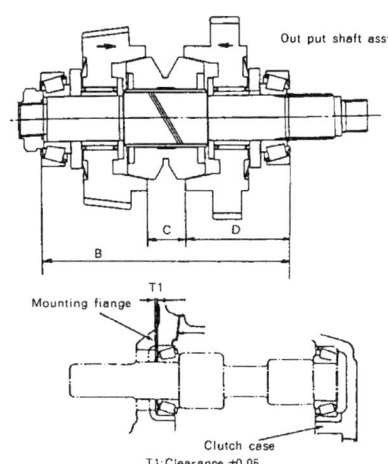

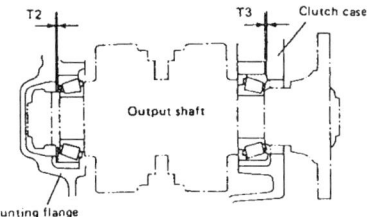

  (c) Measure lengths (D) and (C) from the outer race end of the clutch case bearing included in the output shaft assembly.

NOTE: Before measuring length (D) and (C), press the forward large gear and the reverse large gear to the drive cone until there is no clearance.

  (d) Obtain thicknesses (T_2) and (T_3) by the following formulas:

$T_2 = A + A' - B - T_3$ (T_2: Clearance $\pm^{0.1mm}_{0}$)

T_3(KM3A) $= A' - 50 - C/2 - D$ (Tolerance ± 0.05mm)

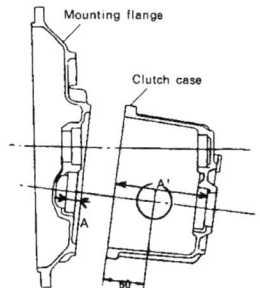

1. Assemble the outer bearing race without inserting shims into the clutch case body and flange, and then assemble only the input shaft.
(Caution): The outer bearing race should be inserted all the way to the bottom. Do not suspend it halfway.
2. Fasten the case body and the flange by tightening 2 bolts diagonally.
3. Fasten the dial gauge to the flange and fit the needle to the end face of the input shaft.
4. Move the input shaft up and down manually and read the dial gauge figure to decide the shim thickness.
(Note): The bearing installation hole does not make a right angle to the joint face of the case and flange. Accordingly, precise measurement at the service site is not possible.

Printed in Japan
A0A1015-9110SP

Chapter 7 Reduction and Reversing Gear
3. Inspection and Servicing

(3) Standard size of parts

mm(in.)

	A+A'	B	C	D	Drive cone neutral center position
KM3P2	138.40~138.75 (5.4488~5.4626)	136.56~138.10 (5.3794~5.4370)	20.50~21.10 (0.8071~0.8307)	57.83~58.65 (2.2768~2.3091)	50 (1.9685)

NOTE: Compare your measurements with the above standard size. If your measurements differ largely from the standard sizes, measurements may not be correct. Check and measure again.

(4) Adjusting shim set

	Part No.	Tickness.mm(in.)	No.of shims
Input and Output shaft	177088-02300	1.0(0.0394)	1
		0.5(0.0197)	1
		0.3(0.0118)	2
		0.1(0.0039)	3

13-13. Torque limiter

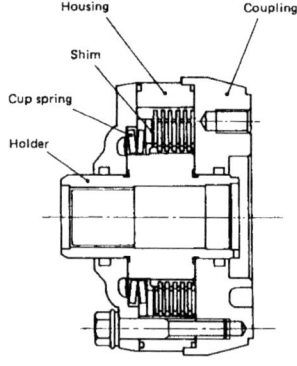
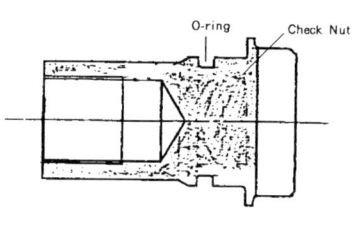

The torque limiter assembly includes these parts. The conversion to the torque limiter specification is easy by exchanging the standard shaft coupling. (Use the check nut, not the end nut, to install the torque limiter.)

4. Disassembly

4-1. Dismantling the clutch
(1) Remove the remote control cable.
(2) Remove the clutch assembly from the engine mounting flange.

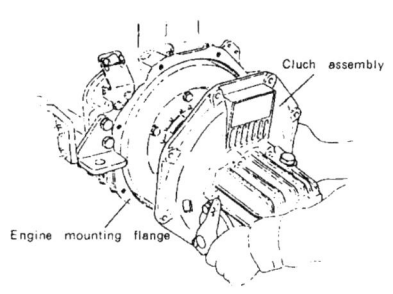

(3) Drain the lubricating oil.
   Drain the lubricating oil by loosening the plug at the bottom of the clutch case.

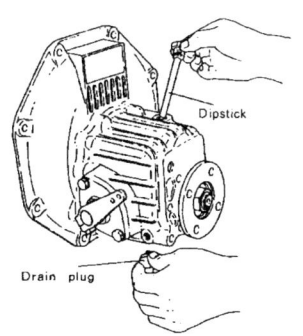

(4) Remove the end nut and output shaft coupling.

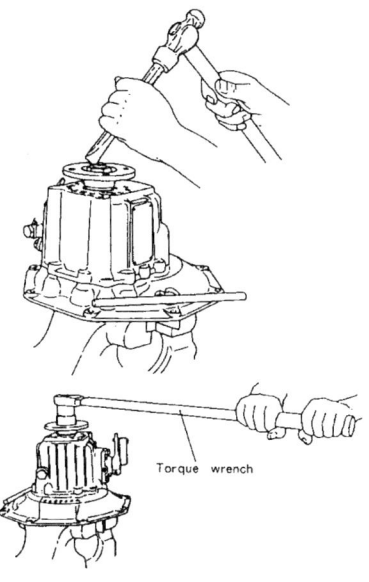

NOTE: Take care as it has a left-handed thread.

(5) Remove the oil dip stick and O-ring.
(6) Remove the fixing bolts on the side cover, and also remove the shift lever shaft, shift lever and shifter.

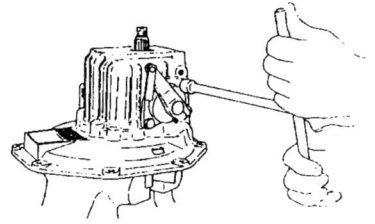

Chapter 7 Reduction and Reversing Gear
4. Disassembly

3JH2 Series

(7) Remove the bolts which secure the mounting flange to the case body, give light taps to the left and right with a plastic headed hammer while supporting the clutch case with your hand, then remove the mounting flange.

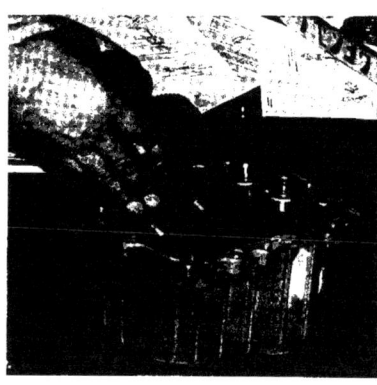

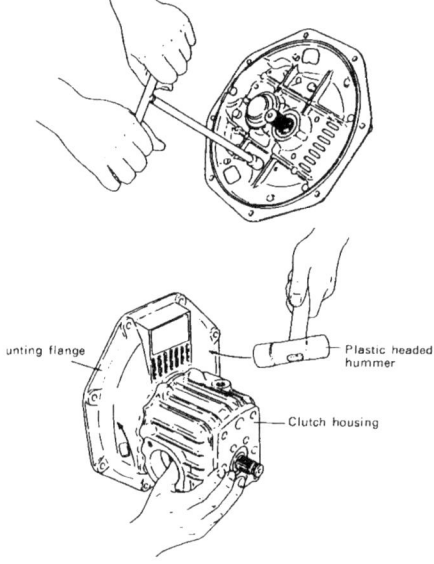

(9) Take out the intermediate shaft and input shaft and intermediate shaft.

(8) Withdraw the output shaft assembly.

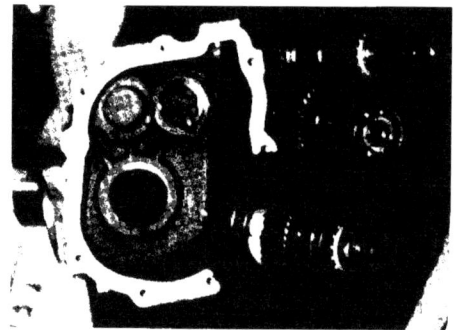

Printed in Japan
A0A1015-9110SP

Chapter 7 Reduction and Reversing Gear
4. Disassembly
3JH2 Series

(10) Remove the oil seal of the output shaft from the case body.

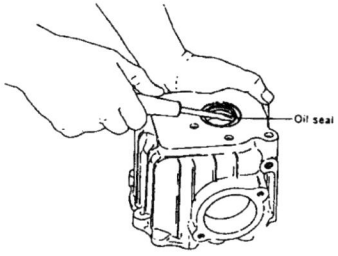

(11) Remove the outer bearing race from the case body by using the special tool.

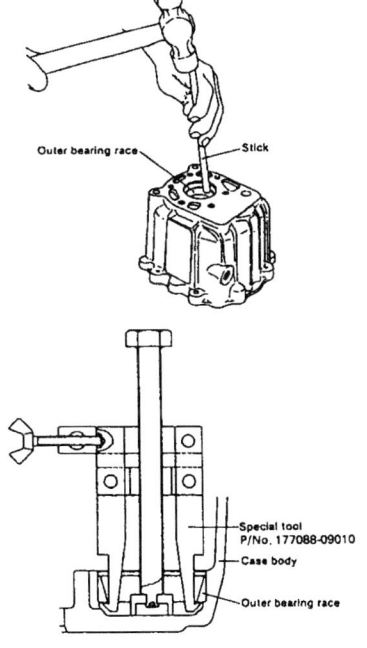

(12) Remove the oil seal of the input shaft from the mounting flange.
(13) Remove the outer bearing race from the mounting flange in the same way as with the case body.
(14) Remove each adjusting plate from the input our output shaft.

NOTE: The same adjusting plates can be reused when the following parts are not replaced. When any part is replaced however, readjustment is necessary.

4-2 Removal of the output shaft

(1) Take out the reverse large gear, thrust collar A, cup spring and inner bearing race.
The reverse large gear must be withdrawn using a pulley extracter, by fixing the nut at the forward end in a vice.

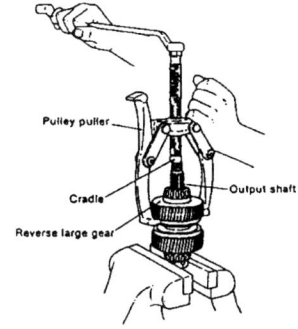

(2) Loosen the calking of the forward nut and remove the nut.
Remove the nut by using a torque wrench after setting the output shaft coupling and fixing the coupling bolt in a vice.

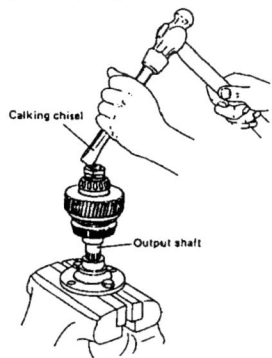

Printed in Japan
A0A1015-9110SP

Chapter 7 Reduction and Reversing Gear
4. Disassembly

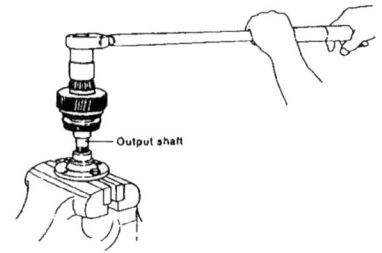

(4) While gripping the drive cone, tap the end of the shaft with a plastic headed hammer, and withdraw the thrust extractor may be used.

(3) Place the pulley extractor against the end surface of the forward large gear, and withdraw the forward large gear, thrust collar A, cup spring, and inner bearing race.

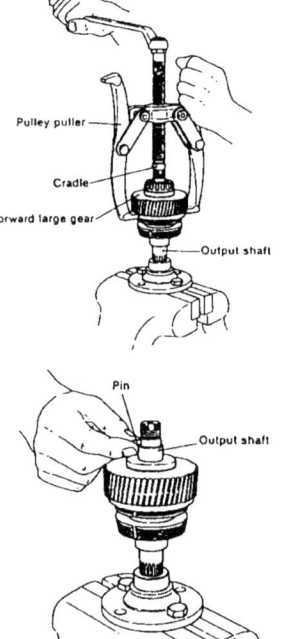

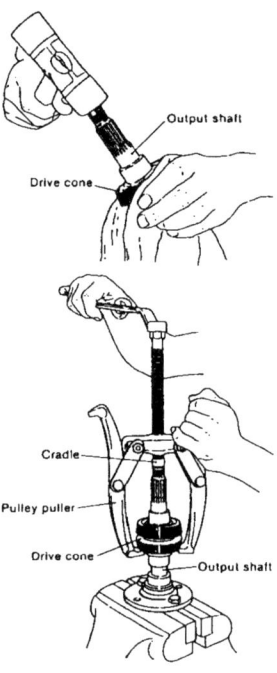

NOTE: Take care as the nut has left-handed thread.

Chapter 7 Reduction and Reversing Gear
4. Disassembly   *3JH2 Series*

4-3 Removal of the intermediate shaft.
(1)Remove the ball bearing using a pulley.

(2)Remove the ball bearing opposite narrow end using screw driver.

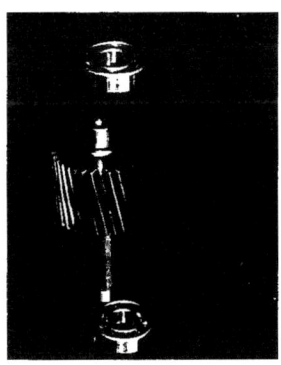

4-4 Dismantling the shifting device
(1)Take out the shifter and shifter spring.

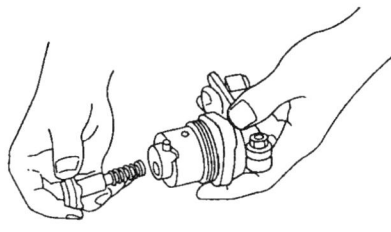

(2)Remove the stopper bolt of the shifter and shim.

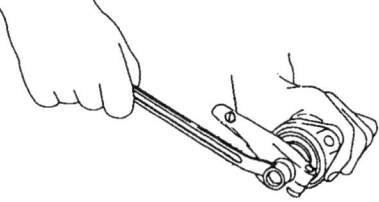

(3)Loosen the bolt of the shift lever and remove the shift lever from the shift lever shaft.

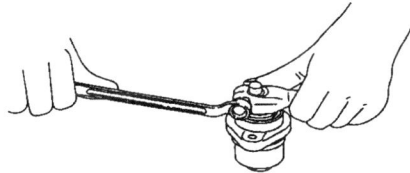

(4)Remove the shift lever to the anti-shif lever side.

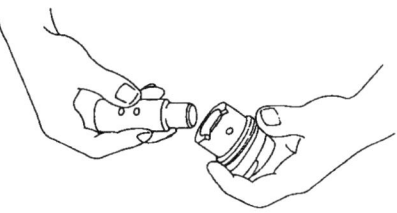

(5)Remove the oil-seal and O-ring.

7-24

Printed in Japan
A0A1015-9110SP

5. Reassembly

5-1 Reassembly of output shaft
(1) Fit the forward side thrust collar B onto the shaft.
(2) Drive in the forward end inner needle bearing race using a jig.

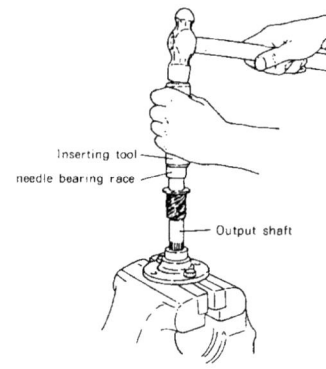

(3) Assemble the needle bearing and forward large gear.
NOTE: Check that the forward large gear rotates smoothly.
(4) Fit the cup spring, Pin and thrust collar A, and dive in the inner bearing race using a jig.

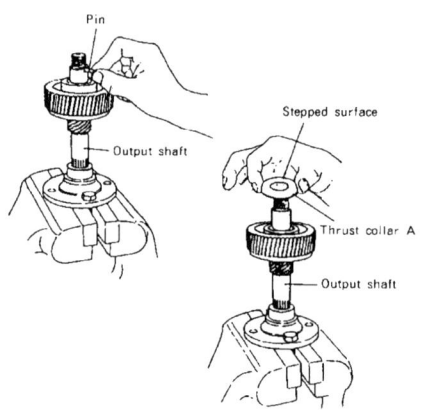

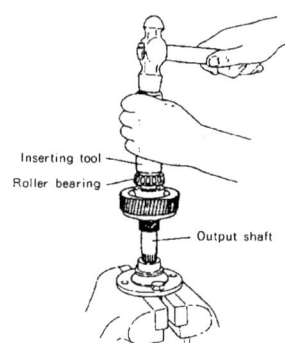

NOTE: 1) Drive in with a plastic headed hammer. Do not hit it hard.
2) When fitting the thrust collar A, note the fitting direction. Fit it keeping the stepped surface toward the roller bearing side.
3) Note that the pin cannot be fitted after the inner bearing race has been driven in.
4) Check that the forward large gear rotates smoothly.

(5) Set and tighten the forward end nut. Insert the bolt into the coupling, and fix it in a vice, keeping the spline part upward.
Insert the shaft into the spline of the coupling, fit the spacer, and tighten the nut with a torque wrench.

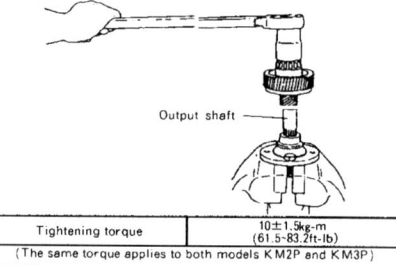

Tightening torque	10±1.5kg-m (61.5-83.2ft-lb)

(The same torque applies to both models KM2P and KM3P)

NOTE: 1) Take care as it is a left-handed thread.
2) Use the reverse side nut used before dismantling at the forward eng. This is to provide effective calking to the nut by changing the calking position.

Chapter 7 Reduction and Reversing Gear
5. Reassembly

5-2 Reassembly of the clutch
(1) Fit the oil seal, bearing outer races and shim (output shaft side) in the clutch case.
(2) Insert the input shaft into the clutch case.
(3) Drive the intermediate shaft into the clutch case.

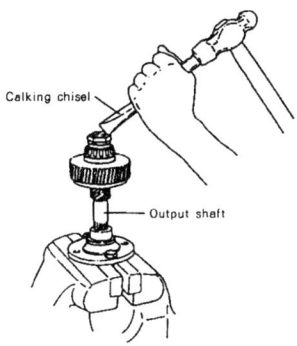

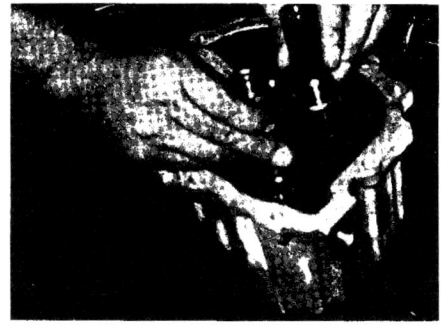

(6) Insert the drive cone while keeping the output shaft set for reverse.

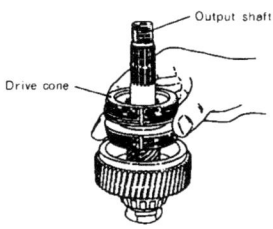

(4) Insert the output shaft into the clutch case.

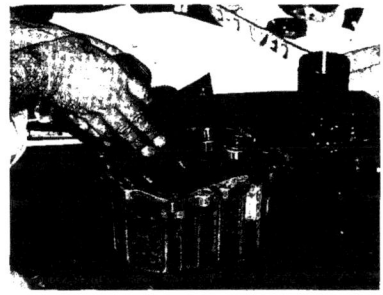

(7) Apply procedures 1 through 4 to the forward end.

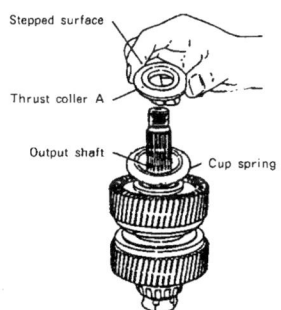

NOTE: 1) Fit thrust collar A so that the stepped surface faces the roller bearing side.
2) Check that the reverse large gear rotates smoothly.

Chapter 7 Reduction and Reversing Gear
5. Reassembly

3JH2 Series

(5) Fit the adjusting plate to the mounting flange, and drive in the outer bearing race.
   NOTE: *The outer bearing race can be easily driven in by heating the mounting flange to about 100°C, or by cooling the outer race with liquid hydrogen.*
(6) Apply non-drying liquid packing around the outer surface of the oil seal, and insert the oil seal into the mounting flange while keeping the spring part of the oil seal facing the inside of the case.
(7) Apply non-drying liquid packing to the matching surfaces of the mounting flange end the case body.

(8) Insert the input shaft and output shaft into the shaft holes of the mounting flange, assemble the mounting flange on the case body, and tighten the bolt.

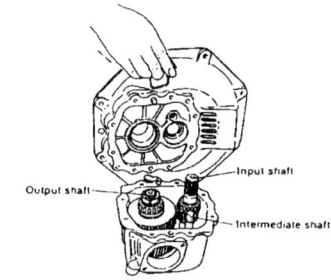

NOTE: *Apply non-drying liquid packing to either the mounting flange or the case body.*

(9) Assemble the output shaft coupling on the output shaft, and fit the O-ring.
(10) Tighten the end nut by using a torque wrench, then calk it.

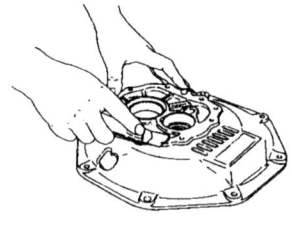

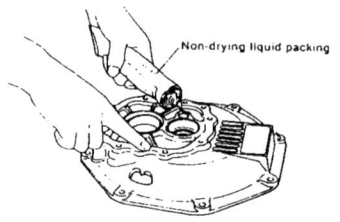

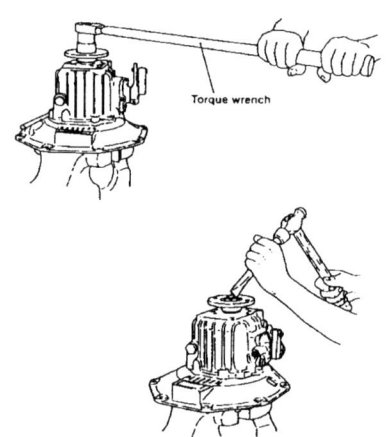

NOTE: *Take care as it is a left-handed thread.*

Tightening torque	10±1.5kg-m (61.5~83.2ft-lb)

(The same torque applies to both models KM2P and KM3P)

Chapter 7 Reduction and Reversing Gear
5. Reassembly
3JH2 Series

5-3 Reassembly of the shifting device
(1) Fit the oil seal and O-ring to the side cover.

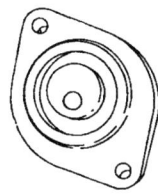

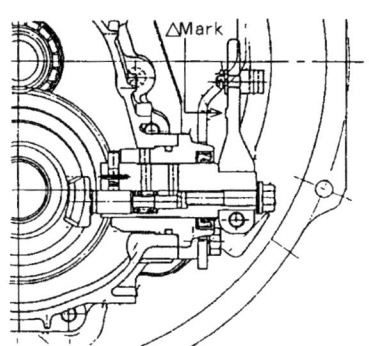

(2) Insert the shift lever shaft to the side cover.

(4) Insert the shifter spring and shifter to the shift lever shaft.
(5) Fit the side cover assembly to the clutch case.

NOTE: 1) Check the direction of the shifter (Top and bottom side).
2) The shift lever may not turn smoothly if the clutch case is not filled with lubricating oil.

(6) Fit the shim and stopper bolt to the shift lever shaft.
NOTE: Apply non-drying liquid packing or seal-tape to the thread of the stopper bolt.

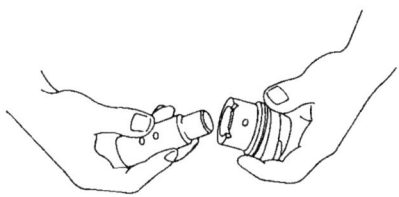

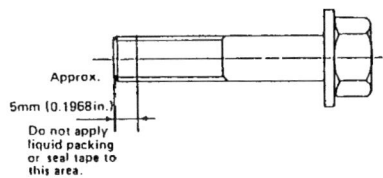

(3) Fit the shift lever to the shift lever shaft.
NOTE: Check the direction of the shift lever △ mark.

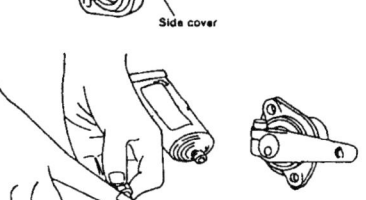

(7) Fit the pivot to the shift lever.

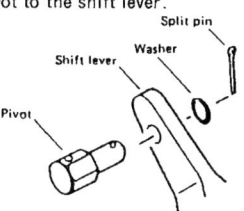

Chapter 7 Reduction and Reversing Gear
1. Construction

3JH2 series

Marine Gear Models
KM3P1, KM3P3, KM35P1
for Engine Models 3JH25A/3JH30A

1. Construction

1-1. Construction

These clutches are a cone-type, mechanically operated clutch.

When the drive cone (which is connected to the output shaft by the lead spline) is moved forward or backward, its taper contacts with the large gear and transfers power to the output shaft.

The construction is simple when compared with other-types of clutch and if serves to reduce the number of components, making for a lighter, more compact unit which can be operated smoothly. Although it is small, the power transmission efficiency is high even under a heavy load. Its durability is high and it is also reliable because high grade materials are used for the shaft and gear, and. a taper roller bearing is incorporated.

Power transmission is smooth because connection

with the engine is made through the damper disc

- The drive cone is made from special aluminum bronze, which has both higher wear-resistance and durability.
  The drive cone is connected with the output shaft through the thread spline. The taper angle, diameter of the drive cone, twist angle, and diameter of the thread spline, are designed to give the greatest efficiency, thus ensuring that the drive cone can be readily engaged or disengaged.
- Helical gears are used for greater strength.
  The intermediate shaft is supported at 2 points to reduce deflection and gear noise.
- The clutch ease and mounting flange are made from an aluminum alloy of special composition to reduce weight.

It is also anticorrosive against seawater.
- As the damper disc is fitted to the input shaft, power can be transmitted smoothly.
- There is small clearance between the dipstick and the inside of the dipstick tube. A small hole in the dipstick works as a breather.
- when the load on the propeller is removed, the engagement of the drive cone and the large gear is maintained by the shifter and V-groove of the drive cone.
  Even when the drive cone's tapered area and V-groove are worn, this engagement is maintained by the shift lever device and accordingly no adjustment of the remote control cable is required.
- The cup spring on the rear of the larger gear absorbs rotational fluctuations and stabilizes the engagement of the drive cone and the larger gear.
  Thus, the durability of the cone against wear is enhanced.

NOTE:

KM3P3 marine gear differs from KM3P1 as follows.
- *Torque !imiter applied to KM3P3.*

KM35P1 marlne gear differs from KM3P1 as follows.
- *Output shaft dia. 28mm. (KM3P1 : 25mm).*
- *Drive corn the same as the one for KM4A marine gear.*
- *Marine gear oil reserve capacity up.*
  0.5L (0.35L KM3P1)

Chapter 7 Reduction and Reversing Gear
1. Construction _____ *3JH2 series*

1.2 Specifications

Mode			KM3P1	KM3P3	KM35P1	
For engine models			3JH25A		3JH30A	
Clutch			Constant mesh gear with servo cone clutch (wet type)			
Reduction ratio	Forward		2.36	2.61	2.36	2.61
	Reverse		3.16	3.16	3.16	3.16
Propeller shaft mirr1 (Forward)		(min^{-1})	1356	1226	1229	1111
Direction of rotation	Input shaft		Counter-clockwise, viewed from stern			
	Forward		Clockwise, viewed from stern			
	Output shaft Reverse		Counter-clockwise, viewed from stern			
Remote control	Control head		Single lever control			
	Cable		Morse. 33-C (cable travel 76.2mm)			
	Clamp		YANMAR made. standard accessory			
	Cable connector		YANMAR made, standard accessory			
Output shaft coupling	Outer diameter	(mm)	100			
	Pitch circle diameter	(mm)	78			
	Connecting bolt holes	(mm)	4-1 0.5			
Position of shift lever			Right side, viewed from stern			
Lubricating oil			API CC SAE 20/30			
Lubricating oil capscity		(ℓ)	0.35		0.5	
Dry mass		(kg)	12	15	12	

Note:
Torque limiter should be installed on KM3P3
No torque limiter installed on KM3P1 & KM35P1

Reduction ratio	No. of blade	Diameter of the propeller (mm)	Moment of inertia N-m^2 (kg-m^2=GD^2)	Material
2.36	3	450	1.49 (0.15)	Bronze
	4	425		
2.61	3	470	1.86 (0.19)	
	4	440		
	4	460		

Chapter 7 Reduction and Reversing Gear
1. Construction

3JH2 series

1-3 Power transmission system
1-3.1 Arrangement of shafts and gears

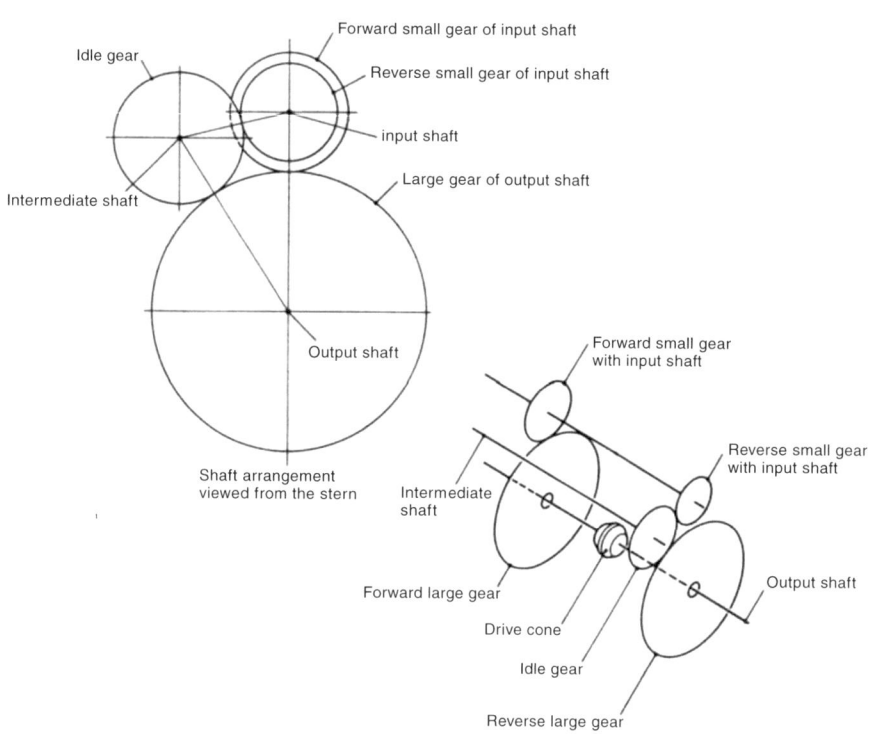

1-3.2 Reduction ratio
Forward

Model	No. of teeth of forward small gear Zif	No. of teeth of forward 18rge gear Zof	Reduction retio Zof/Zif
KM3P1, KM3P3, KM35P1	25	59	59/25 = 2.36
	23	60	60/23 = 2.61

Reverse

Model	No. of teeth of reverse small gesr Zif	No. of teeth of intemediate shaft gear Zi	No. of teeth of reverse large gear Zdr	Reduction ratio Zi/Zir · Zdr/Zi
KM3P1 KM3P3 KM35P1	19	26	60	60/19 = 3.16

Printed in Japan
A0A1015-0302

7-31

Chapter 7 Reduction and Reversing Gear
1. Construction
3JH2 series

1-3-3 Power transmission routine-Forward

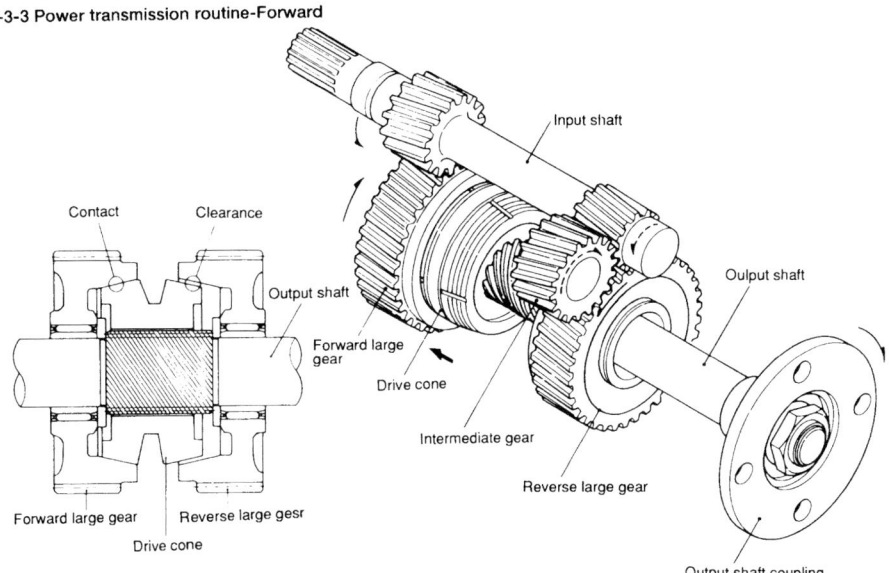

1-3-4 Power transmission routine-Reverse

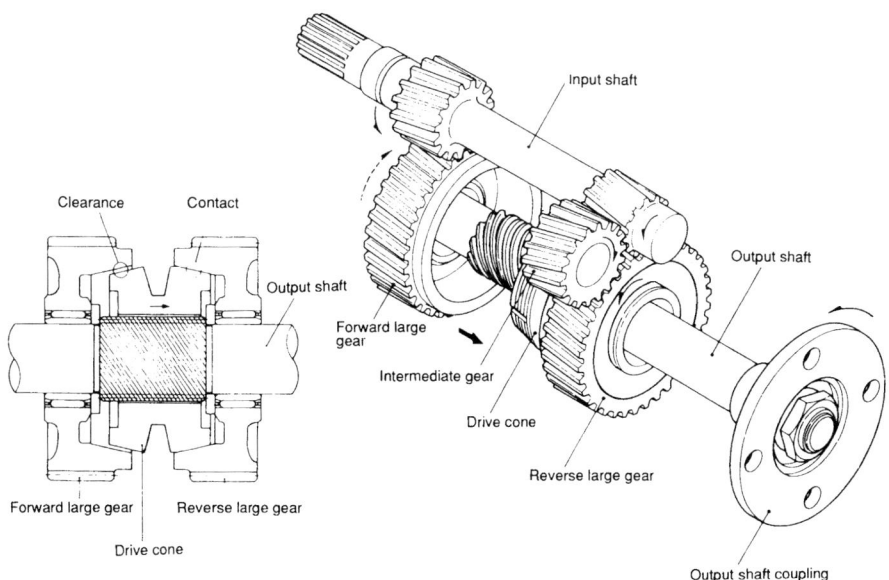

7-32

Printed in Japan
A0A1015-0302

Chapter 7 Reduction and Reversing Gear
1. Construction

3JH2 series

1-4 Drawing

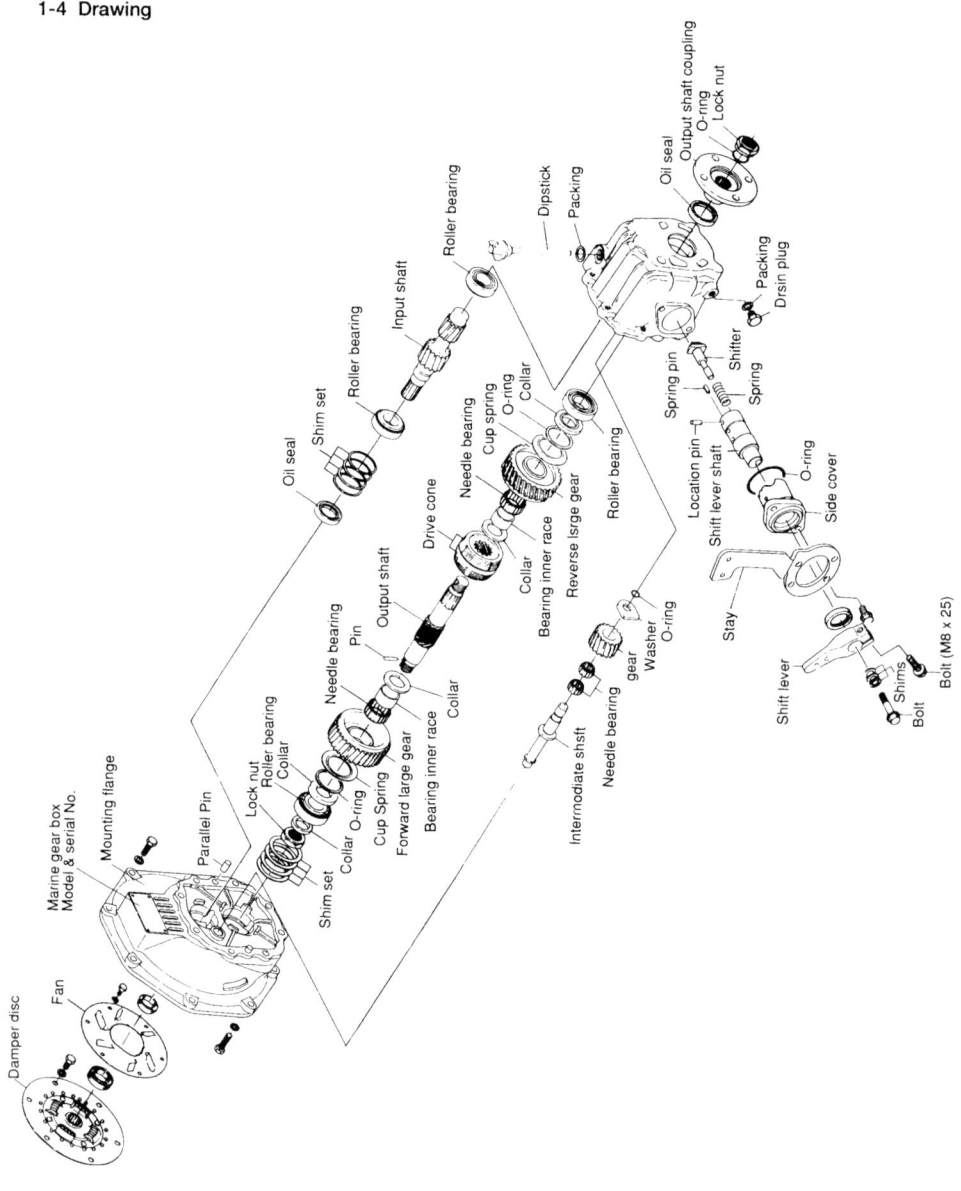

Chapter 7 Reduction and Reversing Gear
1. Construction _____*3JH2 series*

1-5 Sectional view

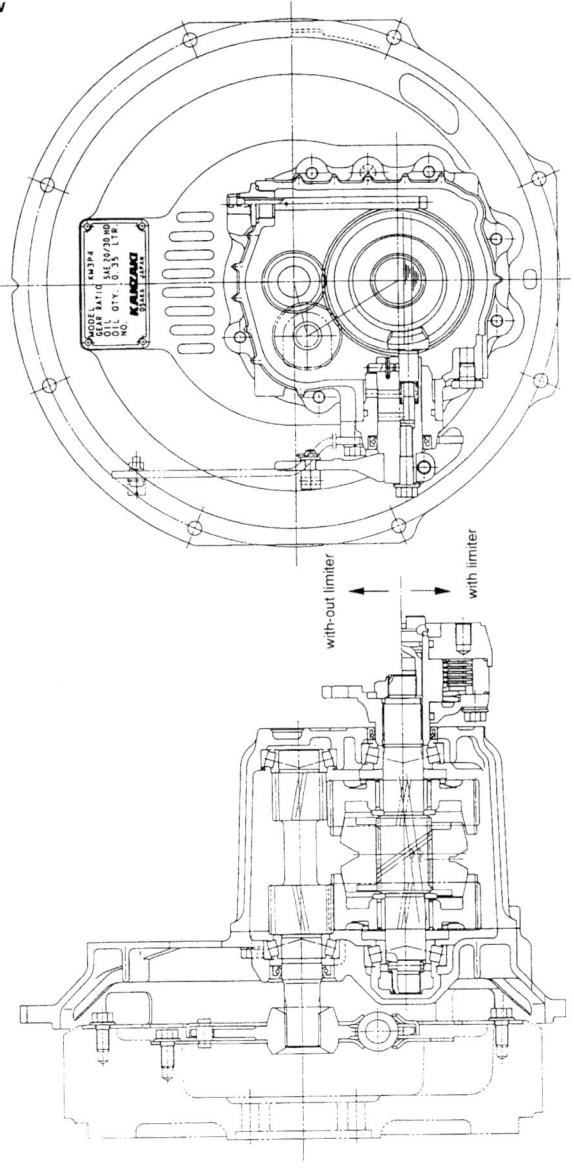

Chapter 7 Reduction and Reversing Gear
2. Shifting Device

2. Shifting Device

2-1 Construction of shifting mechanism

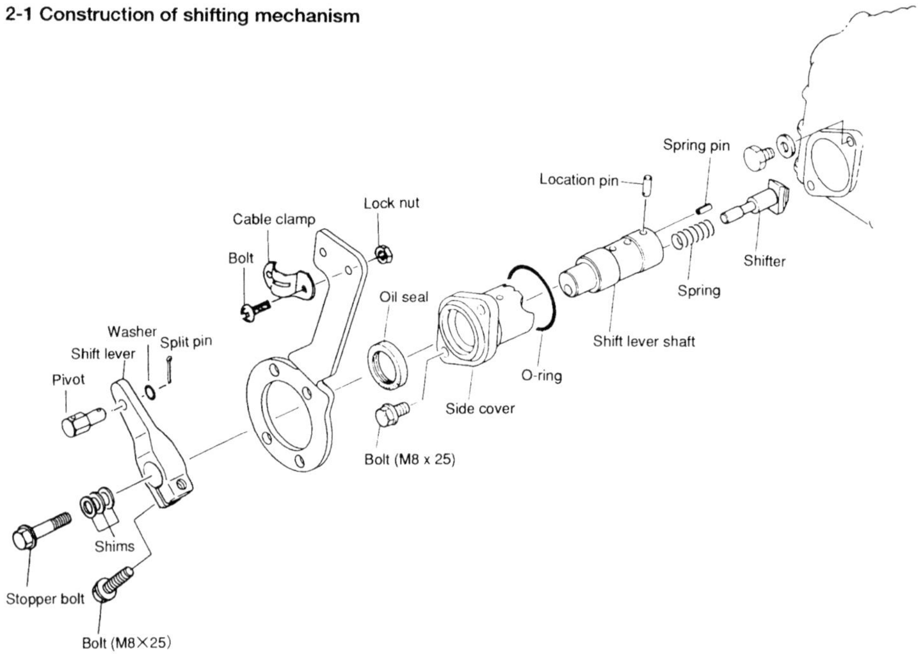

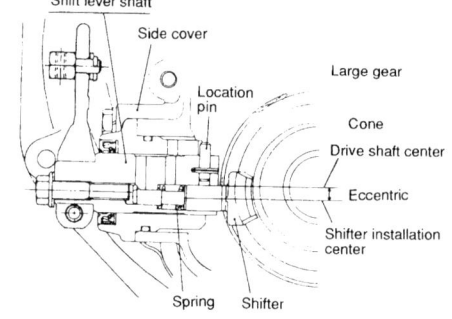

The shift lever shaft is installed on the side cover with neutral, forward and reverse positions provided on this cover. The neutral, forward and reverse location pins of the shift lever shaft are constantly inserted into their respective grooves on the shift lever by the tension of the shifter spring. The shifter is set on the eccentric hole of the shift lever shaft and moves the drive cone in the neutral position either to the forward or reverse positions, and then back to the neutral positions. (The shift lever shaft moves slightly to the shift lever or drive cone side when the shift lever is placed in the forward on reverse positions.)

Chapter 7 Reduction and Reversing Gear
2. Shifting Device

3JH2 series

2-2 Forward and reverse clutch operation
(Neutral ⇒ Forward; Neutral ⇒ Reverse)

When the shift lever is moved to the forward position from the neutral position, the shift lever shaft starts to revolve, and the location pin disengages from the neutral V-groove position of the side cover. (Shift lever moves approx. 0.5mm to the drive cone side.) At this time the shifter, which is set on the eccentric hole of the shift lever shaft, moves the drive cone's V-groove to the forward large gear.

When the location pin of the shift lever shaft falls in the forward position groove of the side cover, (the shift lever shaft moves to the shift lever side approx. 3mm), and the shifter stars to press the drive cone V-groove to the forward large gear side through the spring force.

2-3 Engagement and disengagement of clutch
(Forward ⇒ Neutral; Reverse ⇒ Neutral)

When the shift lever is moved to the forward position from the neutral position, the shift lever shaft starts to revolve, and the location pin disengages from the forward position groove of the side cover. (The shift lever shaft moves approx. 3mm to the drive cone side.) At this time, the shifter which is set on the eccentric hole of the shift lever shaft is moved to the neutral side (reverse large gear side). The drive cone, however, is engaged with the forward large gear through the torque force produced by the revolving centrifugal force.

Further, when the shift lever shaft starts to revolve, and the positioning pin falls in to the neutral V-groove position of the side cover (the shift lever shaft travels approx. 5mm to the shift lever side), the shifter moves to the shift lever side(to the spring side) while moving the V-groove of the drive cone to the reverse large gear side. The movement of the shifter to the shift lever side, however, is stopped when the shifter end contacts the stopper bolt. The shifter only works to press the V-groove of the drive cone to the reverse large gear side. Thus, the drive cone is disengaged from the forward large gear. After this disengagement, the transmission torque of the drive cone is decreased to zero and the shift lever is returned to the neutral position by the spring force.

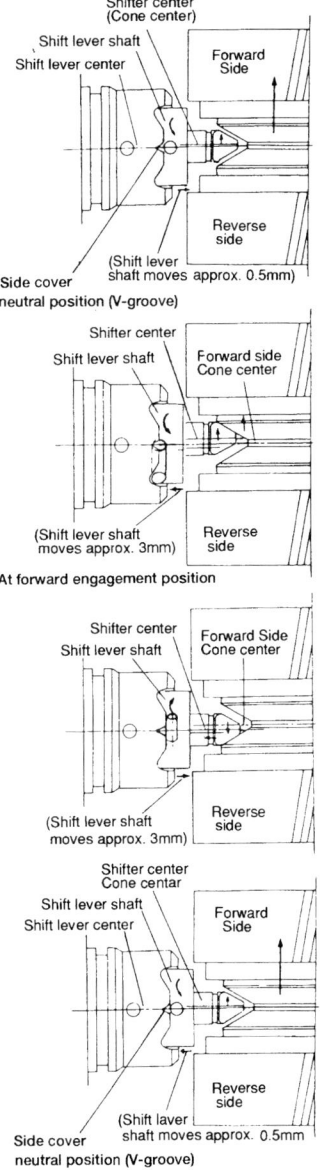

At forward engagement position

7-36

Printed in Japan
_A0A1015-0302_

Chapter 7 Reduction and Reversing Gear
2. Shifting Device

3JH2 series

2-4 Clutch shifting force

Shifting position / shifting direction	Shift lever position at 56mm	Remote control handle postition at 170mm (Cable length, 4m)
Engaging force at 1000rpm	3~4 kg	4~5 kg
Disengaging force at 1000rpm	3.5~5 kg	4~6 kg

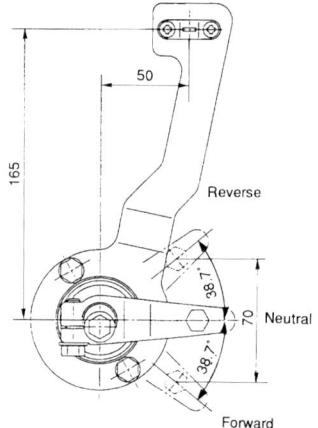

2-5 Adjustment of shifting device
Whenever the side cover, shift lever shaft, shifter, stopper bolt or drive cone is replaced, be sure to adjust the clearance between the shifter end and the stopper bolt by using shims. When the adjustment of this clearance is not proper the drive cone may be properly fitted When the shift lever is moved to the neutral position either from the forward or reverse position.

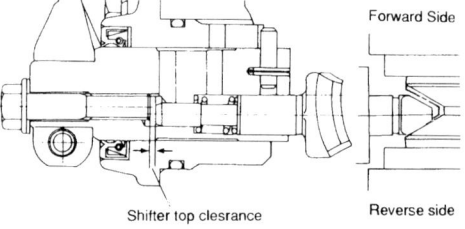

Shifter top clesrance

Chapter 7 Reduction and Reversing Gear
2. Shifting Device

3JH2 series

2-5-1 Measurement and adjustment of clearance

(a) Assemble the shifting mechanism (without installing the stopper bolt of the shifter) to the marine gear case.

NOTE : Ensure the correct direction of the shifter before assembly.

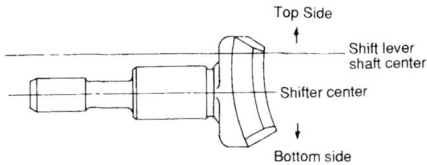

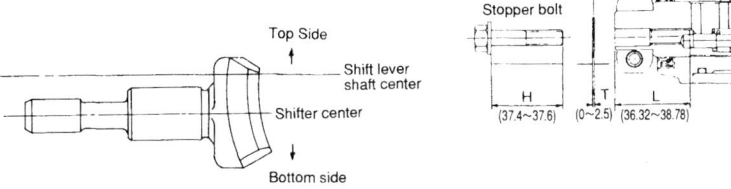

(b) Turn the shift lever 10~15 degree either to the forward or reverse position from the neutral position.
(c) Measure the L-distance between the shift lever shaft end surface and the shifter's end.
(d) Measure the H-distance (the distance from the neck of the stopper bolt to its end).

(e) Obtain the shim thickness T" by the following formula.

$$T = (H - L + 1.25) \pm 0.1 mm$$

NOTE : Shim set includes one piece each of 1mm, 0.4mm, 0.3mm, 0.25mm shims.
(YANMAR Part No. 177088-06380)

(f) Insert shim (s) of proper thickness to the stopper bolt side and tighten to the shift lever shaft.
NOTE : When tightening the stopper bolt, apply either a non-drying type liquid packing (TREE BOND No.1215), or a seal tape around the bolt threads .

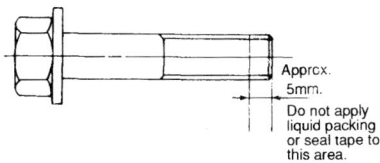

2-5-2 Inspect for the following points (to be inspected every 2-3 months)
(1) Looseness at the connection of the cable connector and the remote control cable.
(2) Looseness of the attaching nut of the cable connector and the shift lever.

7-38

Printed in Japan
A0A1015-0302

Chapter 7 Reduction and Reversing Gear
2. Shifting Device

_____ 3JH2 series

2-6 Adjustment of the remote control head
Marine gear box control side
(1) Equal distribution of the control lever stroke.

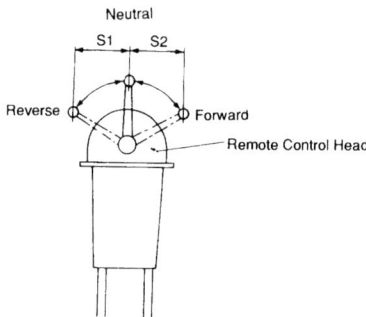

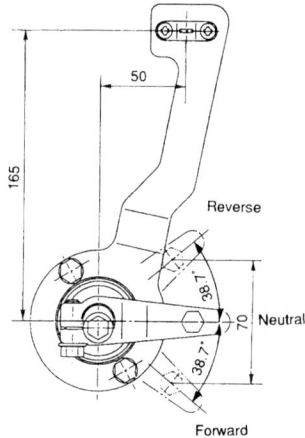

The stroke between the neutral position → forward position (S2), and the neutral position → reverse position (S1) must be equalized.
When either stroke is too short, clutch engagement becomes faulty.

(2) Equalizing the travel distance of the control cable.
After ensuring the equal distribution of the stroke described in (1), connect the cable to the control head. Adjust that the cable shift travel of the S_1 and S_2 control lever strokes becomes identical.

2-7 Cautions
(1) Always stop the engine when attaching, adjusting, and inspecting.
(2) When conducting inspection immediately after stopping the engine, do not touch the clutch.
The oil temperature is often raised to around 90°C (194°F).
(3) Half-clutch operation is not possible with this design and construction. Do not use with the shift lever halfway to the engaged position.

NOTE : *The dual (Two) lever remote control device cannot be usded.*

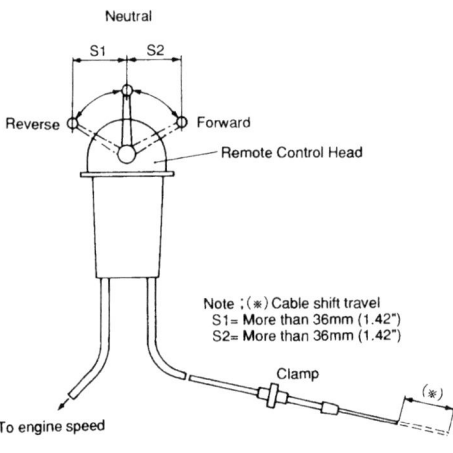

Printed in Japan
A0A1015-0302

3. Inspection and Servicing

3-1 Clutch case
(1) Check the clutch case with a test hammer for cracking.
Perform a color check when required.
If the case is cracked, replace it.
(2) Check for staining on the inside surface of the bearing section.
Also, measure the inside diameter of the case.
Replace the case if it is worn beyond the wear limit.

3-2 Bearing
(1) Rusting and damage.
If the bearing is rusted or the taper roller retainer is damages, replace the bearing.
(2) Make sure that the bearings rotates smoothly.
If rotation is not smooth, if there is any binding, or if any abnormal sound is evident, replace the baring.

3-3 Gear
Check the surface, tooth face conditions and backlash of each gear. Replace any defective part.
(1) Tooth surface wear.
Check the tooth surface for pitting, abnormal wear, dents, and cracks. Repair the lightly damaged gears and replace heavily damaged gears.
(2) Tooth surface contact.
Check the tooth surface contact. The amount of tooth surface contact between the tooth crest and tooth flank must be at least 70% of the tooth width.
(3) Backlash.
Measure the backlash of each gear, and replace the gear when it is worn beyond the wear limit.   mm

	Maintenance standard	Wear limit
Input shaft forward gear and output shaft forward large gear	0.06~0.12	0.2
Input shaft reverse gear and intermediate gear	0.06~0.12	0.2
Intermediate gear and output shaft reverse large gear	0.06~0.12	0.2

3-4 Forward and reverse large gears
(1) Contact surface with drive cone.
Visually inspect the tapered surface of the forward and reverse large gears where they make contact with the drive cone to check if any abnormal condition or sign of overheating exists.
If any defect is found, replace the gear.

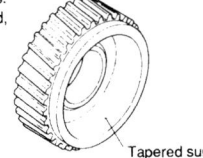
Tapered surface

(2) Forward/reverse large gear needle bearing.
When an abnormal sound is produced at the needle bearing, visually inspect the rollers; replace the bearing if the rollers are faulty.

Rollers

3-5 Drive cone
(1) Visually inspect that part of the surface that comes into contact with the circumferential triangular slot to check for signs of scoring, overheating or wear. If deep scoring or signs of overheating are found, replace the cone.

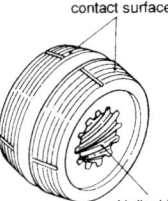
contact surface
Helical involute spline

(2) Check the helical involute spline for any abnormal condition on the tooth surface, and repair or replace the part should any defect be found.
(3) Measure the amount of wear on the tapered contact surface of the drive cone, and replace the cone when the wear exceeds the specified limit.

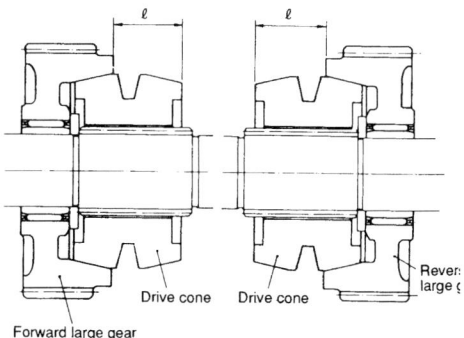
Drive cone   Drive cone
Forward large gear   Reverse large g

Chapter 7 Reduction and Reversing Gear
3. Inspection and Servicing

3JH2 series

mm

Dimensions		Standard dimensions	Limited dimensions
Dimensions	KM3P1 KM3P3	32.7-33.3	32.4
	KM35P1	29.25-29.75	28.1

NOTE : When dismantled, the forward of reverse direction of the drive cone must be clearly identified.

(4) If the wear of the V-groove of the drive cone is excessive, replace the part.

NOTE : When replacing the drive cone, the new cone and forward large gear and reverse large gear must be lapped prior to assembly.
The lapping procedure is described below.

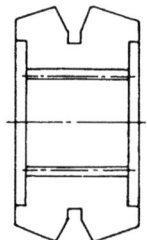

3-5-1 Lapping Procedure for Drive Cone

(1) Coat the lapping powder onto the cave of the clutch gear (Lapping powder : 67 micron silicon carbide #280)

(2) Set the large gear on the output shaft with a needle bearing and then set the drive cone on the output shaft.

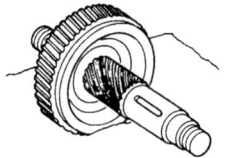

(3) Lap the large gear's cave and drive cone, pushing them together by hand.

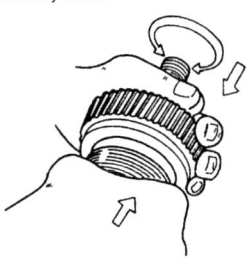

(4) Push and turn the large gear about 5 times both clockwise and counter-clockwise.

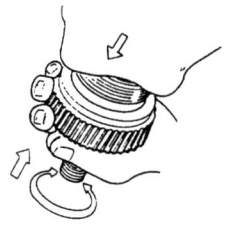

(5) After lapping them, wash them with washing oil. The lapped parts should be cleaned completely.

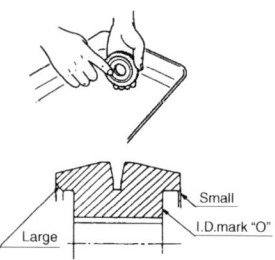

NOTE :
- Do not mix the combination of the lapped parts. The washing oil should be changed frequently in order to prevent residual powder being left on the parts.
  When assembling the drive cone, be sure to check its alignment. The larger chamfering face should be on the forward large gear side.

Chapter 7 Reduction and Reversing Gear
3. Inspection and Servicing _____ *3JH2 series*

3-6 Thrust collar

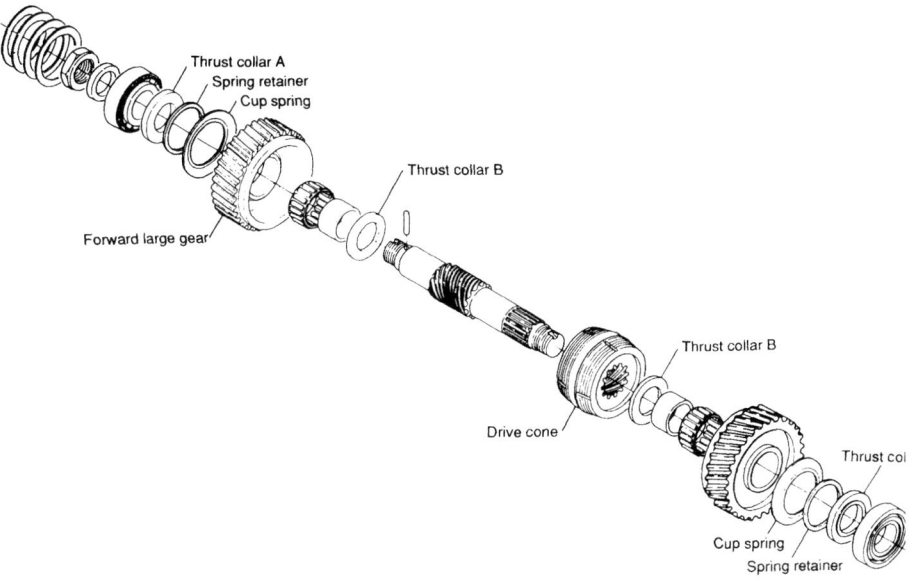

Chapter 7 Reduction and Reversing Gear
3. Inspection and Servicing

3JH2 series

(1) Visually inspect the sliding surface of thrust collar A or B to check for signs of overheating, scoring, or cracks.
Replace the collar if any abnormal condition is found.

(2) Measure the thickness of thrust collar A or B, and replace it when the dimension exceeds the specified limit.

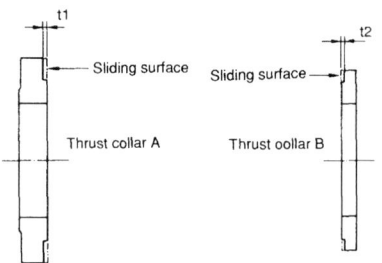

Stepped wear	Limit for use
Thrust collar A, t1	0.05
Thrust collar B, t2	0.20

mm

3-7 Cup spring and spring retainer

(1) Check for cracks and damage to the cup spring and spring retainer.
Replace the part if defective.

(2) Measure the free length of the cup spring and the thickness of the spring retainer. If the length or the thickness deviates from the standard size, replace the part.

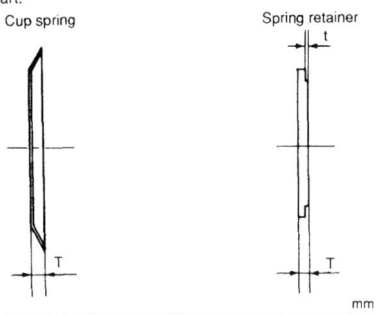

	Standard	Limit
Cup spring.T	2.8~3.1	2.6
Spring retainer,T	2.92~3.08	2.8
Spring retainer,t	—	0.1

mm

3-8 Oil seal of output shaft

Visually inspect the oil seal of the output shaft to check if there is any damage or oil leakage; replace the seal when any abnormal condition is found.

3-9 Input shaft

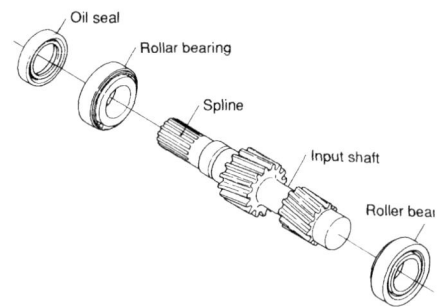

(1) Spline part
Whenever uneven wear and/or scratches are found, replace with a new part.

(2) Surface of oil seal.
If the sealing surface of the oil seal is worn or scratched, replace.

3-10 Output shaft

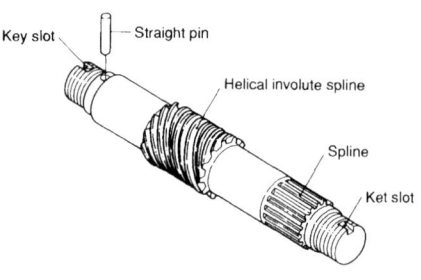

(1) Visually inspect the spline and the helical involute spline, and repair or replace a part when any abnormal condition is found on its surface.

Chapter 7 Reduction and Reversing Gear
3. Inspection and Servicing
3JH2 series

3-11 Intermediate shaft

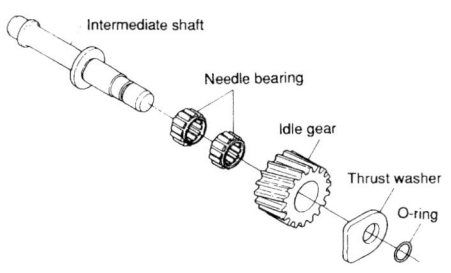

(1) Needle bearing dimensions, staining.
Check the surface of the roller to see whether the needle bearing sticks or is damaged. Replace if necessary.

3-12 Shifting device
3-12-1 Shifter

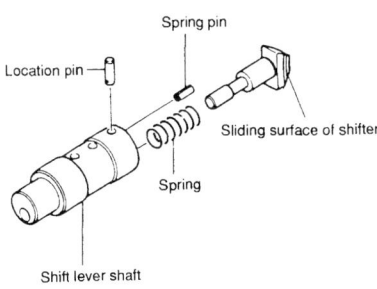

(1) Visually inspect the surface in contact with the drive cone, and replace the shifter when signs of overheating, damage or wear are found.
(2) Measure the shaft diameter of the shifter. Replace the shaft if the size deviates from the standard.

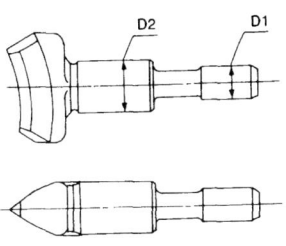

mm

	Standard	Limit
D1	66.9~67.0	65
D2	11.966~11.984	11.95
Shift lever shaft, Shifter insert hole	12.0~12.018	12.05

3-12-2 Shift lever shaft and location pin

(1) Check the shift lever shaft and location pin for damage or distortion, and replace defective parts. If the location pin must be replaced, replace it together with the shift lever shaft.
(2) Measure the diameter of the shift lever shaft and the shifter insertion hole. Replace the part if the size deviates from the standard value.

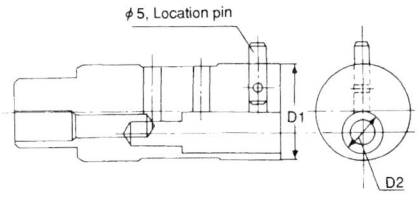

mm

	Standard	Limit
D1	27.959~27.98	27.90
D2	12.0~12.018	12.05
Side cover, Shift insert hole	28.0~28.021	28.08

Chapter 7 Reduction and Reversing Gear
3. Inspection and Servicing
3JH2 series

3-12-3 Shifter spring
(1) Check the spring for scratches or corrosion.
(2) Measure the free length of the spring.

Shifter spring	Standard	Limt
Free length	22.6mm	19.8mm
Spring constant	0.854kgf/mm	—
Length when attached	14.35mm	—
Load when attached	7.046kg	6.08kg

3-12-4 Stopper bolt
Check the stopper bolt. If it is worn or stepped, replace.

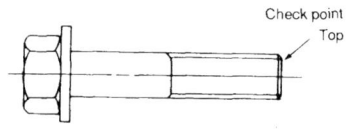

3-12-5 Side cover and oil seal
(1) Check the neutral, forward and reverse position grooves.
Replace if the grooves are worn.
(2) Measure the insertion hole of the shift lever s haft.
Replace if the size deviates from the standard value.
(3) Check the oil seal and the O-ring for damage.
Replace if the part is defective.

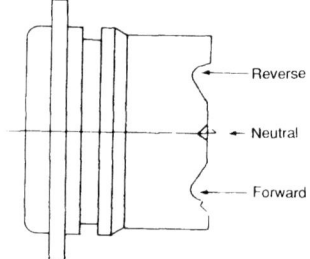

3-13 Damper disc

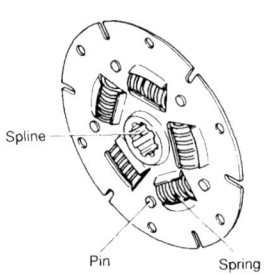

(1) Spline part.
Whenever uneven wear and/or scratches are found, replace with a new part.
(2) Spring.
Whenever uneven wear and/or scratches are found, replace with a new part.
(3) Pin wear
Whenever uneven wear and/or scratches are found, replace with a new part.
(4) Whenever a crack or damage to the spring slot is found replace the defective part with a new one.

3-14 Shim adjustment for output and input shafts

Check the thickness of shims for both input and output shafts. When the component parts are not replaced after dismantling, the same shims can be reused. When the clutch case and flange or any one of the following parts is replaced the thickness of shim must be determined in the following manner.

For input shaft part : input shaft, bearing.
For output shaft parts : output shaft, thrust collar A, thrustcollar B, gear, bearing.

Chapter 7 Reduction and Reversing Gear
3. Inspection and Servicing

(1) Shim thickness (T_1) measurement of output shaft
  (a) Measure the bearing insertion hole depth (A) of the mounting flange, and the bearing insertion hole depth (A') of the clutch case.
  (b) Measure the length (B) between the bearing outer race of the input shaft assembly.
  (c) Obtain the (T_1) thickness by the following formula :
  $T_1 = A + A' - B$ (T_1 : Clearance ± 0.05mm)

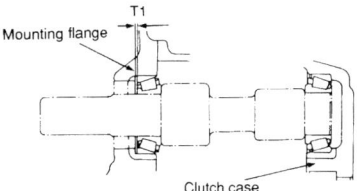

Mounting flange
Clutch case

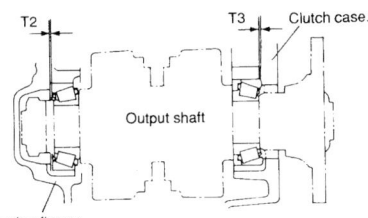

Output shaft
Mounting flange

  (c) Measure the (F) and (E) length from the outer race end of the clutch case bearing included in the output shaft assembly.
  NOTE : Before measuring the (F) and (E) length, press the forward large gear and the reverse large gear to the drive cone until there is no clearance among them.

  (d) Obtain the (T_2) and (T_3) thicknesses by the following formulas :

  $T_2 = C + C' - D - T_3$ (Clearance $^{+0.1mm}_{0}$)

  T_3(KM3P) $= C' - 47.3 - \dfrac{E}{2} - F$ (Clearance ± 0.05mm)

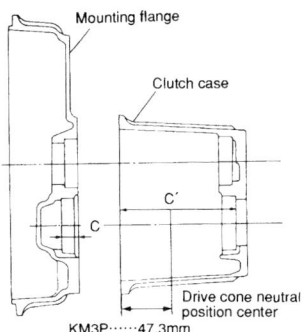

Mounting flange
Clutch case
Drive cone neutral position center
KM3P······47.3mm

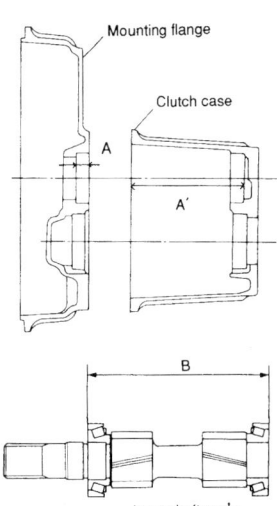

Mounting flange
Clutch case
Input shaft ass'y

(2) Shim thickness (T_2, T_3) measurement of output shaft
  (a) Measure the bearing insertion hole depth (C) of the mounting flange, and the bearing insertion hole depth (C') of the clutch case.
  (b) Measure the length (D) between the bearing outer races.
  NOTE : Tighten the mounting flange nut of the output shaft assembly with the specified torque. Press-fit the inner race of the clutch case roller bearing to the large gear side.

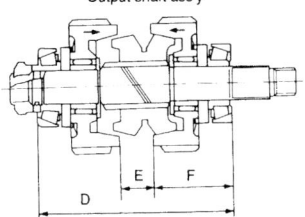

Output shaft ass'y

Chapter 7 Reduction and Reversing Gear
3. Inspection and Servicing

3JH2 series

(3) Standard size of parts

mm

	A+A'	B	C+C'	D	E	F	Drive cone neutral center position
KM3P	132.40~132.75	131.20~132.10	141.20~141.55	139.56~141.00	23.50~24.10	57.83~58.65	47.3

NOTE : Compare your measurements with the above standard size. If your measurements largely differ from the standard sizes, measurements may not be correct. Check and measure again.

(4) Adjusting shim set

	Tickness. mm (in.)	No. of shims
Input shaft	0.5	1
	0.4	1
	0.3	2
Output shaft	1.0	1
	0.5	1
	0.3	2
	0.1	3

3-15 Torque limiter

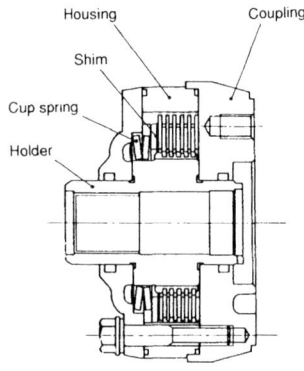
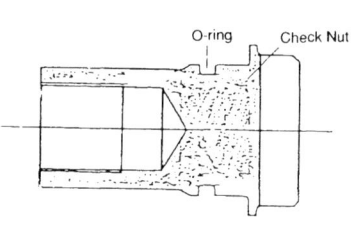

The torque limiter assembly includes these parts.
The conversion to the torque limiter specification is easy by exchanging the standard shaft coupling. (Use the check nut, not the end nut, to install the torque limiter.)

4. Disassembly

4-1. Dismantling the clutch

(1) Remove the remote control of cable.
(2) Remove the clutch assembly from the engine mounting flange.

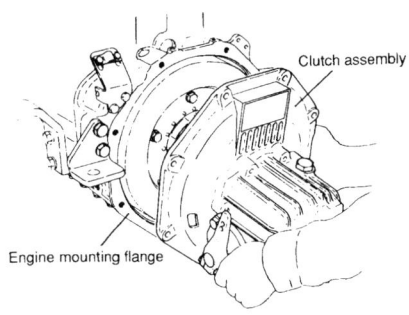
Clutch assembly
Engine mounting flange

(3) Drain the lubricating oil.
   Drain the lubricating oil by loosening the plug at the bottom of the clutch case.

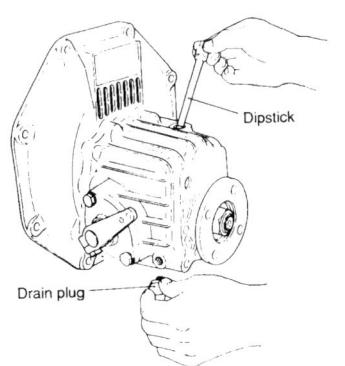
Dipstick
Drain plug

(4) Remove the end nut and output shaft coupling.

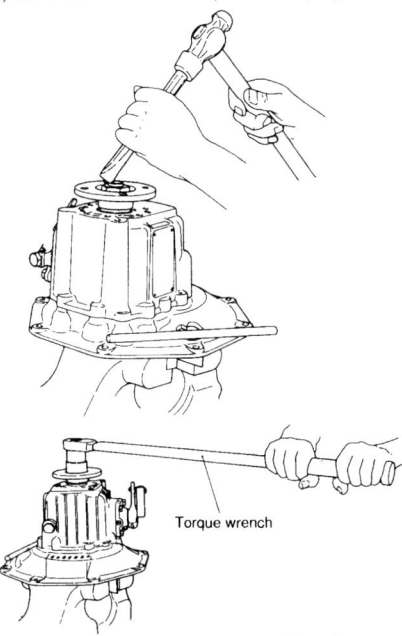
Torque wrench

NOTE : Take care as it has a left-handed thread.

(5) Remove the oil dip stick and O-ring.
(6) Remove the fixing bolts on the side cover, and also remove the shift lever shaft, shift lever and shifter.

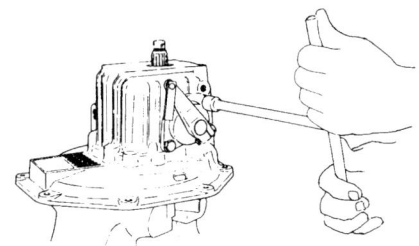

Chapter 7 Reduction and Reversing Gear
4. Disassembly

3JH2 series

(7) Remove the bolts which secure the mounting flange to the case body, give light taps to the left and right with a plastic headed hammer while supporting the clutch case with your hand, then remove the mounting flange.

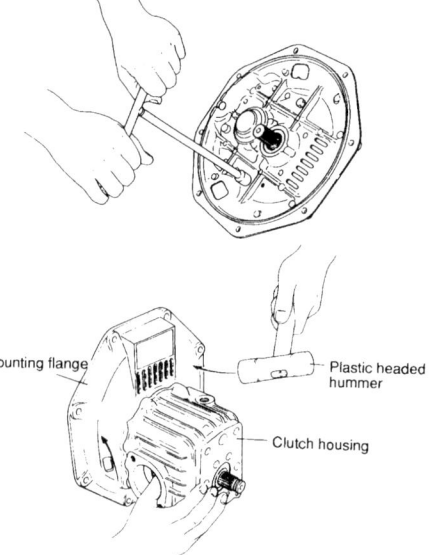

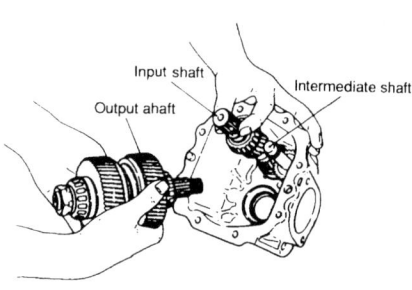

(9) Take out the intermediate shaft and input shaft. When taking out the intermediate shaft, place a bolt or spacer on the shaft hole of the case, and drive the shaft out by tapping it lightly.

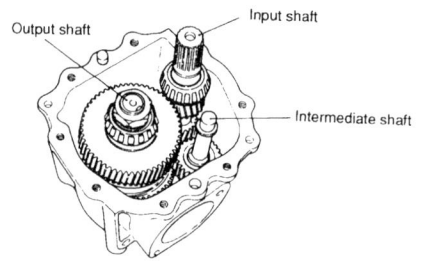

(8) Withdraw the output shaft assembly.

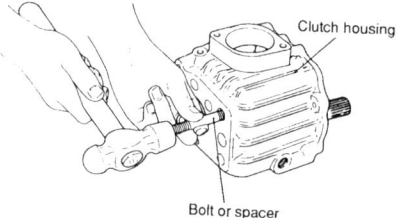

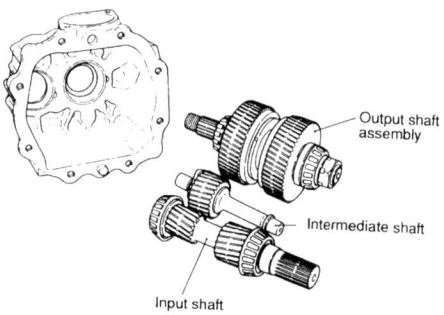

Printed in Japan
A0A1015-0302

7-49

Chapter 7 Reduction and Reversing Gear
4. Disassembly
3JH2 series

(10) Remove the oil seal of the output shaft from the case body.

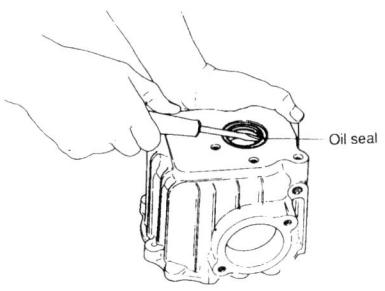
Oil seal

(11) Remove the outer bearing race from the case body by using the special tool.

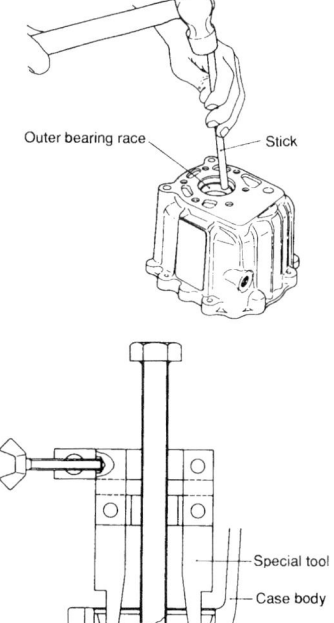
Outer bearing race — Stick
Special tool
Case body
Outer bearing race

(12) Remove the oil seal of the input shaft from the mounting flange.
(13) Remove the outer bearing race from the mounting flange in the same way as with the case body.
(14) Remove each adjusting plate from the input our output shaft.

NOTE : *The same adjusting plates can be revsed when the following parts are not replaced.*
When any part is replaced however, readjustment is necessary.

4-2 Removal of the output shaft

(1) Take out the reverse large gear, thrust collar A, cup spring, spring retainer and inner bearing race.
The reverse large gear must be withdrawn using a pulley extracter, by fixing the nut at the forward end in a vice.

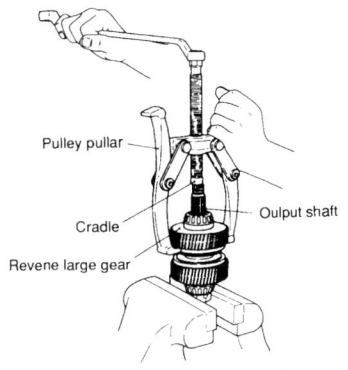
Pulley pullar
Cradle
Revene large gear
Output shaft

(2) Loosen the calking of the forward nut and remove the nut and spacer.
Remove the nut by using a torque wrench after setting the output shaft coupling and fixing the coupling bolt in a vice.

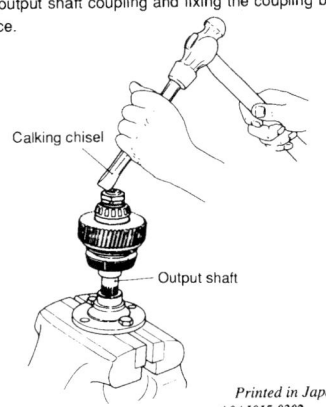
Calking chisel
Output shaft

Printed in Japan
A0A1015-0302

Chapter 7 Reduction and Reversing Gear
4. Disassembly

3JH2 series

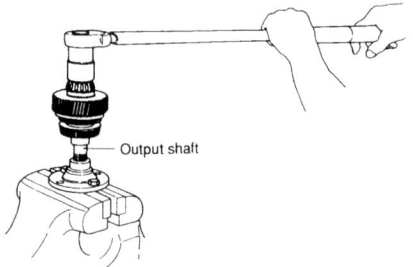

(3) Place the pulley extractor against the end surface of the forward large gear, and withdraw the forward large gear, thrust collar A, cup spring, spring retainer and inner bearing race.

(4) While gripping the drive cone, tap the end of the shaft with a plastic headed hammer, and withdraw the thrust collar B and inner needle bearing race. A pulley extractor may be used.

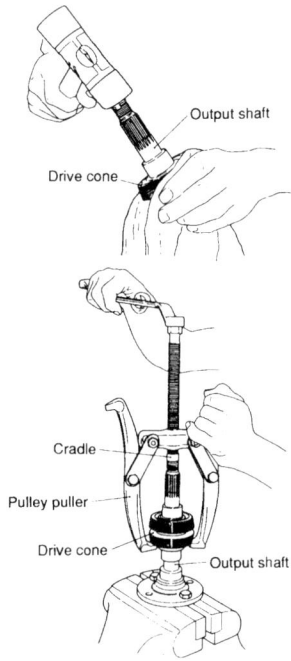

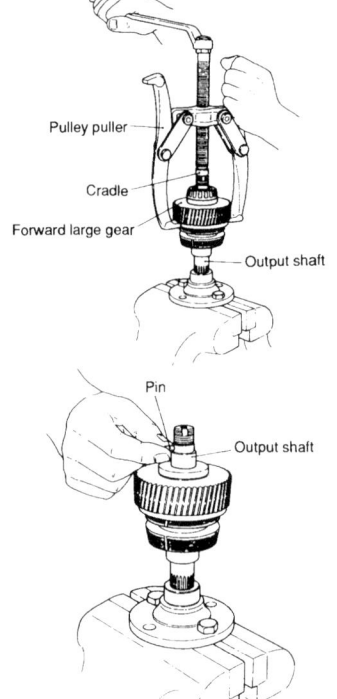

NOTE : Take care as the nut has left-handed thread.

4-3 Removal of the intermediate shaft.
(1) Remove the "O" ring.
(2) Remove the thrust washer.
(3) Remove the intermediate gear and needle bearing.

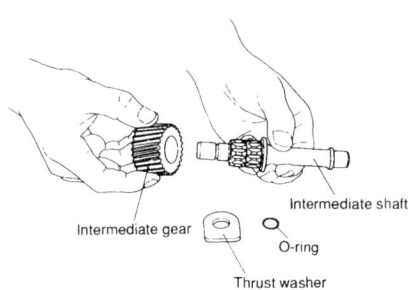

Chapter 7 Reduction and Reversing Gear
4. Disassembly _____ *3JH2 series*

4-4 Dismantling the shifting device
(1) Take out the shifter and shifter spring.

(4) Remove the shift lever to the anti-shif lever side.

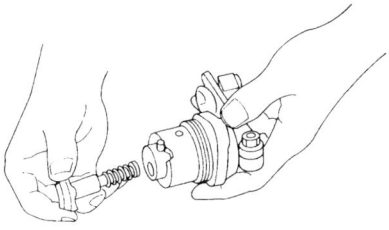

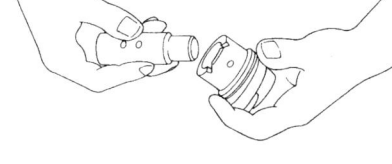

(2) Remove the stopper bolt of the shifter and shim.

(5) Remove the oil-seal and O-ring.

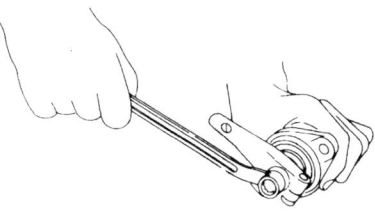

(3) Loosen the bolt of the shift lever and remove the shift lever from the shift lever shaft.

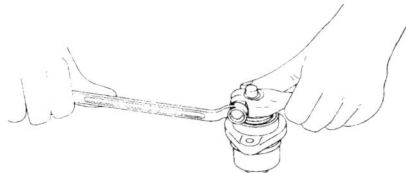

5. Reassembly

5-1 Reassembly of output shaft
(1) Fit the forward side thrust collar B onto the shaft.
(2) Drive in the forward end inner needle bearing race using a jig.

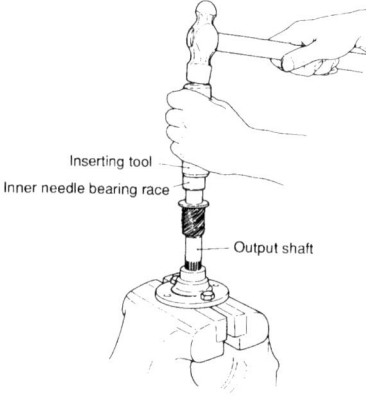

(3) Assemble the needle bearing and forward large gear.

NOTE : Check that the forward large gear rotates smoothly.

(4) Fit the cup spring, spring retainer, thrust collar A and Pin, and driven in the inner bearing race using a jig.

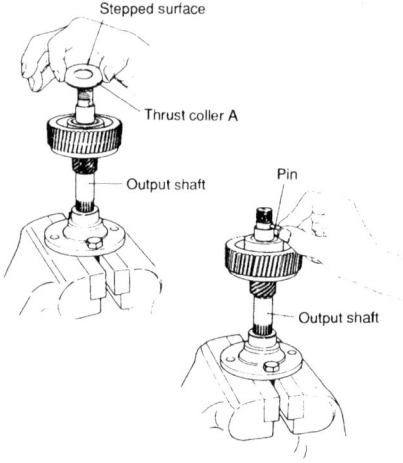

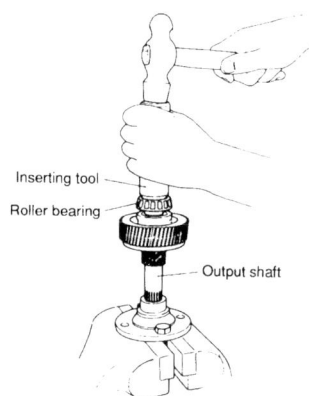

NOTE : 1) Drive in with a plastic headed hammer. Do not hit it hard.
        2) When fitting the thrust collar A, note the fitting direction. Fit it keeping the stepped surface toward the roller bearing side.
        3) Note that the pin cannot be fitted after the inner bearing race has been driven in.
        4) Check that the forward large gear rotates smoothly.

(5) Assemble the collar and pin so that the pin is in the groove of the collar.
(6) Set and tighten the forward end nut. Insert the bolt into the coupling, and fix it in a vice, keeping the spline part upward.
Insert the shaft into the spline of the coupling, fit the spacer, and tighten the nut with a torque wrench.

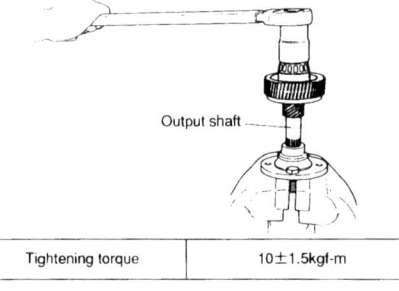

Tightening torque	10±1.5kgf-m

NOTES : 1) Take care as it is a left-handed thread.
         2) Use the reverse side nut used before dismantling as the forward end nut. This is so as not to match the calked portion to the same point.

Chapter 7 Reduction and Reversing Gear
5. Reassembly

5-2 Reassembly of the clutch
(1) Fit the oil seal, bearing outer races and shim (output shaft side) in the clutch case.
(2) Insert the input shaft into the clutch case.
(3) Drive the intermediate shaft into the clutch case.

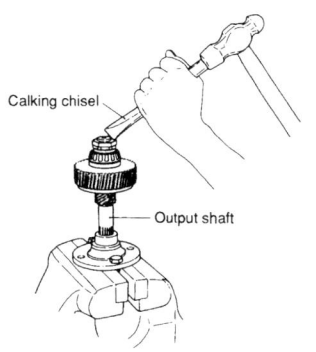

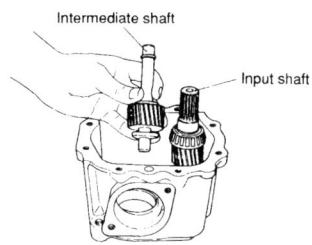

(7) Insert the drive cone while keeping the output shaft set for reverse.

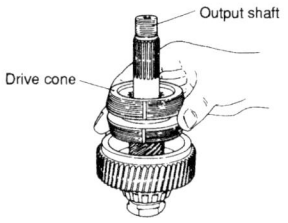

NOTES : 1) If the output shaft is not fitted into the clutch case before driving-in the intermediate shaft, it cannot be assembled.
2) Note the assembly direction of the thrust washer.

(4) Insert the output shaft into the clutch case.

(8) Apply procedures 1 through 4 to the forward end.

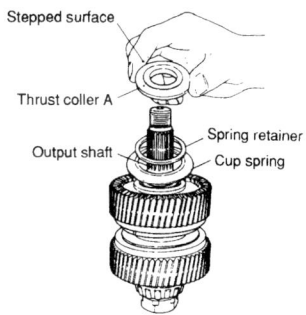

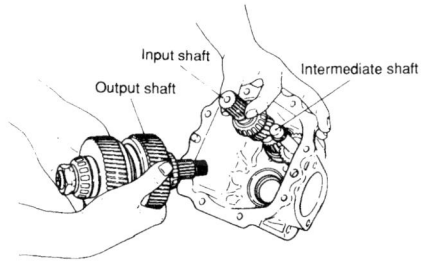

NOTE :1) Fit thrust collar A so that the stepped surface faces the roller bearing side.
2) Check that the reverse large gear rotates smoothly.

Chapter 7 Reduction and Reversing Gear
5. Reassembly

3JH2 series

(5) Fit the adjusting plate to the mounting flange, and drive in the outer bearing race.
NOTE : *The outer bearing race can be easily driven in by heating the mounting flange to about 100°C, or by cooling the outer race with liquid hydrogen.*
(6) Apply non-drying liquid packing around the outer surface of the oil seal, and insert the oil seal into the mounting flange while keeping the spring part of the oil seal facing the inside of the case.
(7) Apply non-drying liquid packing to the matching surfaces of the mounting flange end the case body.

(8) Insert the input shaft and output shaft into the shaft holes of the mounting flange, assemble the mounting flange on the case body, and tighten the bolt.

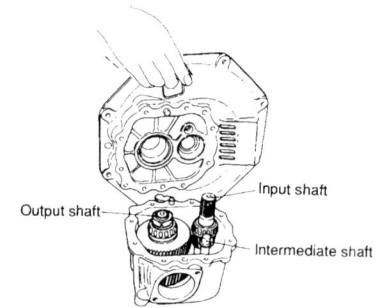

Output shaft — Input shaft — Intermediate shaft

NOTE : *Apply non-drying liquid packing to either the mounting flange or the case body.*

(9) Assemble the output shaft coupling on the output shaft, and fit the O-ring.
(10) Tighten the end nut by using a torque wrench, then calk it.

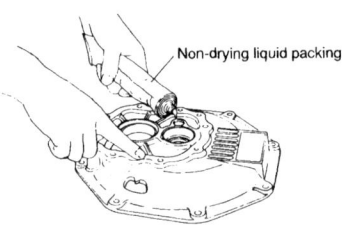

Non-drying liquid packing

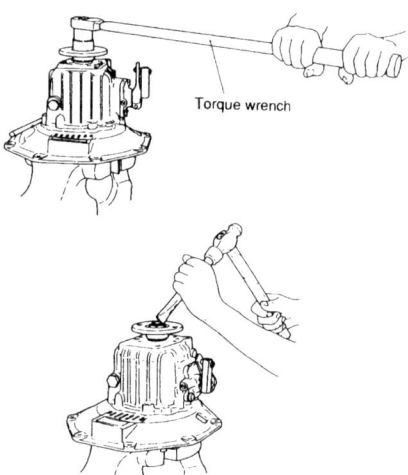

Torque wrench

NOTE : *Take care as it is a left-handed thread.*

Tightening torque	10±1.5kgf-m

5-3 Reassembly of the shiating device

(1) Fit the oil seal and O-ring to the side cover.

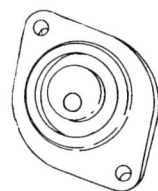

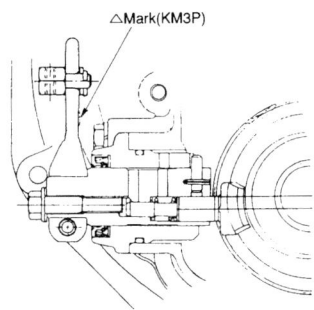
△Mark(KM3P)

(2) Insert the shift lever shaft to the side cover.

(4) Insert the shiater spring and shifter to the shift lever shaft.
(5) Fit the side cover assembly to the clutch case.

NOTE : 1) Check the direction of the shifter (Top and bottom side).
2) The shift lever may not turn smoothly if the clutch case is not filled with lubricating oil.

(6) Fit the shim and stopper bolt to the shift lever shaft.

NOTE : Apply non-drying liquid packing or sealtape to the thread of the stopper bolt.

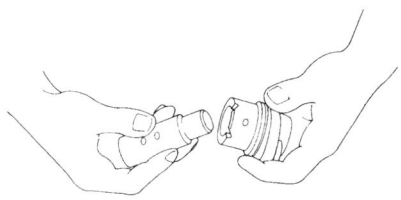

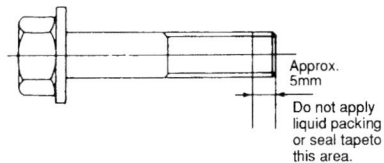

Approx. 5mm
Do not apply liquid packing or seal tapeto this area.

(3) Fit the shift lever to the shift lever shaft.

NOTE : Check the dlrection of the shift lever △ mark.

(7) Fit the cable connector to the shift lever.

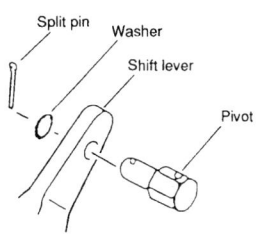

Split pin   Washer
            Shift lever
                        Pivot

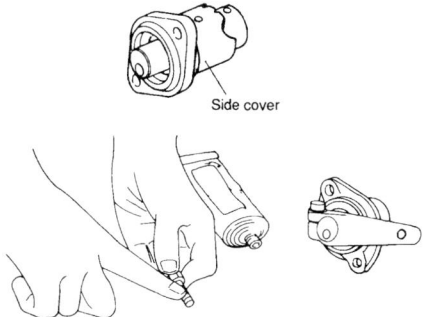

Side cover

CHAPTER 8
REMOTO CONTROL

1. Remote Control System ·· 8-1
2. Remote Control Installation ································· 8-2
3. Remote Control Inspection ··································· 8-5
4. Remote Control ADJUSTMENT ···················· 8-6
5. Disassembly ·· 8-13

1. Remote Control System

1-1 Construction of remote control system

The remote control permits one handed control of the engine speed, changing from forward to reverse, and stopping.

Fittings which allow for easy connection of the remote control cables with the fuel injection pump and transmission are provided with the remote control set.

The use of Morse remote control cables, clamps and a remote control head, are also provided for. The device to stop the engine is electric and will be explained under the section on electrical equipment.

1-2 Remote control device components

	Morse description	Yanmar Part No.
Remote control head	Morse MT2 top mounting single lever	41730-000680
	Morse MV side mounting single lever	128170-86500
Remote control cable	Morse 33C x 4m (13.12ft.)	41710-000360
	Morse 33C x 7m (23.00ft.)	129470-86500
Engine stop cable	Yanmar 4m (13.12ft)	129470-67550
	Yanmar 7m (22.96ft)	129470-67560

(1) Remote control handle

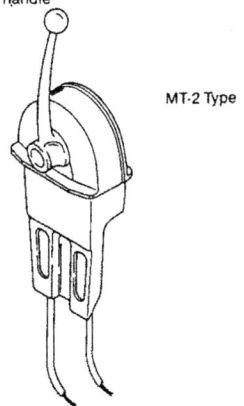

MT-2 Type

The model MT-2 remote control has been designed so that operation of the clutch (shift) and governor (throttle) can be effected with one lever.

Two cables are required for the MT-2 single, one for the clutch and the other for the governor.

When warming up the engine, to freely control the governor separately from the clutch put the lever in-neutral, the central position, and pull the knob in the center of the control lever. When the lever is returned to the neutral position, the knob automatically returns to its original position, and the clutch is free. The governor can then be freely operated.

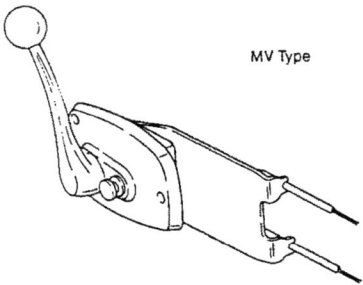

MV Type

The MV type controller has been designed so that operation of the clutch and throttle can be effected with one lever. When the button next to the control lever is pulled out with the lever in the central position, it holds the clutch in the neutral position so that the throttle can be opened all the way and warm up the engine.

When the engine is warmed up, return the handle to the central position and push the button back in. Control of the clutch and throttle is thus effected with one handle.

(2) Remote control cable

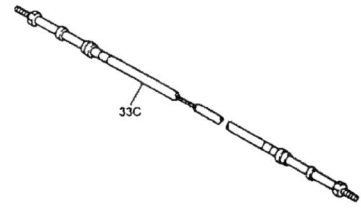

Use only Super-Responsive Morse Control Cables. These are designed specifically for use with Morse control heads. This engineered system of Morse cables, control head and engine connection kits ensures dependable, smooth operation with an absolute minimum of backlash.

(3) Engine stop cable

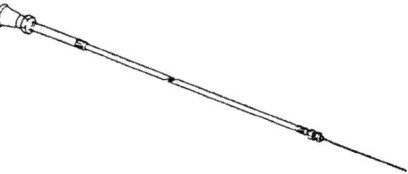

2. Remote Control Installation

2-1 Speed control

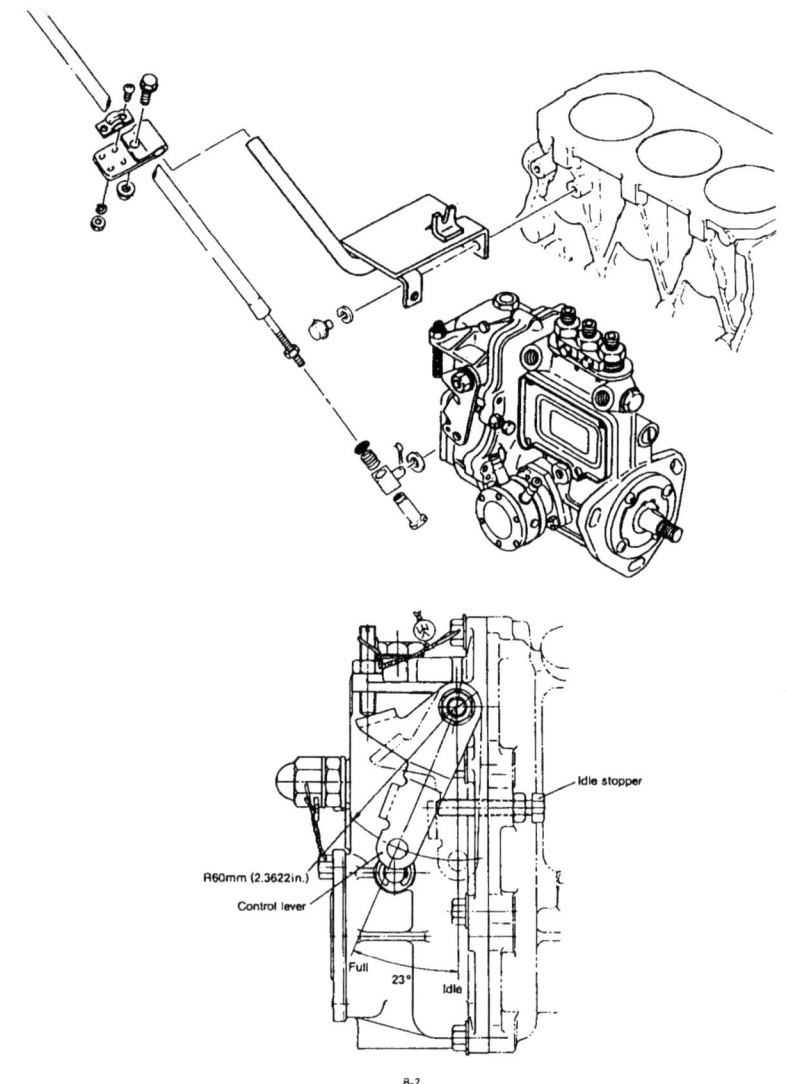

Chapter 8 Remote Control
2. Remote Control Installation

2-2 Clutch control

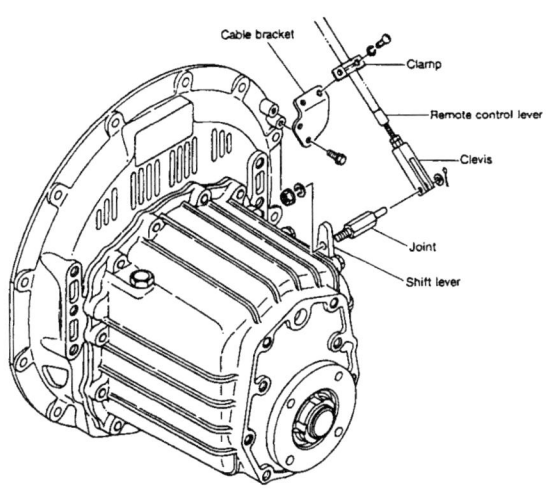

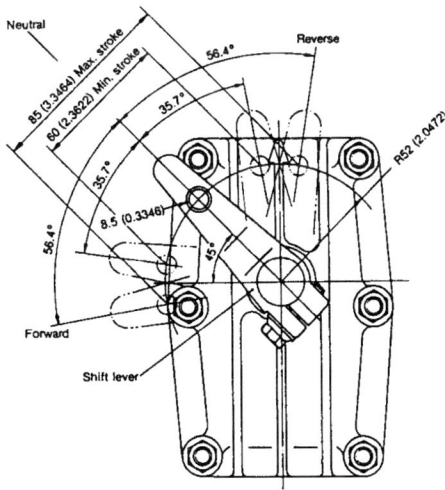

mm (in.)

Chapter 8 Remote Control
2. Remote Control Installation

2-3 Engine stop

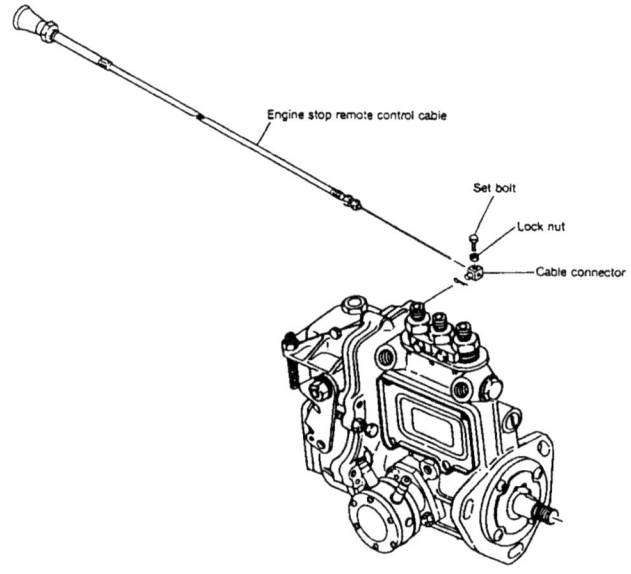

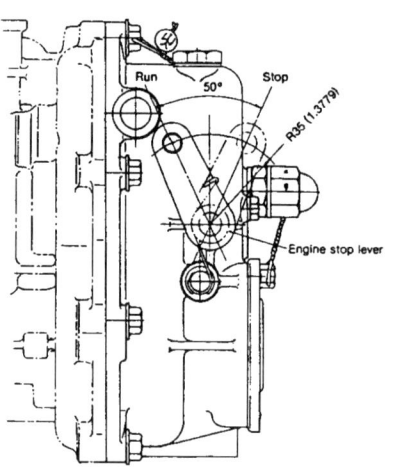

mm (in.)

3. Remote Control Inspection

(1) When the control lever movement does not coincide with operation of the engine, check the cable end stop nut to see whether or not it is loose, and readjust/retighten when necessary.

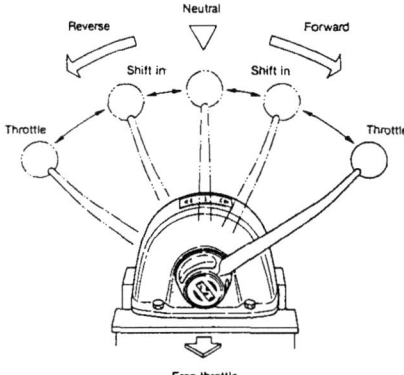

Free throttle

(2) Too many bends (turns) in the cable or bends at too extreme an angle will make it difficult to turn the handle. Reroute the cable to reduce the number of bends or enlarge the bending radius as much as possible (to 200mm or more).
(3) Check for loose cable bracket/clamp bolts or nuts and retighten as necessary.
(4) Check cable connection screwheads, cable sleeves and other metal parts for rust or corrosion. Clean off minor rust and wax or grease the parts. Replace if the parts are heavily rusted or corroded.

4. Remote Control Adjustment

(1) Shift lever adjustment
Move the lever several times—the movement of the clutch lever on the engine from forward, neutral and reverse must coincide with the forward, neutral and reverse on the control lever. If they do not coincide, adjust the fittings as necessary (first engine side, then controller side).

(2) Throttle lever adjustment
Move the control lever all the way to full throttle several times, and then return. The throttle lever on the engine must lightly push against the idle switch when it is returned. If it is properly adjusted, the knob can be easily pulled out when the lever is in the neutral position, and will automatically return when the control lever is brought back to the neutral position. If the control lever presses too hard against the knob, it may not return automatically, in which case the cable end must be adjusted as explained for the clutch. The knob cannot be pulled out when the lever is not in the neutral (central) position.

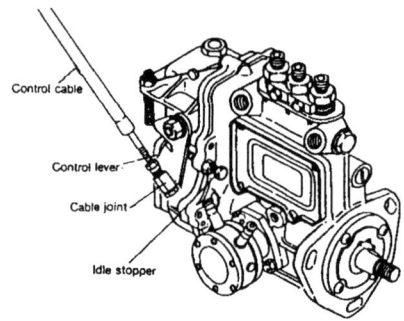

CHAPTER 9
ELECTRICAL SYSTEM

1. Electrical System ·· 9-1
2. Battery ·· 9-5
3. Starter Motor ··· 9-8
4. Alternator ·· 9-24
5. Instrument Panel ·· 9-34
6. Warning Devices ··· 9-36
7. Air Heater (Optional) ·· 9-39
8. Electric Type Engine Stop Device (Optional) ··· 9-40
9. Tachometer ··· 9-42
10. Alternator 12V/80A (Optional) ······················· 9-45

Chapter 9 Electrical System
1. Electrical System — 3JH2 Series

1. Electrical System

System diagram of electric parts (B2-type)

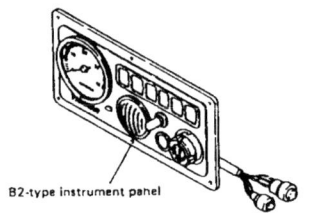

B2-type instrument panel

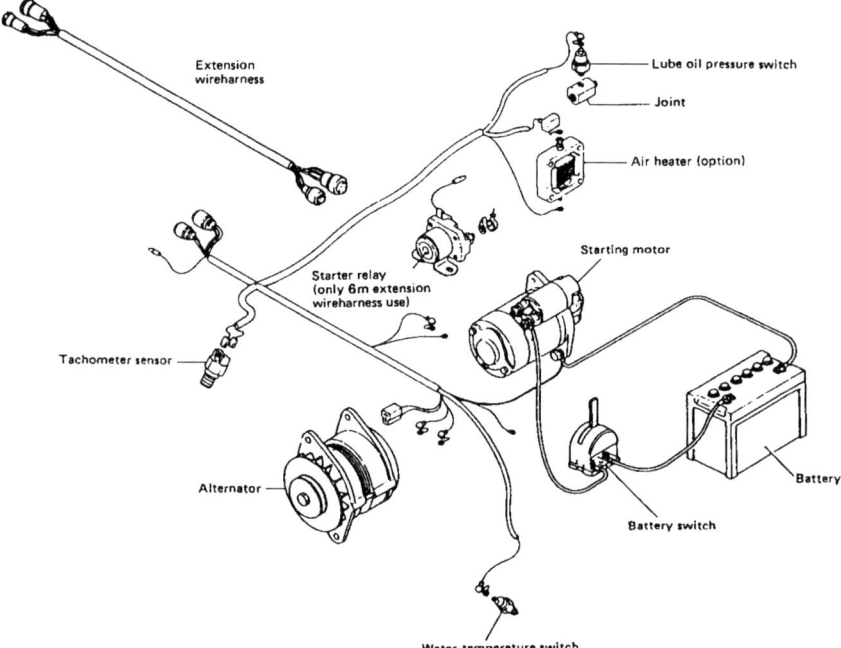

Chapter 9 Electrical System
1. Electrical System

3JH2 Series

C-type

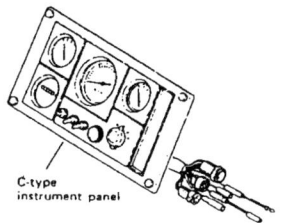

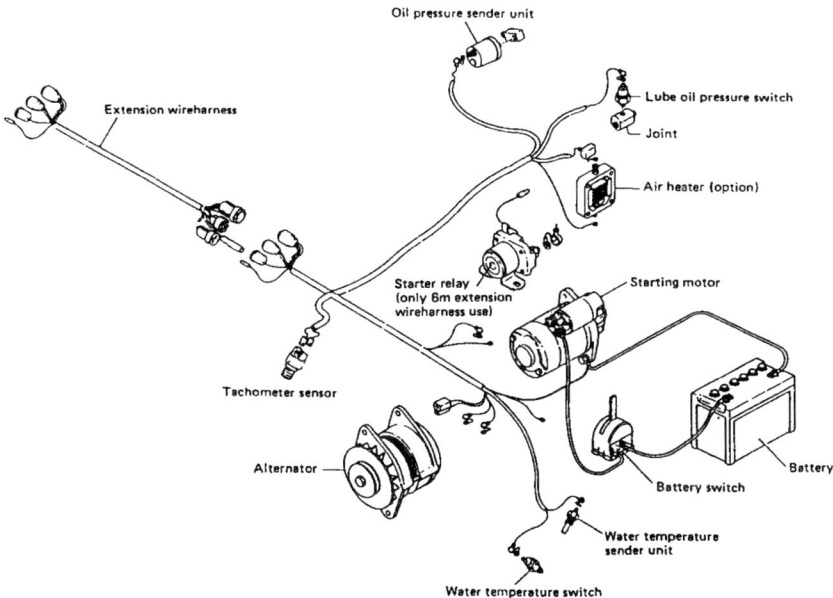

Chapter 9 Electrical System
1. Electrical System

3JH2 Series

1-2 Wiring diagram

1-2.1 For B-type instrument panel

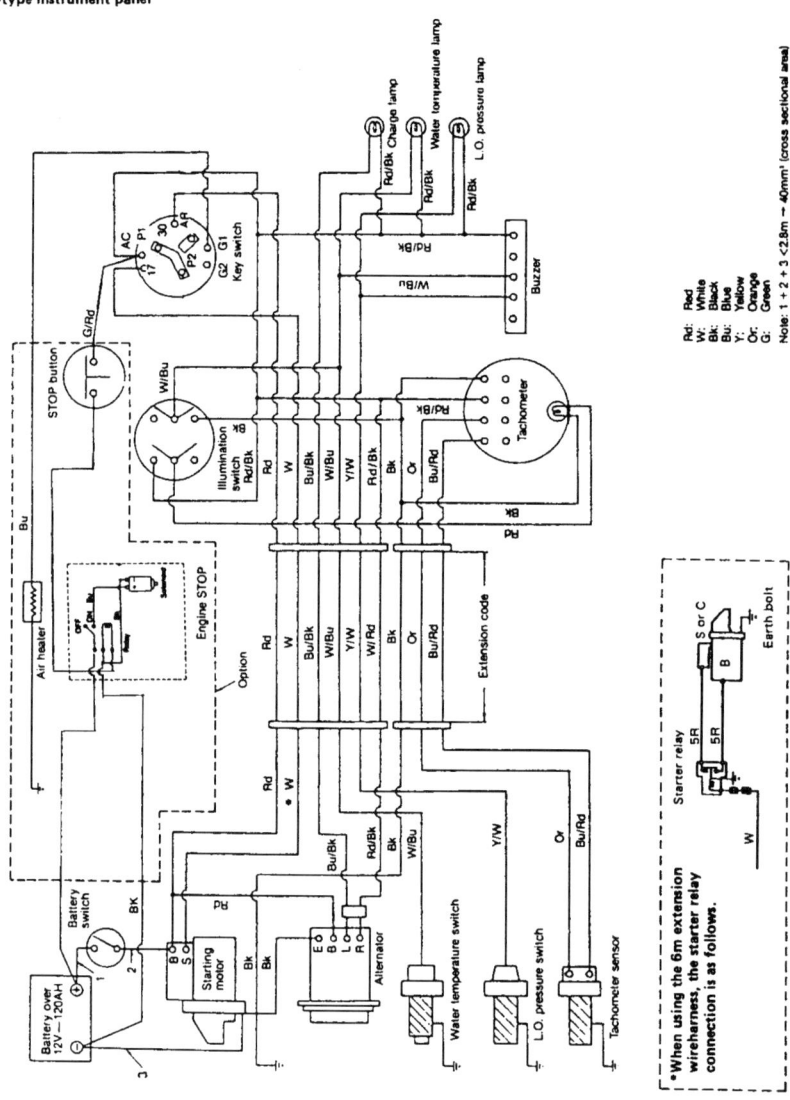

Chapter 9 Electrical System
1. Electrical System

1-2.2 For C-type instrument panel

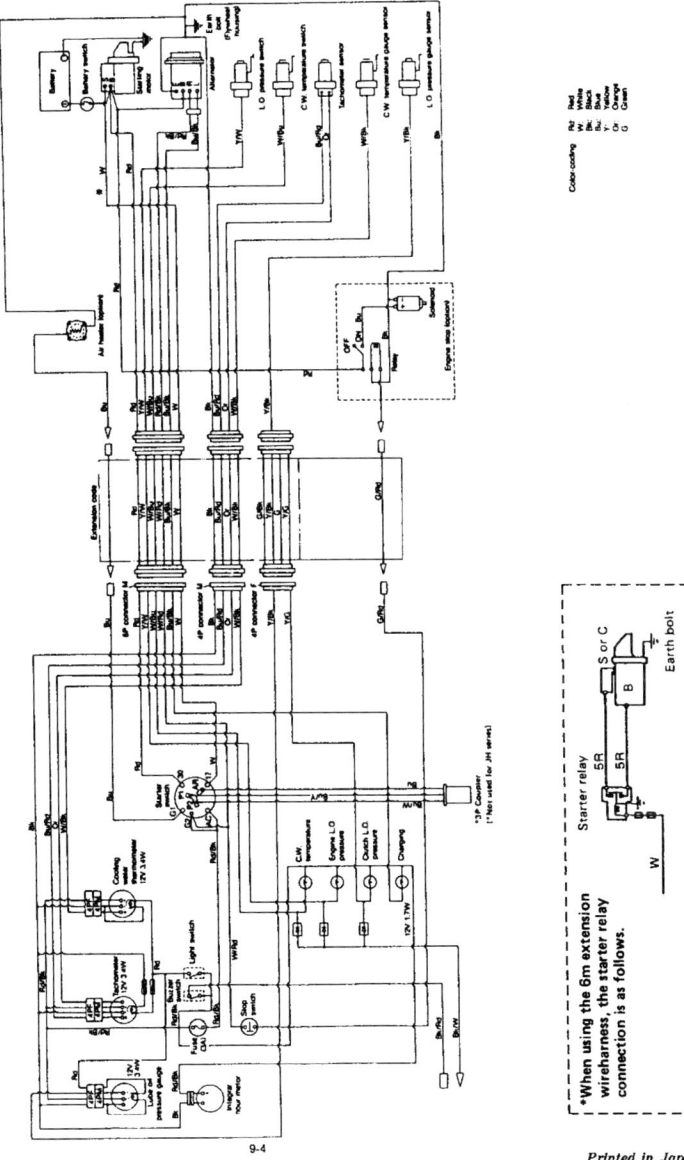

Chapter 9 Electrical System
1. Electrical System

3JH2 series

3JH25A/30A

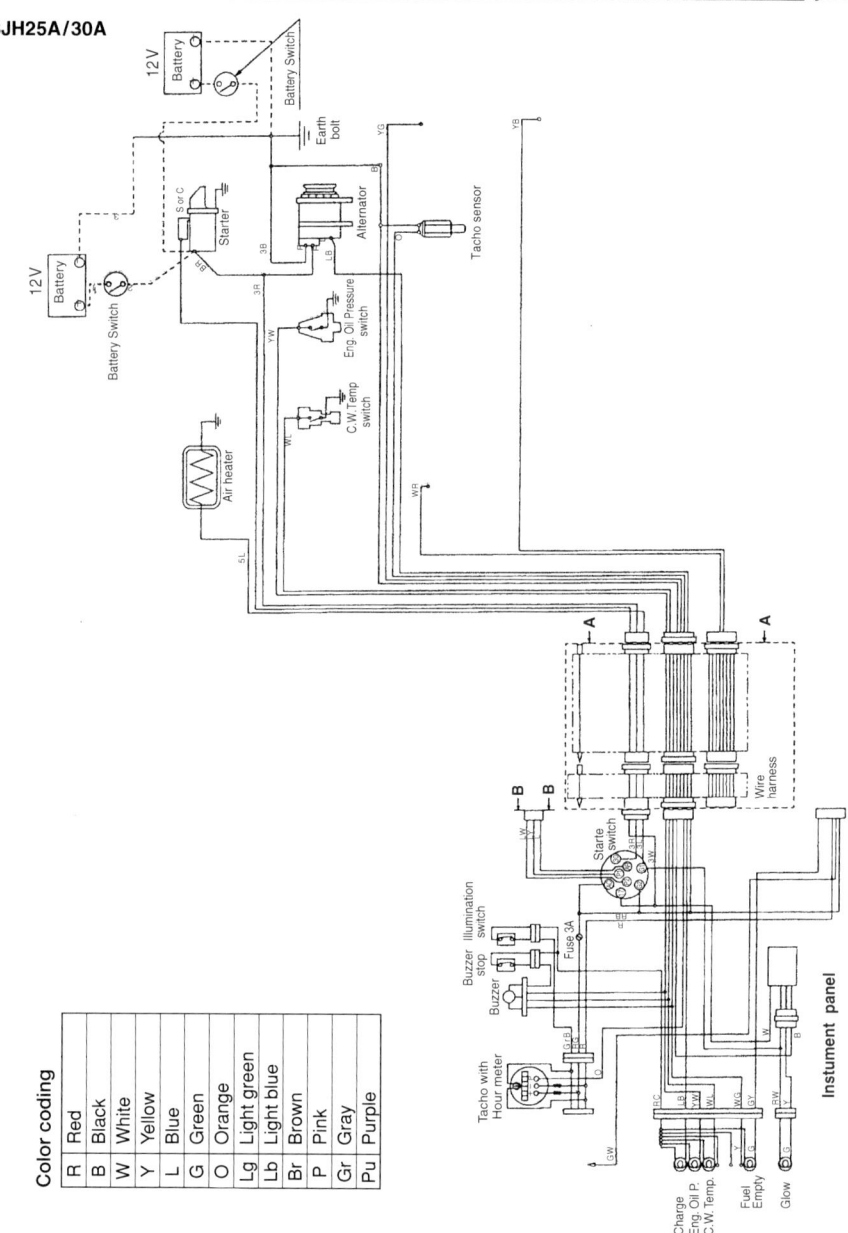

2. Battery

2-1 Construction

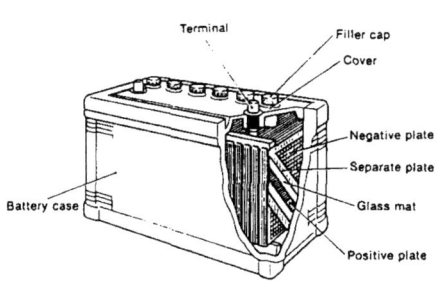

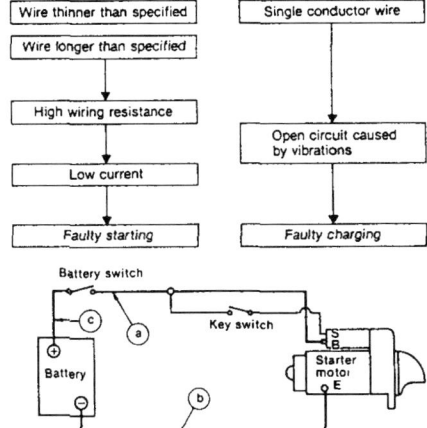

The battery utilizes chemical action to convert chemical energy to electrical energy. This engine uses a lead acid battery which stores a fixed amount of power that can be used when required. After use, the battery can be recharged and used again.
As shown in the figure, a nonconductive container is filled with dilute sulfuric acid electrolyte. Lead dioxide positive plates and lead dioxide negative plates separated by glass mats are stacked alternately in the electrolyte. The positive and negative plates are connected to their respective terminals.
Power is removed from the battery by connecting the load across these two terminals.
When the battery is discharging, an electric current flows from the positive plates to the negative plates. When the battery is being charged, electric current is passed through the battery in the opposite direction by an external power source.

2-2 Battery capacity and battery cables

2-2.1 Battery capacity
Since the battery has a minimum capacity of 12V, 70AH, it can be used for 100 ~ 150AH.

Battery capacity	minimum	12V — 100AH
	standard	12V — 120AH
	cold weather	12V — 150AH
Full charged specific gravity		1.26

2-2.2 Battery cable
Wiring must be performed with the specified electric wire. Thick, short wiring should be used to connect the battery to the starter, (soft automotive low-voltage wire [AV wire]). Using wire other than that specified may cause the following troubles:

The overall lengths of the wire between the battery (+) terminal and the starter (B) terminal, and between the battery (-) terminal and the starter (E) terminal, should be determined according to the following table.

Voltage system	Allowable wiring voltage drop	Conductor cross-section area	a+b+c allowable length
12V	0.2V or less/100A	20mm² (0.0311 in.²)	Up to 2.5m (98.43 in.)
		40mm² (0.062 in.²)	Up to 5m (196.87 in.)

Note: Excessive resistance in the key switch circuit (between the battery and start [S] terminals) can cause improper pinion engagement. To prevent this, follow the wiring diagram carefully.

2-3 Inspection
The quality of the battery governs the starting performance of the engine. Therefore the battery must be routinely inspected to ensure that it functions perfectly at all times.

2-3.1 Visual inspection
(1) Inspect the case for cracks, damage and electrolyte leakage.
(2) Inspect the battery holder for tightness, corrosion, and damage.
(3) Inspect the terminals for rusting and corrosion, and check the cables for damage.
(4) Inspect the caps for cracking, electrolyte leakage and clogged vent holes.
Correct any abnormal conditions found. Clean off rusted terminals with a wire brush before reconnecting the battery cable.

2-3.2 Checking the electrolyte
(1) Electrolyte level

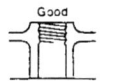
Good

Low

High

Check the electrolyte level every 7 to 10 days. The electrolyte must always be 10 ~ 20mm (0.3937 ~ 0.7874in.) over the top of the plates.

NOTES: 1. The "LEVEL" line on a transparent plastic battery case indicates the height of the electrolyte.
2. Always use distilled water to bring up the electrolyte level.
3. When the electrolyte has leaked out, add dilute sulfuric acid with the same specific gravity as the electrolyte.

(2) Measuring the specific gravity of the electrolyte
1) Draw some of the electrolyte up into a hydrometer.

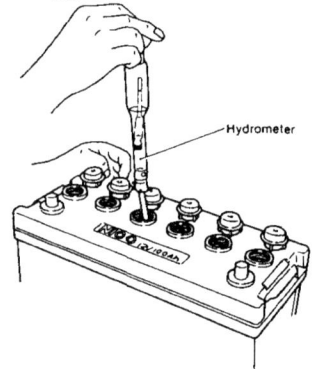
Hydrometer

2) Take the specific gravity reading at the top of the scale of the hydrometer.

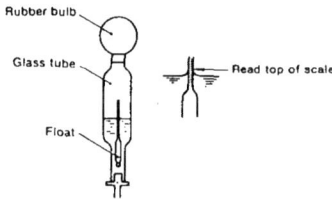
Rubber bulb
Glass tube
Read top of scale
Float

3) The battery is fully charged if the specific gravity is 1.260 at an electrolyte temperature of 20°C. The battery is discharged if the specific gravity is 1.200 (50%). If the specific gravity is below 1.200, recharge the battery.
4) If the difference in the specific gravity among the cells of the battery is ±0.01, the battery is OK.
5) Measure the temperature of the electrolyte.
Since the specific gravity changes with the temperature, 20°C is used as the reference temperature.
Reading the specific gravity at 20°C
$S_{20} = St + 0.0007 (t - 20)$
S_{20}: Specific gravity at the standard temperature of 20°C
St: Specific gravity of the electrolyte at t°C
0.0007: Specific gravity change per 1°C
t: Temperature of electrolyte

2-3.3 Voltage test
Using a battery tester, the amount of discharge can be determined by measuring the voltage drop which occurs while the battery is being discharged with a large current.

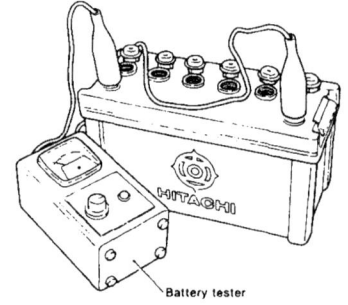
Battery tester

(1) Connect the tester to the battery.
12V battery tester
Adjust the current (A).
(2) Connect the (+) lead of the tester to the (+) battery terminal, and the (−) tester lead to the (−) battery terminal.
(3) Push the TEST button, wait 5 seconds, and then read the meter.
• Repeat the test twice to make sure that the meter indication remains the same.

2-3.4 Washing the battery
(1) Wash the outside of the battery with a brush while running cold or warm water over the battery. (Make sure that no water gets into the battery.)
(2) When the terminals or other metal parts are corroded due to exposure to electrolyte leakage, wash off all the acid.
(3) Check the vent holes of the caps and clean if clogged.
(4) After washing the battery, dry it with compressed air, connect the battery cable, and coat the terminals with grease. Since the grease acts as an insulator, do not coat the terminals before connecting the cables.

Printed in Japan
A0A1015-9110SP

2-4 Charging

2-4.1 Charging methods
There are two methods of charging a battery: normal and rapid.
Rapid charging should only be used in emergencies.
- Normal charging...Should be conducted at a current of 1/10 or less of the indicated battery capacity (10A or less for a 100AH battery).
- Rapid charging...Rapid charging is done over a short period of time at a current of 1/5 ~ 1/2 the indicated battery capacity (20A ~ 50A for a 100AH battery). However, since rapid charging causes the electrolyte temperature to rise too high, special care must be exercised.

2-4.2 Charging procedure
(1) Check the specific gravity and adjust the electrolyte level.
(2) Disconnect the battery cables.
(3) Connect the red clip of the charger to the (+) battery terminal and connect the black clip to the (−) terminal.

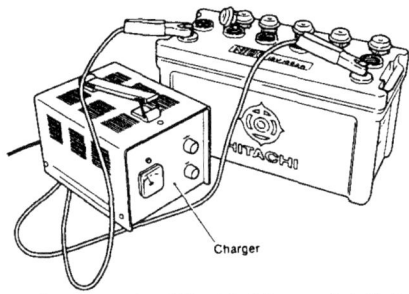
Charger

(4) Set the current to 1/10 ~ 1/5 of the capacity indicated on the outside of the battery.
(5) Periodically measure the specific gravity during charging to make sure that the specific gravity remains at a high fixed value. Also check whether gas is being generated.

2-4.3 Charging precautions
(1) Remove the battery caps to vent the gas during charging.
(2) While charging, ventilate the room and prohibit smoking, welding, etc.
(3) The electrolyte temperature should not exceed 45°C during charging.
(4) Since an alternator is used on this engine, when charging with a charger, always disconnect the battery (+) cable to prevent destruction of the diodes.
(Before disconnecting the (+) battery cable, disconnect the (−) battery cable [ground side].)

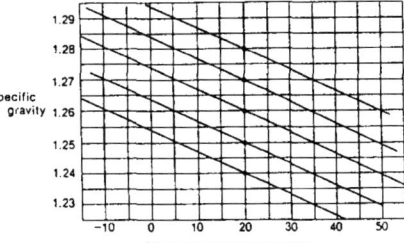
Electrolyte temperature and specific gravity

2-5 Battery storage precautions
The life of a battery depends considerably on how it is handled. Generally speaking, however, after about two years its performance will deteriorate, starting will become difficult, and the battery will not fully recover its original charge even after recharging. Then it must be replaced.

(1) Since the battery will self-discharge about 0.5%/day even when not in use, it must be charged 1 or 2 times a month when it is being stored.

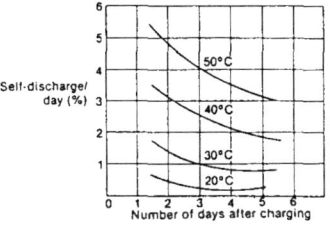

(2) If charging by the engine alternator is insufficient because of frequent starts and stops, the battery will rapidly lose power.
Charge the battery as soon as possible after it is used under these conditions.
(3) An easy-to-use battery charger that permits home charging is available from Yanmar. Take proper care of the battery by using the charger as a set with a hydrometer.
When the specific gravity has dropped to about 1.16 and the engine will not start, charge the battery up to a specific gravity of 1.26 (24 hours).
(4) Before putting the battery in storage for long periods, charge it for about 8 hours to prevent rapid aging.

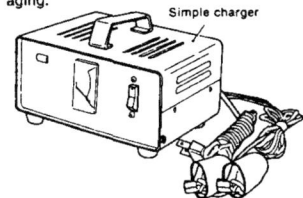
Simple charger

Chapter 9 Electrical System
3. Starter Motor

3JH2 Series

3. Starter Motor

1. The Reduction Starter System
 1-1 The Reduction Starters
  While these only had specialized applications in the past, they currently are being widely adopted because of their compact, lightweight design.
  Although smaller than the direct-drive type starter with its armature and pinion driven at the same speed, the gear reduction starter actually reduces the motor speed to approximately 27% prior to driving the pinion.
  It does this without reducing output, hence its name.
  Furthermore, use of heat-resistant insulating materials and advanced production technology makes the compact, light weight design possible and improves its starting capabilities in cold regions.

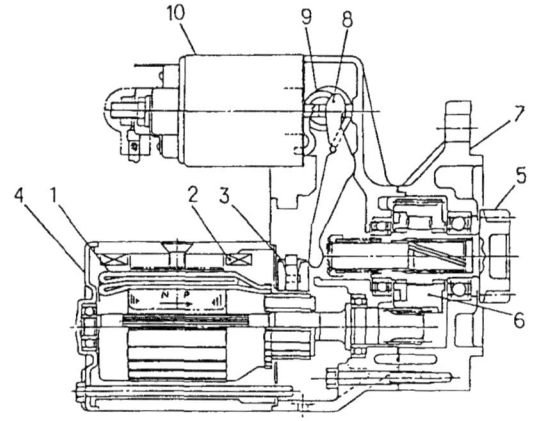

1. Armature
2. Field Coil
3. Brush
4. Rear Cover
5. Pinion Shaft
6. Pinion Clutch
7. Gear Case
8. Shift Lever
9. Torsion Spring
10. Magnetic Switch

Fig.1 Reduction Starter Construction

Chapter 9 Electrical System
3. Starter Motor   3JH2 Series

1-2 The Engagement Mechanism

This type utilizes the electromagnetic force. The pinion is engaged with the ring gear by means of the torsion spring and shift lever. The plunger is shifted by the attracting force and depresses the pinion. When the pinion does not strike the ring gear, smooth engagement occurs, then the contacts close to start the motor.

Also, when the pinion strikes the ring gear teeth, it compresses the torsion spring and loses the contacts. When the current flows through the motor and the armature starts rotating, the pinion is depressed strongly on the ring gear and rotated by means of torsion spring pressure and the helical spline's force. Then, the pinion teeth are arranged in engagement with the ring gear teeth. When the key start switch is turned OFF, the magnetic switch is demagnetized, and the pinion is returned by the torsion spring force. Simultaneously, the contacts open to stop motor operation. In Fig. 2. engagement between the pinion and ring gear is illustrated.

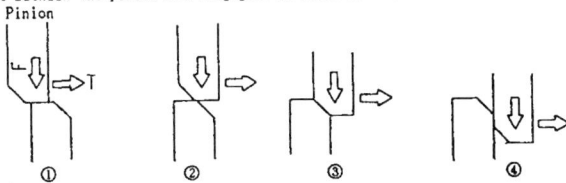

Fig. 2. Engagement of Pinion and Ring Gear

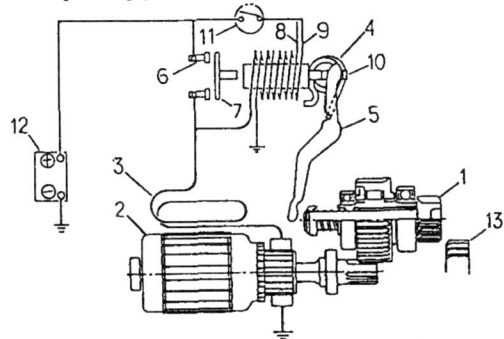

1. Pinion
2. Armature
3. Field Coil
4. Torsion Spring
5. Shift lever
6. Stationary contact
7. Movable Contactor
8. Shunt coil (Holding Coil)
9. Series Coil (Attracting Coil)
10. Plunger
11. Key Start Switch
12. Battery
13. Ring Gear

Fig. 3. Schematic Layout of Reduction Starter's Electrical Circuit

2. Removal
   1) Disconnect the battery's negative or ⊖ side cable at the battery.
   2) Disconnect the battery's posistive or ⊕ cable and the main harness' feed wire from the magnetic switch of the reduction starter.
   3) Disconnect the battery's negative or ⊖ cable at the reduction starter.
   4) Remove the reduction starter retaining bolts and lockwashers. Then withdraw the motor assembly.

Chapter 9 Electrical System
3. Starter Motor

3JH2 Series

3. TROUBLESHOOTING THE STARTER SYSTEM:

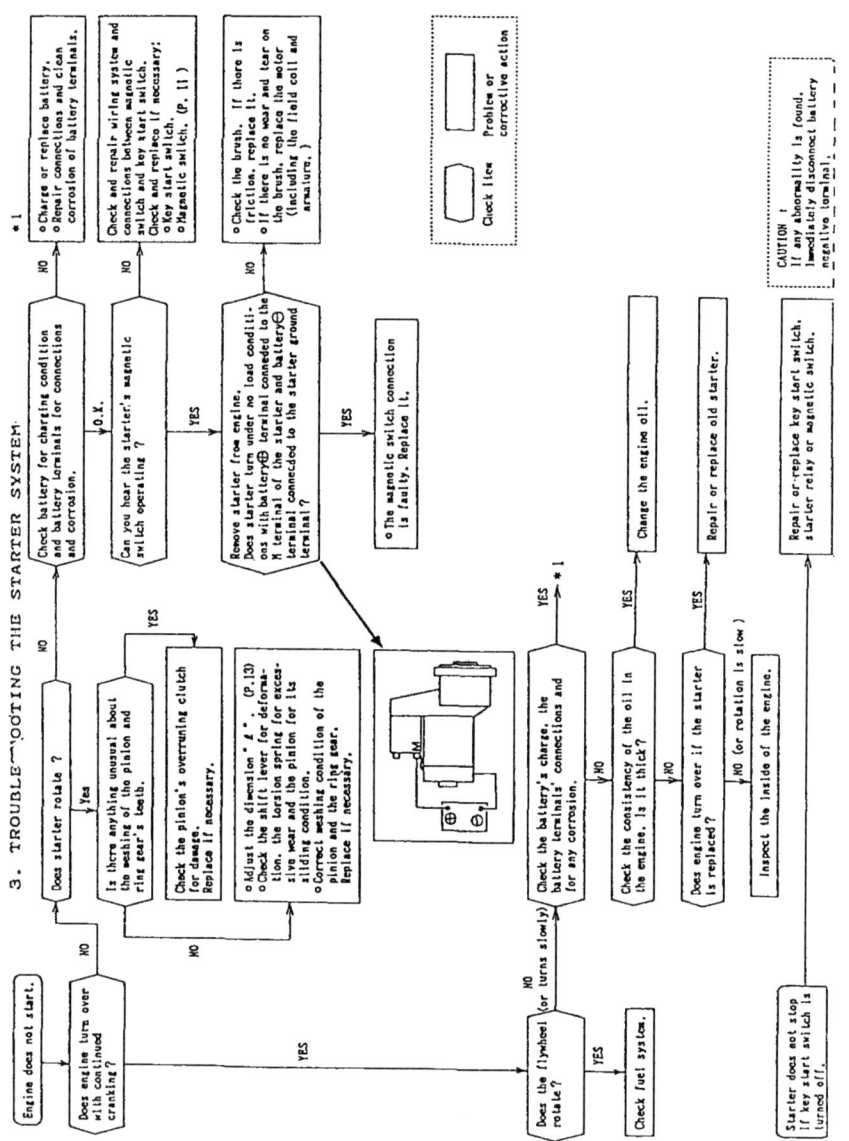

9-10

Printed in Japan
A0A1015-9110SP

Chapter 9 Electrical System
3. Starter Motor

___3JH2 Series___

4. Disassembly
   ▲ 1) The Magnetic Switch's 8 mm Nut
      2) The 5 mm Through Bolts (2)
   ▲ 3) The Rear Cover
   ▲ 4) The Brush Holder
      5) Yoke Assembly
   ▲ 6) Armature
      7) The 6 mm Bolts (2)
      8) Magnetic Switch
   ▲ 9) Torsion Spring
      10) Dust Cover
   ▲11) Shift Lever
      12) The 6 mm Bolts (3)
      13) Gear Case
   ▲14) Center Housing
   ▲15) The Pinion Stopper Clip
      16) Pinion Stopper
      17) Retaining Spring
      18) Pinion Shaft
   ▲19) Clutch Assembly

   ▲: Disassembly Reference Exhibit Is Provided

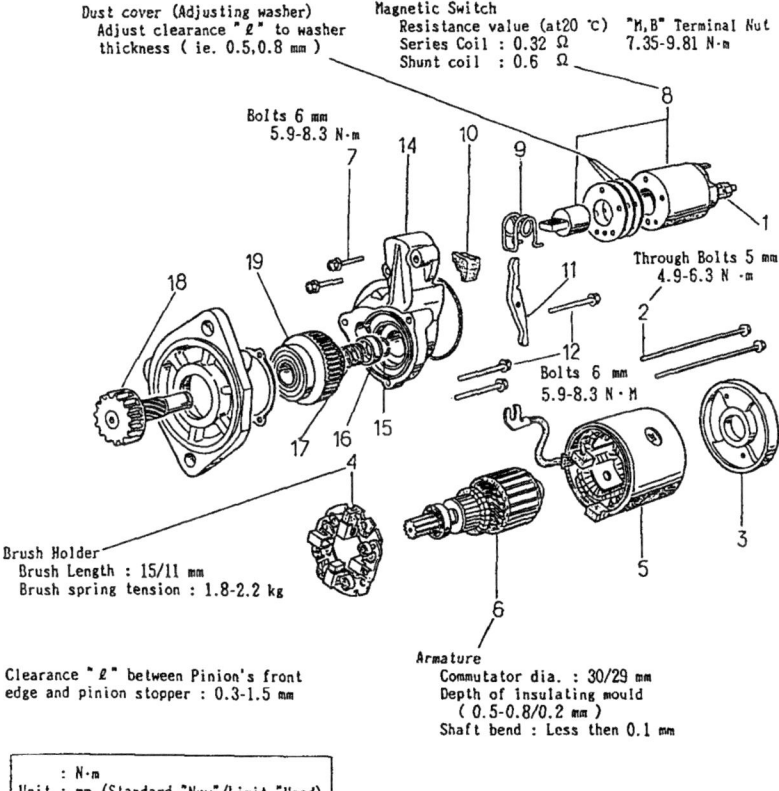

Dust cover (Adjusting washer)
Adjust clearance "ℓ" to washer thickness (ie. 0.5, 0.8 mm)

Magnetic Switch
Resistance value (at 20 °C)
Series Coil : 0.32 Ω
Shunt coil : 0.6 Ω

"M,B" Terminal Nut
7.35-9.81 N·m

Bolts 6 mm
5.9-8.3 N·m

Through Bolts 5 mm
4.9-6.3 N·m

Bolts 6 mm
5.9-8.3 N·M

Brush Holder
Brush Length : 15/11 mm
Brush spring tension : 1.8-2.2 kg

Clearance "ℓ" between Pinion's front edge and pinion stopper : 0.3-1.5 mm

Armature
Commutator dia. : 30/29 mm
Depth of insulating mould
(0.5-0.8/0.2 mm)
Shaft bend : Less then 0.1 mm

: N·m
Unit : mm (Standard "New"/Limit "Used")

Fig. 4. Exhibit of Disassembled Parts

Chapter 9 Electrical System
3. Starter Motor

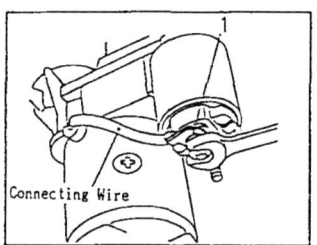

Fig. 5

1) The Magnetic Switch's 8 mm Nut

   Remove the magnetic switch's 8 mm nut and disconnect the connecting wire.

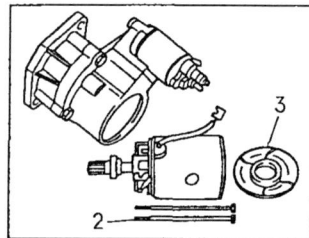

Fig. 6

2) The 5 mm Through Bolts (2)
3) The Rear Cover

   The rear cover is disassembled by removing the 5 mm through bolts.

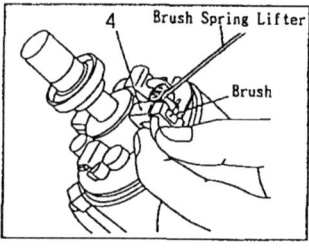

Fig. 7

4) The Brush Holder

   Pull the brush spring up with a brush spring lifter tool so that the ⊖ side brush is separated from the surface of the commutator (otherwise, the brush holder keeps the brush in contact with the commutator). Remove the ⊕ side brush from the brush holder.

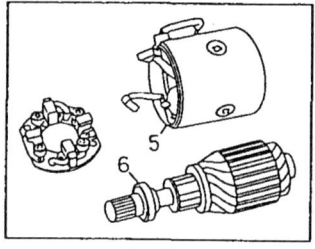

Fig. 8

5) Yoke Assembly
6) Armature

   The armature and the yoke assembly can be disassembled once the brush holder is removed.

Chapter 9 Electrical System
3. Starter Motor — 3JH2 Series

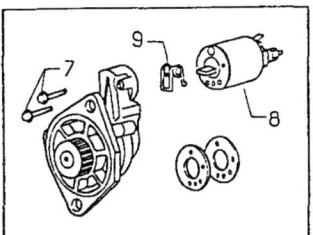

Fig. 9

7) The 6 mm Bolts (2)
8) Magnetic Switch
9) Torsion Spring

The magnetic switch can be disassembled once the 6 mm Bolts are removed. Next, the torsion spring is disassembled from the magnetic switch.

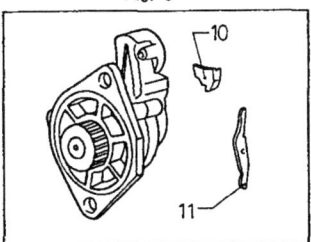

Fig. 10

10) Dust Cover
11) Shift lever

The shift lever can be removed once the dust cover is disassembled from the gear case.

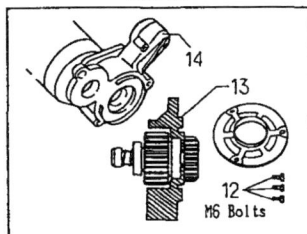

Fig. 11

12) The 6 mm Bolts (3)
13) Gear Case and Pinion Clutch ASSY.
14) Center Housing
20) Gasket

The gear case and the Center Housing can disassembled after the 6 mm Bolts have been removed.

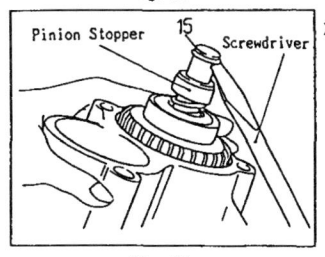

Fig. 12

15) The Pinion Stopper Clip

The pinion stopper clip is removed with a standard screwdriver while the pinion stopper is pushed toward the pinion.

Printed in Japan
A0A1015-9110SP

Chapter 9 Electrical System
3. Starter Motor
                                                         3JH2 Series

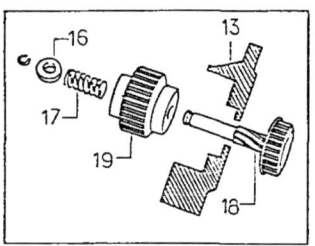

Fig. 13

13) Gear Case
16) Pinion Stopper
17) Retaining Spring
18) Pinion Shaft
19) Clutch Assembly

The pinion stopper, retaining spring, pinion shaft and the clutch assembly can be disassembled once the pinion stopper clip has been removed.

-End of Disassembly-

Chapter 9 Electrical System
3. Starter Motor

5. Inspection and Repair

5-1 Armature
(1) Check the diameter of the Commutator

If the outside diameter of the commutator is below the minimum limit then replace it.

(mm)

Standard (New)	Limit (Used)
30	29

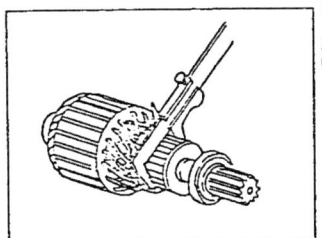

Fig. 14

(2) Continuity Test for the Armature Coil

Use a tester to check for continuity between parallel points on the commutator. If there is continuity, the armature is still good.

No continuity : (Disconnected coil)
Replace the armature.

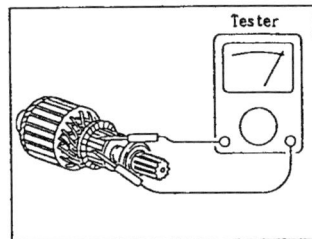

Fig. 15

(3) Insulation Test for the Armature Coil

Use a tester to check for continuity between a point on the commutator and the shaft or the core.
If there is no continuity the armature is still good.

Continuity Exists : (Short circuited coil)
Replace the armature.

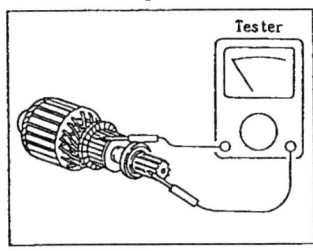

Fig. 16

(4) Check for Surface Distortion on the Armature and the Commutator

Use a dial gauge to measure the distortion of the outside surfaces of the armature core and the commutator. If it is above the limit, then repair or replace it.

(mm)

	Standard (New)	Limit (Used)
Armature	0.05 (MAX)	0.1
Commutator	0.05 (MAX)	0.1

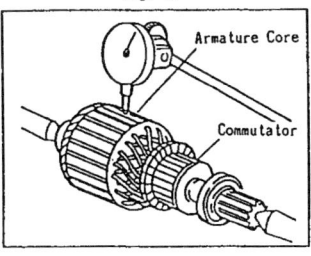

Fig. 17

Chapter 9 Electrical System
3. Starter Motor

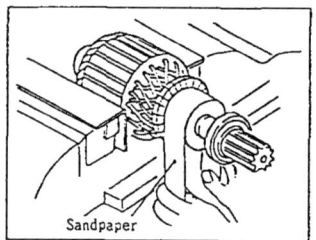

Fig. 18

(5) Check the Surface of the Commutator

If the commutator surface is rough, then please use No. 500-600 sandpaper to make it smooth.

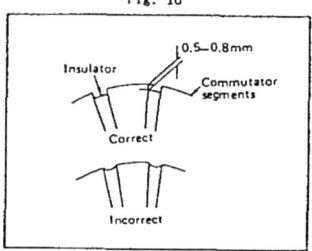

Fig. 19

(6) Check the Depth of Insulating Material from the Commutator Surface

If the depth of the insulating material from the commutator segments is less then the limit, than please repair it by filing it down.

(mm)

Standard (New)	Limit (Used)
0.5 ~ 0.8	0.2

5-2 The Field Coil
(1) Continuity Test for the Field Coil

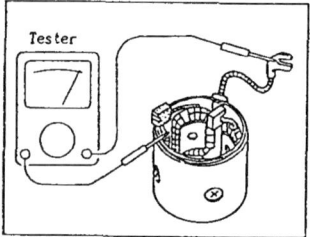

Fig. 20

Check for continuity between the field coils' terminals with a tester. If there is continuity, then it is still good.

No continuity : (Disconnected coil)
                Replace the field coil.

(2) Insulation Test for the Field Coil

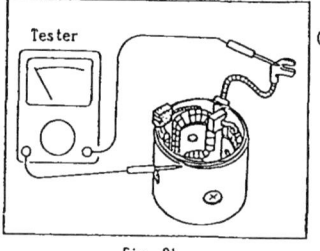

Fig. 21

Check for continuity between the yoke and one terminals of each coil with a tester.
If there is no continuity the field coils are still good.

Continuity Exists : (Short circuited coil)
                    Replace the field coils.

Chapter 9 Electrical System
3. Starter Motor

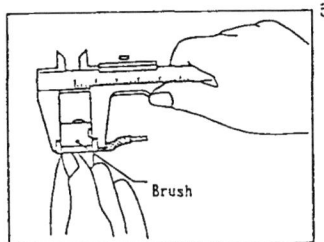

Fig. 22

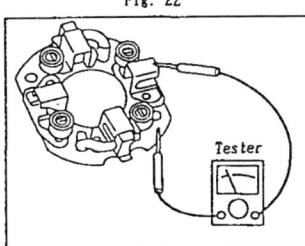

Fig. 23

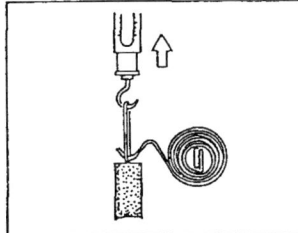

Fig. 24

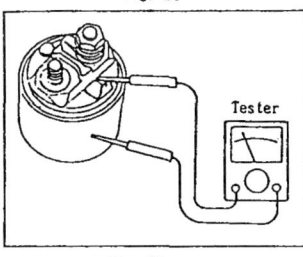

Fig. 25

5-3 Brushes

Measure the length of the brushes and if they are under the limit, replace them.

(mm)

Standard (New)	Limit (Used)
15	11

5-4 Brush Holder

Insulation Test for the Brush Holder

Check for continuity between the brush holder's positive side and its base (negative side) with a tester. If there is no continuity the brush holder is still good.

Continuity Exists : (Unsatisfactory insulation)
Replace the brush holder.

(3) Inspection of the Brush Springs

Check the weight of the brush springs.

Standard Weight (Kg)
1.8 ~ 2.2

5-5 Magnetic Switch

(1) Continuity Test for the Shunt Coil

Check for continuity between the "S" terminals and "M" (the switch body) with a tester. If there is continuity, then it is still good.

No continuity : (Disconnected coil)
Replace the magnetic switch.

Chapter 9 Electrical System
3. Starter Motor _____ 3JH2 Series

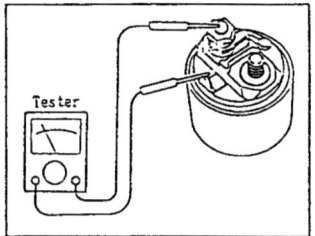

Fig. 26

(2) Continuity Test for the Series Coil

Check for continuity between the "S" and "M" terminals with a tester. If there is continuity, then it is still good.

No continuity : (Disconnected coil)
Replace the magnetic switch.

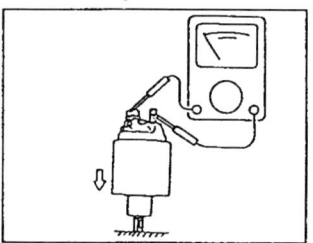

Fig. 27

(3) Continuity Test for Contact-Points

Put the plunger on the under side and then push the magnetic switch down. At this time, check for continuity between the "B" and "M" terminals with a tester. If there is continuity, then it is still good.

No continuity : (Insufficient Continuity)
Replace the magnetic switch.

5-6 Pinion Clutch

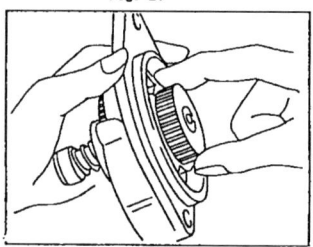

Fig. 28

(1) Inspection of the Pinion

Rotate the pinion manually. While rotating it in the direction of normal operation, smoothly reverse the direction of rotation to confirm that it locks. In the event of any irregularity, replace it.

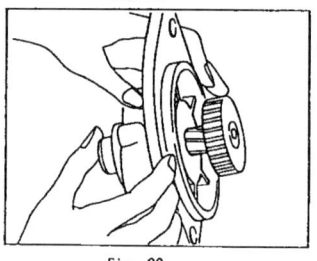

Fig. 29

(2) Pinion Sliding Test

Check to see if the pinion slides up smoothly when the end is pushed. If there are scratches, rust or if the required force seems too strong, please repair it. If too much grease is applied to the pinion shaft, Then it will seem hard to slide.

Printed in Japan
A0A1015-9110SP

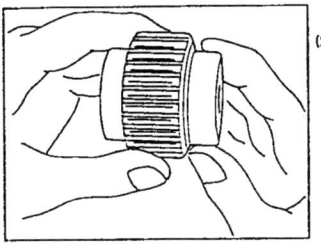

Fig. 30

(2) Inspection of the Ball Bearings

Rotate the ball bearings outer ring surface with your finger tips and check to see if it rocks perpendicularly to the direction of rotation.

Chapter 9 Electrical System
3. Starter Motor

6. Reassembly

Reassembly is in the reverse order of disassembly. However, note the following points.

1. Tightening Torques : Refer to page 5 of the reference materials for the tightening torques of particular screws.

2. The Places to Apply Grease :
   - ①······· The moving parts of shift lever.
   - ②······· The sliding surface of magnetic switch plunger.
       The surface of pinion.
   - ③······· The toothed wheel inside the gear case.

Part Item	Grease	①	②	③
		Shell Alvania Grease No. 2	Aero Shell Grease No. 7	Epnoc Grease No. 2
Worked Penetration 60 Times at 25℃		280	272	282
Dropping Point		182	260	200
Viscosity	at 37.8 ℃	145	—	—
	at 98.7 ℃	—	32	13.9
Starting Torque /Running Torque (Ball Bearing Dia. 47 mm) g-cm	at -30 ℃	2890/800	—	—
	at -40 ℃	—	520/140	—

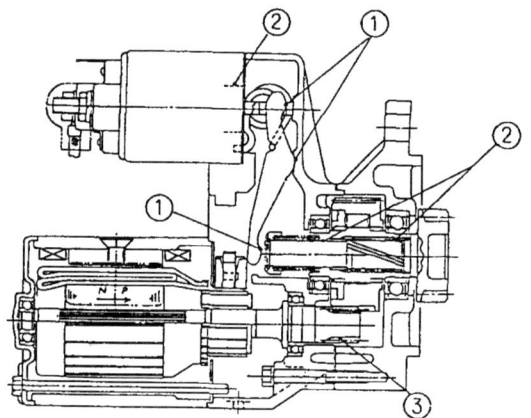

Fig. 31 Kind of Grease

3. Reassembly of the Magnetic Switch

(1) Introduce the torsion springs into the magnetic switch and connect the shifting lever.

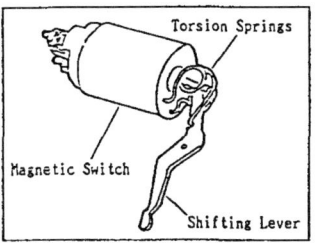
Fig. 32

(2) To connect and stabilize the magnetic switch to the gear case, pull out the pinion and connect the shift lever (connected to the magnetic switch) to the gear case with a 6 mm bolt.
Do not forget to reconnect the dust cover.

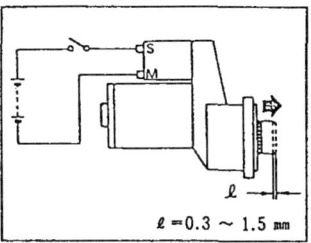
Fig. 33

(4) Measurement of the Pinion's Motion

After connecting the positive $\oplus$ side of the battery to the "S" terminal and the negative $\ominus$ side to the "M" terminal and turning the switch on, measure the amount of movement " ℓ " in the direction of the pinion's thrust.

Standard length " ℓ "
$0.3 \sim 1.5$ mm

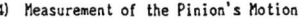
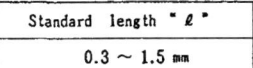

$\ell = 0.3 \sim 1.5$ mm
Fig. 34

Note : When taking the measurement, do so by pushing the pinion softly in the direction of the large arrow.

(5) When the measurement " ℓ " is outside the standard range, adjust the dust cover by inserting it further or loosening it.

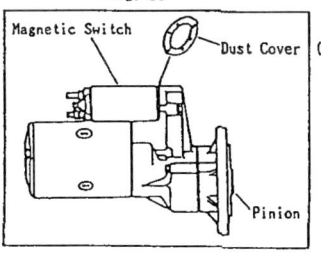
Fig. 35

Chapter 9 Electrical System
3. Starter Motor

3JH2 Series

7. Operation Specifications Check

   Perform the no-load test as instructed because this provides an easy way to confirm the specifications.
   Note: The rating is 30 seconds, so perform the test quickly.

(1) The No-load Test

   Set the starter securely on a test bench and lay the lines as shown in fig. 36. When the switch is turned off, the electric current flows into the starter in no-load operating conditions. With the electric current flowing, measure the voltage and the r.p.m. and see whether they satisfy the specifications.

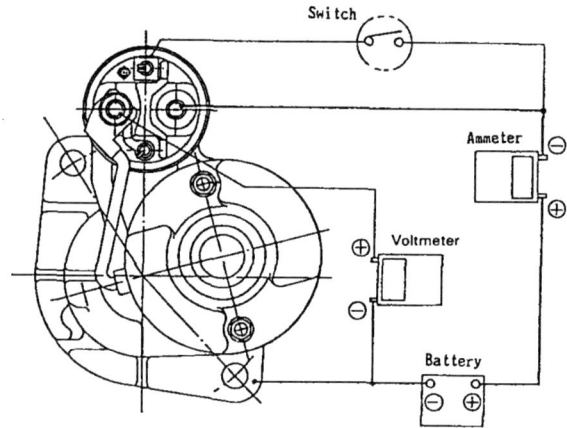

Fig. 36   The No-load Test

Chapter 9 Electrical System
3. Starter Motor
3JH2 Series

8. Appendix
(1) Specifications

Hitachi Model No.		S114-483
YANMAR Part No.		171008-77010
Yoke Diameter	(mm)	80
Nominal power	(kw)	1.4
Nominal voltage	(V)	12
Rating	(sec)	30
Direction of Rotation (Looking from the pinion side)		Clockwise
Number of Pinion Teeth		15
Weigt	(kg)	5.0
No load	Terminal voltage (V) Electric Current (A) Revolutions (rpm)	12 100 (MAX) 4300 (MIN)
Load	Terminal voltage (V) Electric Current (A) Torque (N·m) Revolutions (rpm)	9.8 200 4.5 (MIN) 1900 (MIN)

4. Alternator Standard, 12V/55A

The alternator serves to keep the battery constantly charged. It is installed on the cylinder block by a bracket, and is driven from the V-pulley at the end of the crankshaft by a V-belt.

The type of alternator used in this engine is ideal for high speed engines with a wide range of engine speeds. It contains diodes that convert AC to DC, and an IC regulator that keeps the generated voltage constant even when the engine speed changes.

4-1 Features

The alternator contains a regulator using an IC, and has the following features.

(1) The IC regulator is self-contained, and has no moving parts (mechanical contact points). It therefore has superior features such as freedom from vibration, no fluctuation of voltage during use, and no need for readjustment.
Also, it is of the over-heating compensation type and can automatically adjust the voltage to the most suitable level depending on the operating temperature.
(2) The regulator is integrated within the alternator to simplify external wiring.
(3) It is an alternator designed for compactness, lightness of weight, and high output.
(4) A newly developed U-shaped diode is used to provide increased reliability and easier checking and maintenance.
(5) As the alternator is to be installed on board, the following measures are taken to provide salt-proofing.
 1) The front and rear covers are salt-proofed.
 2) Salt-proof paint is applied to the diode.
 3) The terminal, where the inboard harness is connected to the alternator, is nickel plated.

4-2 Specifications

Model of alternator	LR155-20 (HITACHI)
Model of IC regulator	TRIZ-63 (HITACHI)
Battery voltage	12V
Nominal output	12V/55A
Earth polarity	Negative earth (⊖)
Direction of rotation (viewed from pulley end)	Clockwise
Weight	4.3kg (9.5lb.)
Rated speed	5000 rpm
Operating speed	1000 ~ 9000
Speed for 13.5V	1000 or less
Output current at 20°C	over 53A/5000 rpm
Regulated voltage	14.5 ±0.3V (Standard temperature voltage gradient, −0.01/°C)

4-3 Characteristics

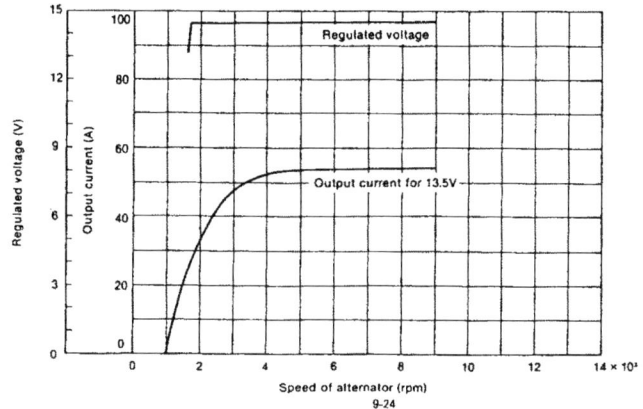

Speed of alternator (rpm)

Chapter 9 Electrical System
4. Alternator 3JH2 Series

4-4 Construction

This is a standard rotating field type three-phase alternator. It consists of six major parts: the pulley, fan, front cover, rotor, stator and rear cover. The IC regulator is an integral part of the alternator.

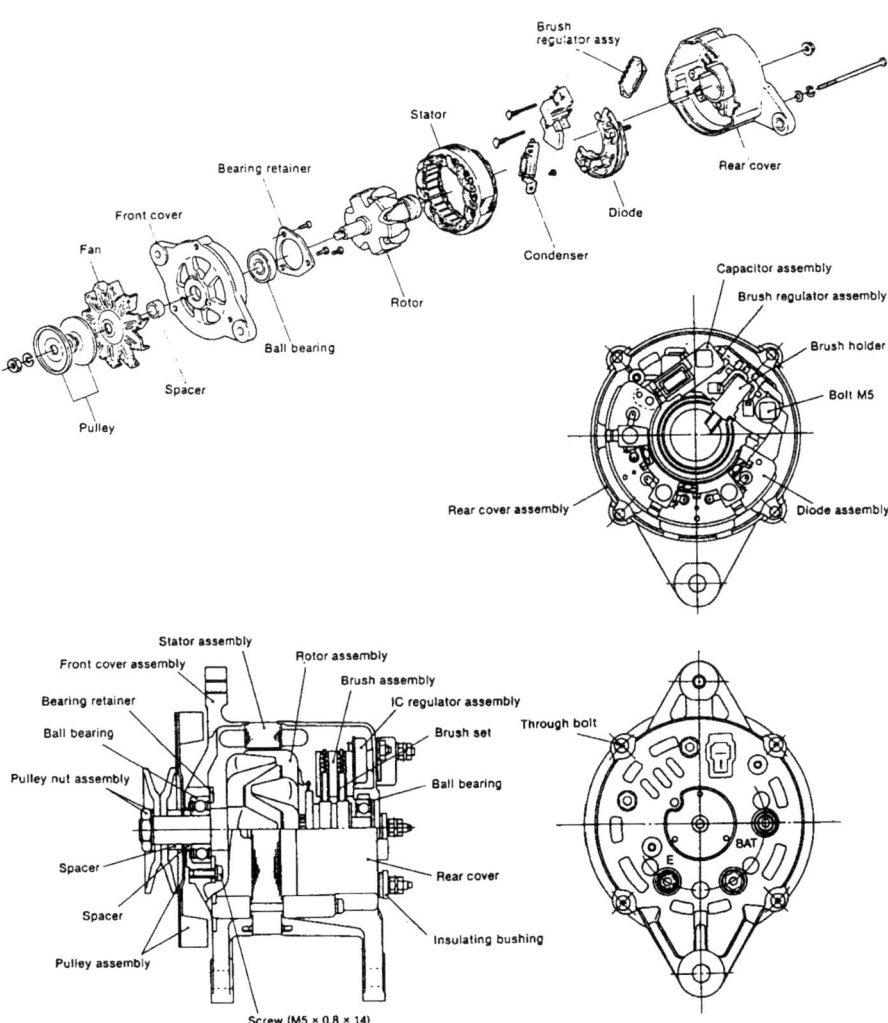

Chapter 9 Electrical System
4. Alternator

3JH2 Series

4-5 Alternator functioning

(1) IC regulator
The IC regulator is the transistor (Tr_1) which is series-connected with the rotor. The IC regulator controls the output voltage of the generator by breaking or conducting the rotor coil (exciting) current.
When the output voltage of the generator is within the standard value, the transistor (Tr_1) turns on. When the voltage exceeds the standard value, the Zener diode goes on and the transistor (Tr_1) turns off.
With the repeated turning on and off of the transistor, the output voltage is kept at the standard value. (Refer to the circuit diagram below.)

(2) Charge lamp
When the transistor (Tr_1) is on, the charge lamp key switch is turned to ON, and current flows to R_1, R_4 and to Tr_1 to light the lamp. When the engine starts to run and output voltage is generated in the stator coil, the current stops flowing to this circuit, turning off the charge lamp.

(3) Circuit diagram

4-6 Handling precautions

(1) Be careful of the battery's polarity (+, − terminals), and do not connect the wrong terminals to the wrong cables, or the battery will be short-circuited by the generator diode.
In this case too much current will flow, the IC regulator and diodes burn out, and the wire harness will burn.
(2) Make sure of the correct connection of each terminal.
(3) When quick-charging, etc., disconnect either the battery terminal on the AC generator or the terminal on the battery.
(4) Do not short-circuit the terminals.
(5) Do not conduct any tests using high tension insulation resistance. (The diodes and IC regulator will burn out.)

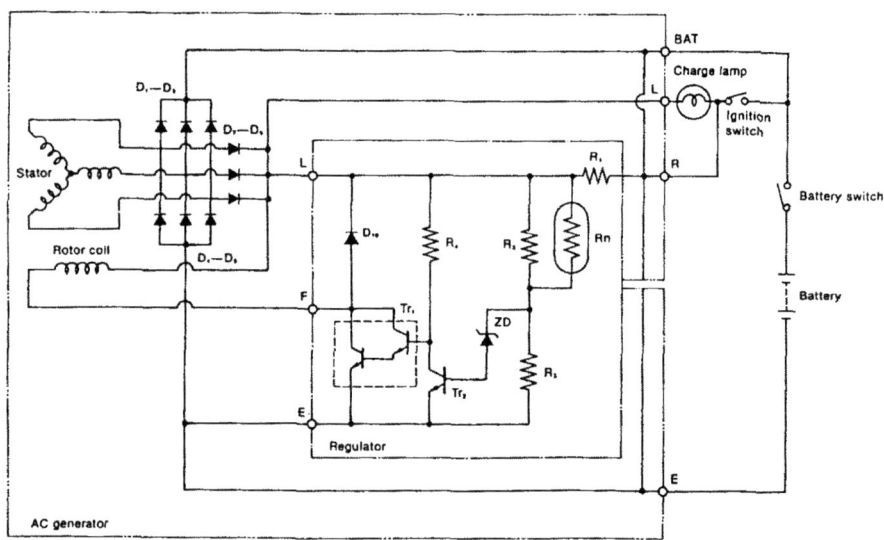

BAT:	Generator output terminal	D_1–D_6:	Output commutation diode
D_{10}:	IC protecting diode	R_1–R_4:	Resistor
L:	Charge lamp terminal	D_7–D_9:	Charging lamp switching diode
ZD:	Zener diode	F:	To supply current to rotor coil
E:	Earth	Rn:	Thermistor
Tr_1, Tr_2:	Transistor		(Temperature gradient resistance)

4-7 Disassembling the alternator

(1) Remove the through-bolt, and separate the front assembly from the rear assembly.

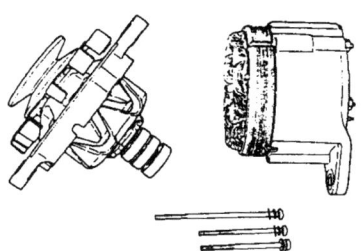

(2) Remove the pulley nut, and pull out the rotor from the front cover.

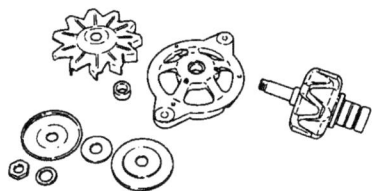

(3) Remove the ø5mm (ø0.1969in.) screw from the front cover, and then remove the ball bearing.

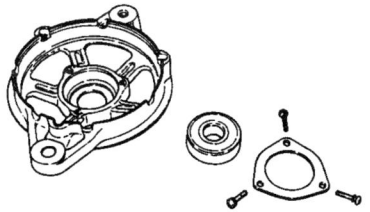

(4) Remove the nut, the brush-holder, and diode fixing nut at the BAT, and the terminal screws of the rear cover. Separate the rear cover from the stator (with the diode and brush holder).

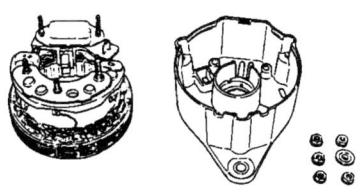

(5) Disconnect the soldered joint of the stator lead wire, and remove the diode and brush regulator assemblies from the stator at the same time.

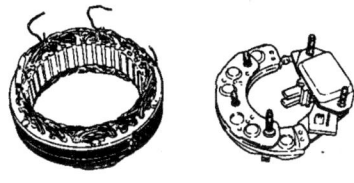

(6) Separating the regulator
1) To separate the regulator, remove the ø3mm (ø0.1181in.) rivet which keeps the diode assembly and the brushless regulator in place, and the soldered joint of the L-terminal.

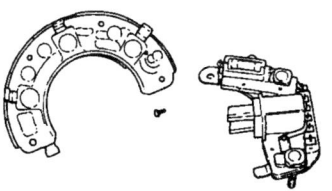

Chapter 9 Electrical System
4. Alternator

3JH2 Series

2) To replace the IC regulator, disconnect the soldered joint of the IC regulator and pull out the two bolts. Do not remove these two bolts except when replacing the IC regulator.

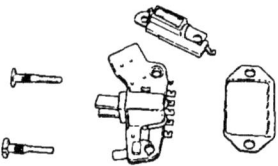

After repeating the above test, if any diode is found to be defective, replace the diode assembly. Since there is no terminal on the auxiliary diode, check the continuity between both ends of the diode.

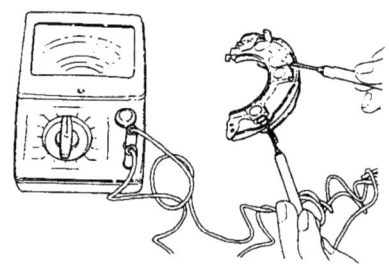

4-8 Inspection and adjustment

(1) Diode

Between terminals		BAT (+ side diode)	
U.V.W.	Tester wire	+ side	− side
	+ side		No continuity
	− side	Continuity	

Between terminals		E (− side diode)	
U.V.W.	Tester wire	+ side	− side
	+ side		Continuity
	− side	No continuity	

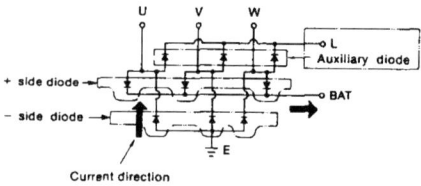

U.V.W.: terminal from the stator coil

Current flows only in one direction in the diode as shown in Fig. 181. Accordingly, when there is continuity between each terminal (e.g. BAT and U), the diode is in normal condition (photo). When there is no continuity, the diode is defective.
When the tester is connected in the reverse of above, there should be no continuity. If there is, the diode is defective.

CAUTION: Do not use high tensile insulation resistance such as meggers, etc. for testing. The diode may burn out.

(2) Rotor
Inspect the slip ring surface, rotor coil continuity and insulation.
1) Inspecting the slip ring surface
Check if the surface of the slip ring is sufficiently smooth. If the surface is rough, grind the surface with No. 500—600 sand paper. If it is contaminated with oil, etc., wipe the surface clean with alcohol.

Slip ring outer dia.	Standard	Wear limit
	⌀31.6mm (1.2441in.)	⌀30.6mm (1.2049in.)

2) Rotor coil continuity test
Check the continuity in the slip ring with the tester. If there is no continuity, there is a wire break. Replace the rotor coil.

Resistance value	Approx. 3.34Ω at 20°C

Printed in Japan
_A0A1015-9110SP_

Chapter 9 Electrical System
4. Alternator — 3JH2 Series

3) Rotor coil insulation test
Check the continuity between the slip ring and the rotor core, or the shaft. If there is continuity, insulation inside the rotor is defective, causing a short with the earth circuit. Replace the rotor coil.

2) Stator coil insulation test
Check the continuity between the terminals and the stator core. If there is continuity, insulation of the stator coil is defective. This will cause a short-circuit with the earth core. Replace the stator coil.

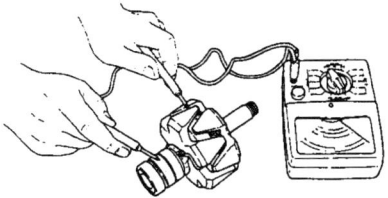

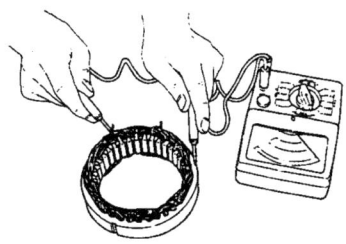

4) Check the rear side ball bearing. If the rotation of the bearing is heavy, or produces abnormal sounds, replace the ball bearing.

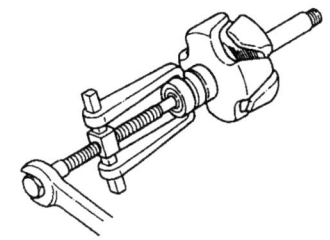

(4) Brush
The brush is hard and wears slowly, but when it is worn beyond the allowable limit, replace it. When replacing the brush, also check the strength of the brush spring. To check, push the spring down to 2mm (0.0787in.) from the end surface of the brush holder, and read the gauge.

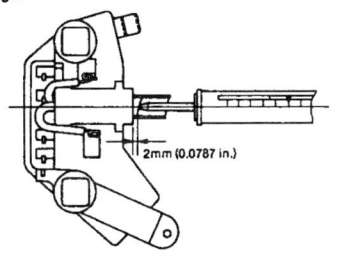

| Brush spring strength | 255—345g (0.56 ~ 0.76lb.) |

(5) Brush wear
Check the brush length.
The brush wears very little, but replace the brush if worn over the wear limit line printed on the brush.

(3) Stator
1) Stator coil continuity test
Check the continuity between each terminal of the stator coil. If there is no continuity, there is a wire break in the stator coil. Replace the stator coil.

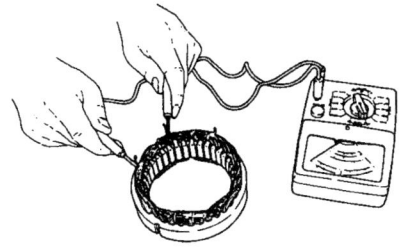

| Resistance value | Approx. 0.077Ω at 20°C
1-phase resistance |

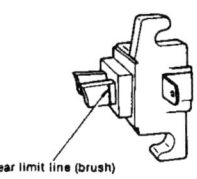

Wear limit line (brush)

mm (in.)

	Maintenance standard	Wear limit
Brush length	16 (0.6299)	9 (0.3543)

Chapter 9 Electrical System
4. Alternator

3JH2 Series

(6) IC regulator
Connect the variable resistance, two 12V batteries, resistor, and voltmeter as shown in the diagram.

1) Use the following measuring devices.
   - Resistor (R.)   100Ω, 2W, 1pc.
   - Variable resistor (Rv) 0—300Ω, 12W, 1pc.
   - Battery (BAT₁, BAT₂)   12V, 2pcs.
   - DC voltmeter   0—30V, 0.5 class 1pc.
                             (measure at 3 points)

2) Check the regulator in the following sequence, according to the diagram.
   a) Check V_3 (BAT₁ + BAT₂ voltage). If the voltage is 20—26V, both BAT₁ and BAT₂ are normal.
   b) While measuring V_2 (F-E terminal voltage), move Rv gradually from the 0-position. Check if there is a point where the V_2 voltage rises sharply from below 2.0V to over 2.0V. If there is no such point, the regulator is defective. Replace the regulator. If there is a sharp voltage rise when testing, return the Rv to the 0-position, and connect the voltmeter to the V_1 position.
   c) While measuring V_1 (voltage between L-E terminals), move Rv gradually from the 0-position. There should be a point where the voltage of V_1 rises sharply by 2—6V. Measure the voltage of V_1 just before this sharp voltage rise. This is the regulating voltage of the regulator. If this voltage of V_1 is within the standard limit, the regulator is normal. If the voltage deviates from the limit, the regulator is defective. Replace the regulator.

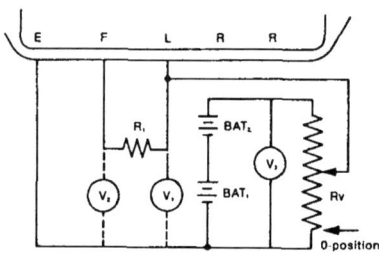

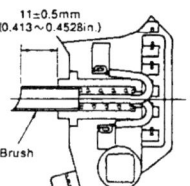

11±0.5mm (0.413~0.4528in.)

Brush

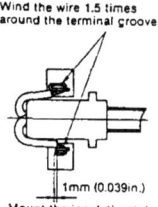

Wind the wire 1.5 times around the terminal groove.

1mm (0.039in.)
Mount the insulation tube on the terminal surface.

NOTES: 1. Use non-acid type paste.
       2. The soldering iron temperature is 300 ~ 350°C.

2) Mount the IC regulator on the brush holder as illustrated, and press in the M5 bolt. Do not forget to assemble the bushing and the connecting plate at the same time.
(If the bushing is left out, the output terminal will be earthed and the battery short-circuited).

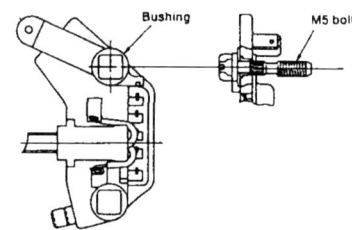

Bushing   M5 bolt

NOTES: 1. Insertion pressure is 100kg (220.5 lbs.)
       2. Insert vertically.

(2) Connecting the brush regulator assembly and diode
1) Check the rivets
   Place the rivets as shown in the figure, and then calk them using the calking tool.

Calking torque	500kg (1102 lbs.)

2) Connect the brush to the diode.
   Insert the brush side terminal into the diode terminal, calk it, and then solder into place.

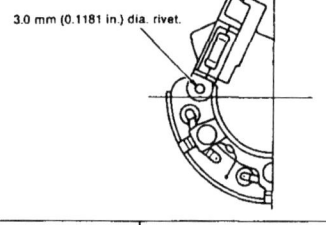

3.0 mm (0.1181 in.) dia. rivet.

Rivetting pressure	500kg (1102 lbs.)

4·9 Reassembling the alternator

Reassembly is done in the reverse order of disassembly. For reassembly, be careful of the following points. (Refer to 4—7 disassembling alternator).
(1) Assembling the brush regulator
 1) Solder the brush.
    Position the brush as shown in the drawing and solder it. Be careful not to let the solder drip into the pig tail (lead wire).

Printed in Japan
A0A1015-9110SP

Chapter 9 Electrical System
4. Alternator

(3) Assembling the rear cover
Insert pins from the outside of the rear cover. Install the brush on the brush holder, then attach the rear cover. After assembly, pull out the pins.

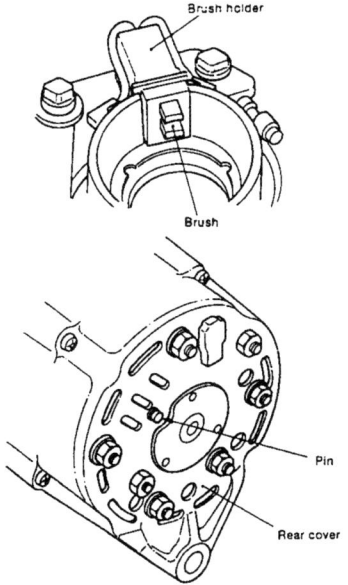

(4) Tightening torques

Positions	Tightening torque kg-cm (ft-lb)
Brush holder fixing	32—40 (2.31 ~ 2.89)
Diode fixing	32—40 (2.31 ~ 2.89)
Bearing retainer fixing	32—40 (2.31 ~ 2.89)
Pulley nut tightening	400—600 (28.93 ~ 43.40)
Through-bolt tightening	32—40 (2.31 ~ 2.89)

4-10 Performance test

Conduct a performance test on the reassembled AC generator as follows. The following is the circuit for the performance test.

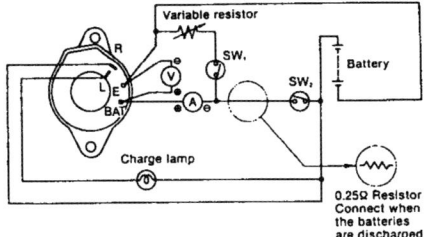

(1) Measuring devices

DC voltmeter	0—15V or 0—30V, 0.5 Class, 1pc.
DC ammeter	0—100A, 1.0 Class, 1pc.
Variable resistor	0—0.25Ω, 1kW, 1pc.
Lamp	12V, 3W
100Ω resistor	3W
0.25Ω resistor	25W

(2) Measuring the regulating voltage
1) When measuring devices are connected in the performance test circuit as shown above, the charge lamp lights.
2) Close SW_2 while keeping SW_1 open and run the AC generator. When the revolutions of the generator are gradually raised, the charge lamp goes off.
3) Raise the revolutions of the AC generator, and read the voltmeter gauge when the revolutions reach about 5,000 rpms.

NOTES: 1. Make sure that the ammeter indication at this time is less than 5A. If the indication is over 5A, connect the 0.25Ω resistor. The voltmeter indication at this time must be within the prescribed regulating voltage value.
2. Raise the AC generator revolutions high to make sure the regulating voltage does not fluctuate along with changes in the revolution speed.

(3) Precautions for measuring the regulating voltage
1) When measuring the voltage, measure the voltage between the AC generator BAT terminal, or Battery + terminal, and AC generator E-terminal.
2) Use a fully charged battery.
3) Measure the voltage quickly.
4) Keep SW_1 open for measurement.

Chapter 9 Electrical System
4. Alternator
3JH2 Series

4-11 Troubleshooting

(1) Charging failure

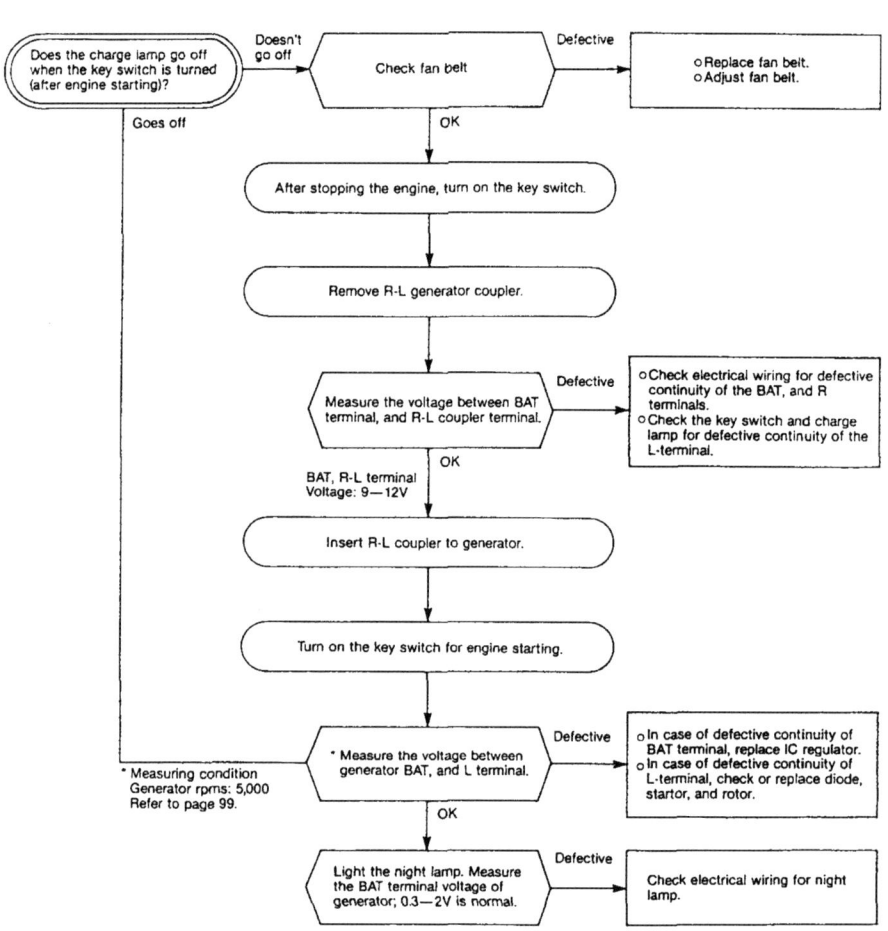

9-32

Printed in Japan
A0A1015-9110SP

Chapter 9 Electrical System
4. Alternator

(2) Overcharging

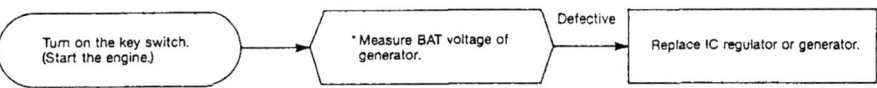

(3) Charge lamp failure

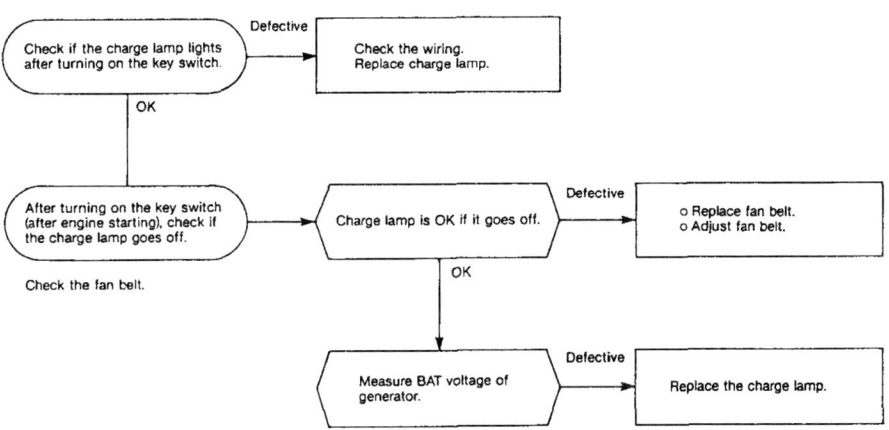

Chapter 9 Electrical System
5. Instrument Panel

3JH2 Series

5. Instrument Panel

5-1 B2-type instrument panel with wiring

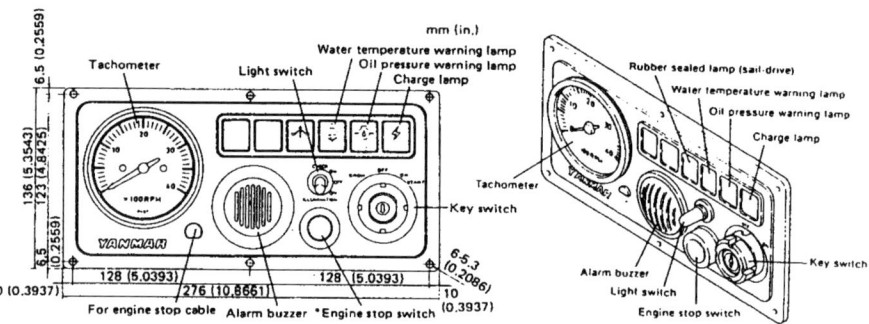

5-2 C-type instrument panel

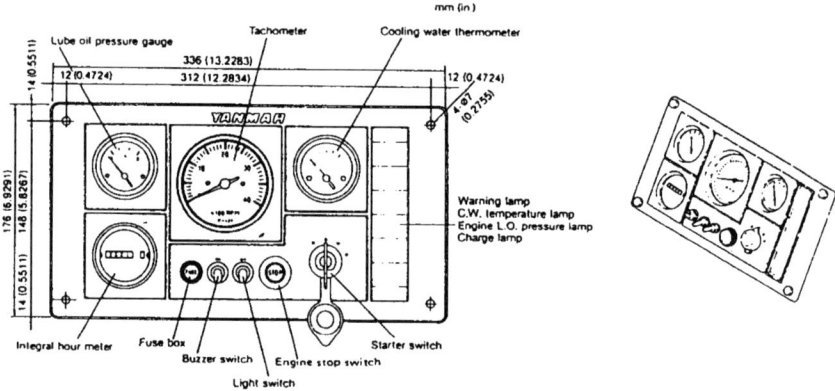

5-5 Extension codes
Extension cord for instrument panel

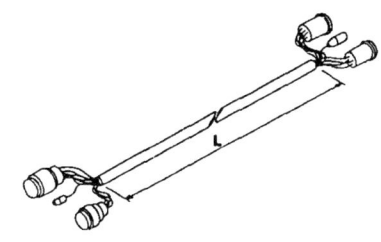

mm(in.)

	Part code No.	L
Extention cord 4M	119171-77710	3750 ~ 3850 (147.63 ~ 151.57)
Extention cord 6M	119171-77701	5750 ~ 5850 (226.38 ~ 230.31)

6. Warning Devices

6-1 Oil pressure alarm

If the engine oil pressure is below 0.1 ~ 0.3 kg/cm² (1.42 ~ 4.26 lb/in.²), with the main switch in the ON position, the contacts of the oil pressure switch are closed by a spring, and the lamp is illuminated through the lamp → oil pressure switch → ground circuit system. If the oil pressure is normal, the switch contacts are opened by the lubricating oil pressure and the lamp remains off.

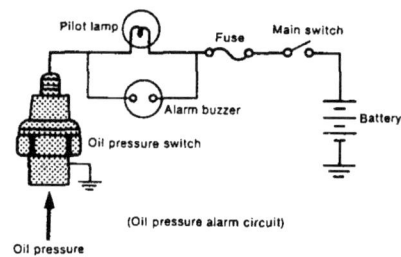

(Oil pressure alarm circuit)

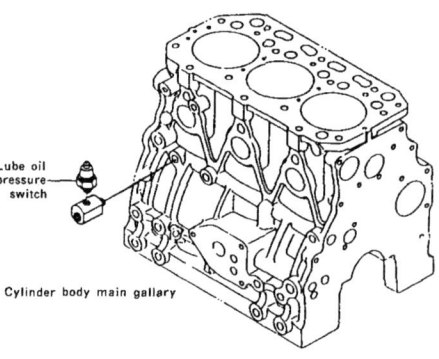

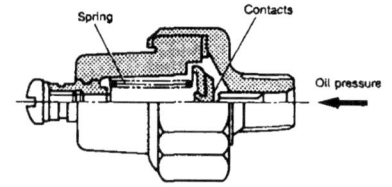

Oil pressure switch

Part No.	124060-39451
Rated voltage	12V
Operation pressure	0.1 ~ 0.3kg/cm² (1.422 ~ 4.266lb/in.²)
Lamp capacity	5W

Inspection

Problem	Inspection item	Inspection method	Corrective action
Lamp not illuminated when main switch set to ON	1. Oil pressure lamp blown out	(1) Visual inspection	Replace lamp
		(2) Lamp not illuminated even when main switch set to ON position and terminals of oil pressure switch grounded	
	2. Operation of oil pressure switch	Lamp illuminated when checked as described in (2) above	Replace oil pressure switch
Lamp not extinguished while engine running	1. Oil level low	Stop engine and check oil level with dipstick	Add oil
	2. Oil pressure low	Measure oil pressure	Repair bearing wear and adjust regulator valve
	3. Oil pressure faulty	Switch faulty if abnormal at (1) and (2) above	Replace oil pressure switch
	4. Wiring between lamp and oil pressure switch faulty	Cut the wiring between the lamp and switch and wire with separate wire	Repair wiring harness

6-2 Cooling water temperature alarm

A water temperature lamp and water temperature gauge, backed up by an alarm in the instrument panel, are used to monitor the temperature of the engine cooling water. A high thermal expansion material is set on the end of the water temperature unit. When the cooling water temperature reaches a specified high temperature, the contacts are closed, and an alarm lamp and buzzer are activated at the instrument panel.

Operating temperature	ON	93 ~ 97°C (199 ~ 206°F)
	OFF	88°C (190°F) or high
Electric capacity		DC 12V, 1A
Response time		with in 60 sec.
Indication color		Green
Part code No.		127610-91350
Tightening torque		2.40 ~ 3.20 kg-m (17.35 ~ 23.14 ft-lb)

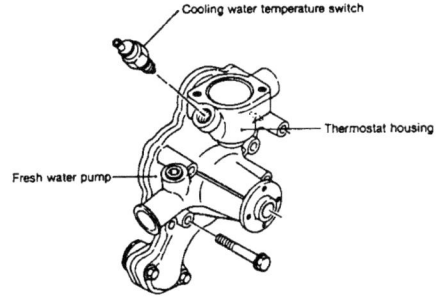

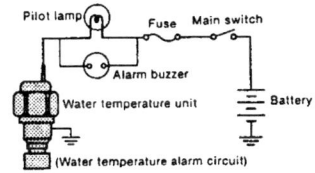
(Water temperature alarm circuit)

6-3 Sender unit for lube oil pressure gauge

The sender unit for the lube oil pressure gauge has a mounting seat for mounting on the lube oil filter bracket. Oil pressure is measured when the oil enters into the main gallery after being fed from the lube oil cooler and passing through the oil pressure control valve. Be sure to mount a vibration damper when mounting the oil pressure sender unit.

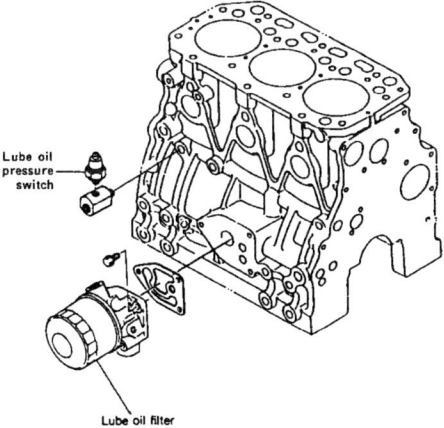

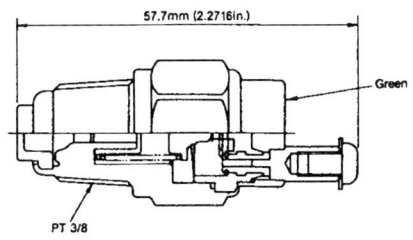

Chapter 9 Electrical System
6. Warning Devices

3JH2 Series

Lube oil pressure sender unit

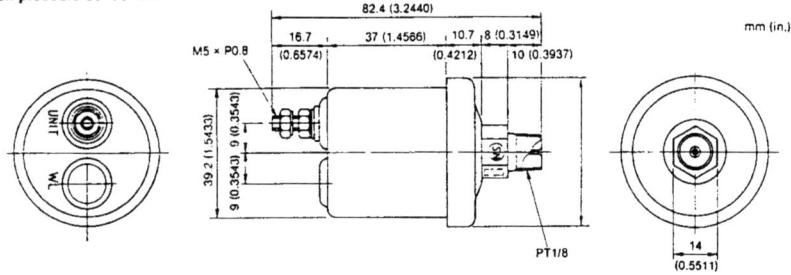

Type	Resistance switch
Rated voltage	DC 12/DC 24
Max. operating pressure	8kg/cm² (113.76 lb/in.²)
Part code No.	144626-91560

6-4 Sender unit for the cooling water temperature gauge

The water temperature sender unit has a mounting seat for mounting on the fresh water pump unit. Water temperature is measured when the cooling water flows into the thermostat housing after leaving the cylinder head.

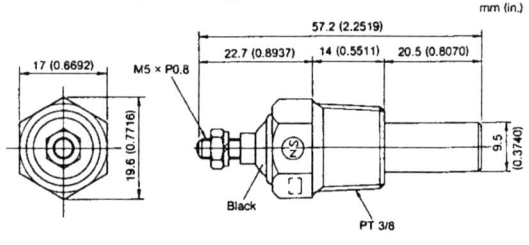
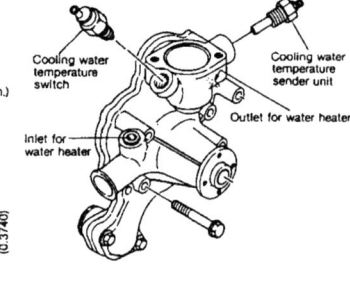

Type	Thermistor switch
Rated voltage	12V/24V
Part code No.	144626-91570

9-38

Printed in Japan
A0A1015-9110SP

7. Air Heater (Optional)

An air heater is available for warming intake air when starting in cold areas in winter. The air heater is mounted between the intake manifold and intake manifold coupling. The device is operated by the glow switch on the instrument panel.

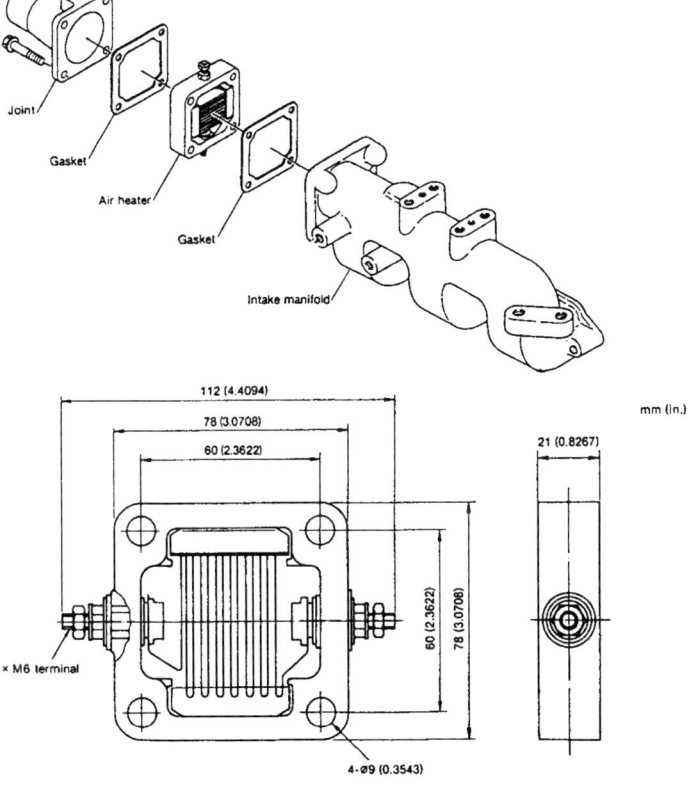

Rated output	400W
Rated current	33.3A
Rated voltage	DC 12V
Rated operating time	Engine operation: 60 sec. Engine stop: 30 sec.
Range of operating temperature	+50°C ~ 30°C (122°F ~ −22°F)
Part code No.	129400-77500

8. Electric type Engine Stopping Device (Optional)

To employ the electric engine stop device, the stop lever of the fuel injection pump is connected to the solenoid with a connection metal.
The device is operated by the stop switch on the instrument panel.

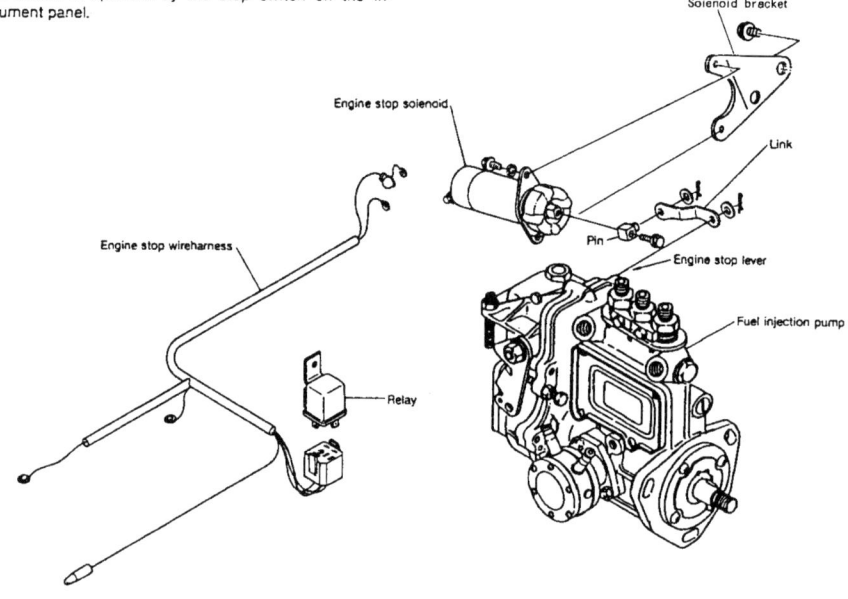

8-1 Solenoid

Solenoid model	1502-12A7U1B
Rated voltage	12V
Loaded current	30A
Loaded force	9kg (19.84lb)
No-load current	0.7A
No-load force	4kg (8.82lb)

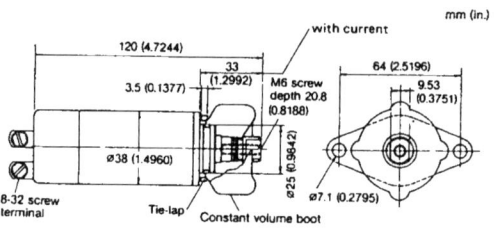

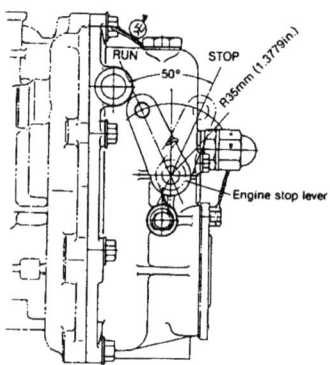

Chapter 9 Electrical System
8. Electric Type Engine Stop Device (Optional)

3JH2 Series

8-2 Relay

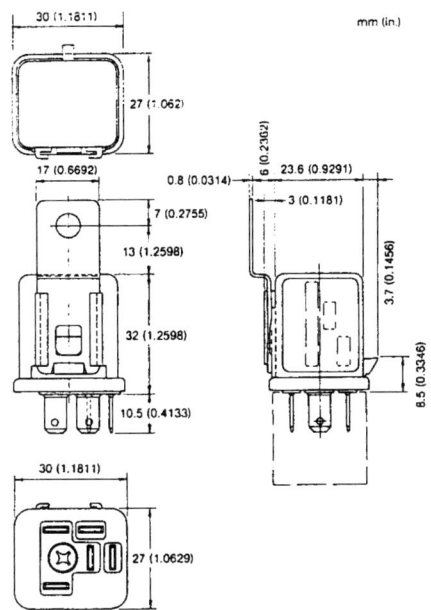

Rated voltage	12V
Contact current	Lamp: 20A, extra-lamp: 25A
Range of operation	−30°C ~ +90°C (−22°F ~ 194°F)
Part code No.	124617-91850

8-3 Wire harness of engine stop

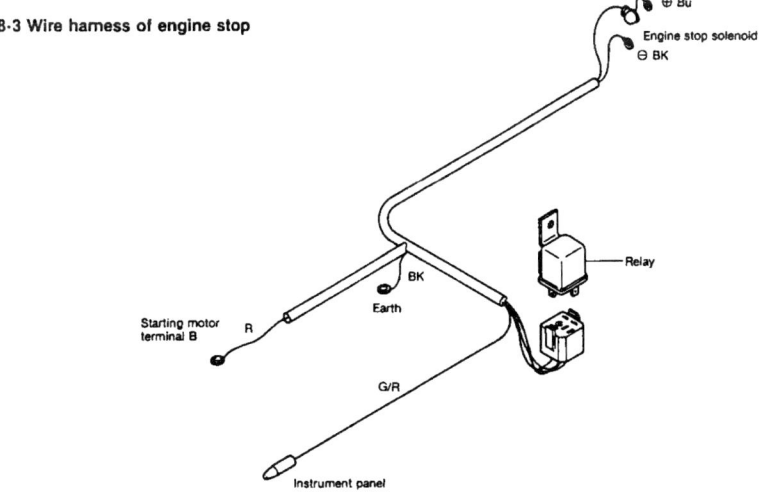

Chapter 9 Electrical System
9. Tachometer

3JH2 Series

9. Tachometer

9-1 Construction of tachometer

The tachometer indicates the number of revolutions per minute by means of an electrical input signal which is generated as a pulse signal from the magnetic pickup sender (MPU sender).
The function of the sender is to convert the rotary motion into an electrical signal by counting the number of teeth of the ring gear connecting with the flywheel housing.

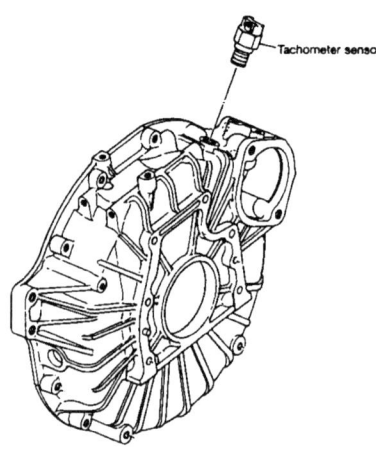

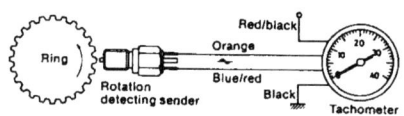

9-2 Specifications and dimensions of tachometer

(1) Specifications

Rated voltage		DC 12V
Range of operating voltage		10 ~ 15V
Illumination		3.4W/12V
Ring gear	No. of teeth	114
	Module	2.54
Part No. of tachometer		120130-91200 (128696-91100)
Part No. of sender unit		128170-91160

(2) Sensitivity limit of sender unit

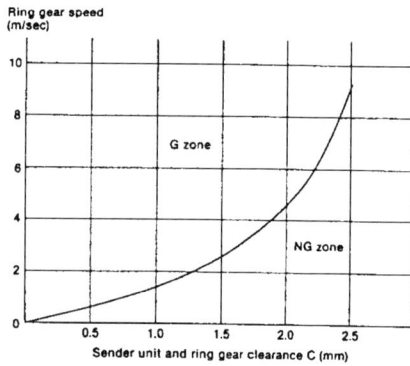

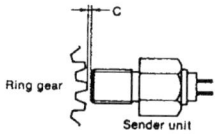

(3) Dimensions of sender unit

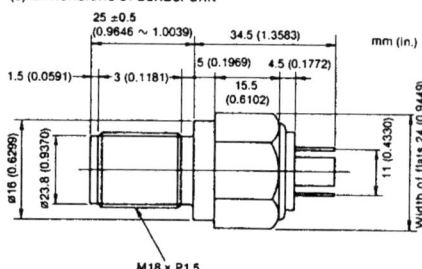

(4) Dimensions and shape of tachometer

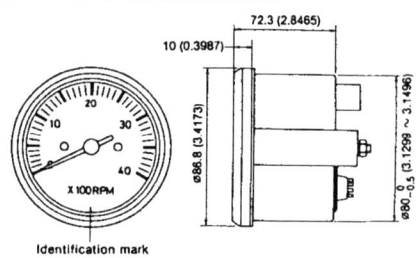

Identification mark

Printed in Japan
A0A1015-9110SP

Chapter 9 Electrical System
9. Tachometer
3JH2 Series

9-3 Measurement of sensor unit characteristics
(1) Measurement of output voltage

Output voltage	1.0V or higher

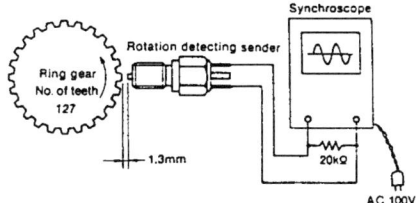

Measuring conditions

Number of teeth of ring gear	114
Gap between the ring gear and sender	1.3mm (0.0511 in.)
Resistance	20kΩ
Speed of ring gear	500 rpm (approx. 800Hz)
Measuring temperature	20°C (68°F)
Measuring instrument	Synchroscope

*Check the output wave pattern and number of pulses when carrying out the output voltage measurement.

(2) Measurement of internal resistance

Measuring conditions

Measuring temperature	20°C (68°F)
Measuring instrument	Digital tester

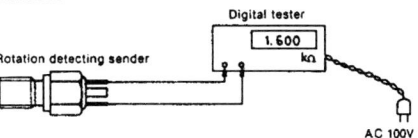

9-4

Fault	Diagnosis		Remedy
Does not function well. 1) Pointer does not move. 2) Functions intermittently.	Check if there is an open-circuit cable connection at the rear of the meter, a loose or disconnected terminal, or bad continuity due to corrosion. ↓	Yes	Make good the connection.
	Disconnect at the instrument terminals, and measure the voltage between the cable terminals. (To be 10 ~ 16V) ↓ Satisfactory	No	If the input voltage is abnormal, check the cause. (e.g. short-circuit, disconnection, or blown fuse, etc.)

9-43

Chapter 9 Electrical System
9. Tachometer

_____ *3JH2 Series*

	Check if the sender is loosely fitted. ↓ No	Yes	Fix the sender securely.
	Measure the internal resistance of the sender. (To be 1.6 ±0.1kΩ at 20°C) ↓	No	Replace the sender.
	Measure the output voltage of the sender. (To be 1V or higher at 20°C)	No	Replace the sender.

10. Alternator 12V/80A (OPTIONAL)

The alternator serves to keep the battery constantly charged. It is installed on the cylinder block by a bracket, and is driven from the V-pulley at the end of the crankshaft by a V-belt.
The type of alternator used in this engine is ideal for high speed engines with a wide range of engine speeds. It contains diodes that convert AC to DC, and an IC regulator that keeps the generated voltage constant even when the engine speed changes.

10-1 Features

The alternator contains a regulator using an IC, and has the following features.
(1) The IC regulator is self-contained, and has no moving parts (mechanical contact points). It therefore has superior features such as freedom from vibration, no fluctuation of voltage during use, and no need for readjustment.
Also, it is of the over-heating compensation type and can automatically adjust the voltage to the most suitable level depending on the operating temperature.
(2) The regulator is integrated within the alternator to simplify external wiring.
(3) It is an alternator designed for compactness, lightness of weight, and high output.
(4) A newly developed U-shaped diode is used to provide increased reliability and easier checking and maintenance.
(5) As the alternator is to be installed on board, the following measures are taken to provide salt-proofing.
  1) The front and rear covers are salt-proofed.
  2) Salt-proof paint is applied to the diode.
  3) The terminal, where the inboard harness is connected to the alternator, is nickel plated.

10-2 Specifications

Model of alternator	LR180-03 (HITACHI)
Model of IC regulator	TRIZ-63 (HITACHI)
Battery voltage	12V
Nominal output	12V/80A
Earth polarity	Negative earth (⊖)
Direction of rotation (viewed from pulley end)	Clockwise
Weight	5.8kg (12.8lb.)
Rated speed	5000 rpm
Operating speed	1000 ~ 9000
Speed for 13.5V	1000 or less
Output current at 20°C	over 78A/5000 rpm
Regulated voltage	14.5 ±0.3V (Standard temperature voltage gradient, −0.01/°C)

10-3 Characteristics

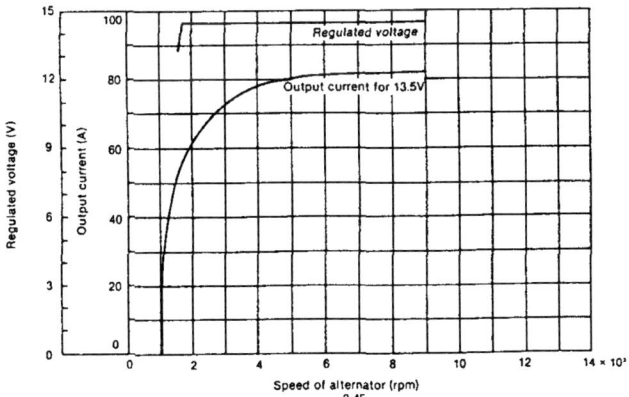

Chapter 9 Electrical System
10. Alternator (OPTIONAL)
3JH2 Series

10-4 Construction

This is a standard rotating field type three-phase alternator. It consists of six major parts: the pulley, fan, front cover, rotor, stator and rear cover. The IC regulator is an integral part of the alternator.

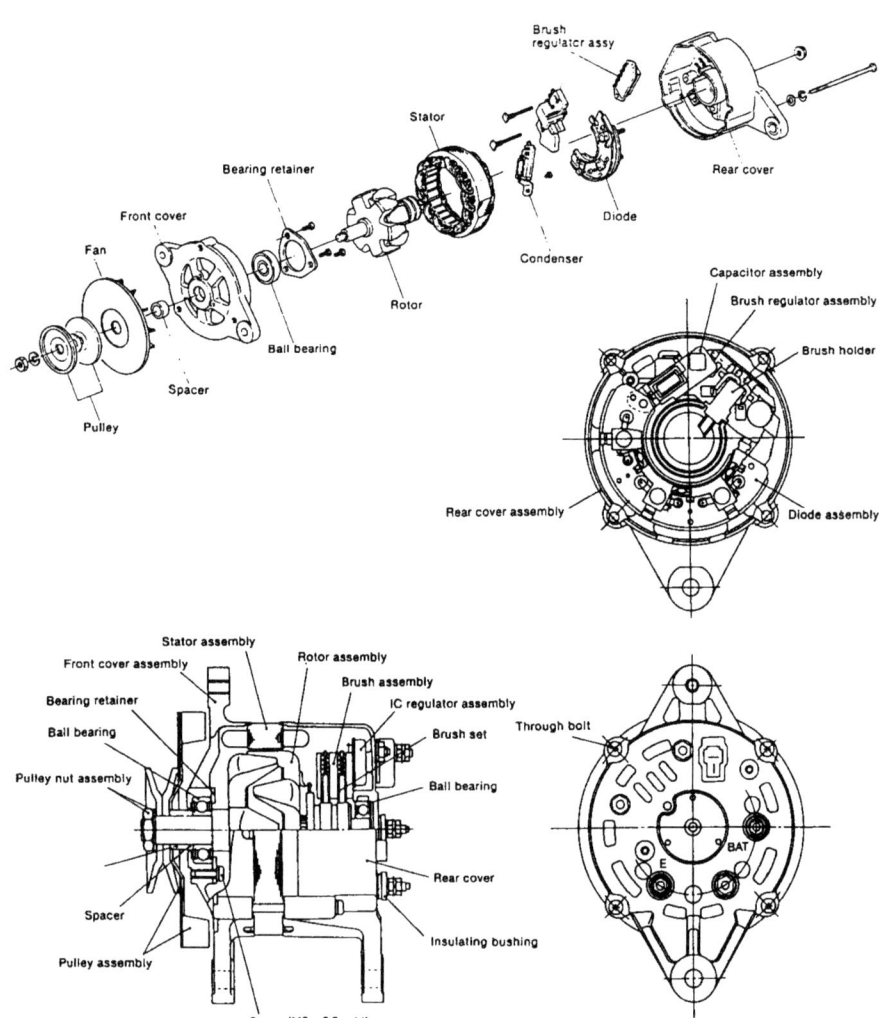

Chapter 9 Electrical System
10. Alternator (OPTIONAL)

3JH2 Series

10-5 Alternator functioning

(1) IC regulator

The IC regulator is the transistor (Tr_1) which is series-connected with the rotor. The IC regulator controls the output voltage of the generator by breaking or conducting the rotor coil (exciting) current.

When the output voltage of the generator is within the standard value, the transistor (Tr_1) turns on. When the voltage exceeds the standard value, the Zener diode goes on and the transistor (Tr_1) turns off.

With the repeated turning on and off of the transistor, the output voltage is kept at the standard value. (Refer to the circuit diagram below.)

(2) Charge lamp

When the transistor (Tr_1) is on, the charge lamp key switch is turned to ON, and current flows to R_1, R_4 and to Tr_1 to light the lamp. When the engine starts to run and output voltage is generated in the stator coil, the current stops flowing to this circuit, turning off the charge lamp.

(3) Circuit diagram

10-6 Handling precautions

(1) Be careful of the battery's polarity (+, − terminals), and do not connect the wrong terminals to the wrong cables, or the battery will be short-circuited by the generator diode.
In this case too much current will flow, the IC regulator and diodes burn out, and the wire harness will burn.
(2) Make sure of the correct connection of each terminal.
(3) When quick-charging, etc., disconnect either the battery terminal on the AC generator or the terminal on the battery.
(4) Do not short-circuit the terminals.
(5) Do not conduct any tests using high tension insulation resistance. (The diodes and IC regulator will burn out.)

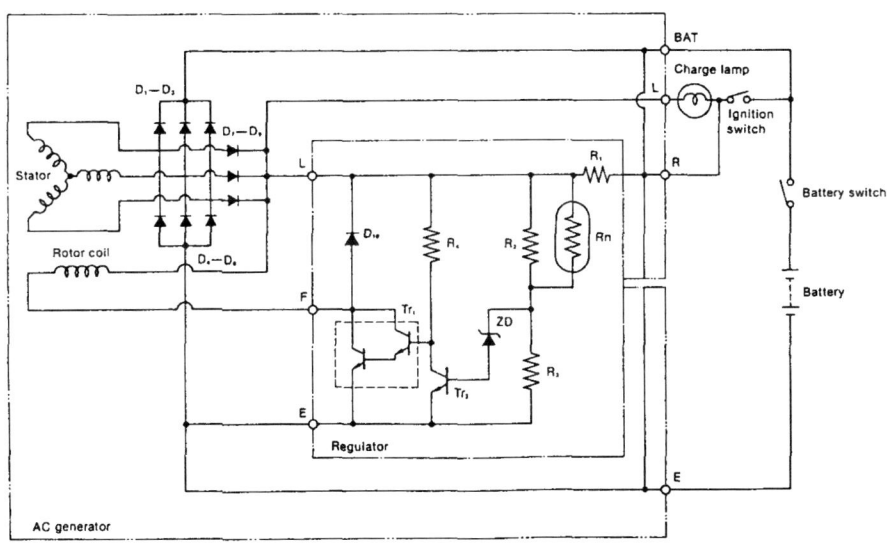

BAT:	Generator output terminal	$D_1 - D_4$:	Output commutation diode
D_{10}:	IC protecting diode	$R_1 - R_4$:	Resistor
L:	Charge lamp terminal	$D_5 - D_6$:	Charging lamp switching diode
ZD:	Zener diode	F:	To supply current to rotor coil
E:	Earth	Rn:	Thermistor
Tr_1, Tr_2:	Transistor		(Temperature gradient resistance)

Chapter 9 Electrical System
10. Alternator (OPTIONAL)

3JH2 Series

10-7 Disassembling the alternator

(1) Remove the through-bolt, and separate the front assembly from the rear assembly.

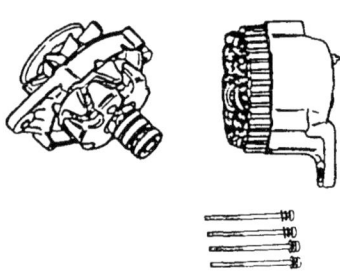

(2) Remove the pulley nut, and pull out the rotor from the front cover.

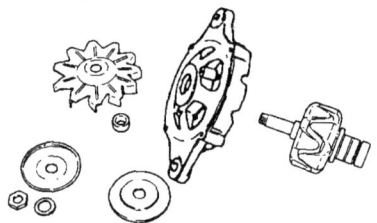

(3) Remove the ø5mm (ø0.1969in.) screw from the front cover, and then remove the ball bearing.

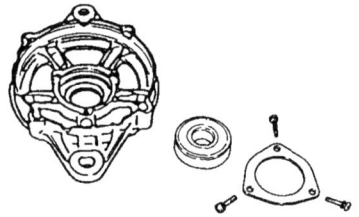

(4) Remove the nut, the brush-holder, and diode fixing nut at the BAT, and the terminal screws of the rear cover. Separate the rear cover from the stator (with the diode and brush holder).

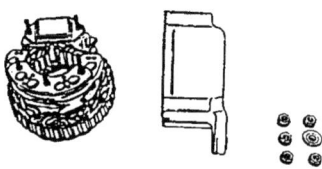

(5) Disconnect the soldered joint of the stator lead wire, and remove the diode and brush regulator assemblies from the stator at the same time.

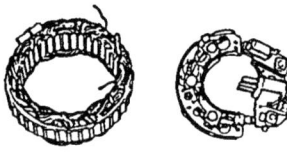

(6) Separating the regulator
1) To separate the regulator, remove the ø3mm (ø0.1181in.) rivet which keeps the diode assembly and the brushless regulator in place, and the soldered joint of the L-terminal.

Printed in Japan
A0A1015-9110SP

Chapter 9 Electrical System
10. Alternator (OPTIONAL)
3JH2 Series

2) To replace the IC regulator, disconnect the soldered joint of the IC regulator and pull out the two bolts. Do not remove these two bolts except when replacing the IC regulator.

After repeating the above test, if any diode is found to be defective, replace the diode assembly. Since there is no terminal on the auxiliary diode, check the continuity between both ends of the diode.

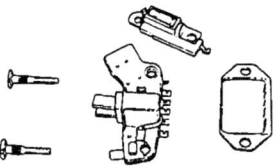

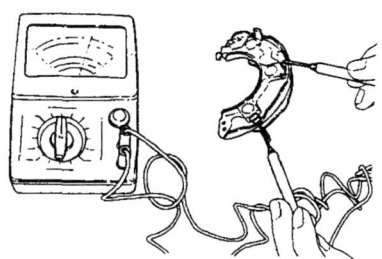

10-8 Inspection and adjustment

(1) Diode

Between terminals		BAT (+ side diode)	
	Tester wire	+ side	− side
U.V.W.	+ side		No continuity
	− side	Continuity	

Between terminals		E (− side diode)	
	Tester wire	+ side	− side
U.V.W.	+ side		Continuity
	− side	No continuity	

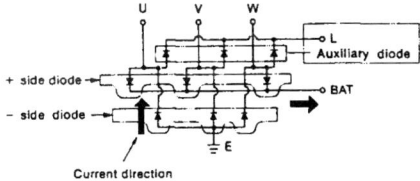

U.V.W.: terminal from the stator coil

Current flows only in one direction in the diode as shown in Fig. 181. Accordingly, when there is continuity between each terminal (e.g. BAT and U), the diode is in normal condition. When there is no continuity, the diode is defective.
When the tester is connected in the reverse of above, there should be no continuity. If there is, the diode is defective.

CAUTION: Do not use high tensile insulation resistance such as meggers, etc. for testing. The diode may burn out.

(2) Rotor
Inspect the slip ring surface, rotor coil continuity and insulation.

1) Inspecting the slip ring surface
Check if the surface of the slip ring is sufficiently smooth. If the surface is rough, grind the surface with No. 500—600 sand paper. If it is contaminated with oil, etc., wipe the surface clean with alcohol.

	Standard	Wear limit
Slip ring outer dia.	ø31.6mm (1.2441in.)	ø30.6mm (1.2049in.)

2) Rotor coil continuity test
Check the continuity in the slip ring with the tester. If there is no continuity, there is a wire break. Replace the rotor coil.

Resistance value	Approx. 2.58 Ω at 20°C

Printed in Japan
A0A1015-9110SP

Chapter 9 Electrical System
10. Alternator (OPTIONAL)

3JH2 Series

3) Rotor coil insulation test
   Check the continuity between the slip ring and the rotor core, or the shaft. If there is continuity, insulation inside the rotor is defective, causing a short with the earth circuit. Replace the rotor coil.

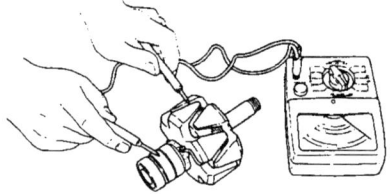

4) Check the rear side ball bearing. If the rotation of the bearing is heavy, or produces abnormal sounds, replace the ball bearing.

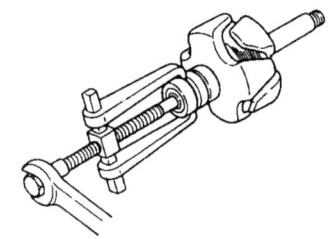

(3) Stator
1) Stator coil continuity test
   Check the continuity between each terminal of the stator coil. If there is no continuity, there is a wire break in the stator coil. Replace the stator coil.

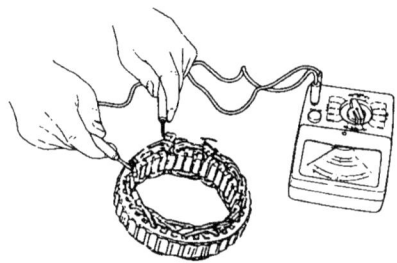

Resistance value	Approx. 0.041Ω at 20°C u, v-phase resistance
	Approx. 0.036Ω at 20°C w-phase resistance

2) Stator coil insulation test
   Check the continuity between the terminals and the stator core. If there is continuity, insulation of the stator coil is defective. This will cause a short-circuit with the earth core. Replace the stator coil.

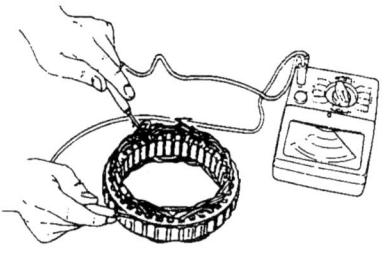

(4) Brush
   The brush is hard and wears slowly, but when it is worn beyond the allowable limit, replace it. When replacing the brush, also check the strength of the brush spring. To check, push the spring down to 2mm (0.0787in.) from the end surface of the brush holder, and read the gauge.

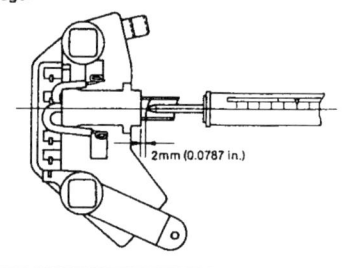

Brush spring strength	255–345g (0.56 ~ 0.76lb.)

(5) Brush wear
   Check the brush length.
   The brush wears very little, but replace the brush if worn over the wear limit line printed on the brush.

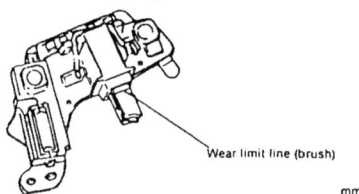

Wear limit line (brush)

mm (in.)

	Maintenance standard	Wear limit
Brush length	16 (0.6299)	9 (0.3543)

9-50

Printed in Japan
_A0A1015-9110SP_

Chapter 9 Electrical System
10. Alternator (OPTIONAL)
3JH2 Series

(6) IC regulator

Connect the variable resistance, two 12V batteries, resistor, and voltmeter as shown in the diagram.

1) Use the following measuring devices.

Resistor (R_1)	100Ω, 2W, 1pc.
Variable resistor (Rv)	0–300Ω, 12W, 1pc.
Battery (BAT_1, BAT_2)	12V, 2pcs.
DC voltmeter	0–30V, 0.5 class 1pc. (measure at 3 points)

2) Check the regulator in the following sequence, according to the diagram.
 a) Check V_2 (BAT_1 + BAT_2 voltage). If the voltage is 20—26V, both BAT_1 and BAT_2 are normal.
 b) While measuring V_2 (F-E terminal voltage), move Rv gradually from the 0-position. Check if there is a point where the V_2 voltage rises sharply from below 2.0V to over 2.0V. If there is no such point, the regulator is defective. Replace the regulator. If there is a sharp voltage rise when testing, return the Rv to the 0-position, and connect the voltmeter to the V_1 position.
 c) While measuring V_1 (voltage between L-E terminals), move Rv gradually from the 0-position. There should be a point where the voltage of V_1 rises sharply by 2–6V. Measure the voltage of V_1 just before this sharp voltage rise. This is the regulating voltage of the regulator. If this voltage of V_1 is within the standard limit, the regulator is normal. If the voltage deviates from the limit, the regulator is defective. Replace the regulator.

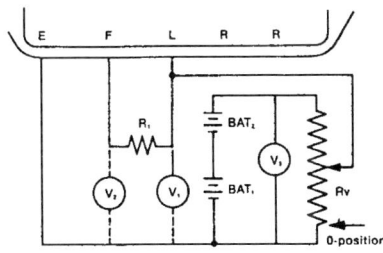

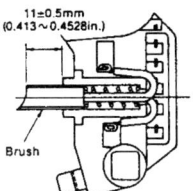

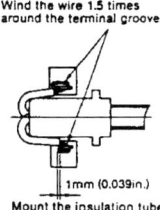

NOTES: 1. Use non-acid type paste.
2. The soldering iron temperature is 300 ~ 350°C.

2) Mount the IC regulator on the brush holder as illustrated, and press in the M5 bolt. Do not forget to assemble the bushing and the connecting plate at the same time.
(If the bushing is left out, the output terminal will be earthed and the battery short-circuited).

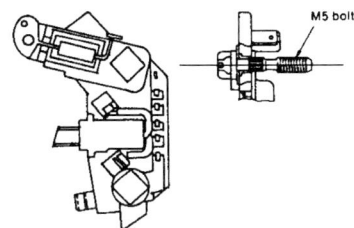

NOTES: 1. Insertion pressure is 100kg (220.5 lbs.)
2. Insert vertically.

(2) Connecting the brush regulator assembly and diode
 1) Check the rivets
 Place the rivets as shown in the figure, and then calk them using the calking tool.

Calking torque	500kg (1102 lbs.)

2) Connect the brush to the diode.
 Insert the brush side terminal into the diode terminal, calk it, and then solder into place.

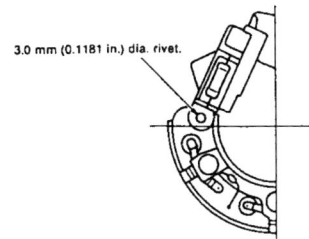

10-9 Reassembling the alternator

Reassembly is done in the reverse order of disassembly. For reassembly, be careful of the following points. (Refer to 4—7 disassembling alternator).

(1) Assembling the brush regulator
 1) Solder the brush.
 Position the brush as shown in the drawing and solder it. Be careful not to let the solder drip into the pig tail (lead wire).

Rivetting pressure	500kg (1102 lbs.)

Chapter 9 Electrical System
10. Alternator (OPTIONAL)
3JH2 Series

(3) Assembling the rear cover
Insert pins from the outside of the rear cover. Install the brush on the brush holder, then attach the rear cover. After assembly, pull out the pins.

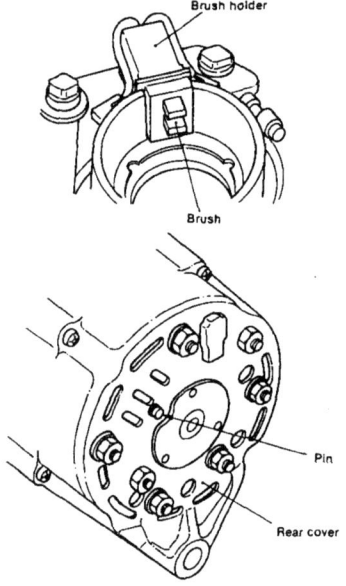

(1) Measuring devices

DC voltmeter	0—15V or 0—30V, 0.5 Class, 1pc.
DC ammeter	0—100A, 1.0 Class, 1pc.
Variable resistor	0—0.25Ω, 1kW, 1pc.
Lamp	12V, 3W
100Ω resistor	3W
0.25Ω resistor	25W

(2) Measuring the regulating voltage
 1) When measuring devices are connected in the performance test circuit as shown above, the charge lamp lights.
 2) Close SW_2 while keeping SW_1 open and run the AC generator. When the revolutions of the generator are gradually raised, the charge lamp goes off.
 3) Raise the revolutions of the AC generator, and read the voltmeter gauge when the revolutions reach about 5,000 rpms.

NOTES: 1. Make sure that the ammeter indication at this time is less than 5A. If the indication is over 5A, connect the 0.25Ω resistor. The voltmeter indication at this time must be within the prescribed regulating voltage value.
2. Raise the AC generator revolutions high to make sure the regulating voltage does not fluctuate along with changes in the revolution speed.

(3) Precautions for measuring the regulating voltage
 1) When measuring the voltage, measure the voltage between the AC generator BAT terminal, or Battery + terminal, and AC generator E-terminal.
 2) Use a fully charged battery.
 3) Measure the voltage quickly.
 4) Keep SW_1 open for measurement.

(4) Tightening torques

Positions	Tightening torque kg-cm (ft-lb)
Brush holder fixing	32—40 (2.31~2.89)
Diode fixing	60—70 (4.33~5.05)
Bearing retainer fixing	32—40 (2.31~2.89)
Pulley nut tightening	400—600 (28.93~43.40)
Through-bolt tightening	32—40 (2.31~2.89)

10-10 Performance test
Conduct a performance test on the reassembled AC generator as follows. The following is the circuit for the performance test.

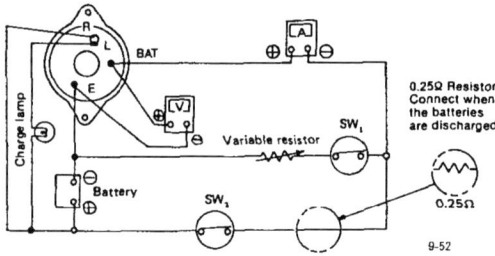

Chapter 9 Electrical System
10. Alternator (OPTIONAL) _____ 3JH2 Series

10-11 Troubleshooting

(1) Charging failure

9-53

Printed in Japan
A0A1015-9110SP

Chapter 9 Electrical System
10. Alternator(OPTIONAL)   3JH2 Series

(2) Overcharging

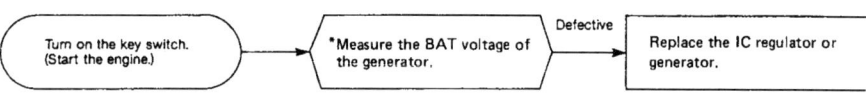

(3) Charge lamp failure

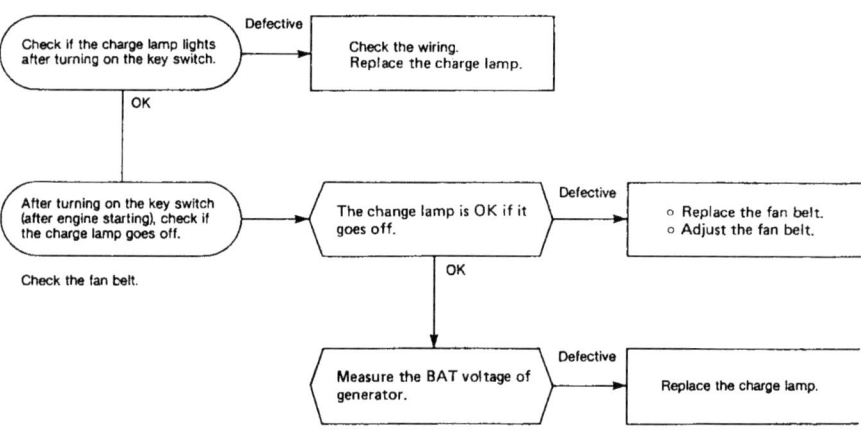

CHAPTER 10
DISASSEMBLY AND REASSEMBLY

1. Disassembly and Reassembly Precautions ··· 10-1
2. Disassembly and Reassembly Tools ············ 10-2
3. Disassembly and Reassembly ······················ 10-9
4. Bolt/nut Tightening Torque ························ 10-32
5. Test Running ··· 10-33

1. Disassembly and Reassembly Precautions

(1) Disassembly
- Take sufficient time to accurately pin-point the cause of the trouble, and disassemble only those parts which are necessary.
- Be careful to keep all disassembled parts in order.
- Prepare disassembly tools.
- Prepare a cleaner and cleaning can.
- Clear an adequate area for parts and prepare a container(s).
- Drain cooling water (sea water, fresh water) and lube oil.
- Close the Kingston cock.

(2) Reassembly
- Sufficiently clean and inspect all parts to be assembled.
- Coat sliding and rotating parts with new engine oil when assembling.
- Replace all gaskets and O-rings.
- Use a liquid packing agent as necessary to prevent oil/water leaks.
- Check the oil and thrust clearances, etc. of parts when assembling.
- Make sure you use the correct bolt/nut/washer. Tighten main bolts/nuts to the specified torque. Be especially careful not to overtighten the aluminum alloy part mounting bolts.
- Align match marks (if any) when assembling. Make sure that the correct sets of parts are used for bearings, pistons, and other parts where required.

2. Disassembly and Reassembly Tools

The following tools are required when disassembling and reassembling the engine.
Please use them as instructed.

2-1. General Handtools

Name of tool	Illustration	Remarks
Wrench		Size: 10 × 13
Wrench		Size: 12 × 14
Wrench		Size: 17 × 19
Wrench		Size: 22 × 24
Screwdriver		
Steel hammer		Local supply

Chapter 10 Disassembly and Reassembly
2. Disassembly and Reassembly Tools _____ *3JH2 Series*

Name of tool	Illustration	Remarks
Copper hammer		Local supply
Mallet		Local supply
Nippers		Local supply
Pliers		Local supply
Offset wrench		Local supply 1 set
Box spanner		Local supply 1 set
Scraper		Local supply

Chapter 10 Disassembly and Reassembly
2. Disassembly and Reassembly Tools   3JH2 Series

Name of tool	Illustration	Remarks
Lead rod		Local supply
File		Local supply 1 set
Rod spanner for hexagon socket head screws		Local supply Size: 6mm (0.2362in.) 8mm (0.3150in.) 10mm (0.3937in.)
Starling Pliers Hole type Shaft type	S—0 H4 ~ H8 S = Hole type H = Shaft type	Local supply

Chapter 10 Disassembly and Reassembly
2. Disassembly and Reassembly Tools

_____ 3JH2 Series

2-2 Special Handtools

Name of tool	Shape and size	Application
Piston pin insertion/ extraction tool	mm (in.) 20 (0.7874) / 80 (3.1496) 12 (0.4724) / 20 (0.7874) Part No. 128670-92260	Piston pin extractor Extraction of piston pin Insertion of piston pin
Connecting rod small end bushing insertion/ extraction tool	mm (in.) 20 (0.7874) / 80 (3.1496) 25.4 ~ 25.7 (1.0000 ~ 1.0118) 28.4 ~ 28.7 (1.1181 ~ 1.1299)	Extraction
Intake and exhaust valve insertion/ extraction tool	mm (in.) ø25 (0.9843) ø100 (3.9370) 15 (0.5906) ø13.5 (0.5315)	
Lubricating oil No.2 filter case remover		

Printed in Japan
A0A1015-9110SP

Chapter 10 Disassembly and Reassembly
2. Disassembly and Reassembly Tools

3JH2 Series

Name of tool	Shape and size	Application
Piston ring compressor		Piston insertion guide
Valve lapping handle		Lapping tool
Valve lapping powder		
Feeler gauge		
Pulley puller	Local supply	Removing the coupling

Chapter 10 Disassembly and Reassembly
2. Disassembly and Reassembly Tools
                                                                    3JH2 Series

2-3 Measuring Instruments

Name of tool	Shape and size	Application
Vernier calipers		0.05mm (0.0020in.), 0 ~ 150mm (0 ~ 5.9055in.)
Micrometer		0.01mm (0.0004in.) 0 ~ 25mm (0 ~ 0.9843in.), 25 ~ 50mm (0.9843 ~ 1.9685in.), 50 ~ 75mm (1.9685 ~ 2.9528in.), 75 ~ 100mm (2.9528 ~ 3.9370in.), 100 ~ 125mm (3.9730 ~ 4.9213in.), 125 ~ 150mm (4.9213 ~ 5.9055in.).
Cylinder gauge		0.01mm (0.0004in.), 18 ~ 35mm (0.7087 ~ 1.3780in.), 35 ~ 60mm (1.3780 ~ 2.3622in.), 50 ~ 100mm (1.9685 ~ 3.9370in.).
Thickiness gauge		0.05 ~ 2mm (0.0020 ~ 0.0787in.)
Torque wrench		0 ~ 13kg-m. (0 ~ 94ft-lb)
Nozzle tester		0 ~ 500kg/cm^2 (0 ~ 7111.7lb/in.^{2})

Chapter 10 Disassembly and Reassembly
2. Disassembly and Reassembly Tools

2-4 Other

Supplementary packing agent

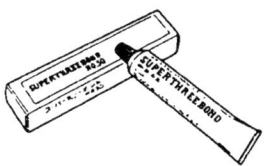

Type	Use
"Three Bond 3B8-005"	White. Since "Three Bond 3B8-005" is a nonorganic solvent, it does not penetrate asbestos sheets made principally or completely of asbestos. Always use it with grey asbestos sheet packing for complete oil tightness. When "Three Bond 3B8-005" is difficult to obtain, use silicon nonsolvent type "Three Bond No. 50."
"Three Bond No. 50"	Grey. Silicon nonsolvent type liquid packing. Semidry type packing agent coated on mating faces to prevent oil and gas leakage. Does not penetrate asbestos sheet and assures complete oil tightness.
"Three Bond No. 1"	Reddish brown. Paste type wet viscous liquid packing. Ideal for mating faces which are removed but reinstalled. Particularly used to prevent water leakage and to prevent seizing of bolts and nuts.

The surface to be coated must be thoroughly cleaned with thinner or benzene and completely dry. Moreover, coating must be thin and uniform.

Products of Three Bond Co., Ltd.

Paint

Color spray

Only Metallic Ecole Silver is used on this engine.

Wipe the surface to be painted with thinner or benzene, shake the spray can well, push the button at the top of the can and spray the paint onto the surface from a distance of 30 ~ 40 cm.

Paint

Type
White paint
(Mixed oil paint)

Usage point
Cylinder liner
insertion hole

Use
Paint parts that contact with the cylinder body when inserting the cylinder liner to prevent rusting and water leakage.

Yanmar cleaner (Ref.)

Cooling passage cleaner is mixed by adding one part "Unicon 146" to about 16 parts water (specific gravity ratio). To use, drain the water from the cooling system, fill the system with cleaner, allowing it to stand overnight (10 ~ 15 hours). Then drain out the cleaner, refill the system with water, and operate the engine for at least one hour.

NEJI LOCK SUPER   203M: a locking agent for screws (Ref.)

For coating on screws and bolts to prevent loosening, rusting, and leaking. To use, wipe off all oil and water on the threads of studs, coat the threads with screw lock, tighten the stud bolt, and allow them to stand until the screw lock hardens. Use screw lock on the oil intake pipe threads, oil pressure switch threads, fuel injection timing shim faces, and front axle bracket mounting bolts.

Printed in Japan
A0A1015-9110SP

3. Disassembly and Reassembly

3-1 Disassembly

For engines mounted in an engine room, remove the piping and wiring connecting them to the ship.

(1) Remove the remote control cable (from engine and marine gearbox).
(2) Unplug the extension cord for the instrument panel from the engine.
(3) Remove the wiring between the starting motor and the battery.
(4) Remove the exhaust rubber hose from the mixing elbow.
(5) Remove the fresh water sub-tank rubber hose from the filler cap.
(6) Remove the cooling water (sea water) pump sea water intake hose (after making sure the Kingston cock is closed).
(7) Remove the fuel oil intake rubber hose from the fuel feed pump.
(8) Remove the body fit (reamer) bolts and disassemble the propeller shaft coupling and thrust shaft coupling.
(9) If a driven coupling is mounted to the front drive coupling, disassemble.
(10) Remove the flexible mount nut, lift the engine, and remove it from the engine base.
(Leave the flexible mount attached to the engine base.)

3-1.1 Drain cooling water

(1) Open the sea water drain cock between the sea water pump and lube oil cooler to drain the sea water.
(2) Open the cylinder body drain cock to drain the fresh water from the cylinder head and cylinder body.
(3) Open the fresh water drain cock on the lower part of the fresh water tank to drain the fresh water.

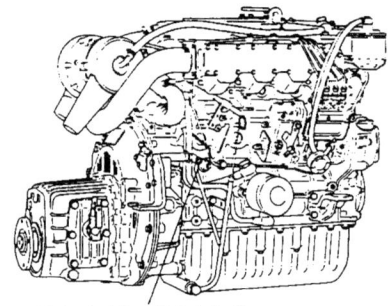

Fresh water drain cock (cylinder block)

3-1.2 Drain lube oil

(1) Remove the pipe coupling bolt which holds the lube oil dip stick guide, and drain the lube oil from the engine.
(2) Remove the drain plug on the lower part of the crank case control side, and drain the lube oil from the marine gearbox.

NOTE: *If a lube oil supply/discharge pump is used for the engine, the intake hose is placed in the dip stick guide, and for the clutch side (gearbox) it is placed in the oil hole on top of the case.*

3-1.3 Removing (electrical) wiring

Remove the wiring from the engine.

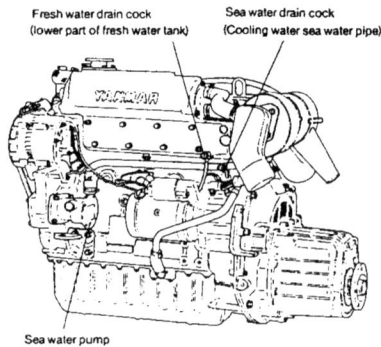

Fresh water drain cock (lower part of fresh water tank)
Sea water drain cock (Cooling water sea water pipe)
Sea water pump

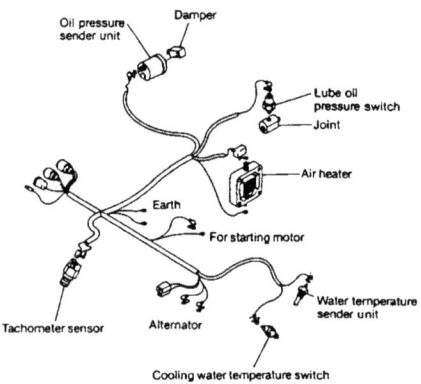

3-1.4 Removing the fuel oil filter & fuel oil pipe

(1) Remove the fuel oil pipe (fuel oil filter—fuel feed pump, fuel oil filter—fuel injection pump).
(2) Remove the fuel oil filter (with bracket) from the intake manifold.

3-1.6 Removing the mixing elbow

(1) Remove cooling water (sea water) pipe rubber (heat exchanger—mixing elbow).
(2) Remove the mixing elbow
 N/A: from the intake manifold intake coupling
 T: from the blower side of the turbocharger

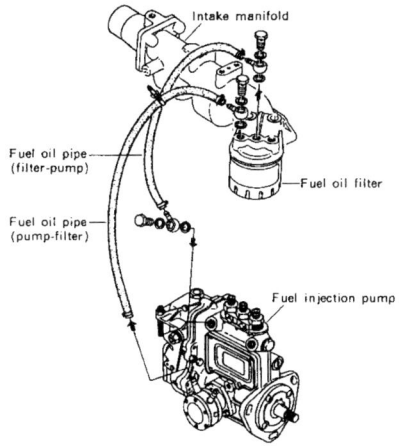

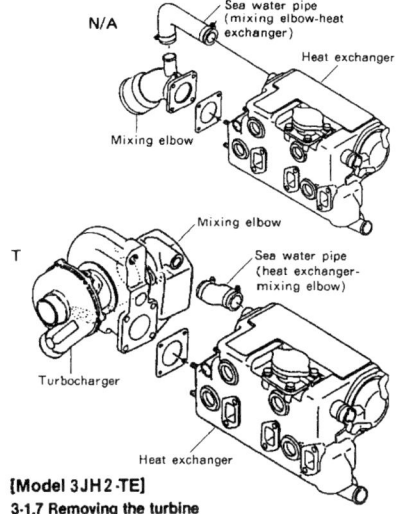

3-1.5 Removing the intake silencer

(1) Remove the breather hose attached to the intake silencer—valve rocker arm chamber cover.
(2) Remove the intake silencer
 N/A: from exhaust manifold outlet
 T: from turbocharger outlet

[Model 3JH2-TE]
3-1.7 Removing the turbine

(1) Remove the intake rubber hose (turbine—intake manifold).
(2) Remove the oil pan side rubber hose for the turbine lube oil return pipe from the oil pan, and the vibration stop from the flywheel housing.
(3) Remove the turbine lube oil pipe (lube oil cooler—turbine).
(4) Remove the turbine from the exhaust manifold.

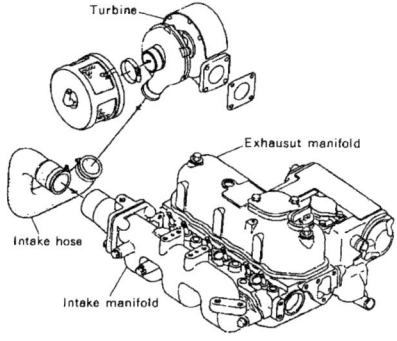

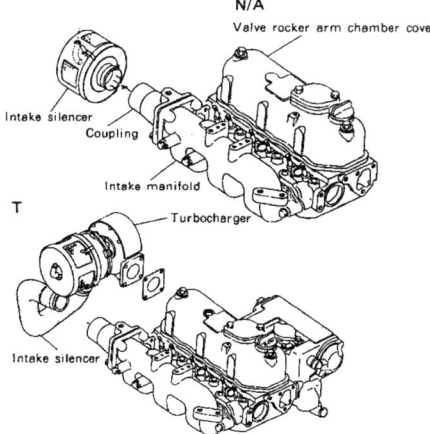

Chapter 10 Disassembly and Reassembly
3. Disassembly and Reassembly
3JH2 Series

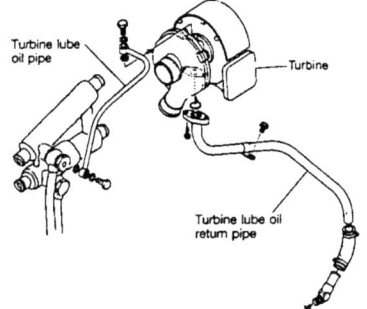

Removing the mixing elbow and the turbocharger.
(1) Remove the fresh water hoses.
    (Turbocharger — heat exchanger)
(2) Remove the lube oil pipes.
    (Lube oil cooler—Turbocharger—Lube oil pump)
(3) Remove the sea water hose.
    (Mixing elbow — heat exchanger)
(4) Remove the mixing elbow from turbocharger.
(5) Remove the air duct rubber hose.
    (Air duct — Turbocharger)
(6) Remove the turbocharger from exhaust manifold.

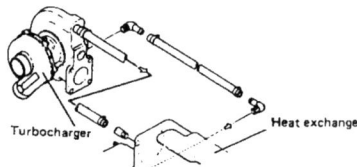

Chapter 10 Disassembly and Reassembly
3. Disassembly and Reassembly

3JH2 Series

3-1.8 Removing the starting motor
Remove the starting motor from the flywheel housing.

[Model: 3JH2E 3JH2-TE]

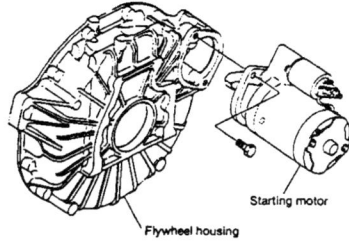

3-1.9 Removing the alternator
(1) Loosen the alternator adjuster bolt and remove the V-belt.
(2) Remove the adjuster from the fresh water pump, and remove the alternator from the gear case (with distance piece).

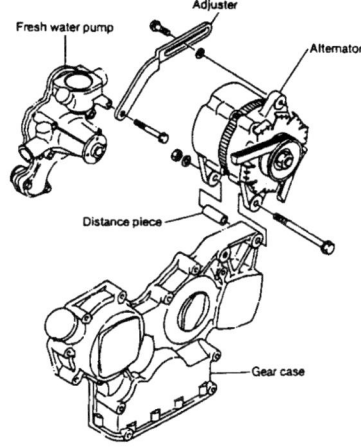

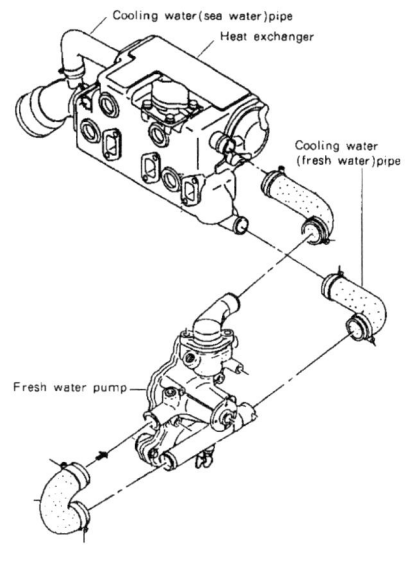

3-1.11 Removing the heat exchanger (exhaust manifold, fresh water tank unit)
Remove the heat exchanger and gasket packing.

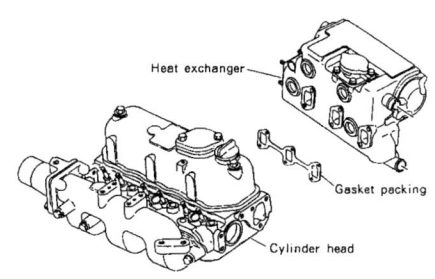

3-1.10 Removing the cooling water pipe
(1) Remove the cooling water (sea water) pipe (lube oil cooler — heat exchanger).
(2) Remove the cooling water (fresh water) pipe (heat exchanger — fresh water pump, fresh water pump — fresh water tank).
(3) Remove the cooling water pipe (lube oil cooler — marine gearbox)

Printed in Japan
A0A1015-9110SP

Chapter 10 Disassembly and Reassembly
3. Disassembly and Reassembly

_____ 3JH2 Series

3-1.12 Removing the cooling water (sea water) pipe (sea water pump—lube oil cooler).

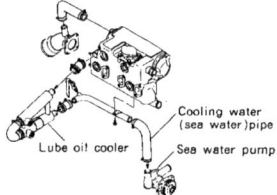

3-1.13 Removing the sea water pump

(1) Pull out the bearing mounts, receptacles from the sea water pump mounting side and from the opposite side of the gear case.
(2) Remove the sea water pump.

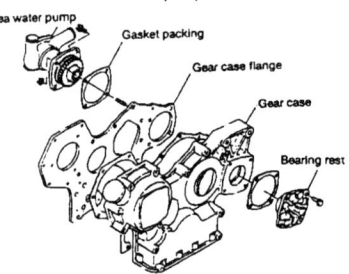

3-1.14 Removing the lube oil filter

(1) Remove the lube oil pipe (lube oil cooler—filter bracket, filter bracket—lube oil cooler).
(2) Remove the filter bracket (with lube oil filter element) from the cylinder block.
(3) Remove the lube oil pipe (cylinder block—fuel injection pump).
(4) Remove the lube oil dipstick and guide.

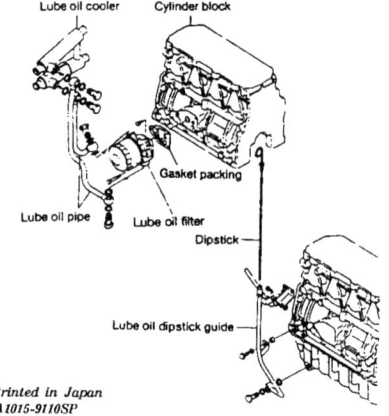

3-1.15 Removing the high pressure fuel pipe

(1) Remove the high pressure fuel pipe vibration stop from the intake manifold.
(2) Loosen the box nuts on both ends of the high pressure fuel pipe and remove the high pressure fuel pipe.
(3) Remove the fuel oil return pipe (fuel injection nozzle—fuel injection pump).

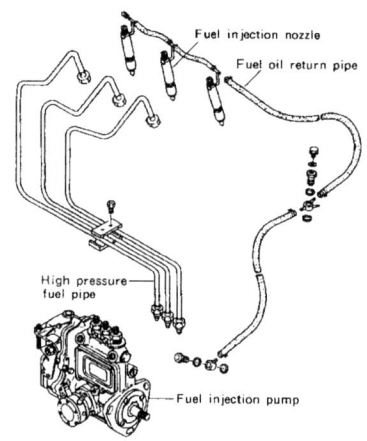

3-1.16 Removing the intake manifold

(1) Remove the governor speed remote control bracket.
(2) Remove the intake manifold and gasket packing.

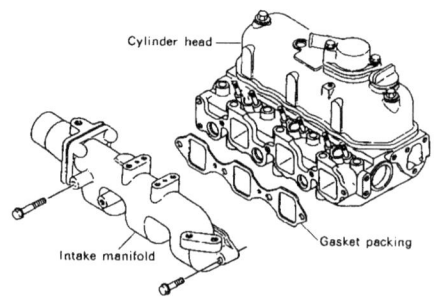

3-1.17 Removing the fresh water pump

Remove the fresh water pump, gasket packing and O-ring.

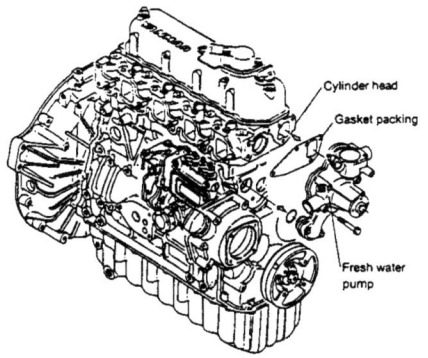

3-1.18 Removing the fuel injection nozzles

Remove the fuel injection nozzle retainer nut, and pull out the fuel injection nozzle retainer and fuel injection nozzle.

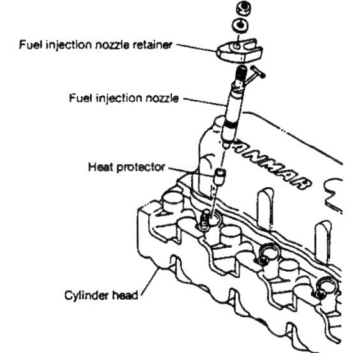

NOTE: *If the heat protector stays in the cylinder head, make a note of the cylinder no. and be sure to remove it when you disassemble the cylinder head.*

3-1.19 Removing the valve elbow shaft assembly

(1) Remove the valve elbow chamber cover.
(2) Remove the valve elbow shaft support mounting bolts(s), and remove the entire valve elbow shaft assembly.
(3) Pull out the push rods.

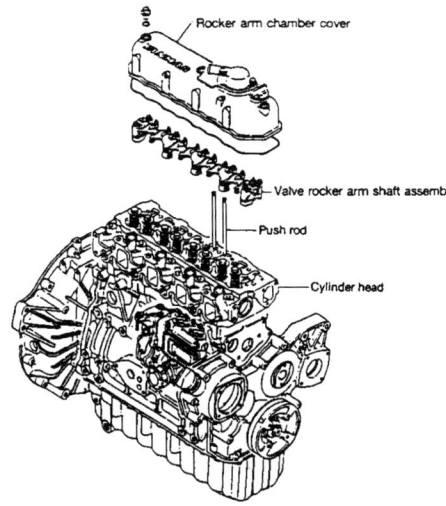

3-1.20 Remvoing the cylinder head

(1) Remove the cylinder head bolts with a torque wrench, and remove the cylinder head.
(2) Remove the cylinder gasket packing.

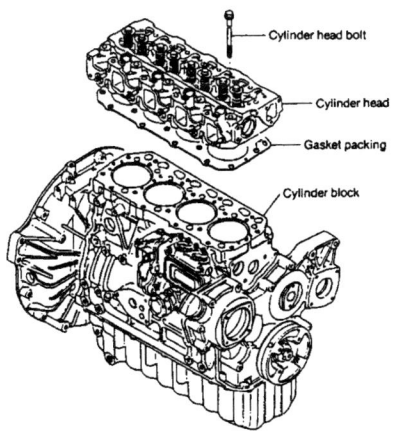

Chapter 10 Disassembly and Reassembly
3. Disassembly and Reassembly

3-1.21 Removing the crankshaft V-pulley
Remove the hex bolts holding the crankshaft V-pulley, and remove the crankshaft V-pulley with an extraction tool.

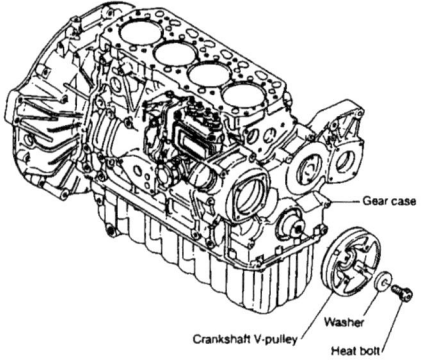

3-1.22 Removing the marine gearbox
(1) Remove the hex bolts from the clutch case flange, and remove the gearbox assembly.
(2) Remove the damper disk from the flywheel.
(3) Remove the fan from the flywheel.

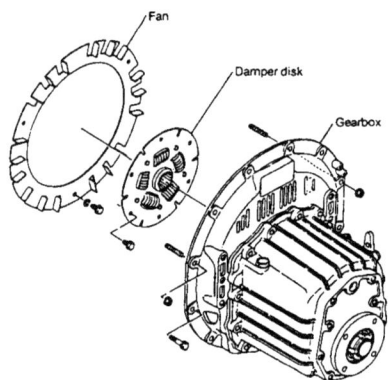

3-1.23 Removing the lube oil cooler
Remove the lube oil cooler from the upper part of the flywheel housing.

MODEL: 4JH2E

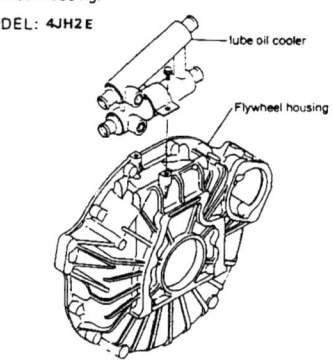

3-1.24 Removing the flywheel
Remove the flywheel mounting bolts and then the flywheel.

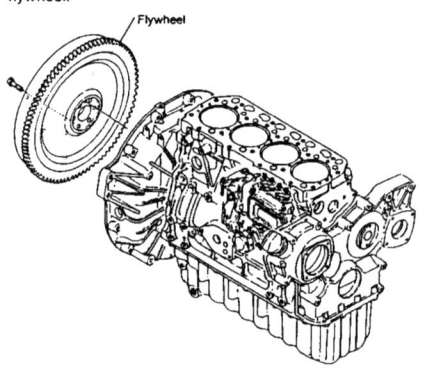

Chapter 10 Disassembly and Reassembly
3. Disassembly and Reassembly

3JH2 Series

3-1.25 Turning the engine over
(1) Place a wood block of appropriate size on the floor, and stand up the engine on the flywheel housing.
(2) Remove the engine mounting feet.

3-1.26 Removing the oil pan
(1) Remove the bracket holding the oil pan and clutch housing.
(2) Remove the oil pan and gasket packing.

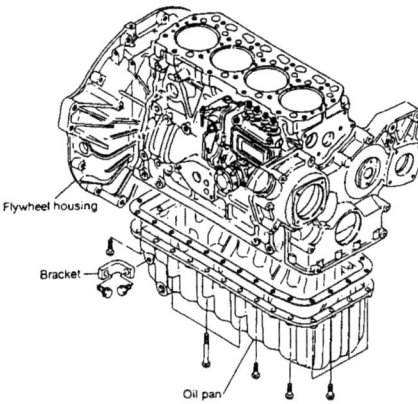

3-1.27 Removing the lube oil intake pipe
Remove the lube oil intake pipe and gasket packing.

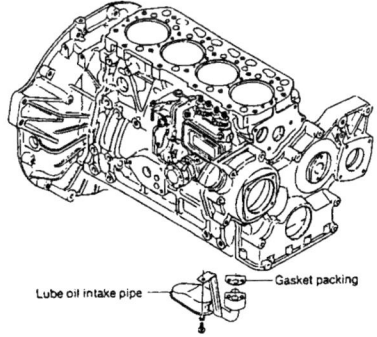

3-1.28 Removing the gear case
Remove the gear case mounting bolts, and remove the gear case from the cylinder block.

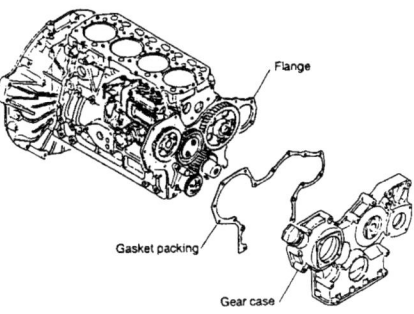

3-1.29 Removing the lube oil pump
Remove the lube oil pump and gasket packing from the gear case flange.

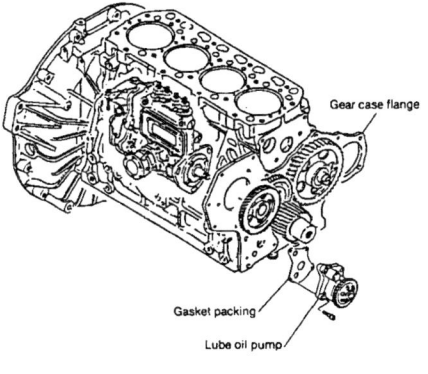

3-1.30 Remove the fuel injection pump

(1) Remove the blind plug mounted to the hub of the automatic advancing timer.
(2) Remove the box nut, and pull out the fuel oil pump drive gear/automatic advancing timer assembly with an extraction tool.
(3) Remove the fuel injection pump and O-ring from the gear case flange.

3-1.32 Removing the pistons and connecting rods

(1) Remove the connecting rod bolt and the large end cap.
(2) Push the connecting rod from the bottom and pull out the piston connecting rod assembly.

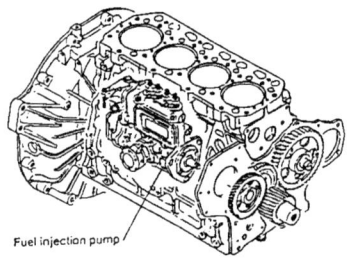

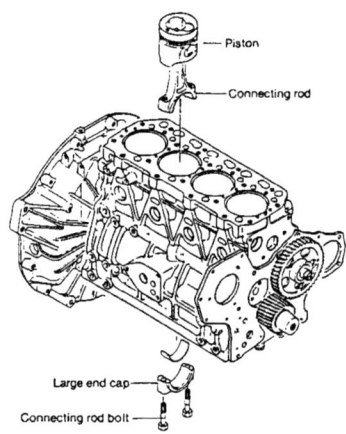

NOTE: Place a tool against the piston cooling nozzle to make sure the nozzle position does not change and it does not get scratches.

3-1.31 Removing the idling gear

Remove the two hex bolts holding the idling shaft, and pull out the idling gear and idling shaft.

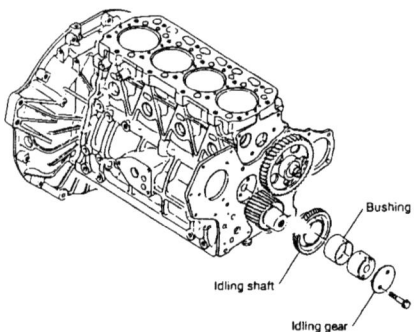

Chapter 10 Disassembly and Reassembly
3. Disassembly and Reassembly

3-1.34 Turning the engine over
Place a wood block of suitable size on the floor and turn the engine over, with the cylinder head mounting surface facing down.

NOTE: Make sure that the cylinder head positioning pins on the cylinder block do not come in contact with the wood block.

3-1.35 Removing the flywheel housing
Remove the flywheel housing from the cylinder block.

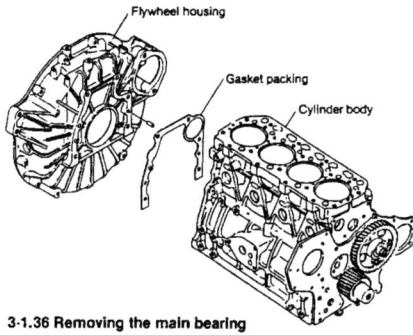

3-1.36 Removing the main bearing
(1) Remove the main bearing bolts.
(2) Remove the main bearing cap and lower main bearing metal.

NOTE: The thrust metal (lower) is mounted to the standard main bearing cap. Be sure to differentiate between mounting surfaces.

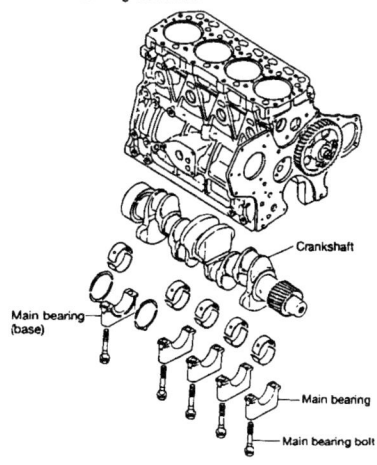

3-1.37 Removing the crankshaft
(1) Remove the crankshaft

NOTE: 1. The thrust metal (upper) is mounted to the standard main bearing. However, in some cases the thrust metal (upper) may be mounted to the crankshaft.
2. Remove the main bearing metal (upper) from the cylinder block.

3-1.38 Removing the camshaft
(1) Loosen the thrust rest mounting bolts out of the holes in the camshaft gear, and remove.
(2) Pull out the camshaft gear and camshaft assembly from the cylinder block.

NOTE: The camshaft gear and camshaft are shrunk fit. They must be heated to 180—200°C to disassemble.

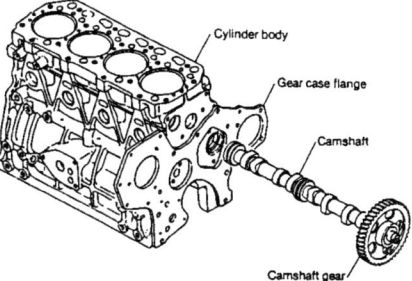

3-1.39 Removing the tappets
Remove the tappets from the tappet holes in the cylinder block.

3-1.40 Removing the gear case flange
(1) Remove the gear case flange from the cylinder block.
(2) Remove the two O-rings from the lube oil passage.

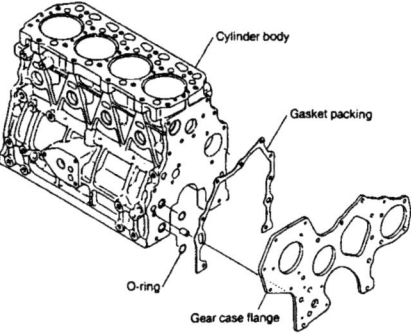

Chapter 10 Disassembly and Reassembly
3. Disassembly and Reassembly
3JH2 Series

3-1.41 Removing the piston cooling nozzle
Remove the piston cooling nozzle mounting nut and then the piston cooling nozzle from the cylinder block.

3-2 Reassembly
3-2.1 Mounting the piston cooling nozzle
Turn the cylinder block upside down and place it on appropriate wood blocks. Mount the piston cooling nozzles.

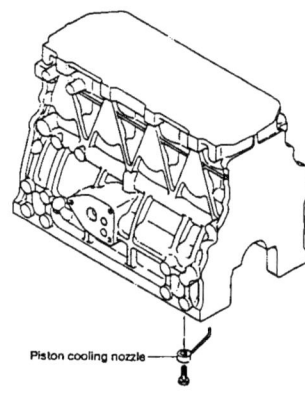

Piston cooling nozzle

3-2.2 Mounting the gear case flange
Mount the gear case flange, gasket packing and lube oil line O-ring onto the cylinder block.

NOTE: 1. When mounting the gear case flange, match up the two cylinder block pipe knock pins.
2. Be sure to coat the cylinder block lube oil line O-ring with grease when assembling, so that it does not get out of place.

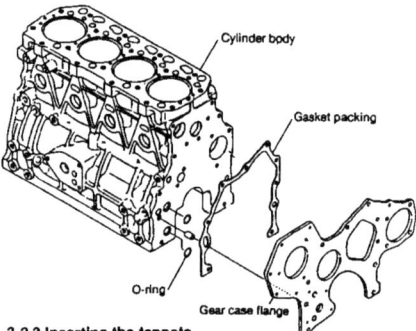

3-2.3 Inserting the tappets
Coat the inside of the cylinder block tappet holes and the outside circumference of the tappets with engine oil, and insert the tappets in the cylinder block.

NOTE: Separate the tappets to make sure that they are reassembled in the same cylinder, intake/exhaust manifold as they came from.

Chapter 10 Disassembly and Reassembly
3. Disassembly and Reassembly   *3JH2 Series*

3-2.4 Mounting the camshaft

(1) If the camshaft and camshaft gear have been disassembled, shrink fit the camshaft and camshaft gear [heat the camshaft gear to 180−200°C (356−392°F) in the hot oil and press fit].

NOTE: When mounting the camshaft and camshaft gear, be sure not to forget assembly of the thrust rest. Also make sure they are assembled with the correct orientation.

(2) Coat the cylinder block camshaft bearings and camshaft with engine oil, insert the camshaft in the cylinder block, and mount the thrust rest with the bolt.

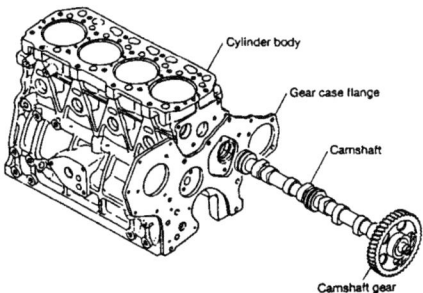

(3) Measure the camshaft side gap.

	mm (in.)
Camshaft side gap	0.05 ~ 0.25 (0.0020 ~ 0.0098in.)

(4) Make sure that the camshaft rotates smoothly.

3-2.5 Mounting the crankshaft

(1) The crankshaft and crankshaft gear are shrink fitted. If the crankshaft and crankshaft gear have been disassembled, they have to be shrink fitted [heat the crank shaft gear to 180°−200°C (356−392°F) in the hot oil and press fit].

(2) Coat the cylinder block crank journal holes and upper part of the main bearing metal with oil and fit the upper main bearing metal onto the cylinder block.

NOTE: 1. Be sure not to confuse the upper and lower main bearing metals. The upper metal has an oil groove.
2. When mounting the thrust metal, fit it so that the surface with the oil groove slit faces outwards, (crankshaft side).

(3) Coat the crank pin and crank journal with engine oil and place them on top of the main bearing metal.

NOTE: 1. Align the crankshaft gear and camshaft gear with the "A" match mark.
2 Position so that the crankshaft gear is on the gear case side.
3. Be careful not to let the thrust metal drop.

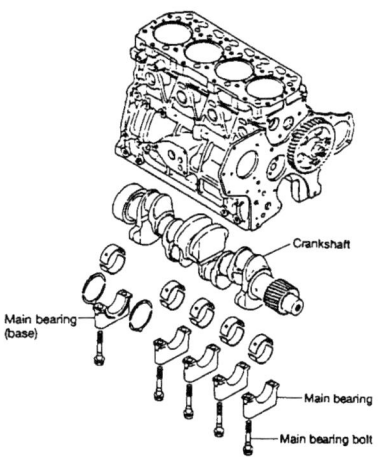

3-2.6 Mounting the main bearing metal with engine oil, and mounting the main bearing cap

NOTE: 1. The lower main bearing metal does not have an oil groove.
2. The standard bearing thrust metal is fitted with the oil groove slit facing outwards.

(2) Coat the main bearing cap bolt washer contact surface and threads with engine oil, place them on the crankshaft journal, and tighten the main bearing bolts to the specified torque.

	kg-m (ft-lb)
Main bearing bolt tightening torque	9.5 ~ 10.5 (68.7 ~ 75.9)

NOTE: 1. The main bearing cap should be fitted with the arrow near the embossed letters "FW" on the cap pointing towards the flywheel.
2. Make sure you have the correct cylinder alignment no.

(3) Measure the crankshaft side clearance.

	mm (in.)
Crankshaft side clearance	0.090 ~ 0.271 (0.0035 ~ 0.0107)

(4) Make sure that the crankshaft rotates smoothly and easily.

3-2.7 Mounting the flywheel housing

(1) Press fit the oil seal in the flywheel housing, and coat the lip of the oil seal with engine oil.
(2) Mount the flywheel housing and gasket packing, matching them up with the cylinder block positioning pins.

NOTE: Trim the gasket packing if it protrudes onto the oil pan mounting surface.

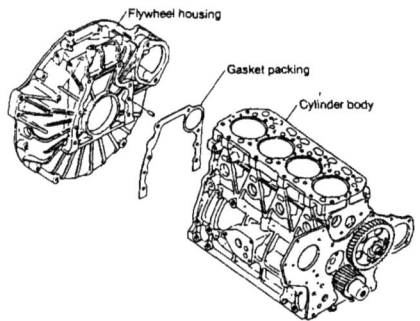

3-2.8 Stand up the cylinder block

On wood blocks, with the flywheel housing facing down. Take care that the gearbox mounting surface does not get scratched.

3-2.10 Mounting the piston and connecting rod

(1) Reassemble the piston and connecting rod.

NOTE: When reassembling the piston and connecting rod, make sure that the parts are assembled with the correct orientation.

(2) Each ring opening (piston/oil rings) should be staggered at gaps of 120°.

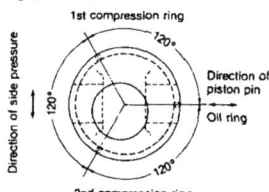

(3) Coat the outside of the piston and the inside of the connecting rod crank pin metal with engine oil and insert the piston with the piston insertion tool.

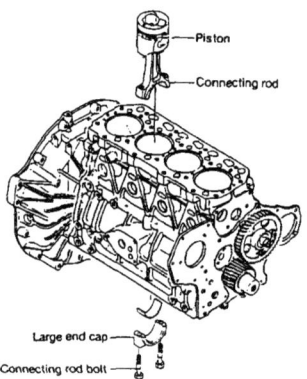

Chapter 10 Disassembly and Reassembly
3. Disassembly and Reassembly
3JH2 Series

NOTE: 1. Insert the piston so that the match mark on the large end of the connecting rod faces the fuel feed pump, and the manufactuer's mark on the stem points toward the flywheel.
2. After inserting the piston, make sure the combustion chamber hollow is facing the fuel feed pump, looking from the top of the piston.

(4) Align the large end match mark, mount the cap, and tighten the connecting rod bolts.

	kg-m (ft-lb)
Connecting rod bolt tightening torque	4.5 ~ 5.0 (32.5 ~ 36.2)

NOTE: If a torque wrench is not available, match up with the mark made before disassembly.

3-2.11 Mounting the idling gear
(1) Fit the idling gear so that the side of the idling shaft with two oil holes faces up.
(2) Align the "A" and "C" camshaft gear and crankshaft gear match marks, match up with idling shaft retaining plate, and tighten the bolts.
(3) Measure the idling gear, camshaft gear and crankshaft gear backlash.

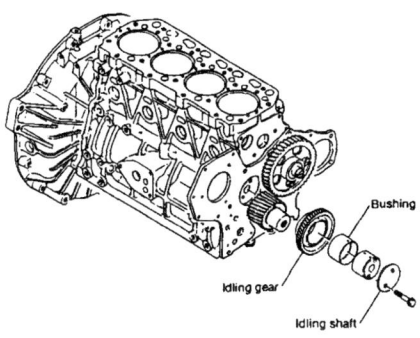
Bushing
Idling gear
Idling shaft

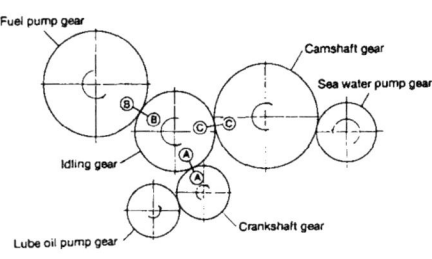
Fuel pump gear
Camshaft gear
Sea water pump gear
Idling gear
Lube oil pump gear
Crankshaft gear
Looking from gear case side

3-2.12 Mounting the fuel injection pump
Lightly fit the fuel injection pump on the gear case.

NOTE: 1. Be careful not to scratch the O-ring between the fuel injection pump and gear case flange.
2. Tighten the fuel injection pump all the way after adjusting injection timing.

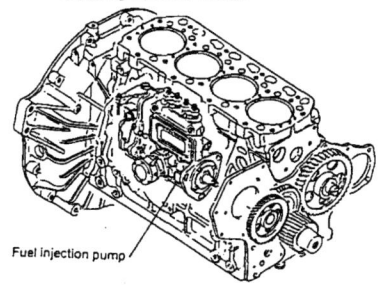
Fuel injection pump

3-2.13 Mounting the fuel feed pump drive gear and automatic advancing timer.
(1) When the drive gear and automatic advancing time have been disassembled, coat all sliding parts in bot assemblies with grease.
(2) Align the "B" match marks on the fuel pump drive gea and idling gear.
(3) Tighten all box nuts holding the fuel feed pump to th specified torque.

	kg-m (ft-l
Box nut tightening torque	6 ~ 7 (43.4 ~ 50.6)

(4) Grease parts around the box nuts (lithium grease) ar tighten the blind plug.
(5) Measure the backlash of the fuel feed pump drive gear

3-2.14 Mounting the lube oil pump
(1) Mount the lube oil pump on the gear case flange.
(2) Measure the backlash of the lube oil pump drive gear.

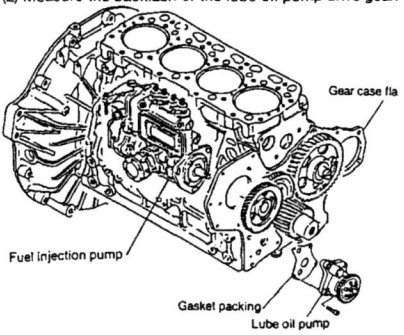
Gear case fla
Fuel injection pump
Gasket packing
Lube oil pump

Printed in Japan
A0A1015-9110SP

3-2.15 Mounting the gear case

(1) Coat the inside and outside of the oil seals with engine oil, and press fit them into the gear case.
(2) Position the two pipe knock pins, and tighten the bolts holding the gear case and gasket packing.

NOTE: Trim the gasket packing if it protrudes onto the oil pan mounting surface.

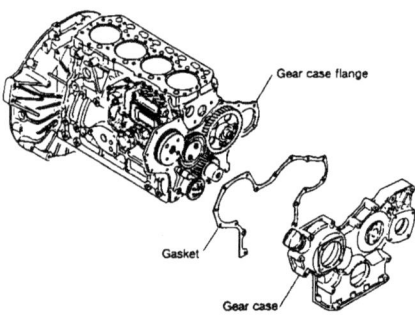

3-2.16 Mounting the lube oil intake pipe

Mount the lube oil intake pipe on the bottom of the cylinder block, using new packing.

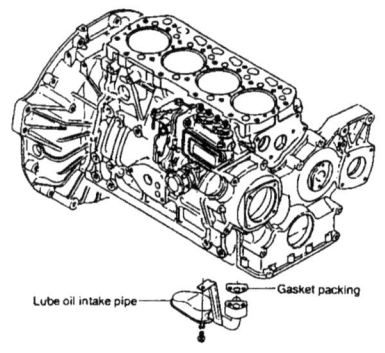

	kg·m (ft-lb)
lube oil intake pipe tightening torque	2.6 (18.8)

3-2.17 Mounting the oil pan

(1) Coat with three bond (3B-1114) the surfaces of the gear case, gear case flange and flywheel that contact with the cylinder block.
(2) Tighten the gasket packing/oil pan bolts.
(3) Mount the bracket that connects the flywheel with the oil pan.

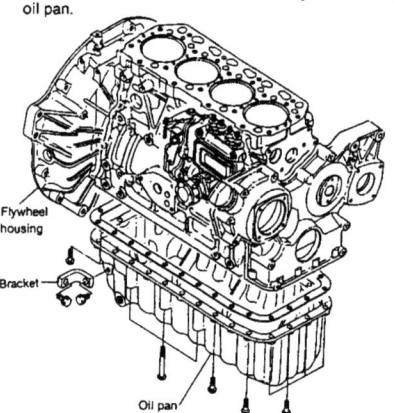

3-2.18 Mounting the engine mounting feet and turning the engine upright.

Place suitable wood blocks below the oil pan and turn the engine upright.

3-2.19 Mounting the flywheel

(1) Coat the flywheel mounting bolt threads with engine oil.
(2) Align the positioning pins, and tighten the flywheel bolts to the specified torque.

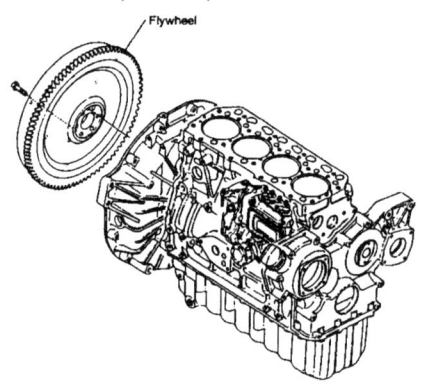

	kg·m (ft-lb)
Flywheel mounting bolt tightening torque	7.0 ~ 8.0 (50.6 ~ 57.9)

3-2.20 Mounting the marine gearbox

(1) Mount the fan and damper disk to the flywheel.
(2) Align the damper disk with the input shaft spline and insert. Tighten the flywheel housing and flange.

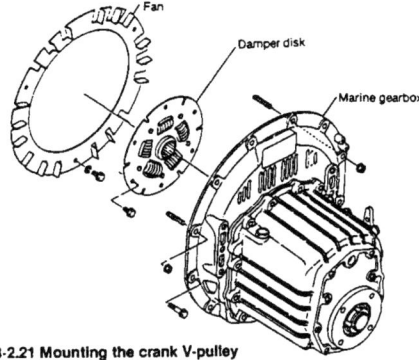

3-2.21 Mounting the crank V-pulley

(1) Coat the oil seal and the section of the shaft with which it comes in contact with oil.
(2) Tighten to the specfied torque.

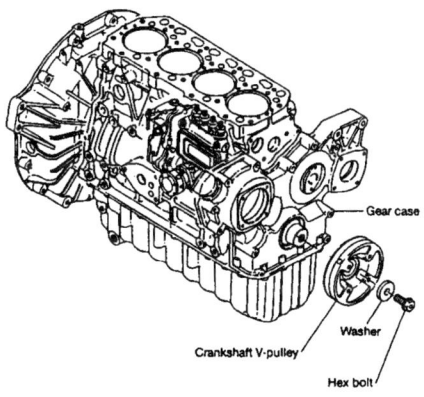

	kg-m (ft-lb)
V-pulley tightening torque	11.5 ~ 12.5 (83.2 ~ 90.4)

3-2.22 Mounting the cylinder head

(1) Fit the gasket packing against the cylinder block, aligning it with the cylinder block positioning pins.

NOTE: *The side on which the engine model is inscribed should face up (cylinder head side).*

(2) Lift the cylinder head horizontally and mount, aligning with the cylinder head gasket.
(3) Coat the mounting bolt washers and threads with engine oil, and lightly tighten the bolts in the specified order. Then tighten completely, in the same order.

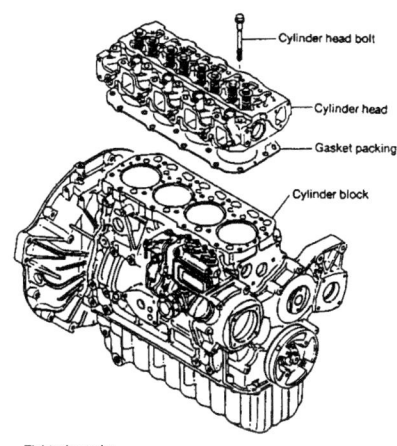

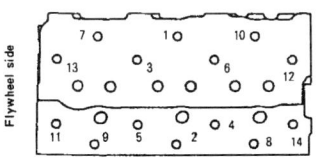

Tightening order

		kg-m (ft-lb)
	Partial	Complete
Cylinder bolt tightening torque	3.5 ~ 4.5 (25.3 ~ 32.5)	7.5 ~ 8.5 (54.2 ~ 61.5)

(4) Measure the top clearance.

	mm (in.)
Top clearance	0.71 ~ 0.89 (0.0279 ~ 0.0350)

Chapter 10 Disassembly and Reassembly
3. Disassembly and Reassembly

3JH2 Series

3-2.23 Mounting the valve rocker arm shaft assembly pushrod

(1) Fit the pushrod to the tappet.
(2) Mount the valve rocker arm shaft assembly.

	kg-m (ft-lb)
Valve rocker arm shaft support tightening torque	2.4 ~ 2.8 (17.4 ~ 20.4)

(3) Adjust valve clearance.

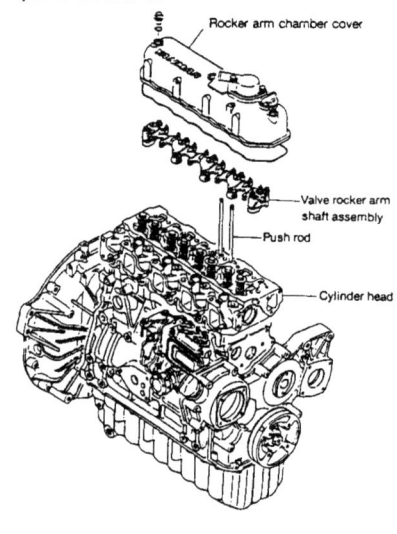

3-2.24 Mounting the fuel injection nozzle

(1) Mount the injection nozzle tip heat protector, and then the fuel injection nozzle.

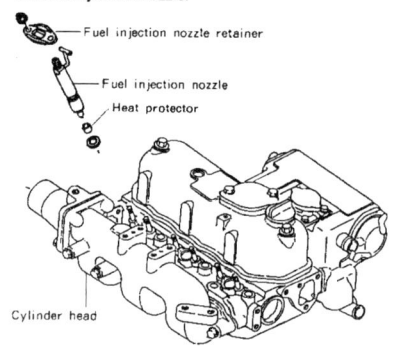

(2) Tighten the fuel injection nozzle retainer nut to the specified torque.

	kg-m (ft-lb)
Fuel injection nozzle retainer tightening torque	2.0 ~ 3.0 (14.5 ~ 21.7)

3-2.25 Mounting the fresh water pump

(1) Thoroughly coat both sides of the packing with adhesive.
(2) Replace the O-ring for the connecting pipe which is inserted in the cylinder block, and tighten the fresh water pump to the specified torque.

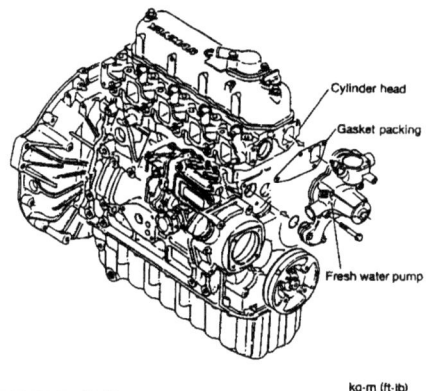

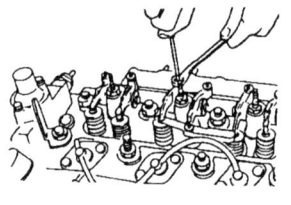

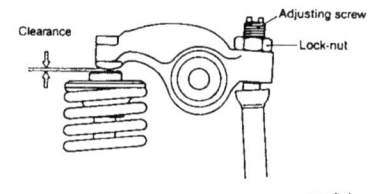

	mm (in.)
Intake/discharge valve clearance	0.2 (0.0079)

	kg-m (ft-lb)
Fresh water pump tightening torque	0.7 ~ 1.1 (5.0 ~ 8.0)

(4) Coat the valve rocker arm and valve spring with engine oil, and mount the valve rocker arm chamber cover.

3-2.26 Mounting the intake manifold

(1) Thoroughly clean the inside of the intake manifold, and mount the gasket packing and intake manifold.
(2) Mount the governor remote control bracket.

3-2.28 Mounting the lube oil cooler

Mount the lube oil cooler to the top of the flywheel housing with the bracket.

MODEL: 4JHE
    4JH-TE

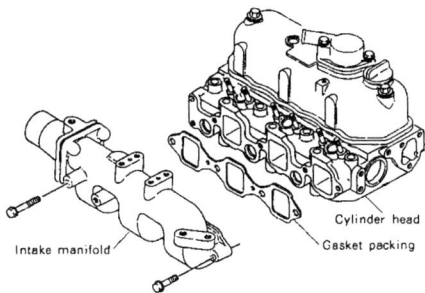

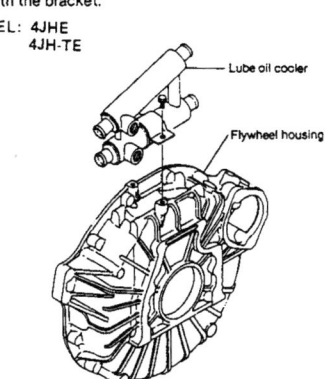

3-2.27 Mounting the high pressure fuel pipe and fuel oil return pipe

(1) Mount the high pressure fuel pipe and then the high pressure fuel pipe vibration stop.

NOTE: *Lightly tighten the box nuts on both ends of the high pressure fuel pipe. Completely tighten after adjusting the injection timing.*

(2) Mount the fuel oil return pipe with the hose clamp (fuel injection nozzle—fuel injection pump)

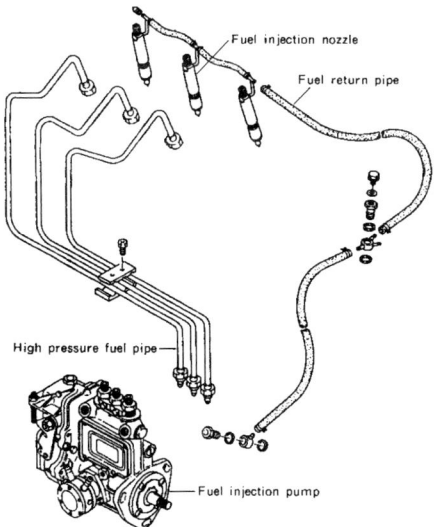

3-2.29 Mounting the lube oil filter

(1) Mount the filter bracket and packing on the cylinder block.
(2) Mount the filter element with the filter remover mounting tool.

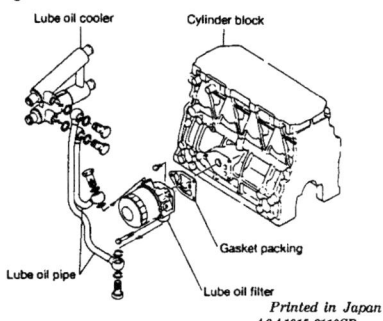

Printed in Japan
A0A1015-9110SP

Chapter 10 Disassembly and Reassembly
3. Disassembly and Reassembly

3-2.30 Mounting the lube oil pipe
(1) Mount the lube oil pipe (filter—lube oil cooler, lube oil cooler—filter).
(2) Mount the lube oil pipe (cylinder block—fuel injection pump).

3-2.31 Mounting the dipstic guide
Mount the dipstick and dipstick guide.

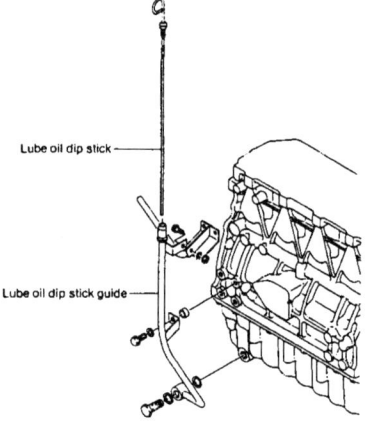

3-2.32 Mounting the sea water pump
(1) Mount the sea water pump assembly to the gear case flange.
(2) Lightly tap the gear case side bearing rest with a wood hammer, and tighten the mounting bolts.

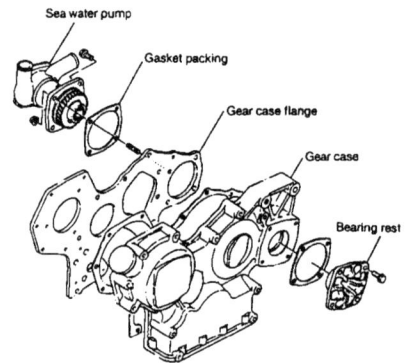

3-2.33 Mounting the cooling sea water pipe
Mount the cooling water pipe with the hose clamp (sea water pump—lube oil cooler).

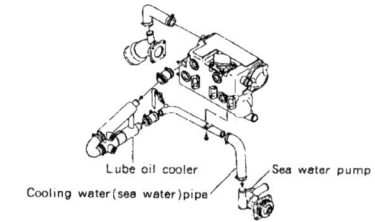

3-2.34 Mounting the heat exchanger (exhaust manifold, fresh water tank unit).
Mount the gasket packing and exhaust manifold.

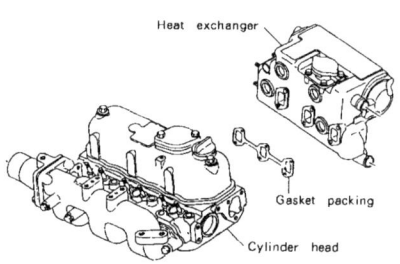

3-2.35 Mounting the cooling water pipe
(1) Mount the cooling fresh water pipe with the hose clamp (fresh water tank — fresh water pump, fresh water pump— heat exchanger).
(2) Mount the cooling sea water pipe with the hose clamp (lube oil cooler — heat exchanger).
(3) Mount the cooling sea water pipe with the hose clamp (lube oil cooler — marine gearbox).

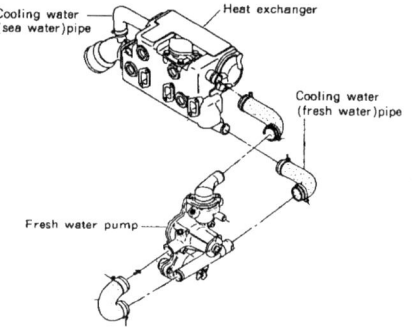

3-2.36 Mounting the alternator

(1) Mount the adjuster on the fresh water pump, the distance piece on the gear case, and then the alternator.
(2) Adjust V-belt tension with the adjuster, and tighten the mounting bolts.

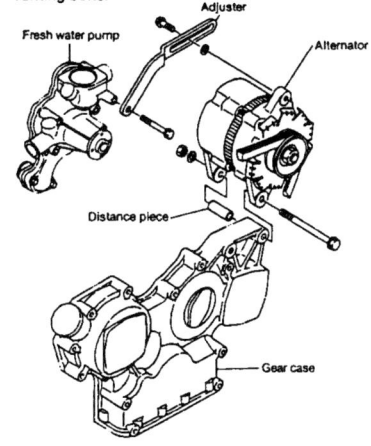

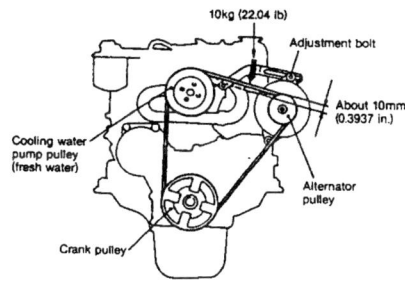

3-2.37 Mounting the starting motor

Fit the starting motor in the flywheel housing.

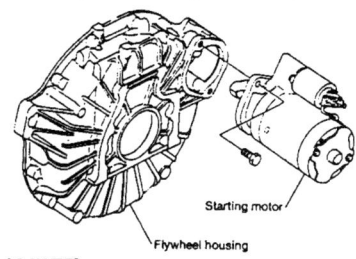

[Model 3JH-TE]

3-2.38 Mounting the turbine

(1) Mount the turbine on the exhaust manifold.

NOTE: *First make sure to tighten the turbine lube oil return pipe.*

(2) Mount the lube oil pipe (lube oil cooler—turbine).
(3) Insert the rubber hose at the end of the lube oil return pipe (turbine—oil pan) into the elbow on the oil pan, and mount with the hose grip.
(4) Mount the intake rubber hose (turbine—intake manifold).

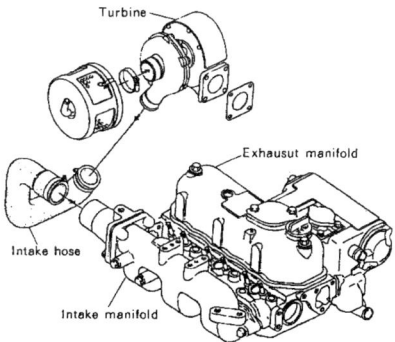

3-2.39 Mounting the mixing elbow

(1) Mount the mixing elbow on the exhaust manifold outlet for model 3JH2E, and on the turbocharger outlet for model 3JH2-TE.
(2) Mount the cooling sea water pipe rubber hose with the hose grip (heat exchanger—mixing elbow).

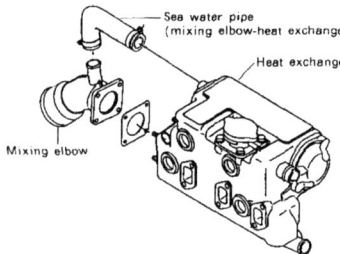

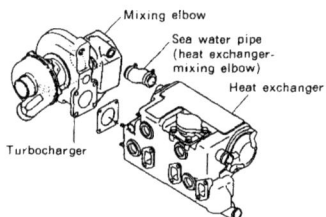

Mounting the mixing elbow and the turbocharger

(1) Mount the turbocharger on the exhaust mainfold.
(2) Mount the air duct rubber hose.
   (Turbocharger — Air duct)
(3) Mount the mixing elbow on the turbocharger.
(4) Mount the sea water hose.
   (Heat exchanger — Mixing elbow)
(5) Mount the lube oil pipes.
   (Lube oil pump — Turbocharger — Lube oil cooler)
(6) Mount the fresh water hoses.
   (Heat exchanger — Turbocharger)

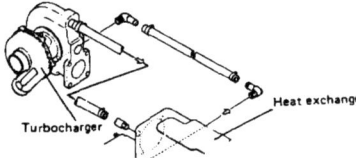

Chapter 10 Disassembly and Reassembly
3. Disassembly and Reassembly
3JH2 Series

3-2.40 Mounting the intake silencer

(1) Mount the intake silencer on the intake manifold inlet coupling for model 3JH2E, and on the turbocharger blower side for model 3JH2-TE.
(2) Mount the breather hose with the hoe clamp (intake silencer—valve rocker arm chamber cover).

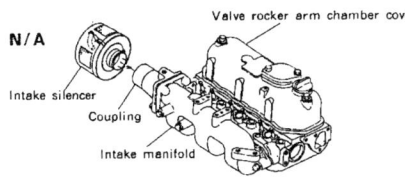

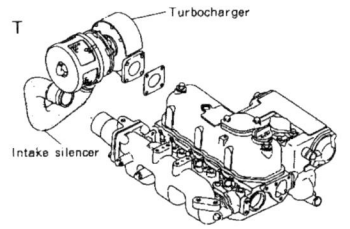

3-2.41 Mounting the fuel filter and fuel oil pipe

(1) Mount the fuel filter.
(2) Mount the fuel oil pipe (fuel feed pump—fuel filter, fuel filter—fuel injection pump).

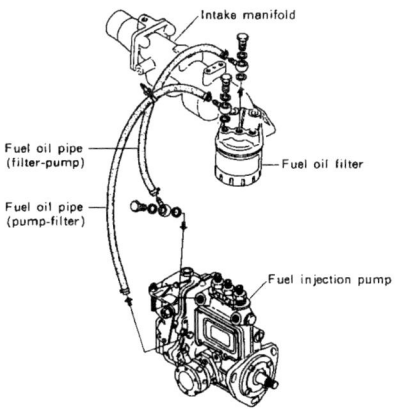

3-2.42 Electrical Wiring

Connect the wiring to the proper terminals, observing the color coding to make sure the connections are correct.

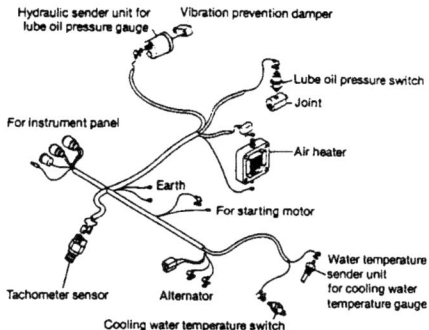

3-2.43 Installation in the ship and completion of the piping and wiring

Mount the engine in the ship after all engine assembly has been completed. Connect the cooling water, fuel oil and other piping on the ship and the exhaust hoses. Connect the battery, instrument panel, remote control and other wiring.

3-2.44 Filling with lube oil

Fill the engine with lube oil from the supply port on top of the gear case and the marine gearbox supply port on top of the clutch case.

		ℓ (in.³)
Lube oil capacity	Engine	6.5 (396.63)
	Gearbox	1.2 (73.22)

Printed in Japan
A0A1015-9110SP

Chapter 10 Disassembly and Reassembly
3. Disassembly and Reassembly

3JH2 Series

3-2.45 Filling with cooling water

(1) Open the fresh water tank cap and fill with water.

	l (in.³)
Fresh water tank capacity	6.7 (408.83)

(2) Fill with water until the level in the sub-tank is between the full and low marks.

	l (in.³)	
	Full	Low
Sub-tank capacity	0.8 (48.82)	0.2 (12.20)

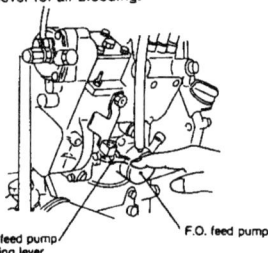

(3) If injection timing is off, change the mounting position using the long hole in the injection pump mounting flange. Turning the fuel feed pump towards the cylinder block slows timing down, while movement in the other directon makes it faster.

Fuel Injection timing (FID)	3JH2E	b.TDC12°
	3JH2-TE	b.TDC17°

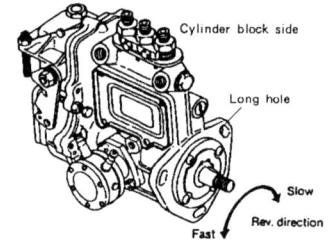

3-2.46 Check fuel injection timing

(1) Open the fuel tank cock and shift the fuel feed pump priming lever for air bleeding.

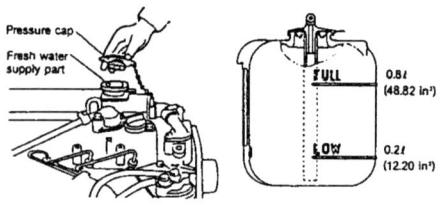

(2) Check injection timing by turning the flywheel and looking through the inspection hole in the flywheel housing.

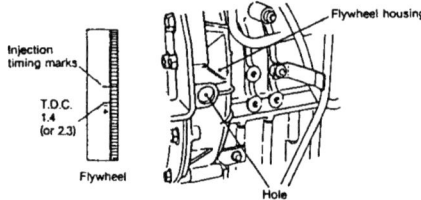

4. Bolt/nut tightening torque

Engine

Description	Thread dia. × pitch mm	Tightening torque kg-m (ft-lb)	Wrench mm (in.)
Cylinder head bolts	M10 × 1.25	7.5 ~ 8.5 (54.24 ~ 61.47)	14 (0.5512)
Connecting rod bolts	M9 × 1.0	5.0 ~ 5.5 (36.16 ~ 39.78)	13 (0.5118)
Flywheel bolts	M10 × 1.25	7.0 ~ 8.0 (50.63 ~ 57.86)	17 (0.6693)
Crankshaft V-pulley bolts	M14 × 1.5	11.5 ~ 12.5 (83.17 ~ 90.41)	19 (0.7480)
Main bearing bolts	M12 × 1.5	10.5 ~ 11.5 (75.94 ~ 83.17)	17 (0.6693)
Fuel pump gear nut	M12 × 1.75	6.0 ~ 7.0 (43.39 ~ 50.63)	17 (0.6693)

Turbocharger (RHB52)

Description	Thread dia. × pitch mm	Tightening torque kg-m (ft-lb)	Wrench mm (in.)
Turbine chamber bolts	M6	10.0 ~ 11.0 (72.33 ~ 79.56)	10 (0.3937)
Blower chamber bolts	M5	3.5 ~ 4.5 (25.31 ~ 32.54)	8 (0.3150)
Thrust metal bolts	M3	0.7 ~ 0.9 (5.06 ~ 6.50)	—
Seal plate screws	M3	0.7 ~ 0.8 (5.06 ~ 5.78)	—
Blower blade nuts	M5	1.8 ~ 2.2 (13.01 ~ 15.91)	8 (0.3150)

5. Test running

5-1. Preliminary Precautions

Before making a test run, make sure of the following points.
(1) Warm the engine up.
(2) Remove any precipitation from the F.O. filter, water separator, and F.O. tank.
(3) Use only lube oil recommended by Yanmar.
(4) Be sure to add Yanmar anti-rust agent to fresh cooling water.
(5) During cold weather, add Yanmar anti-freeze to the cooling water.
(6) Provide good ventilation in the engine room

5-2 Check Points and Precautions During Running

Step	Item	Instructions	Precautions
1	Checks before operation	1) Make sure that the Kingston Cock is open. 2) Make sure there is enough lube oil and (fresh) cooling water. 3) Operate the remote control handle and check if the devices connected to the engine side work properly.	3) Lamp should go off when engine is running.
2	No load operation; warm up operation	1) Glow plug is provided to aid engine starts. When the lube oil temperature is raised to allow the engine to start, the pilot lamp goes off. 2) When the engine is started, check the following: • there is no water and no oil leakage. • gas does not leak when the engine is started. • there are no abnormal indications on the instrument panel. • there is no abnormality in cooling water discharge, engine vibrations, or engine sounds. 3) To warm up the engine, operate at low revolutions for about 5 minutes, then raise the revolutions to the rated rpms and then to max. rpms.	1) Even if one glow plug should break, the remaining plug works. 2) • Fix leaks if any. • Check the intake/exhaust valves, F.O. injection valve, and cylinder head. 3) Do not raise the engine revolutions abruptly.
3	Cruising (load) operation	1) Do not operate the engine at full load yet, but raise the rpms gradually for about 10 minutes until they reach rated rpms. 2) Make sure that exhaust color and temperature are normal. 3) Check the instrument panel and see if the water temperature and oil pressure are normal.	
4	Stopping the engine	1) Before stopping the engine, operate it at 650—700 rpms for about 5 minutes. 2) Raise engine rpms to 1,800 just before stopping the engine and idle the engine for about 3—4 seconds.	1) Stopping the engine suddenly during high speed operation increases the temperature of engine parts. 2) This procedure prevents carbon from being deposited on the valve seats, etc.
5	Checks after stopping the engine	1) Check again for water and oil leaks. 2) Make sure that no nuts and bolts are loose. 3) Close the Kingston and fuel cocks. 4) When the temperature is expected to fall below freezing, drain the cooling water (sea water). 5) Turn off the battery switch.	1) Check the oil seal area. 2) Especially the engine installation bolts. 4) Drain from the sea water pump.

PARTS DIFFERING IN SHAPE

No.	Part			Specification				Reason for Difference	Remarks
				4JH2E Series		3JH2E Series			
				4JH2E	4JH2E-TE	3JH2E	3JH2E-TE		
1	Output	Cont rating		46/3400	57/3400	35/3400	43/3400		
		Max.	Clutch output	Clutch output 48/3600	Clutch output 60/3600	Clutch output 36/3600	Clutch output 45/3600		Indication in nameplate is for flywheel output.
			Flywheel output	Flywheel output 50/3600	Flywheel output 62/3600	Flywheel output 38/3600	Flywheel output 47/3600		
2	Cylinder block CMP			↑	【129573-01000】 for sleeveless cyl. Cyl. block ; 【129402-01010】	↑	【129171-01000】 【129102-01040】	Bore enlargement by sleeveless structure	* Design change in corner of main bearing (2→2.5)
3	Cylinder sleeve			↑	↑	↑	for sleeveless	Bore enlargement by sleeveless structure	
4	Cyl. head gasket			Grommets (at both ends) 4JH2 stamp	【129573 -01340(t=1.3) -01350(t=1.4) -01360(t=1.5) standerd φ82 mm for sleeveless cyl.】	Grommets (at both ends) 3JH2 stamp	129171 -01320(t=1.3) -01330(t=1.4) -01340(t=1.5) φ82	None	Bore enlargement by sleeveless structure
5	Engien name plate			【129570-07010】 Model : 4JH2E	【129571-07010】 Model : 4JH2E-TE	【129170-07010】 Model : 3JH2E	【129171-07010】 Model : 3JH2-TE		
6	Metal cps tightening torque			↑	↑	↑	11±0.5 kg·m	P.max. increase	JH2 mass-produced. As for JH, the torque will be changed to 11kg-m.
7	Rocker arm support			↑	↑	↑	【129155-11260】 -11270 Model of ADC		Rocker arm support of current 4JH is to be changed also to ADC.
8	Supercharger			None	【129571-18000】 52001 HP12NW BRL3511E *MY67*	None	【129171-18000】 34001 HP12NW BRLL338C *MY75*	Combustion performance	RHB52 (Water cooling) MY60 MY34
9	Crankshaft			【129474-21010】 SCM440 Discrimination Stamp : C	【129573-21010】 SCM440 Resintered Discrimination	S50CV 【129170-21010】	SCM440 【129171-21010】	P.max. increase	

No.	Part	(on No.4 arm)	(on high arm)			Purpose	Remarks
10	Flywheel CMP	PCD250 [PCD170] Seat added for YX-15 (8-M8A·6 points)	【12917-21590】 SAE #5			To make it applicable to Bobtail	
11	Piston	【129570-22010】 dia. 82 mm YBPC(Petal) Stamp A	【129572-22010】 dia. 82 mm YBPC(Petal) Stamp C / 【129573-22010】 dia. 82 mm YBPC(Petal) Stamp D	dia. 82 mm YBPC(Petal) Stamp A	【129171-22010】 dia. 82 mm YBPC(Petal) Stamp 3B	Bore enlarging. Combustion performance	4JH2-HTE & 4JH2-DTE differ in combustion chamber only.
12	Piston ring (Top)	【129573-21100】 Chrome-plating on 3 faces	↑	【129120-22100】	【129573-21100】 Chrome-plating on 3 faces	Bore enlargement	Differ in material
	Piston ring(2nd)	【129351-22100】	↑	【129151-22110】	【129351-22100】	Bore enlargement	
	Oil ring	【129573-23010】	↑	【129151-22200】	【129573-22200】	Bore enlargement	Differ in material
13	Conn. rod	【129573-23010】 · Small end : Taper · Small end : Hole dia.= 31 mm · Tightening torque: 5.0–5.5 kg·m		↓	↓	P.max. increase	
14	Piston pin	【129573-22300】 dia. 28 × ℓ 69 mm		↓	↓	P.max. increase	
15	Piston pin metal	【129573-23100】 dia. 28 mm Taper		↓	↓	P.max. increase	
16	Piston pin snap ring	【22252-000280】 Circlip (Flat) For dia. 28 mm hole		↓	↓		
17	Sea water pump	【129573-42500】 Discharge capacity: 3250 ℓ/hr (Cam lift increased) 5 mm		↓	↓	Increase in heat exchanged calorie	That for 4JH2 is changed in design and applied to current 4JH.
18	Fresh water cooler (Body)	【129470-44010】 Cooler inset dia. 76.5 mm Length : 451 mm		【129171-44010】	↓	Increase in heat exchanged calorie	
19	Fresh water cooler (Cooler core)	【129473-44111】 Core dia. 76.5 mm A=0.328m²		【129171-44110】 76.5 × ℓ 269 A=0.229	↓	Increase in heat exchanged calories	
20	Fresh water cooler	【129470-44450】 Cooler inset dia.		↓	↓		

PARTS DIFFERING IN SHAPE

No.	Part	Specification — 4JH2E Series		Specification — 3JH2E Series		Reason for Difference	Remarks
		4JH2E	4JH2E-TE	3JH2E	3JH2E-TE		
21	Fuel injection pump governor	[729570-51300] [B471]	Retraction volume 23.6 m㎥/st. Cut amt.: W/O Boost compensator [729671-51300] [B445]			Combustion performance Standization at acceleration	
22	Fuel injection nozzle	5-0.23φ × 155° 155P235J20	[729595-53100] 5-0.25φ × 145° 140P255ZO	40.24-150 5-0.23φ × 155° 155P235J20 [129100-53000]	5-0.25-140	Combustion performance	
23	Push rod	[119171-14400] d.e. 8.5mm Material=5TKM16C yellow paint	↓	↓	↓	Stress relieving	
24	Cly. head packing	Non-asbestos [Material:SF7000]	↓	↓	↓		Non-asbestos is also to be applied to current 4JH
25	Oil pan		↑	↑ Shallow type	(1)Hole added for front P.T.O bracket (2)Screw hole (M16 × 1.5) for dipstick Added also to non-control side	To make it applicable to twin installation	Oil pan for current 4JH is changed in design also. (Applied also to current 4JHE series)
26	Cover (Thermostat)	[129470-49540]	↓	Added		Following elongation of fresh water cooler (No. 19, 20)	
27	Marine gear Model:KM3A	Input shaft Oil seal : Acryl Shaft,case:oil supply amt increased Length : 7mm increased	↓	[S G GG]	[S G]	Measure for oil leak. Measure for wear out of friction plate. To make it applicable to the clutchless engines	
	Cooling fan	None	None	None	None		
28	Intercooler	None		None	↓	Oil temp. reduced	

#	Item		Previous	Current	Prevention of hose slipping off	A1 pipe is also to be applied to current 4JH-HTE/DTE
29	Air intake duct		None	Aluminum pipe and rubber joint		
30	Starter		Reduction type [129573-77010]	↓	Unification of parts	
31	Wireharness Extension cord		4m : without relay 6m : with/relay	↓	Following change of starter	Optional
32	Marine gear Model:KBW10-E		KBW20 [S][G] Input shaft length : 7 m≈up	↓↓ [S][G]	KBW10-E [S][G] Input shaft length : 7 m≈up	Flywheel changed for application to Bobtail
		Cooling fan	Added Same as KM4A 177073-63190	↓	None	Same as above
33	Head bolt tightening torque		T=9±0.5kg·m at shop assembly (T=8±0.5kg·m at site reassembly)	↓	↓	P.max. increase
34	Flywheel Housing		SAE #4 [129400-01600]	↓	SAE #5 [129171-01600]	↓
35	Foot		—	—	Front:A)129171-08100 :B) ″ -08110	↓
36	Mixing (L)		3 inch	↓	—	2.5 inch [129171-13550]
37	V pulley		[12947-21650]	↓	FC25 [129171-21650]	
38	Lube oil cooler		[129474-33000]	[129474-33000]		[129470-33000]
39	Oil Filter		[129150-35150] φ90 × ℓ80	↓	[119305-35150] φ68 × ℓ65	